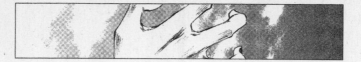

We are all
Born dead.
The end exists
Before anything begins.

If living
Is a constant quest for awareness,
The awareness we gain at the end is the real goal.
In other words, death
Is the discovery and complete understanding
Of the end.

We are not permitted to seek awareness.
Those that cannot transcend death
Will not find awareness in anything.

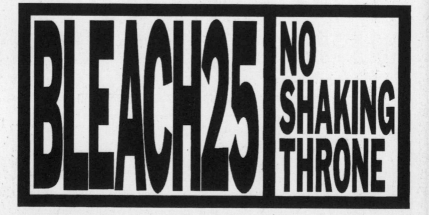

BLEACH 25 NO SHAKING THRONE

STARS AND

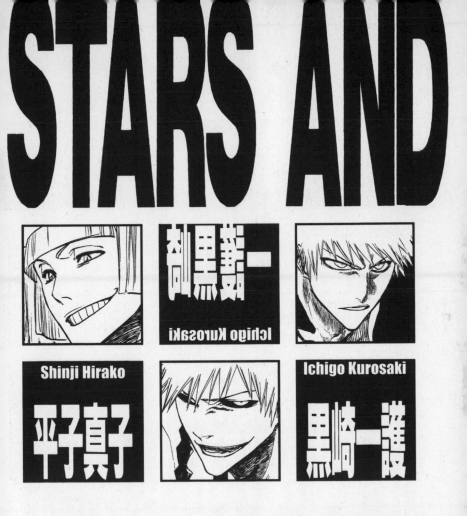

Shinji Hirako

平子真子

Ichigo Kurosaki

黒崎一護

⭐ plot

When Ichigo Kurosaki meets Soul Reaper Rukia Kuchiki his life is changed forever. Soon Ichigo is a Soul Reaper himself, cleansing lost souls called Hollows. After several bouts of severe training, Ichigo is able to rescue Rukia from her date with death in the Soul Society, exposing the sinister plot of Sôsuke Aizen in the process.

Back in the World of the Living, Ichigo continues his job as a Soul Reaper. But when deadly Arrancars begin to show up there, Rukia and a team of Soul Reapers are sent to stop them. In the fierce battles that follow, Ichigo is defeated by an Arrancar named Grimmjow. Faced with his own inadequacy and inability to control his inner Hollow, Ichigo turns at last to a group of rogue Soul Reapers called the Visoreds!!

BLEACH ALL

井上織姫

Orihime Inoue

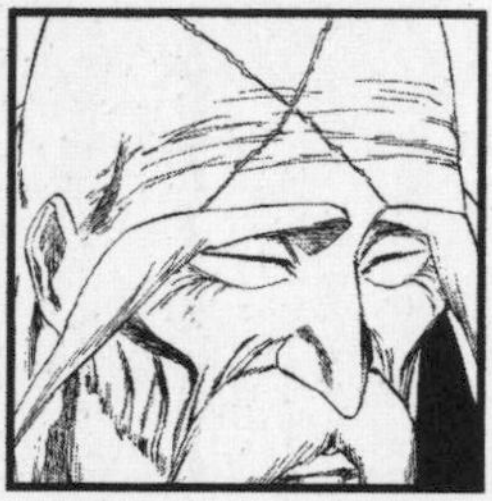

猿柿ひよ里

Hiyori Sarugaki

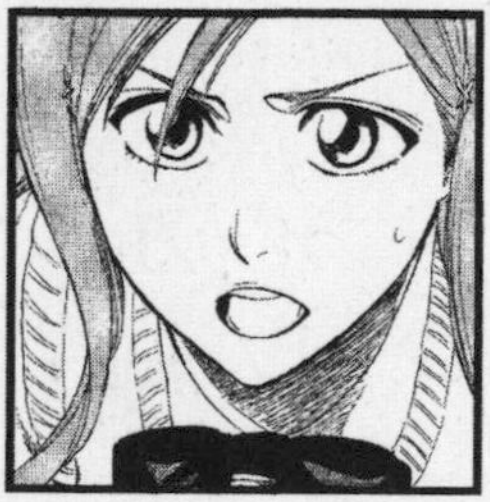

Shigekuni Genryusai Yamamoto

山本元柳斎重國

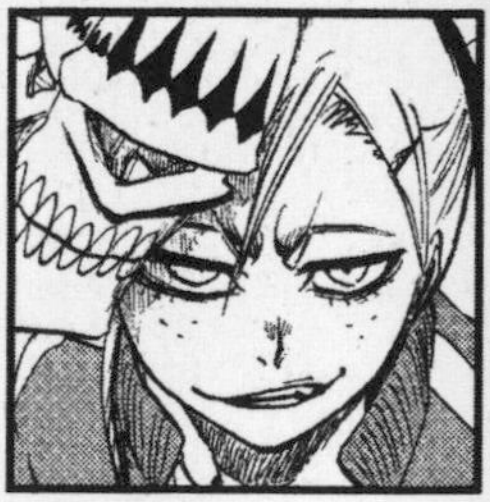

STORIES

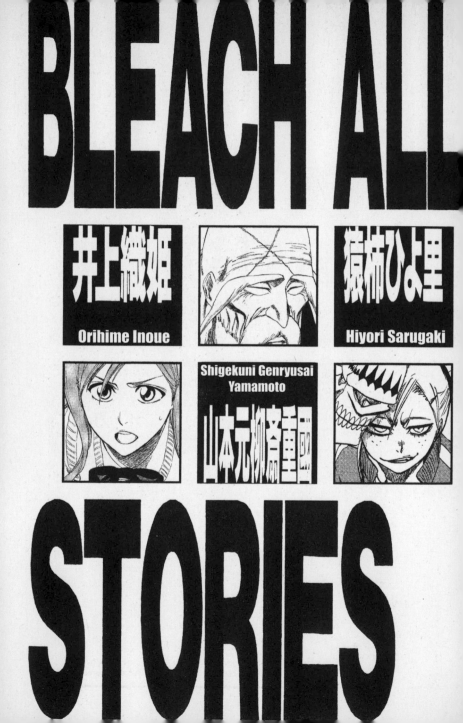

BLEACH 25

NO SHAKING THRONE

Contents

215. Tug Your God Out

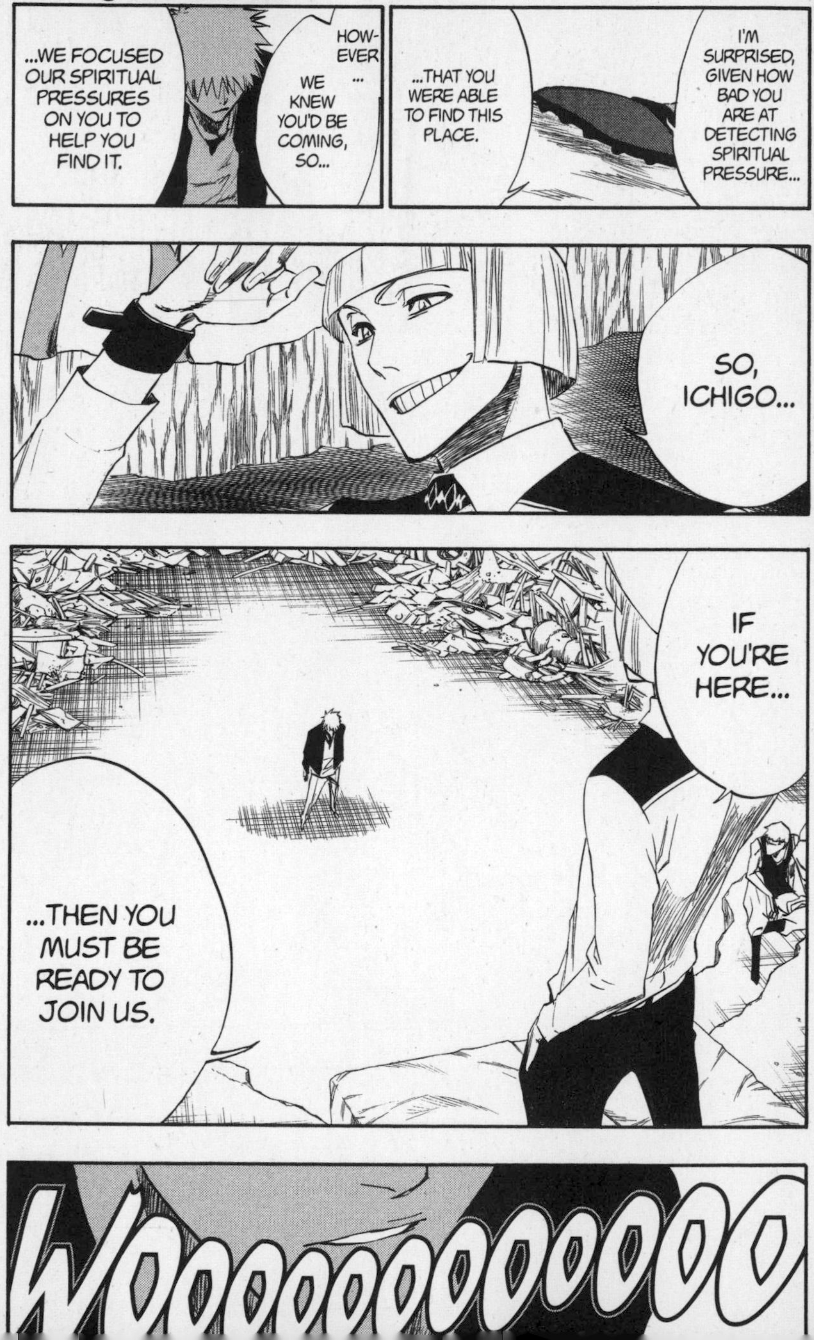
I'M SURPRISED, GIVEN HOW BAD YOU ARE AT DETECTING SPIRITUAL PRESSURE...
...THAT YOU WERE ABLE TO FIND THIS PLACE.
HOWEVER...
WE KNEW YOU'D BE COMING, SO...
...WE FOCUSED OUR SPIRITUAL PRESSURES ON YOU TO HELP YOU FIND IT.
SO, ICHIGO...
IF YOU'RE HERE...
...THEN YOU MUST BE READY TO JOIN US.
WOOOOOOOOOOOO

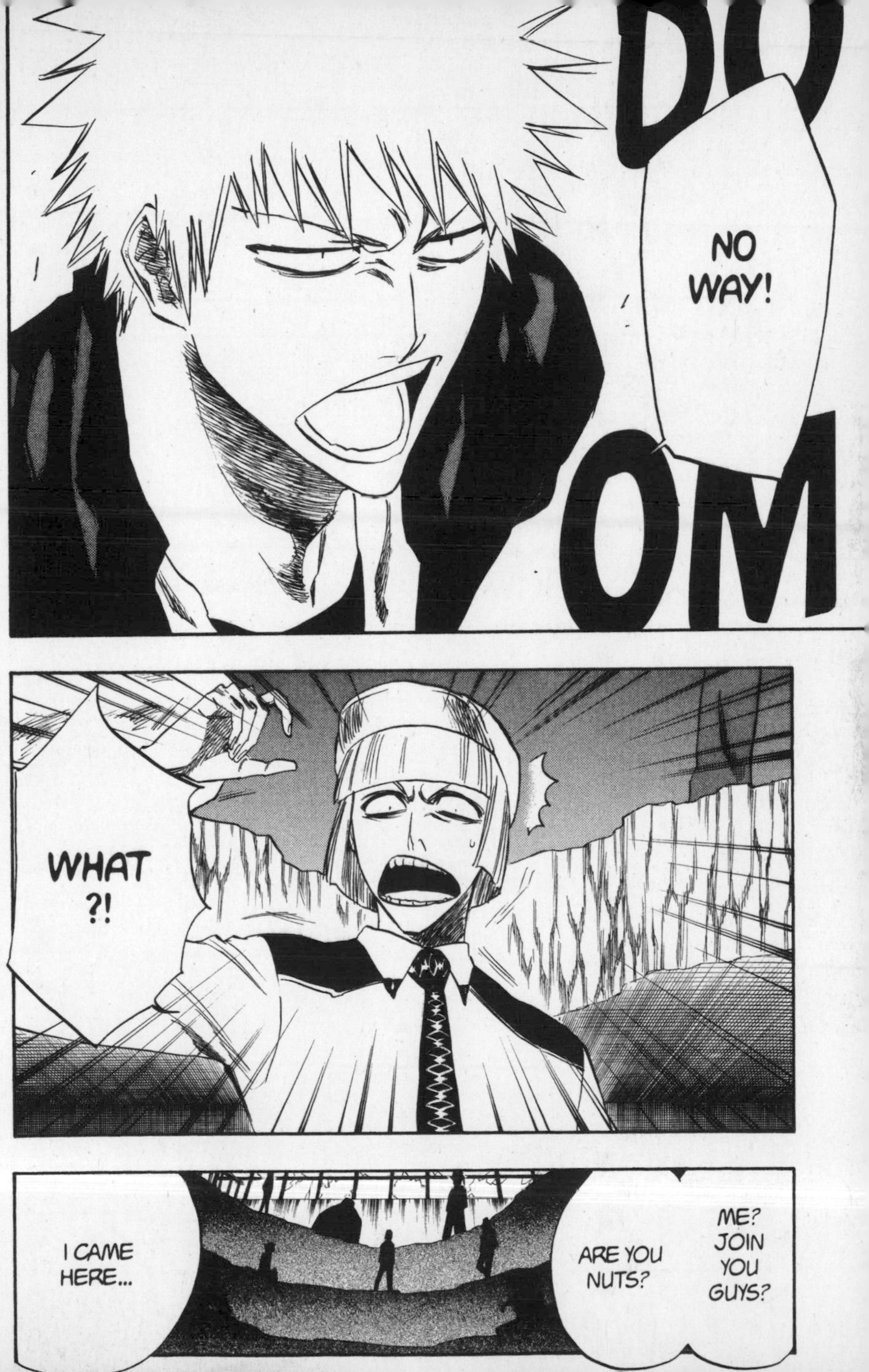
DOOM
NO WAY!
WHAT ?!
ME? JOIN YOU GUYS?
ARE YOU NUTS?
I CAME HERE...

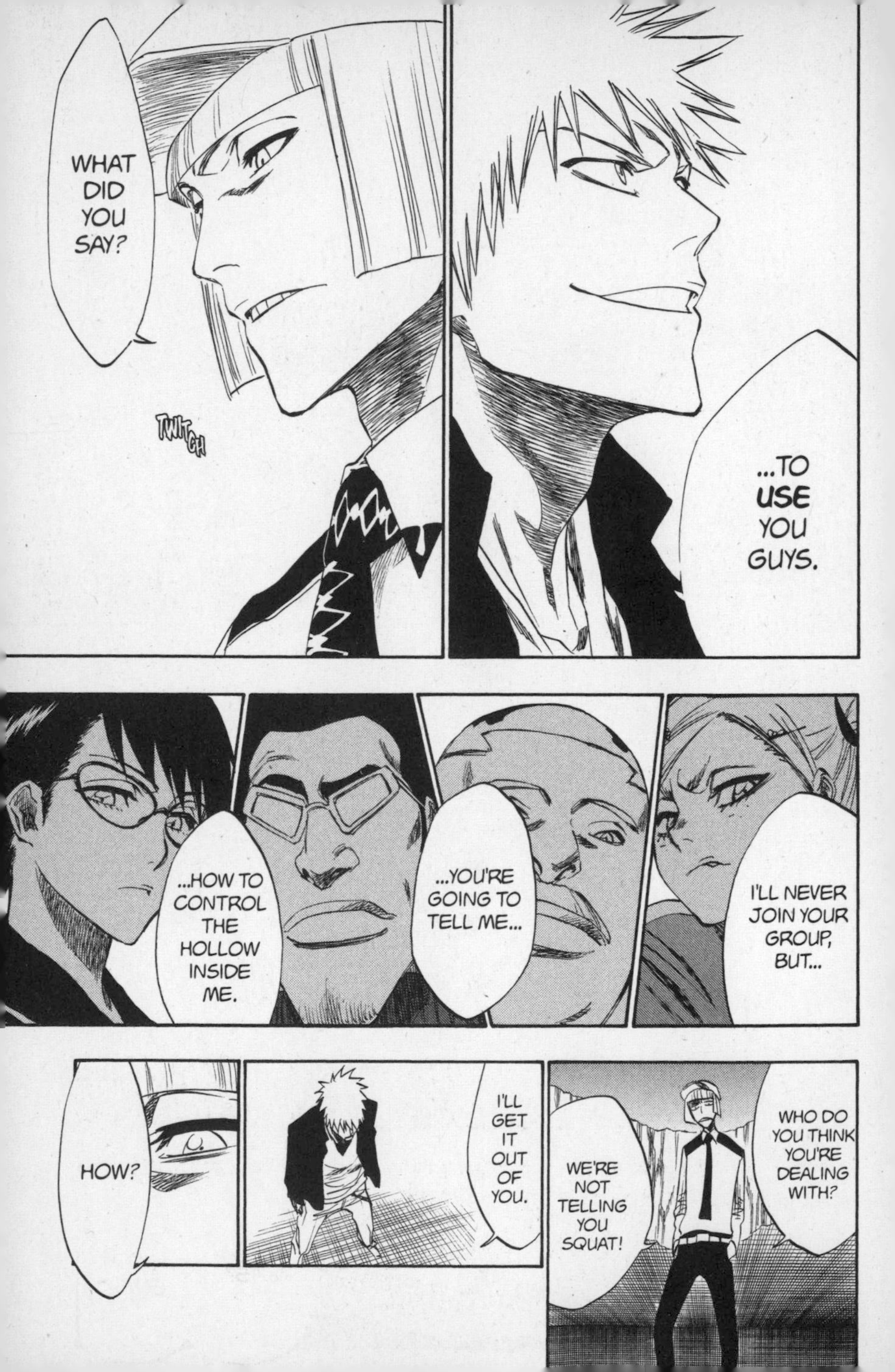
...TO USE YOU GUYS.
WHAT DID YOU SAY?
TWITCH
I'LL NEVER JOIN YOUR GROUP, BUT...
...YOU'RE GOING TO TELL ME...
...HOW TO CONTROL THE HOLLOW INSIDE ME.
WHO DO YOU THINK YOU'RE DEALING WITH?
WE'RE NOT TELLING YOU SQUAT!
I'LL GET IT OUT OF YOU.
HOW?

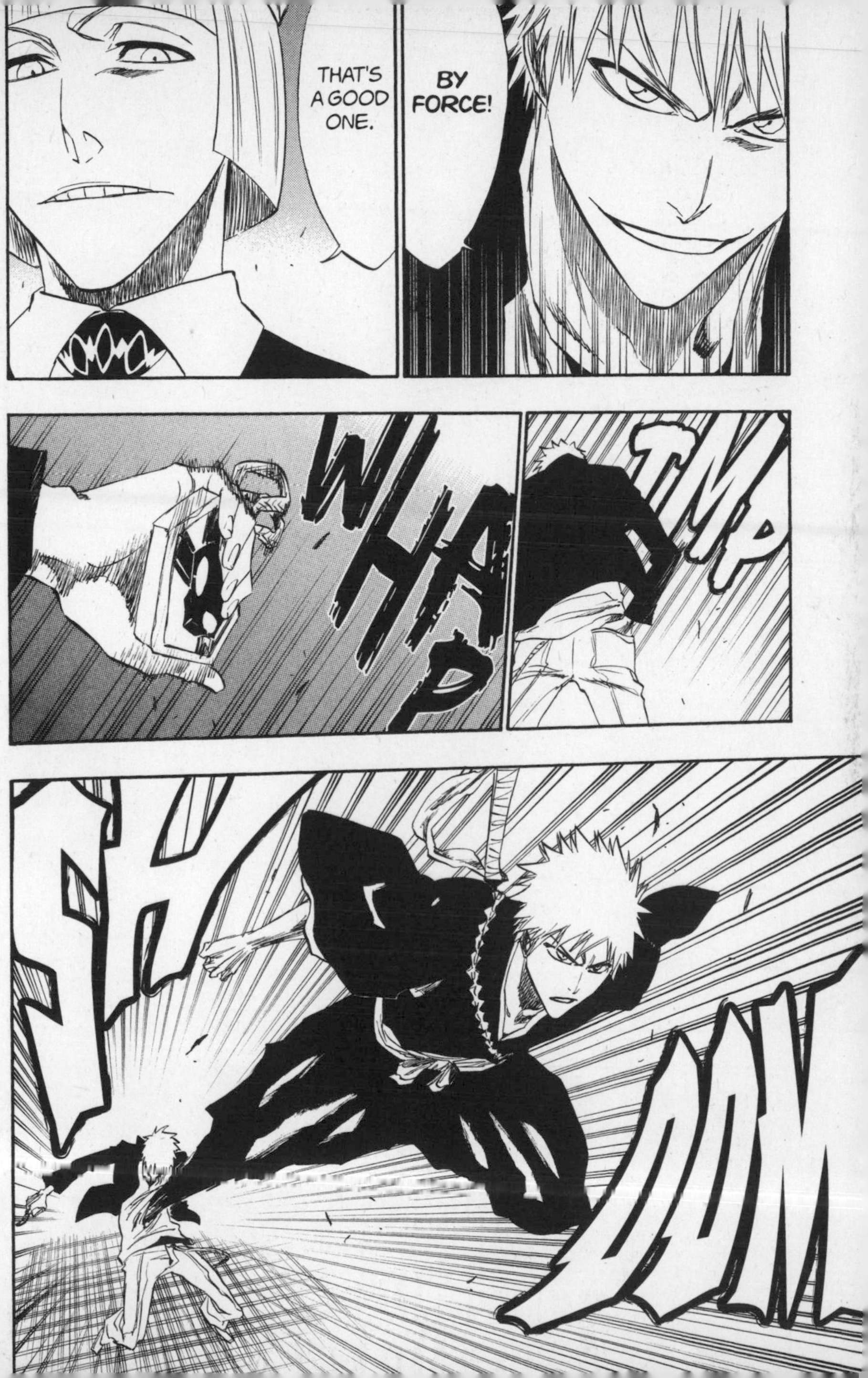
BY FORCE!
THAT'S A GOOD ONE.
TMP
WHAP

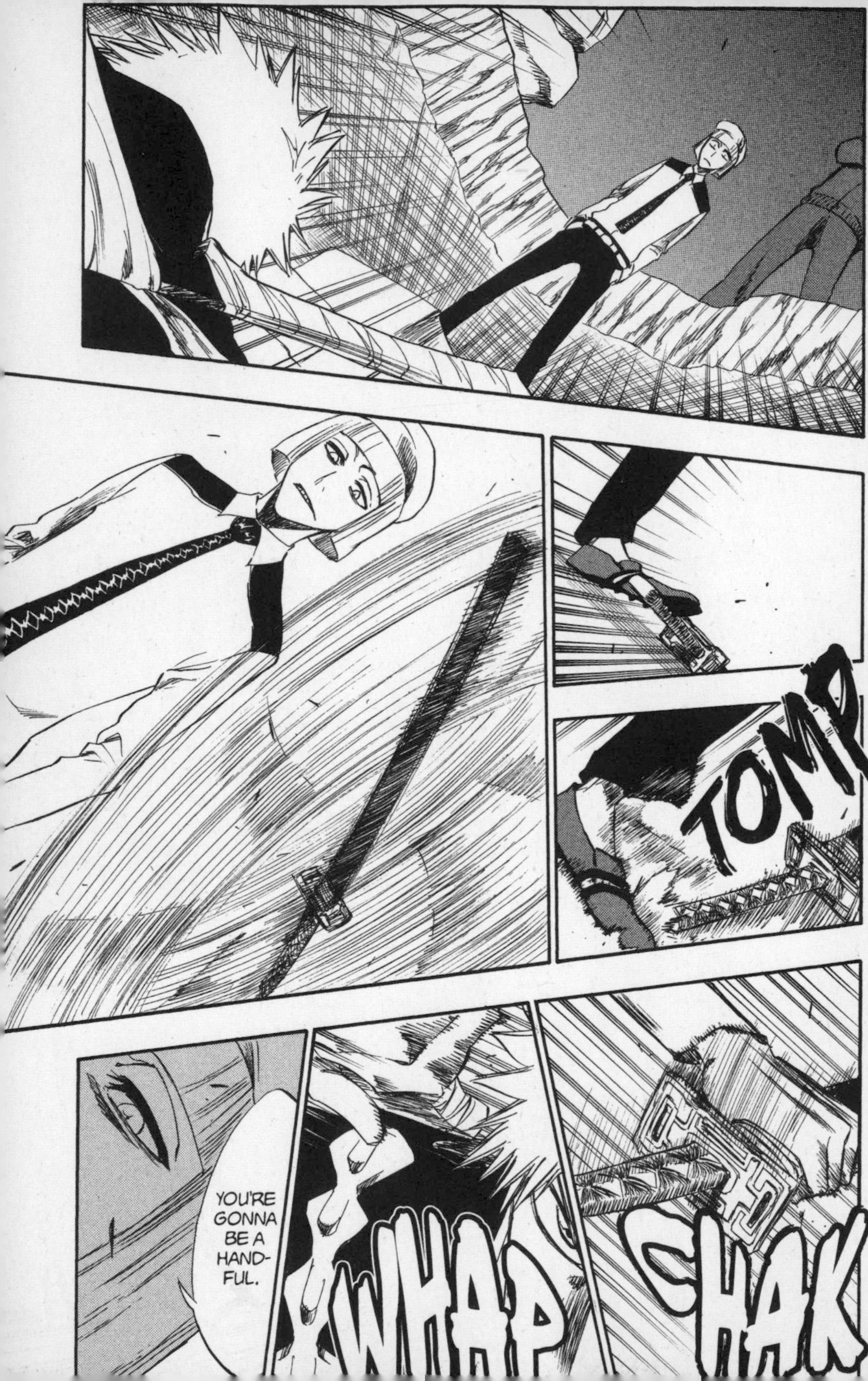
TOMP
CHAK
WHAP
YOU'RE GONNA BE A HAND-FUL.

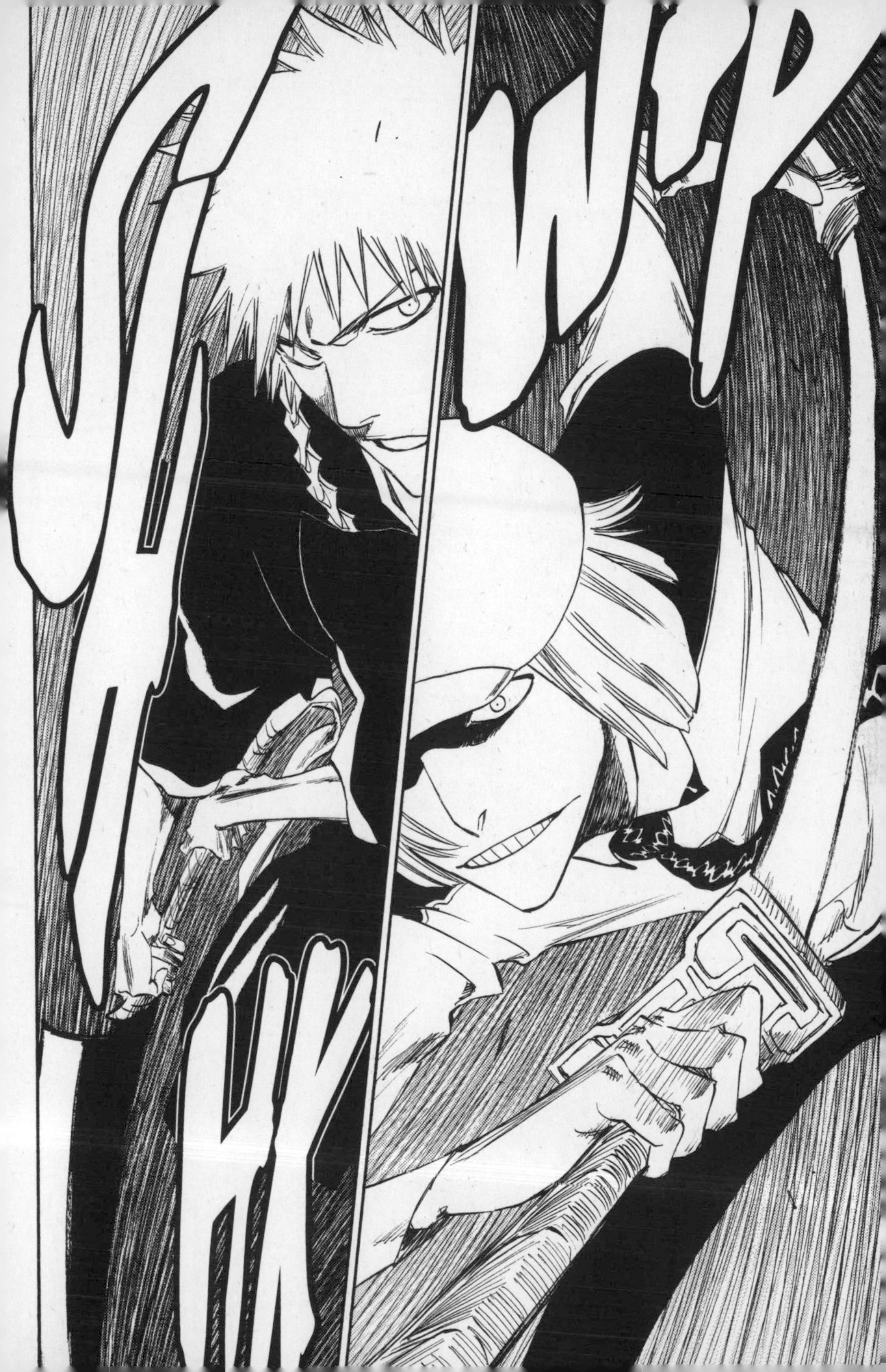

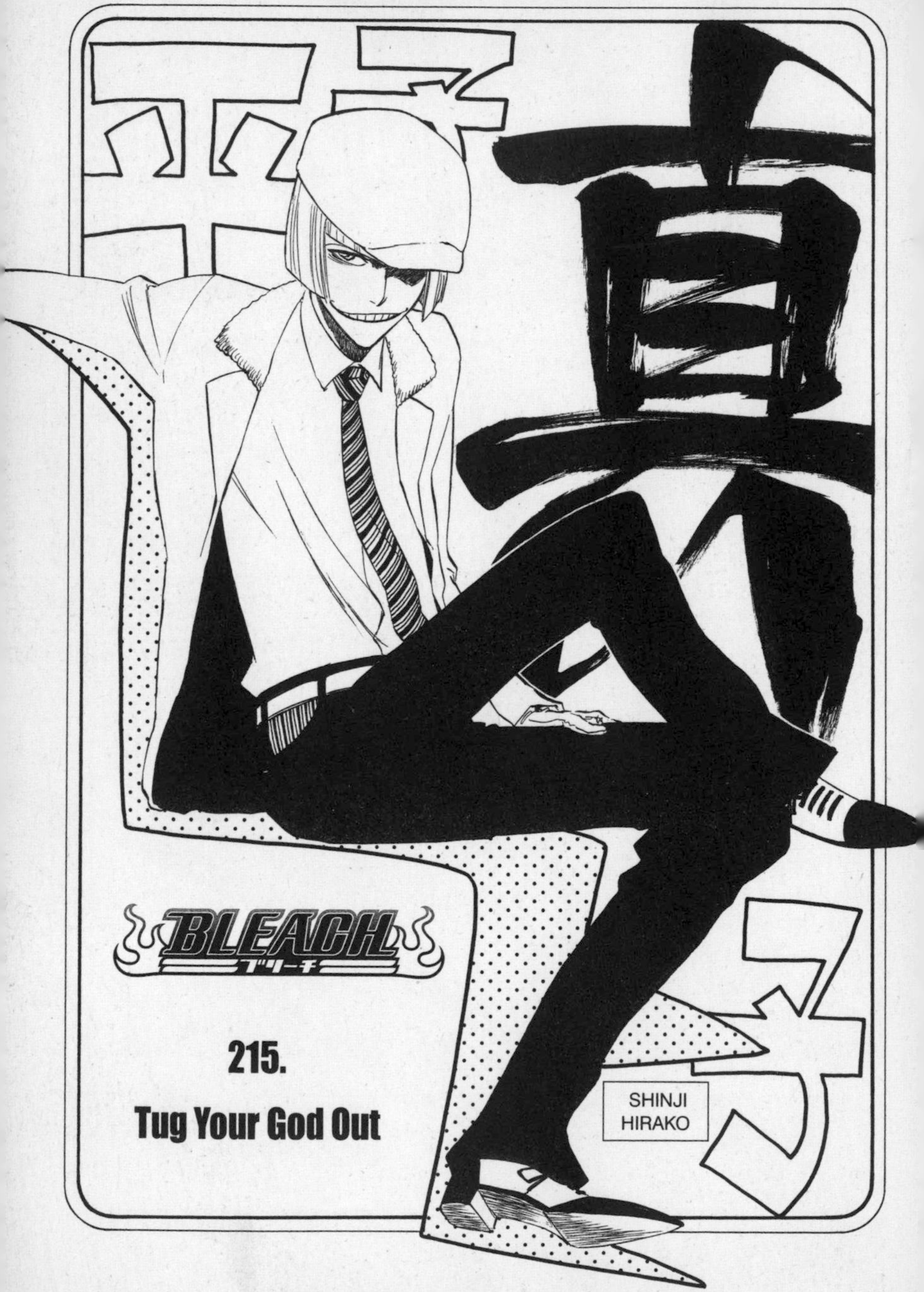
平子真子
BLEACH
ブリーチ
215.
Tug Your God Out
SHINJI
HIRAKO

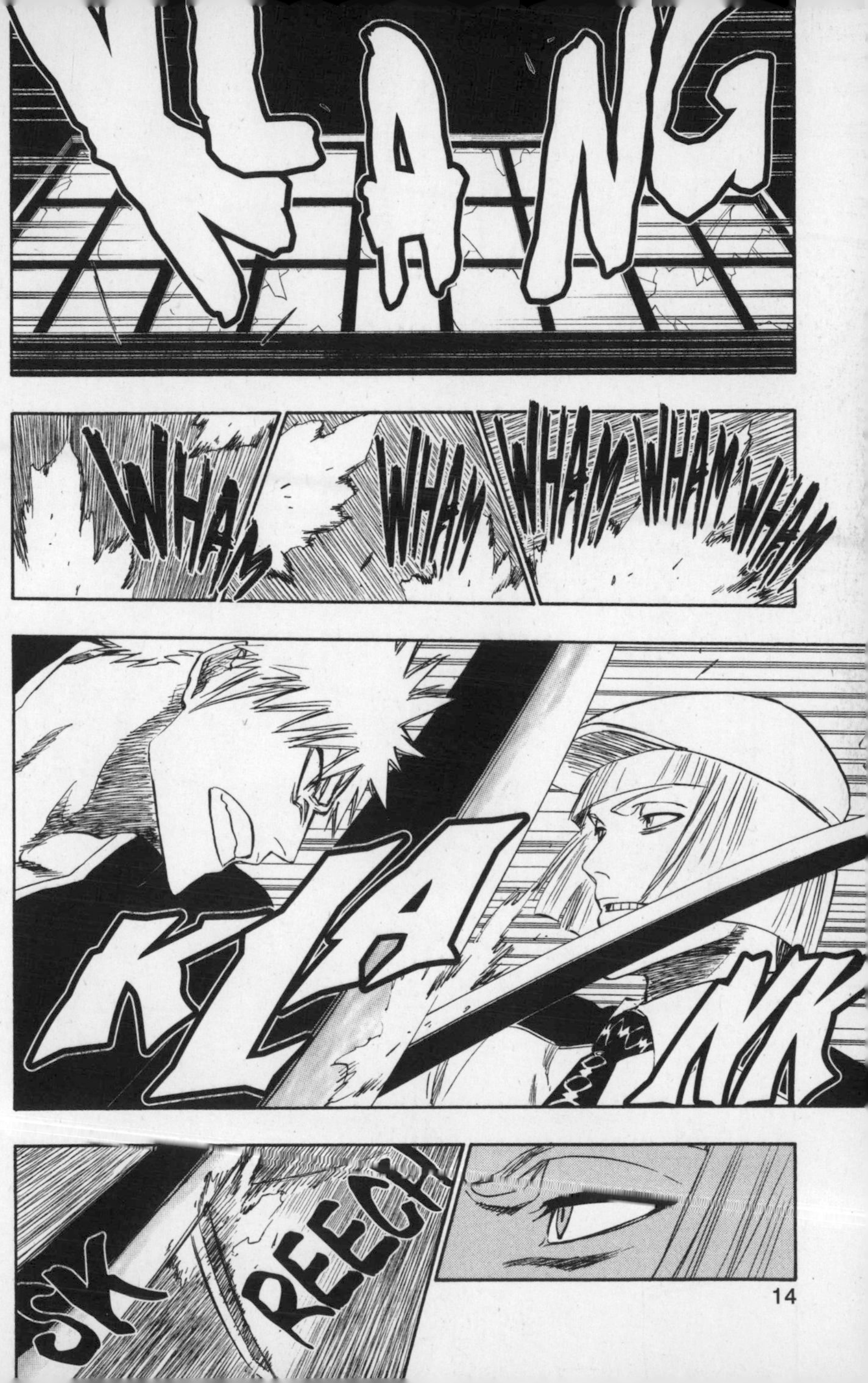
KLANG
WHAM WHAM WHAM
WHAM
WHAM
KLANK
SKREECH

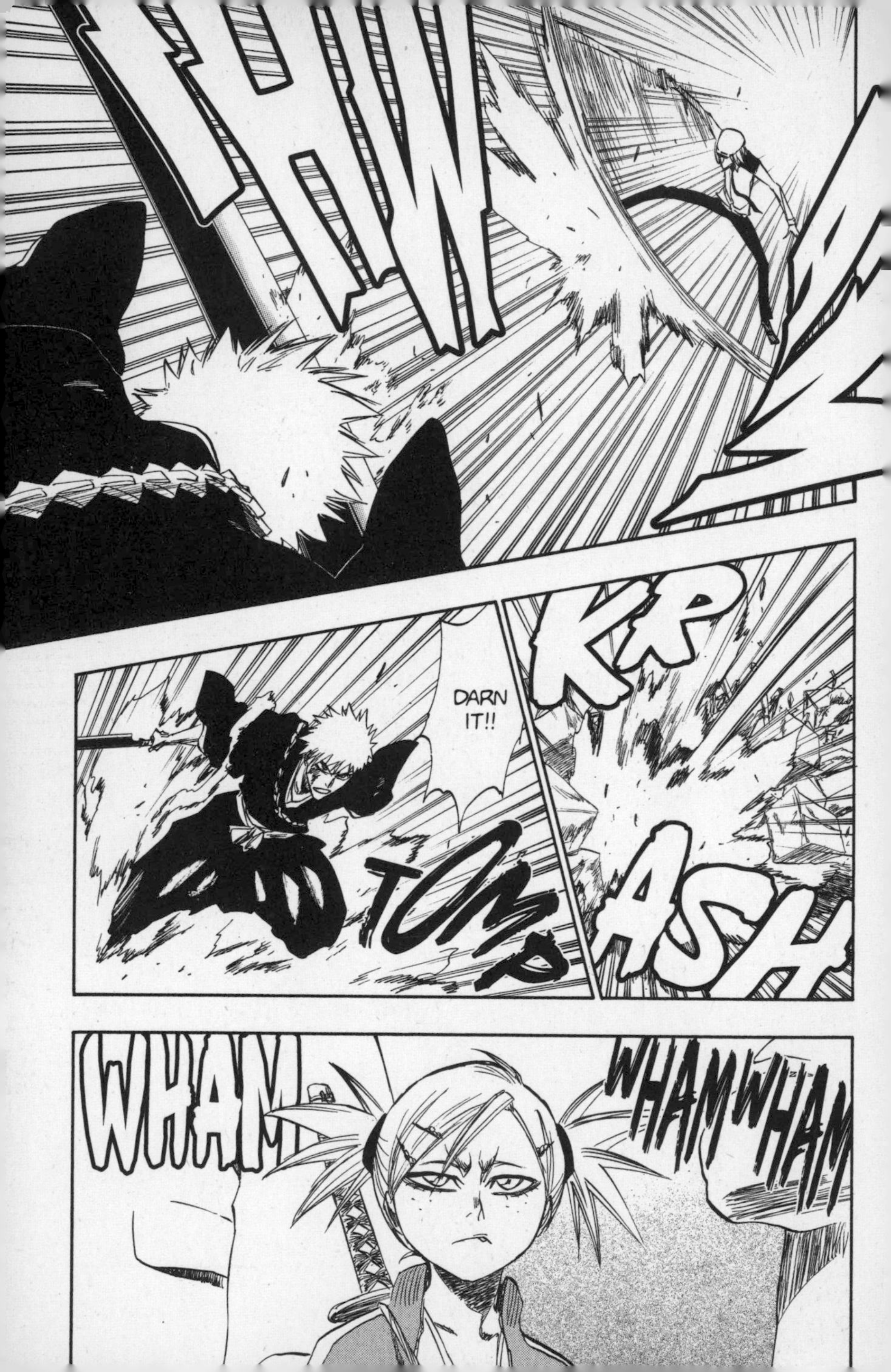
KR
ASH
DARN IT!!
TOMP
WHAM WHAM
WHAM

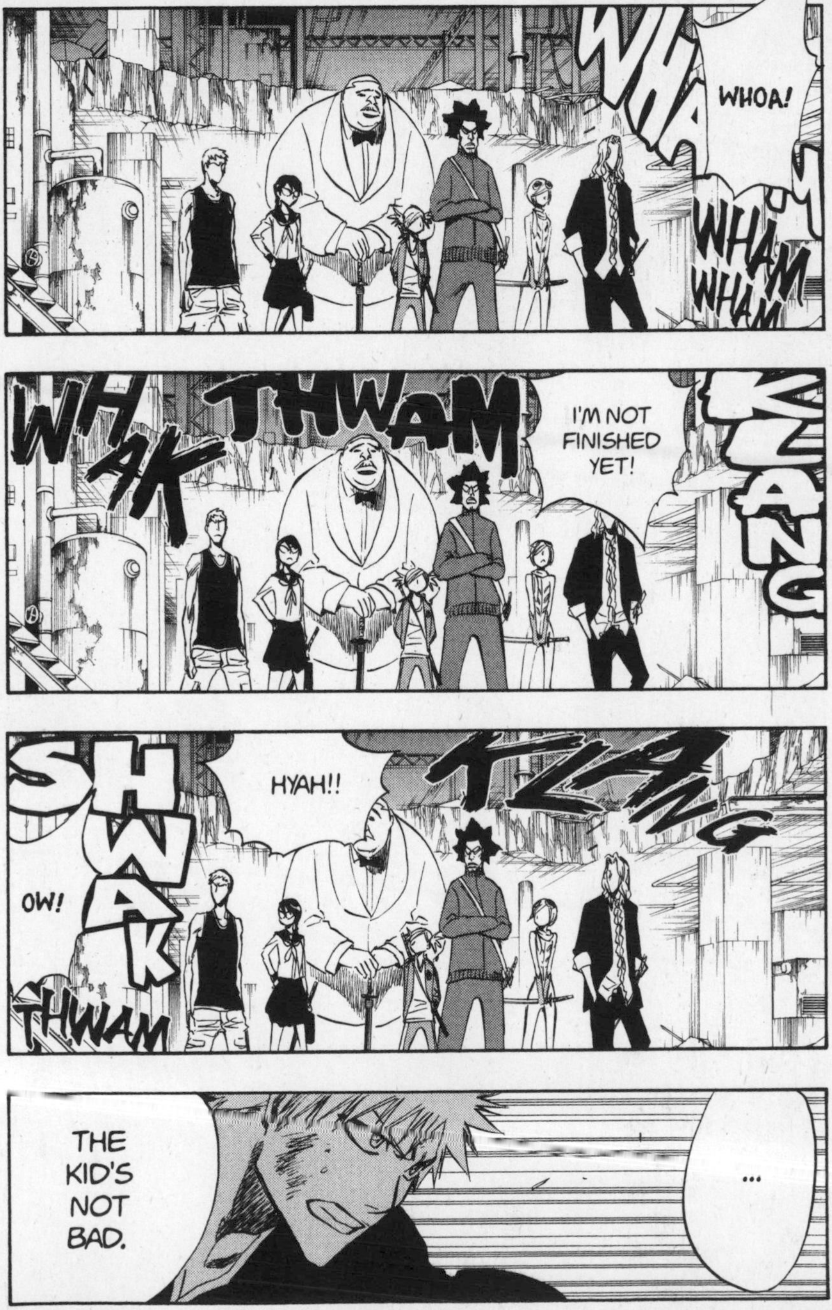
WHOA!
WHAM
WHAM
KLANG
I'M NOT FINISHED YET!
THWAM
WHAK
HYAH!!
SHWAK
OW!
THWAM
...
THE KID'S NOT BAD.

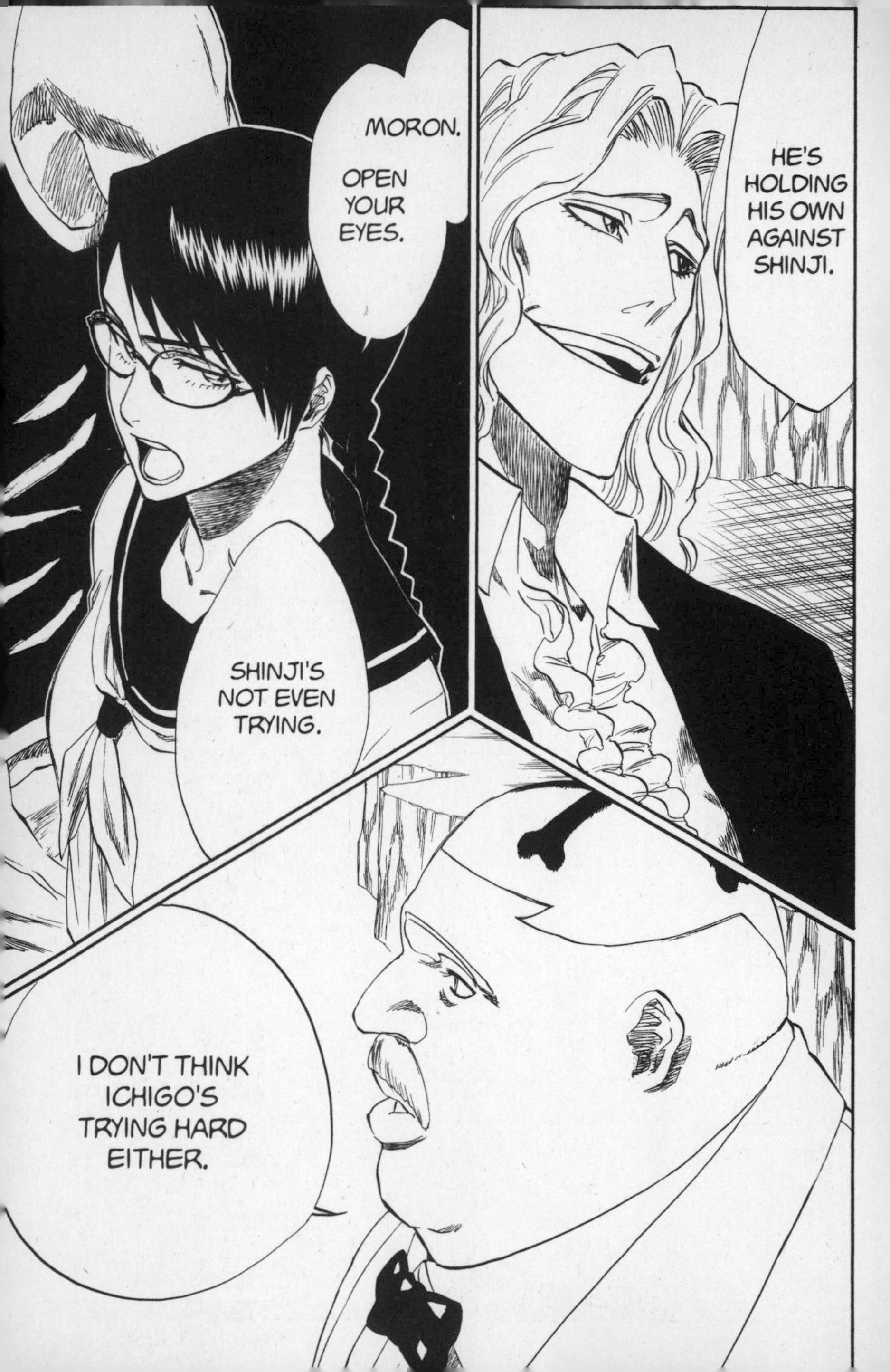
HE'S HOLDING HIS OWN AGAINST SHINJI.
MORON.
OPEN YOUR EYES.
SHINJI'S NOT EVEN TRYING.
I DON'T THINK ICHIGO'S TRYING HARD EITHER.

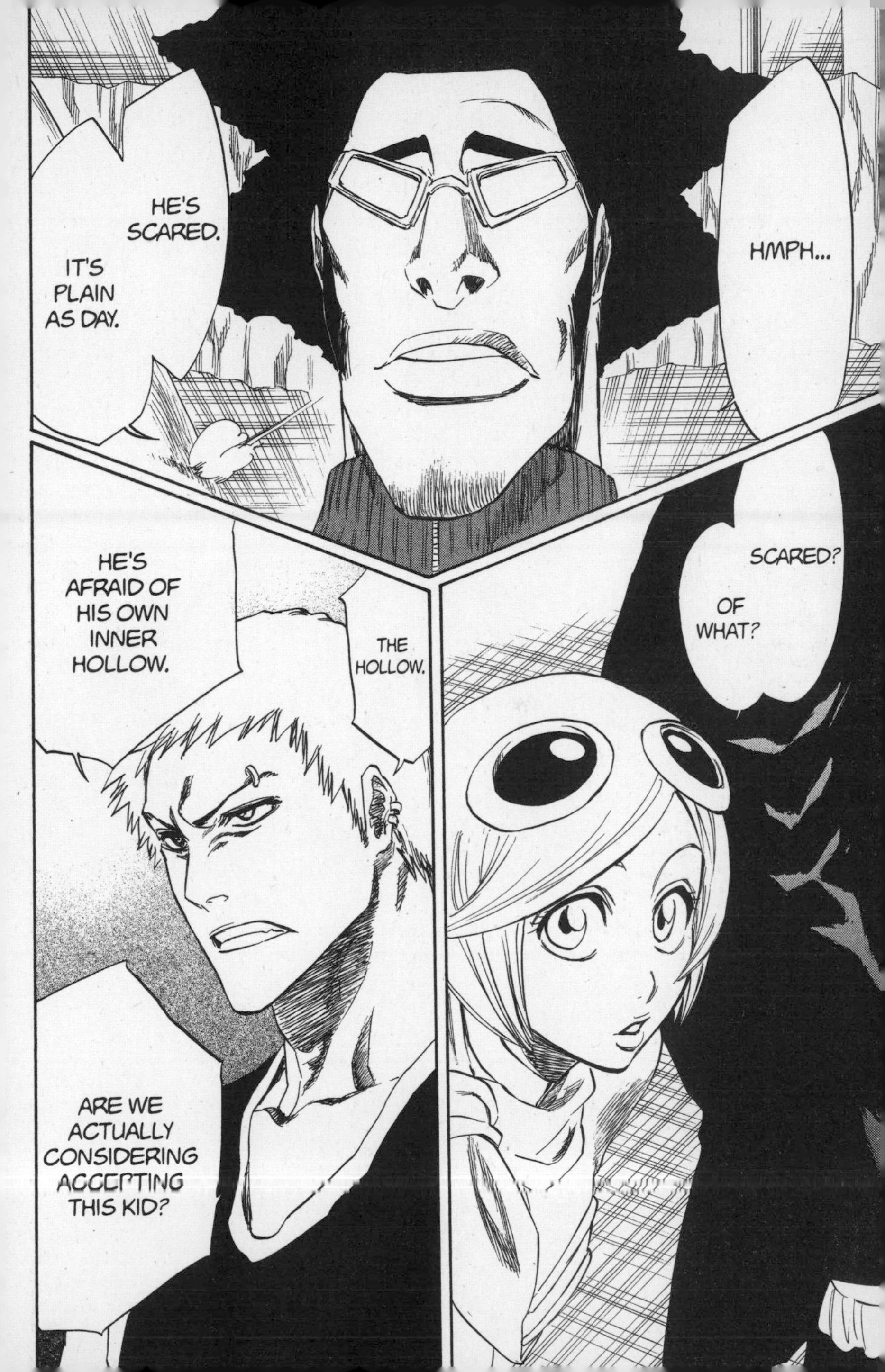
HMPH...
HE'S SCARED.
IT'S PLAIN AS DAY.
SCARED?
OF WHAT?
THE HOLLOW.
HE'S AFRAID OF HIS OWN INNER HOLLOW.
ARE WE ACTUALLY CONSIDERING ACCEPTING THIS KID?

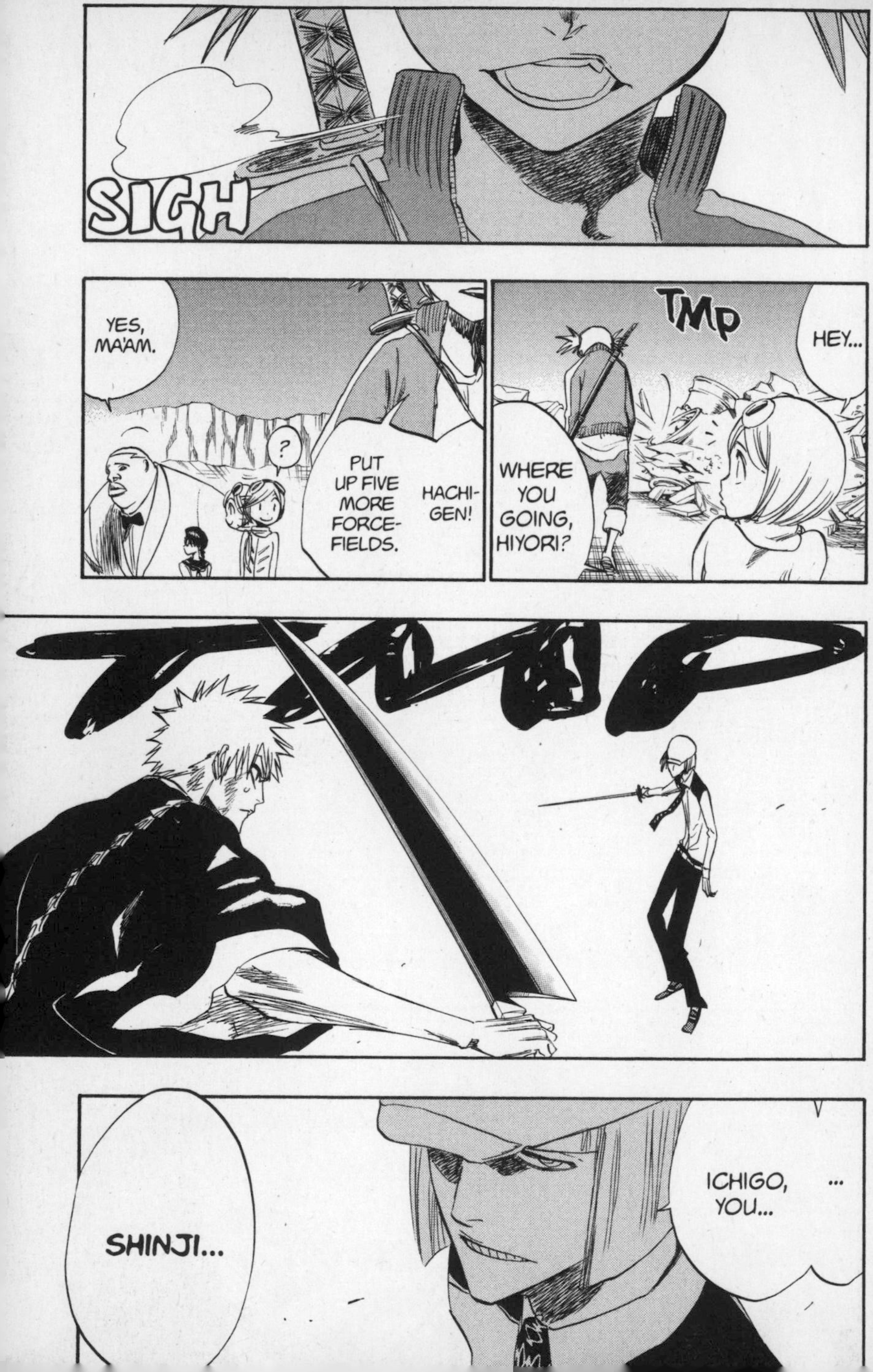
SIGH
HEY...
TMP
WHERE YOU GOING, HIYORI?
HACHIGEN!
PUT UP FIVE MORE FORCE-FIELDS.
YES, MA'AM.
?
TMP
...
ICHIGO, YOU...
SHINJI...

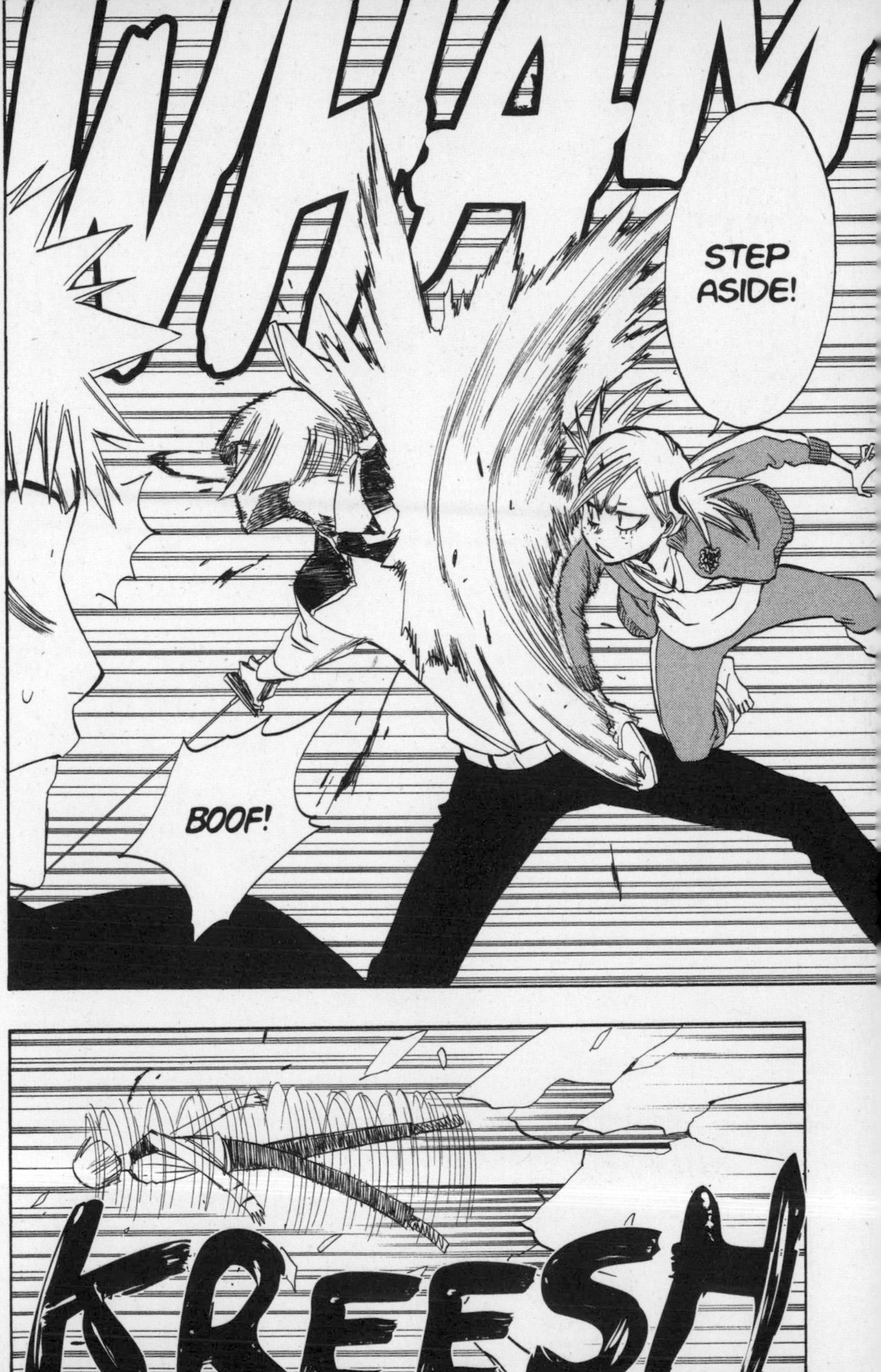
STEP ASIDE!
BOOF!
KREESH!

READ THIS WAY

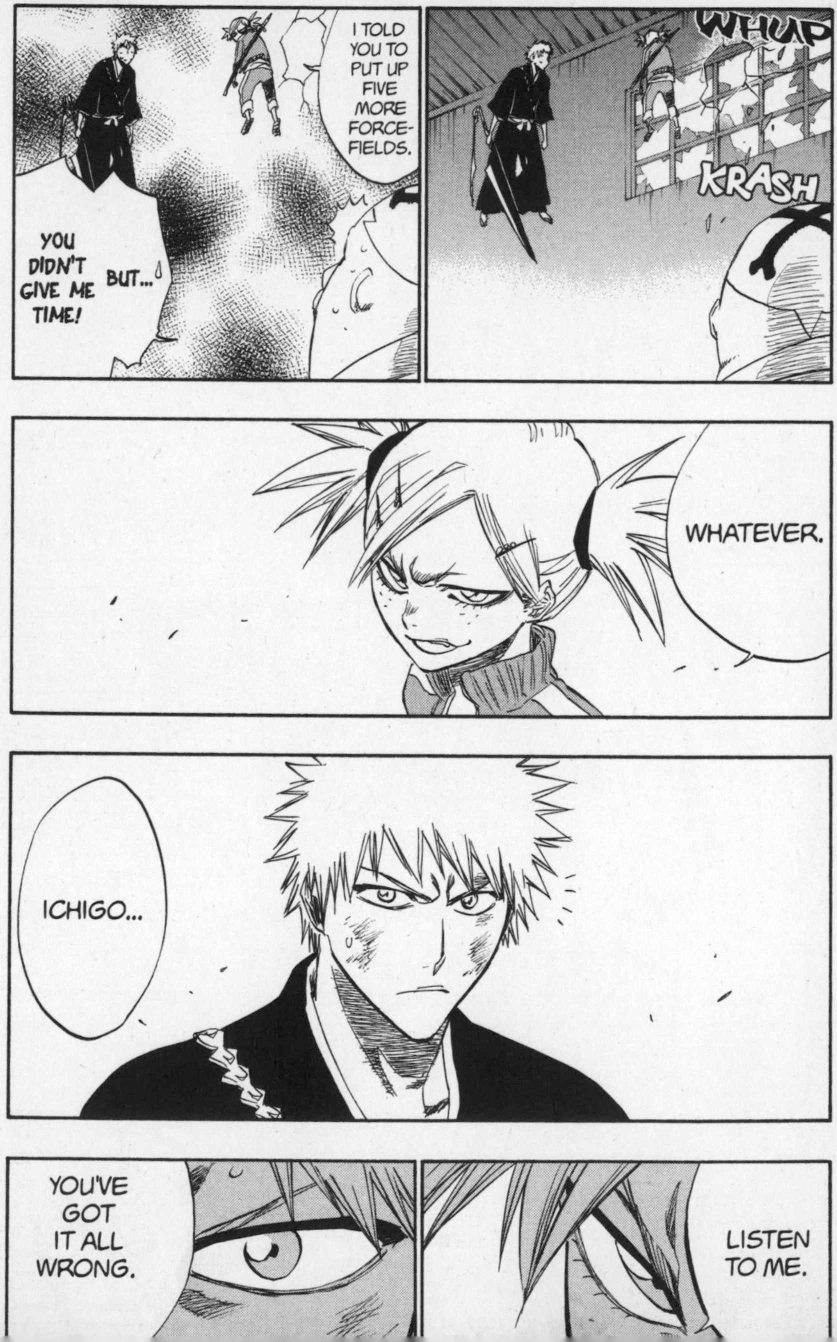
WHUP
KRASH
I TOLD YOU TO PUT UP FIVE MORE FORCE-FIELDS.
BUT...
YOU DIDN'T GIVE ME TIME!
WHATEVER.
ICHIGO...
LISTEN TO ME.
YOU'VE GOT IT ALL WRONG.

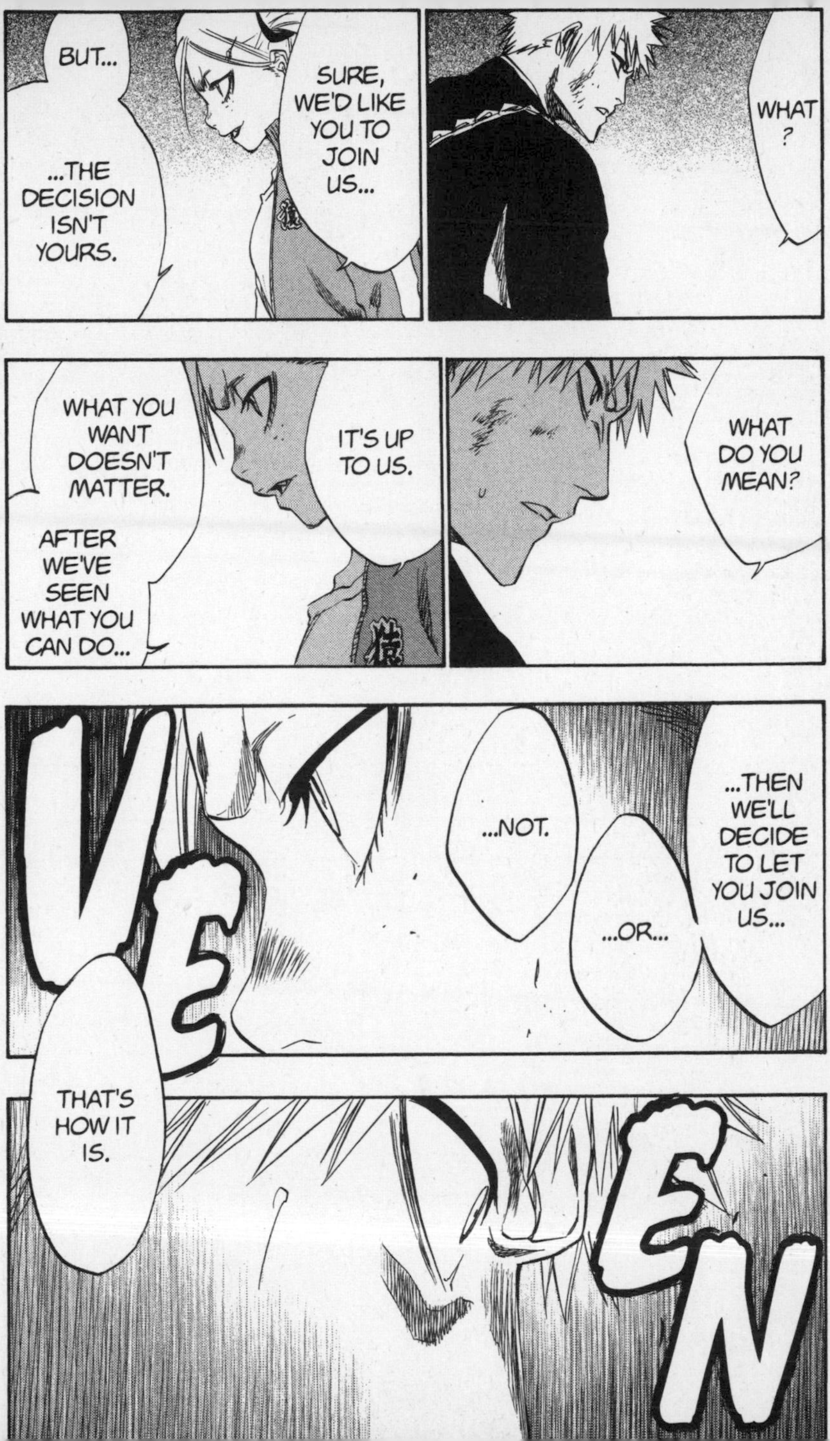
WHAT?
SURE, WE'D LIKE YOU TO JOIN US...
BUT...
...THE DECISION ISN'T YOURS.
WHAT DO YOU MEAN?
IT'S UP TO US.
WHAT YOU WANT DOESN'T MATTER.
AFTER WE'VE SEEN WHAT YOU CAN DO...
...THEN WE'LL DECIDE TO LET YOU JOIN US...
...OR...
...NOT.
VE
THAT'S HOW IT IS.
EN

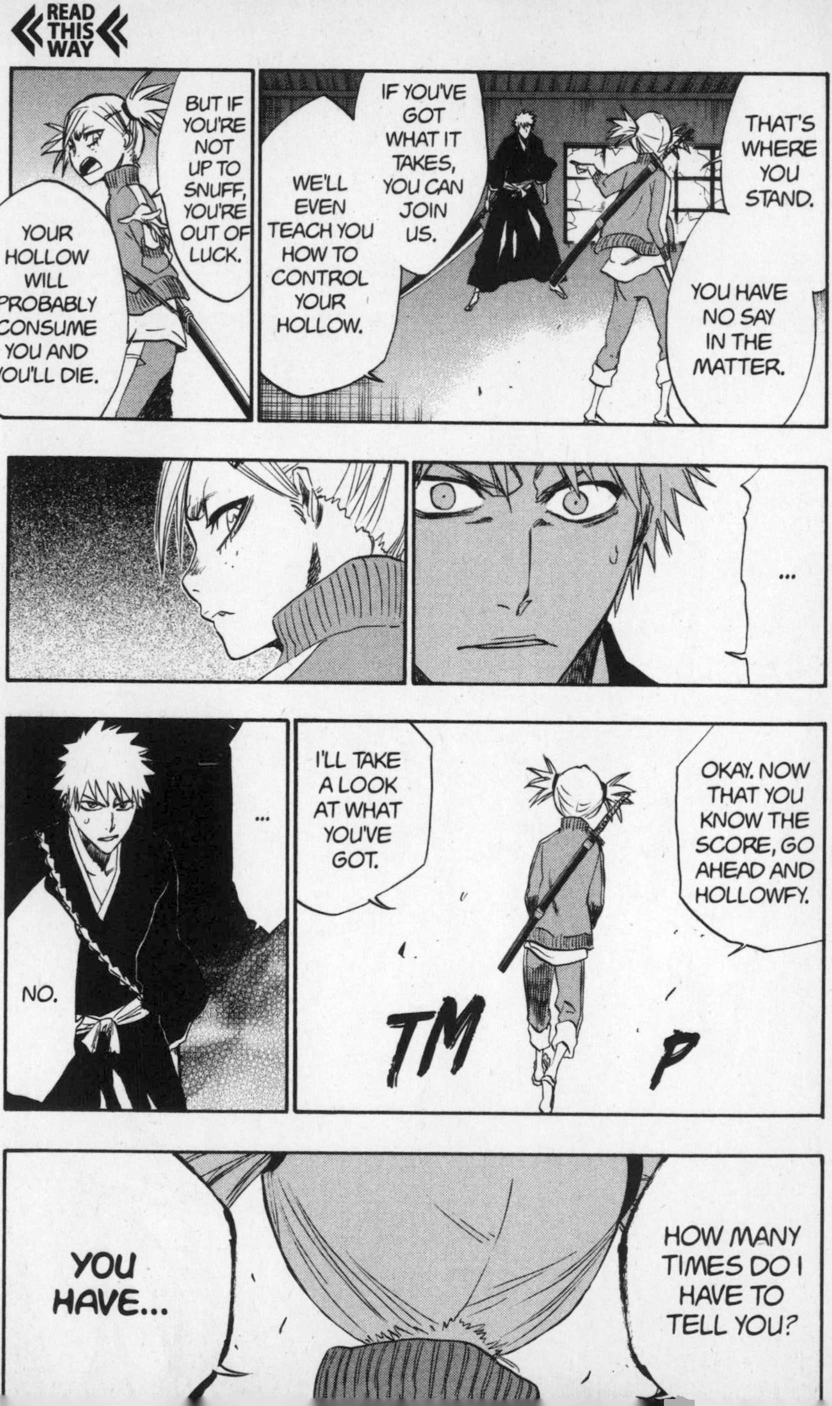
READ THIS WAY
THAT'S WHERE YOU STAND.
YOU HAVE NO SAY IN THE MATTER.
IF YOU'VE GOT WHAT IT TAKES, YOU CAN JOIN US.
WE'LL EVEN TEACH YOU HOW TO CONTROL YOUR HOLLOW.
BUT IF YOU'RE NOT UP TO SNUFF, YOU'RE OUT OF LUCK.
YOUR HOLLOW WILL PROBABLY CONSUME YOU AND YOU'LL DIE.
...
OKAY. NOW THAT YOU KNOW THE SCORE, GO AHEAD AND HOLLOWFY.
TMP
I'LL TAKE A LOOK AT WHAT YOU'VE GOT.
...
NO.
HOW MANY TIMES DO I HAVE TO TELL YOU?
YOU HAVE...

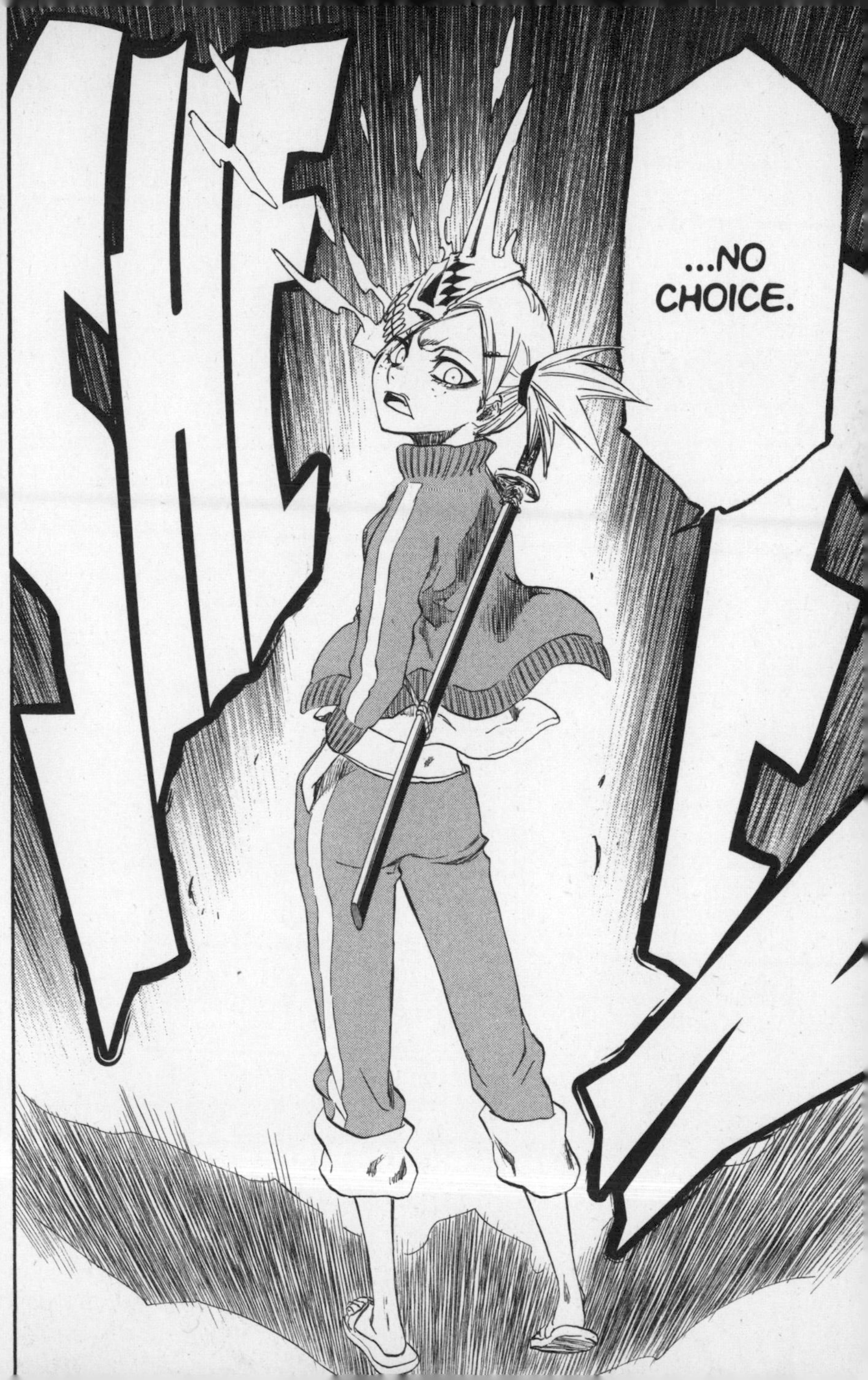
...NO CHOICE.

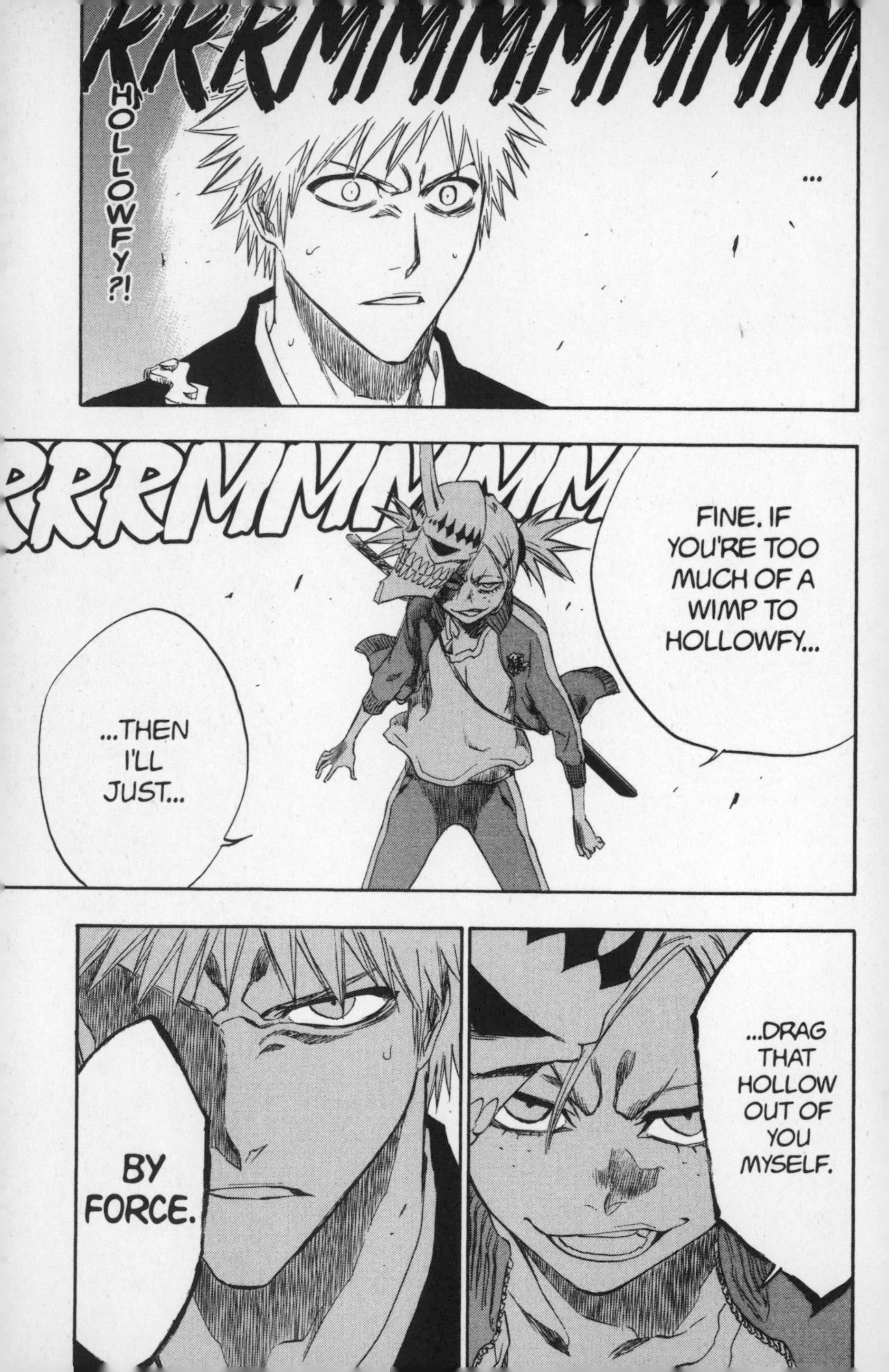
KRRMMMMMMMM
...
HOLLOWFY?!
FINE. IF YOU'RE TOO MUCH OF A WIMP TO HOLLOWFY...
...THEN I'LL JUST...
RRRMMMM
...DRAG THAT HOLLOW OUT OF YOU MYSELF.
BY FORCE.

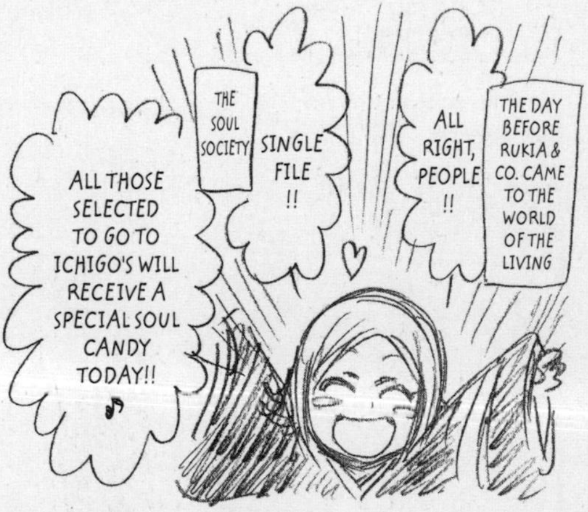
THE DAY BEFORE RUKIA & CO. CAME TO THE WORLD OF THE LIVING
ALL RIGHT, PEOPLE!!
THE SOUL SOCIETY
SINGLE FILE!!
ALL THOSE SELECTED TO GO TO ICHIGO'S WILL RECEIVE A SPECIAL SOUL CANDY TODAY!!

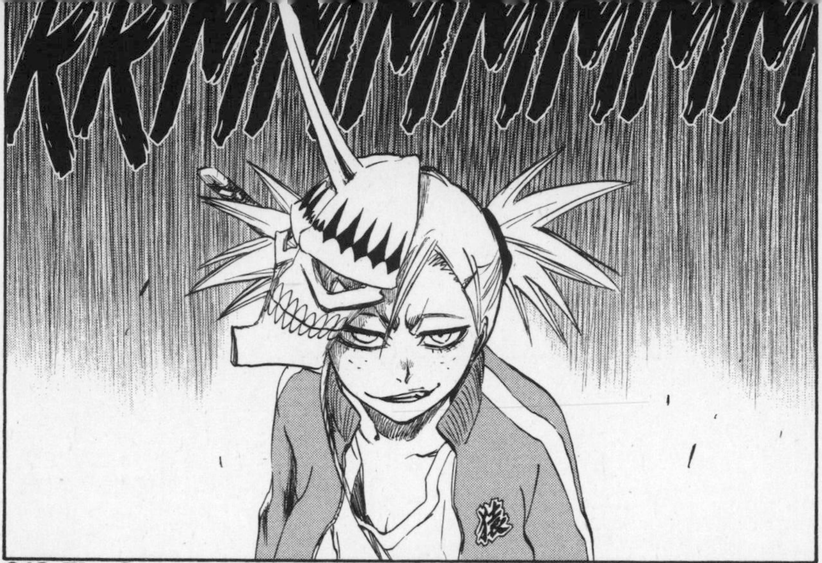
KRMMMMMM

216. The Suppression of Darkness

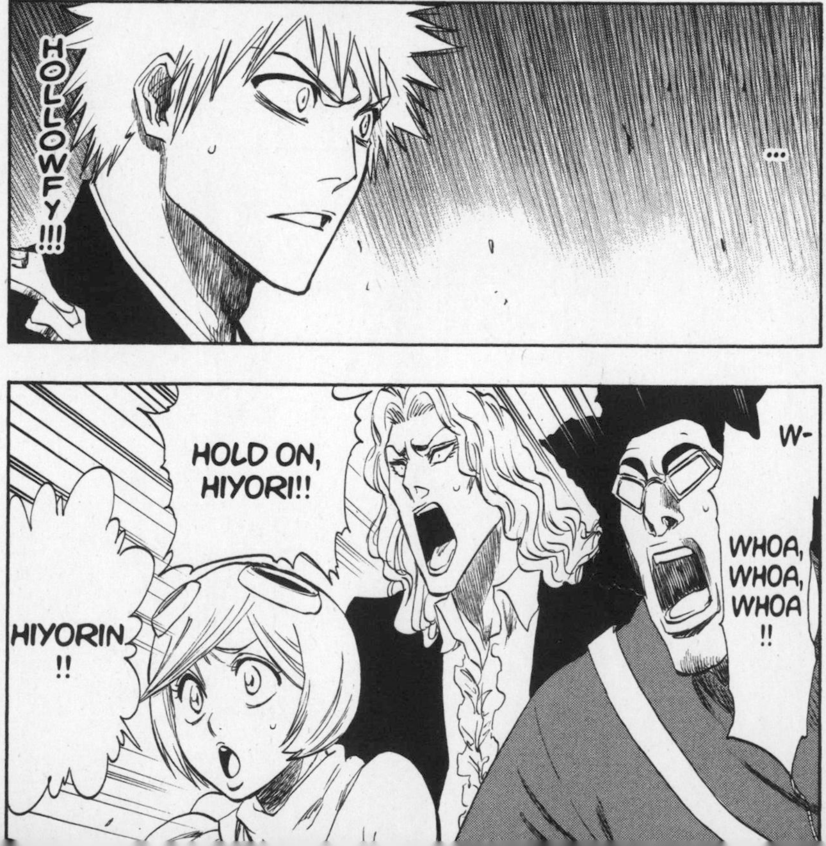
...
HOLLOWFY!!!
W-
WHOA, WHOA, WHOA!!
HOLD ON, HIYORI!!
HIYORIN!!

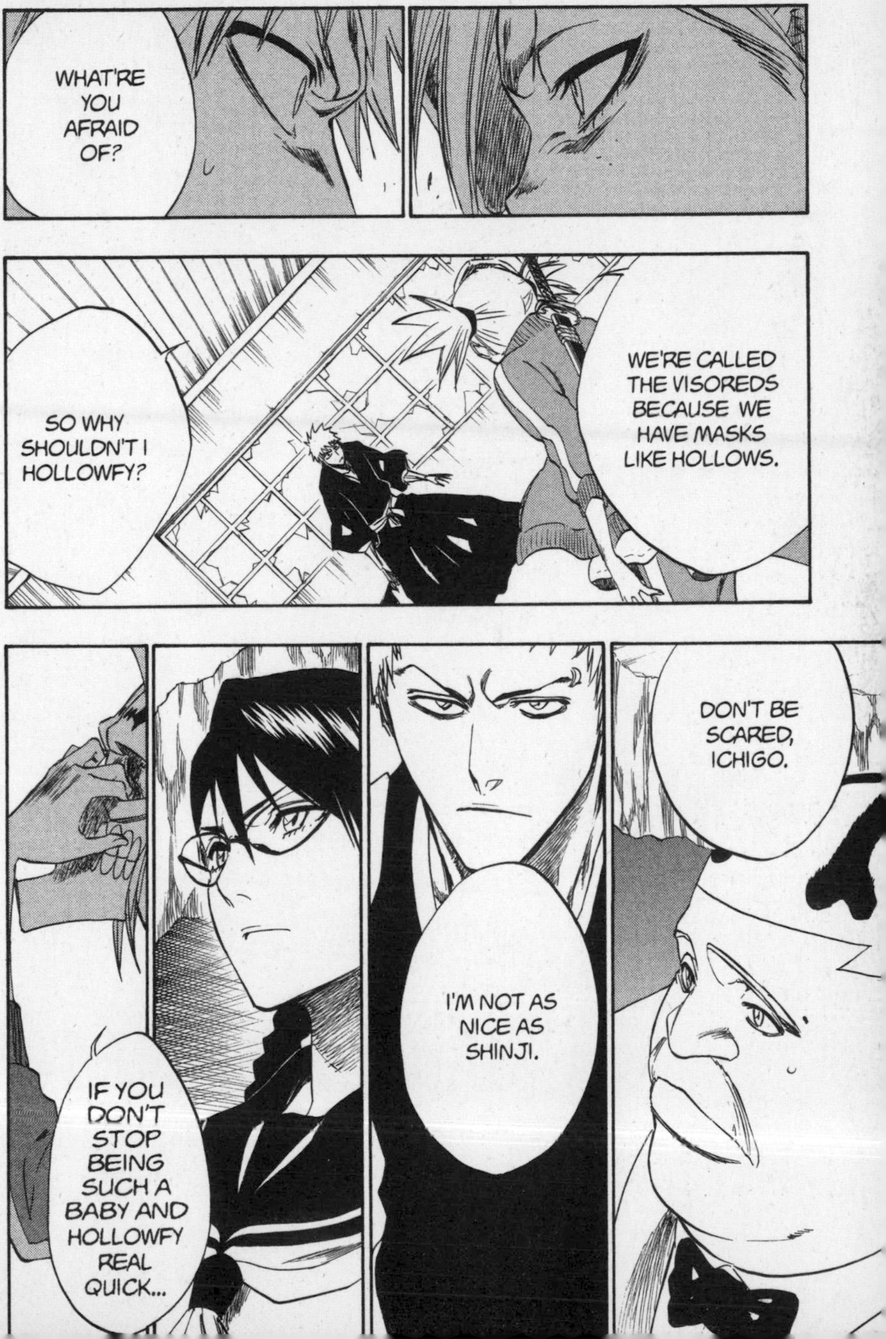
WHAT'RE YOU AFRAID OF?
WE'RE CALLED THE VISOREDS BECAUSE WE HAVE MASKS LIKE HOLLOWS.
SO WHY SHOULDN'T I HOLLOWFY?
DON'T BE SCARED, ICHIGO.
I'M NOT AS NICE AS SHINJI.
IF YOU DON'T STOP BEING SUCH A BABY AND HOLLOWFY REAL QUICK...

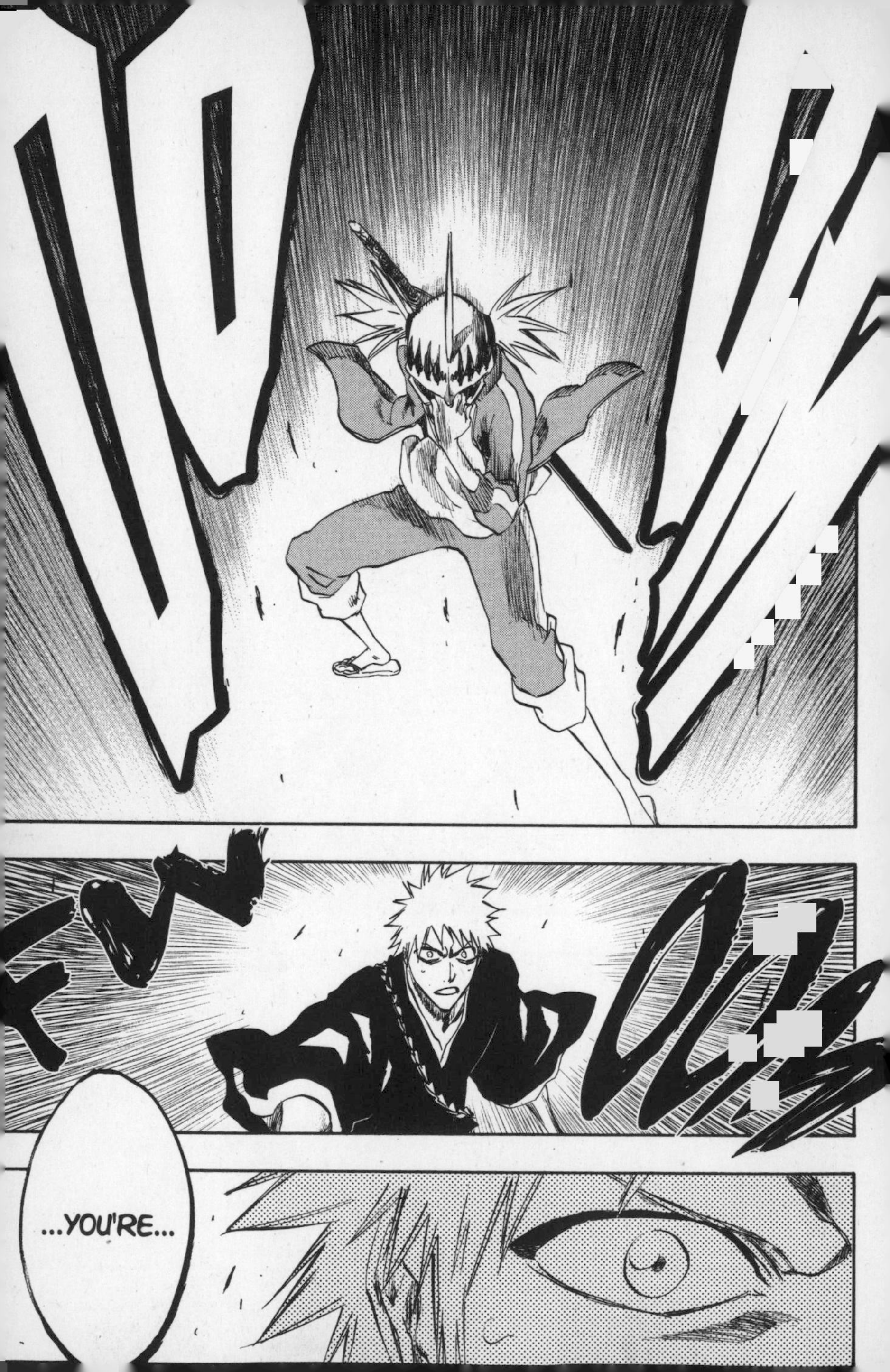
...YOU'RE...

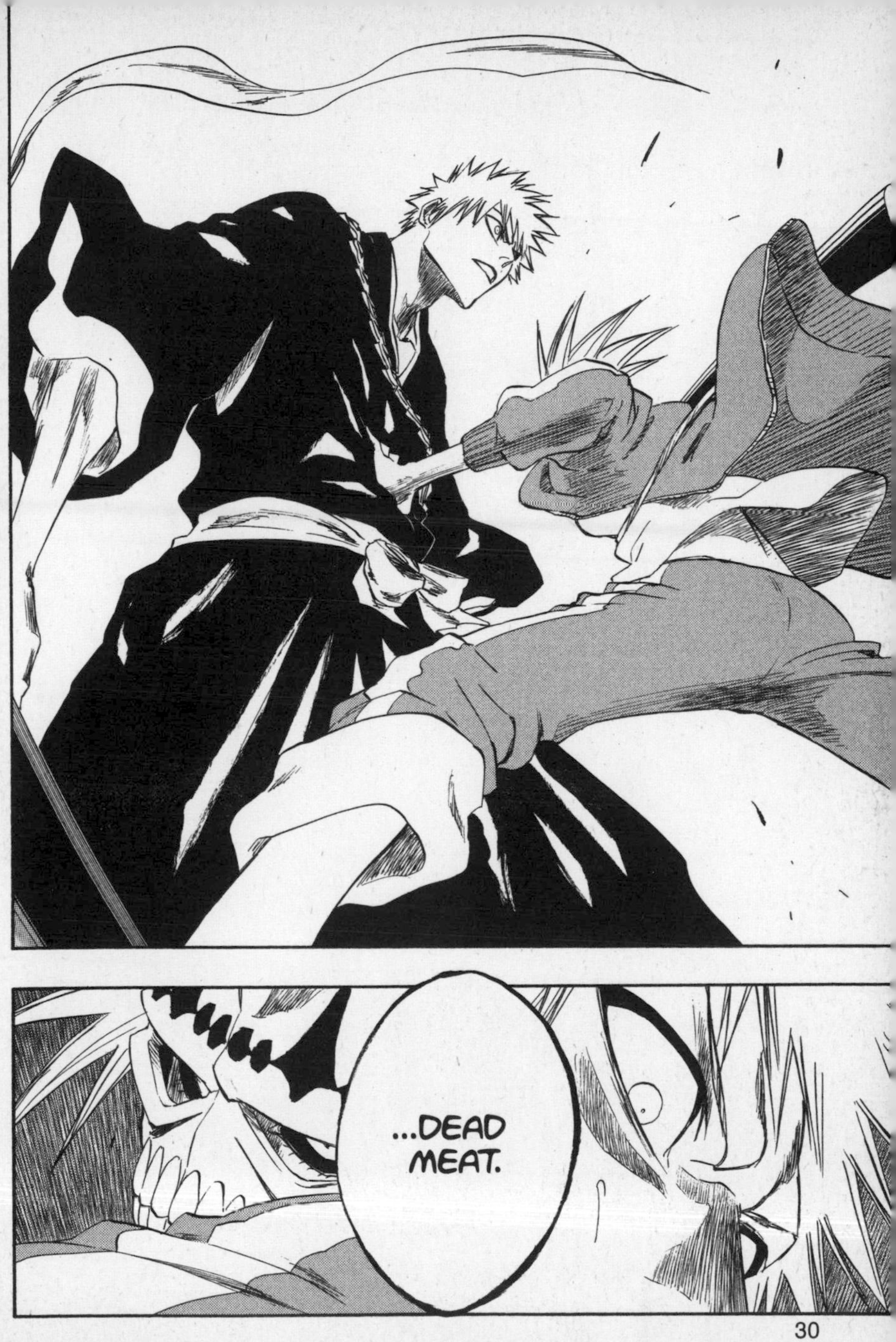
...DEAD
MEAT.

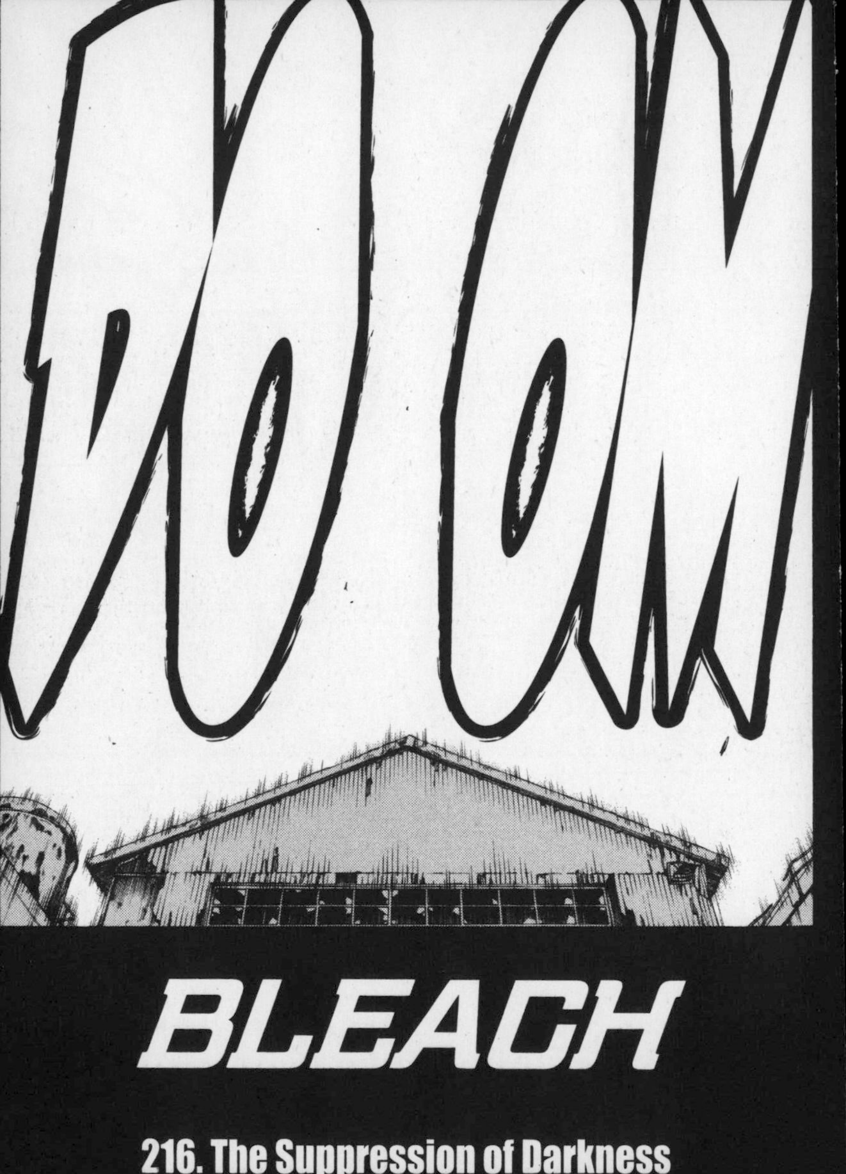

BLEACH

216. The Suppression of Darkness

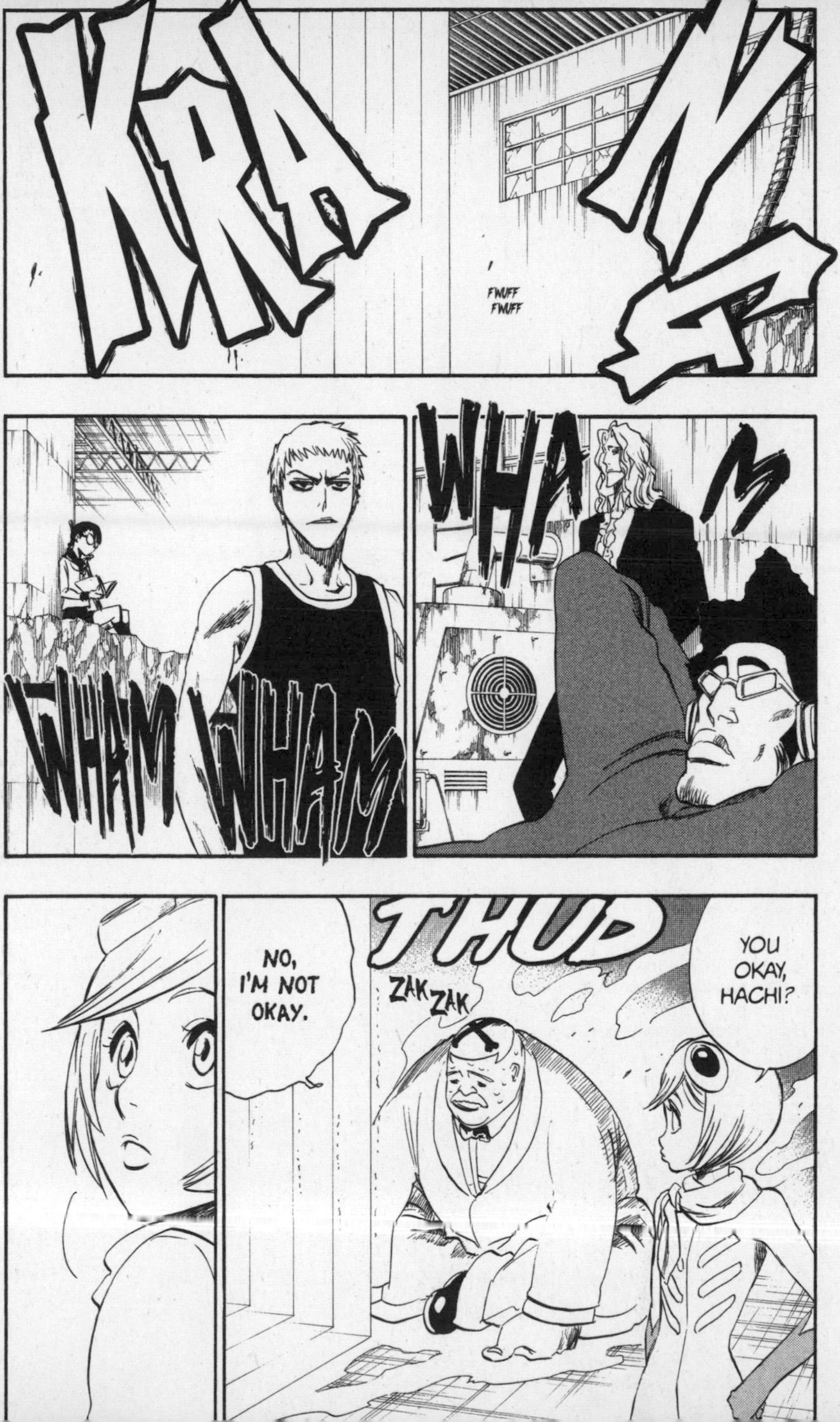
KRANG
FWUFF
FWUFF
WHAM
WHAM
WHAM
THUD
YOU OKAY, HACHI?
NO, I'M NOT OKAY.
ZAK ZAK

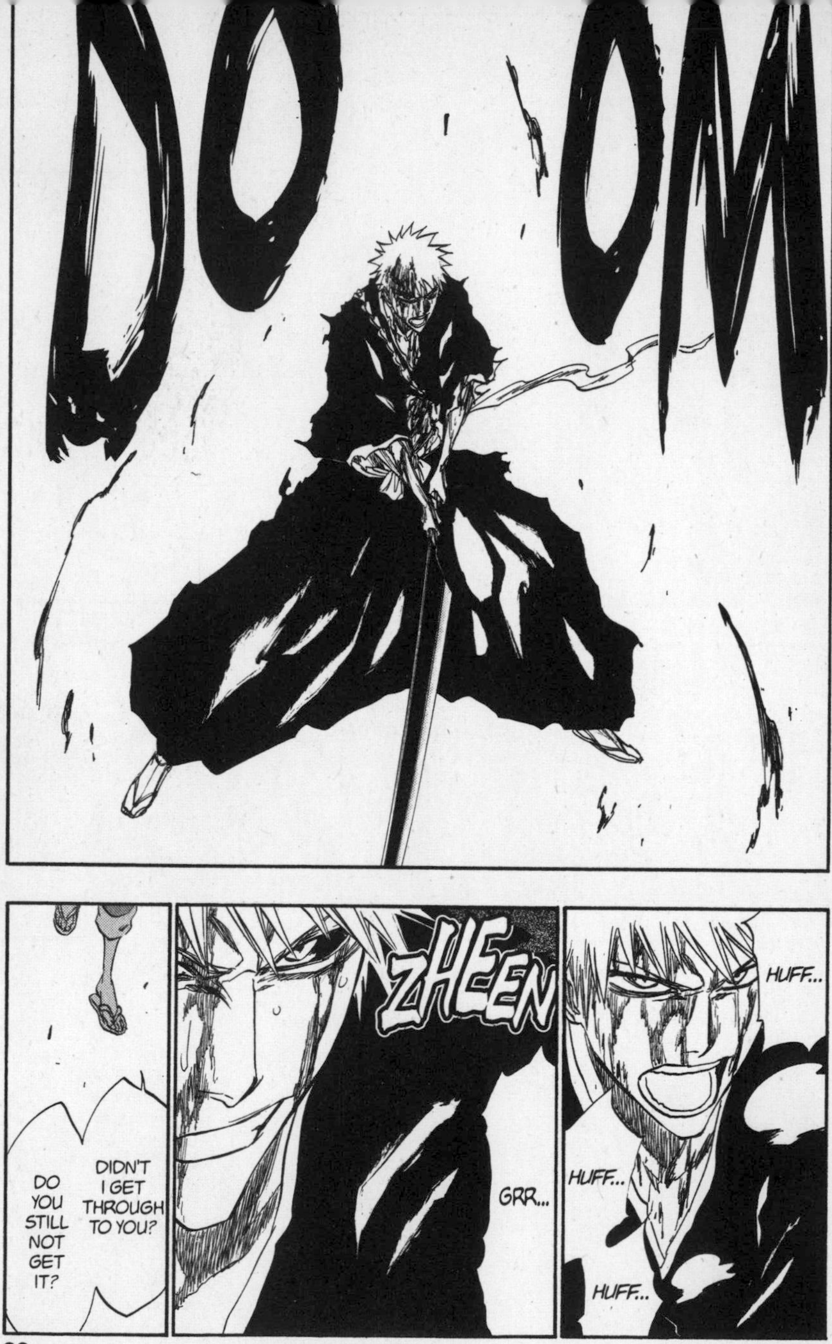
DO OM
HUFF...
HUFF...
HUFF...
ZHEEN
GRR...
DIDN'T I GET THROUGH TO YOU?
DO YOU STILL NOT GET IT?

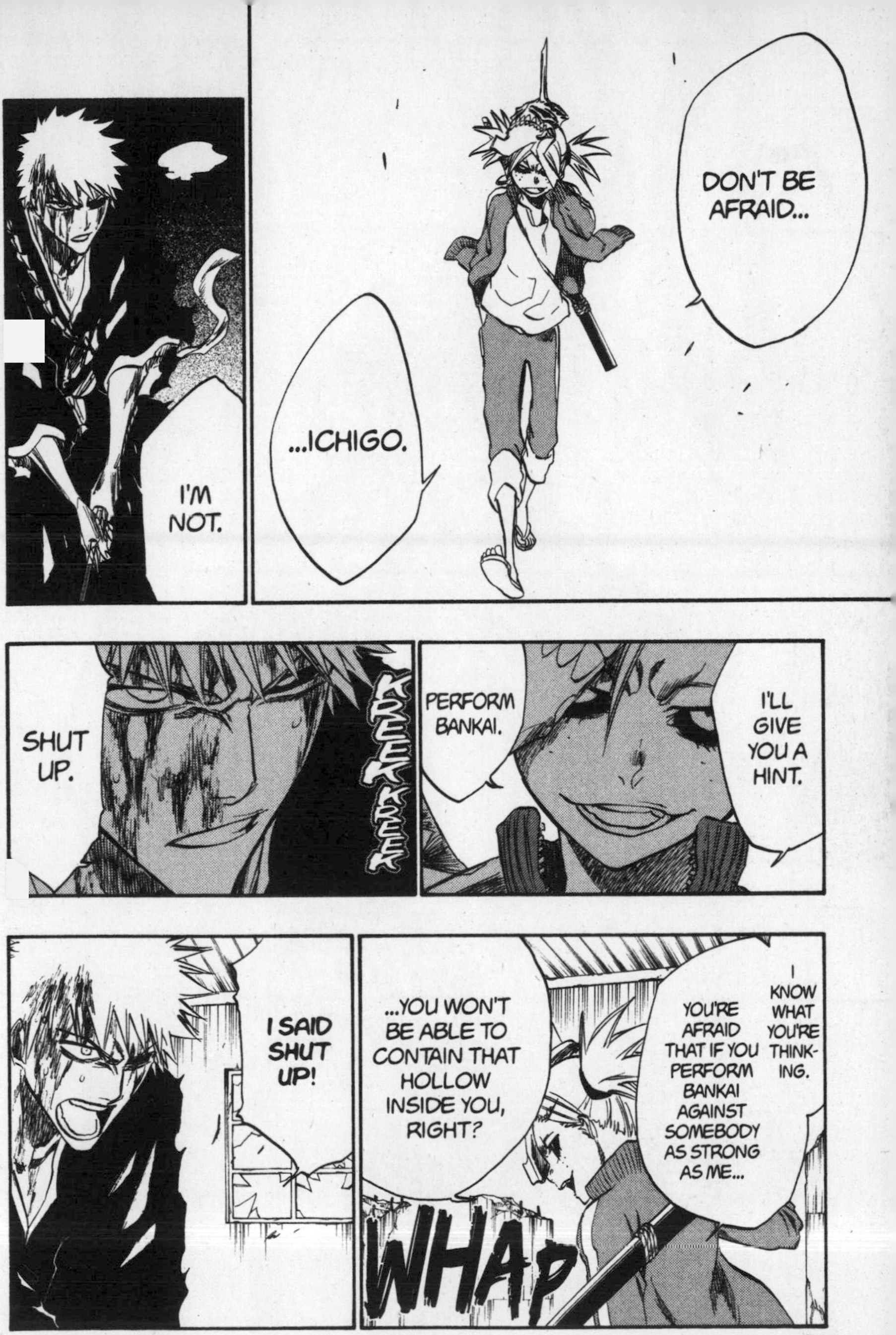
DON'T BE AFRAID...
...ICHIGO.
I'M NOT.
I'LL GIVE YOU A HINT.
PERFORM BANKAI.
KREEK KREEK
SHUT UP.
I KNOW WHAT YOU'RE THINK-ING.
YOU'RE AFRAID THAT IF YOU PERFORM BANKAI AGAINST SOMEBODY AS STRONG AS ME...
...YOU WON'T BE ABLE TO CONTAIN THAT HOLLOW INSIDE YOU, RIGHT?
WHAP
I SAID SHUT UP!

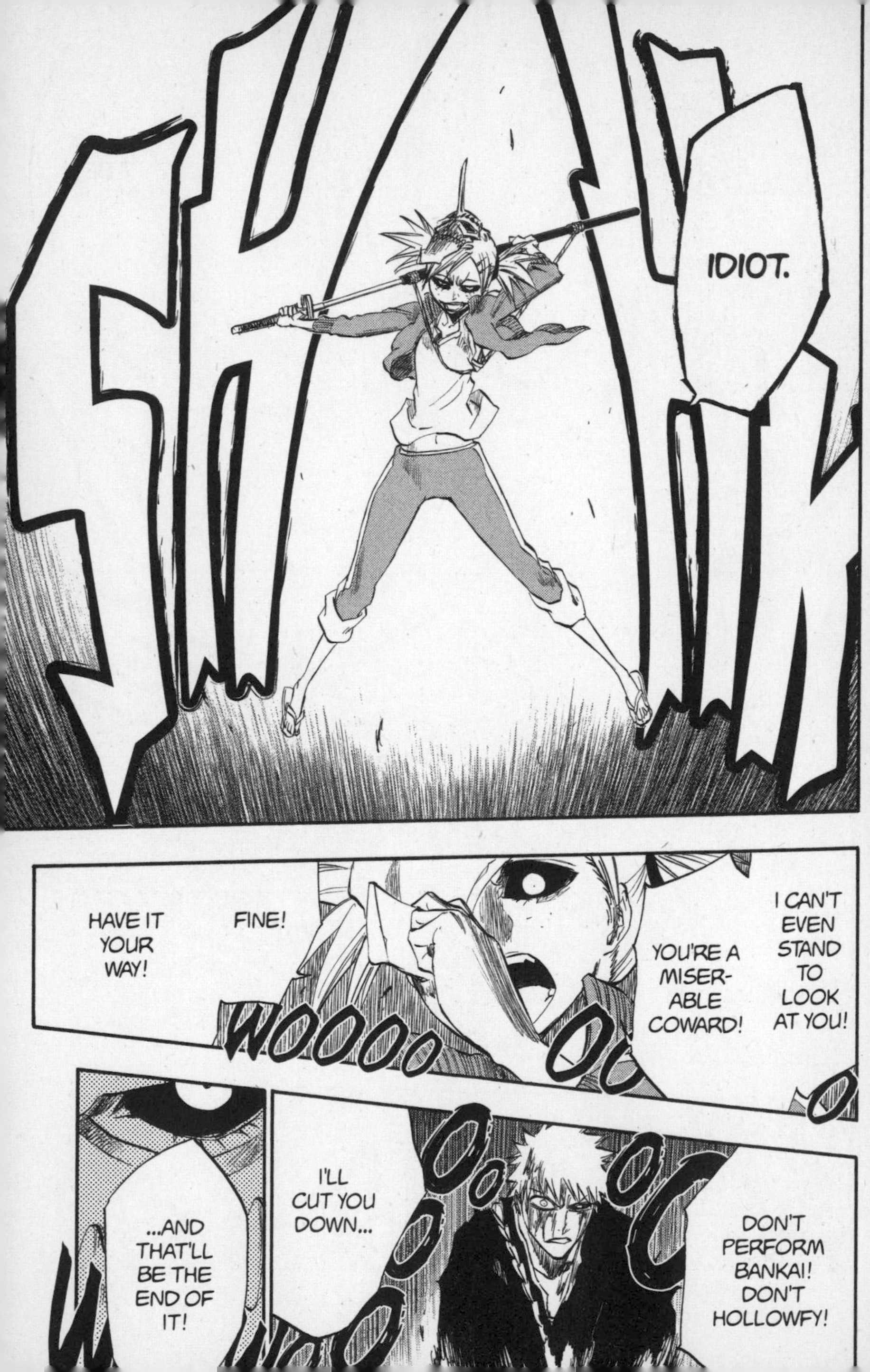
IDIOT.
I CAN'T EVEN STAND TO LOOK AT YOU!
YOU'RE A MISER-ABLE COWARD!
FINE!
HAVE IT YOUR WAY!
WOOOOO
DON'T PERFORM BANKAI! DON'T HOLLOWFY!
I'LL CUT YOU DOWN...
...AND THAT'LL BE THE END OF IT!

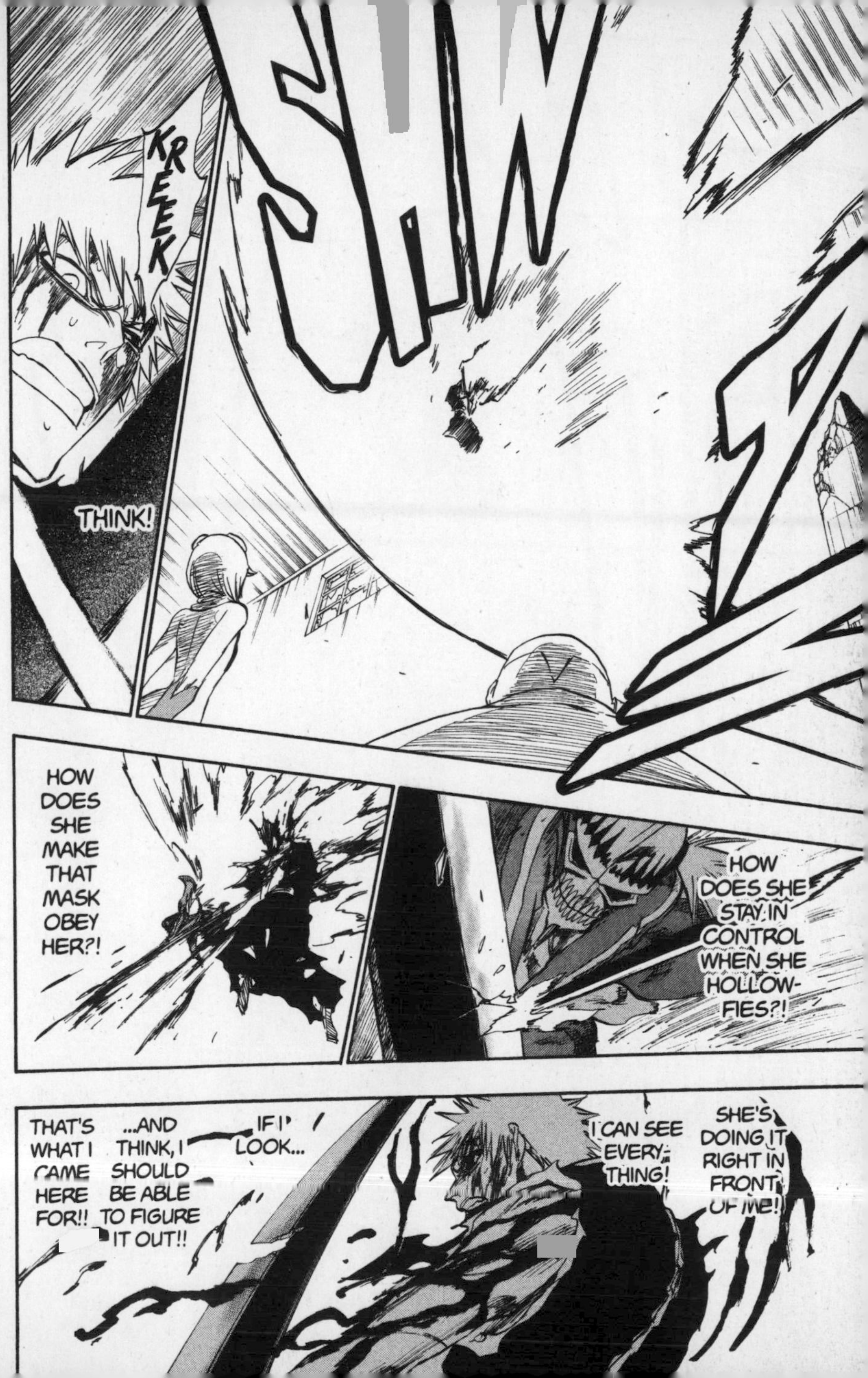
SHW
KREEK
THINK!
HOW DOES SHE STAY IN CONTROL WHEN SHE HOLLOW-FIES?!
HOW DOES SHE MAKE THAT MASK OBEY HER?!
SHE'S DOING IT RIGHT IN FRONT OF ME!
I CAN SEE EVERYTHING!
IF I LOOK...
...AND THINK, I SHOULD BE ABLE TO FIGURE IT OUT!!
THAT'S WHAT I CAME HERE FOR!!

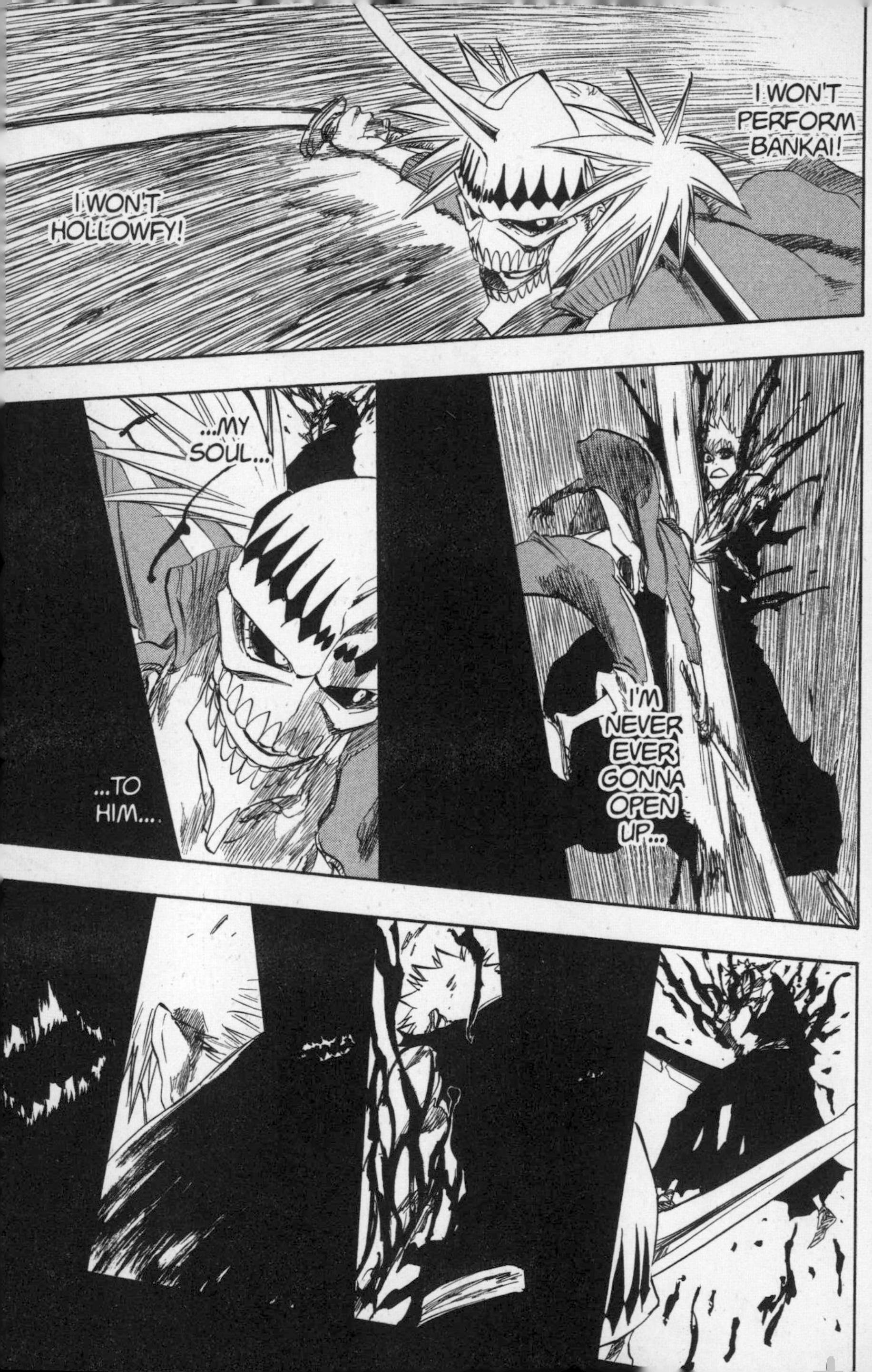
I WON'T PERFORM BANKAI!
I WON'T HOLLOWFY!
I'M NEVER EVER GONNA OPEN UP...
...MY SOUL...
...TO HIM....

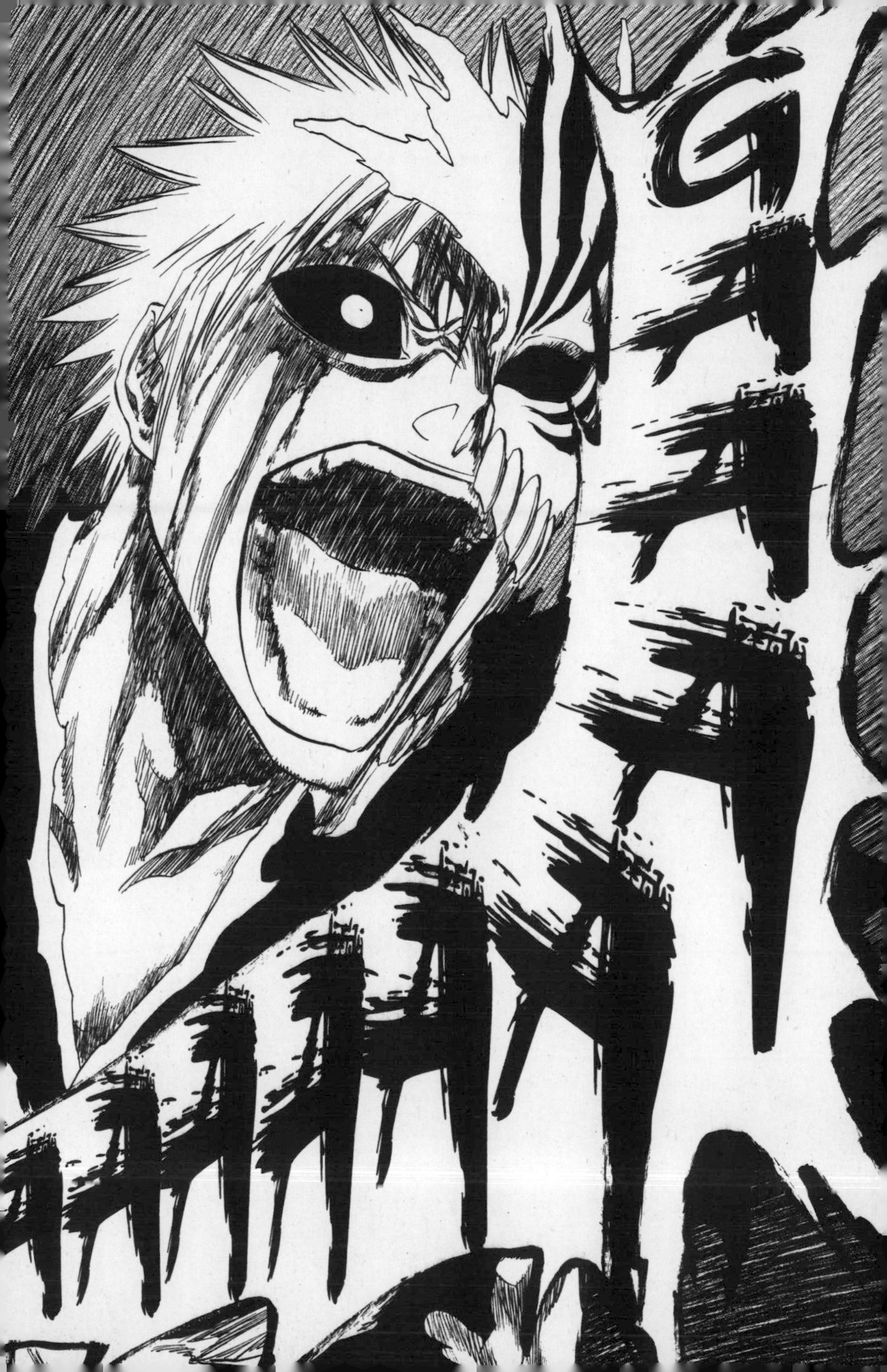

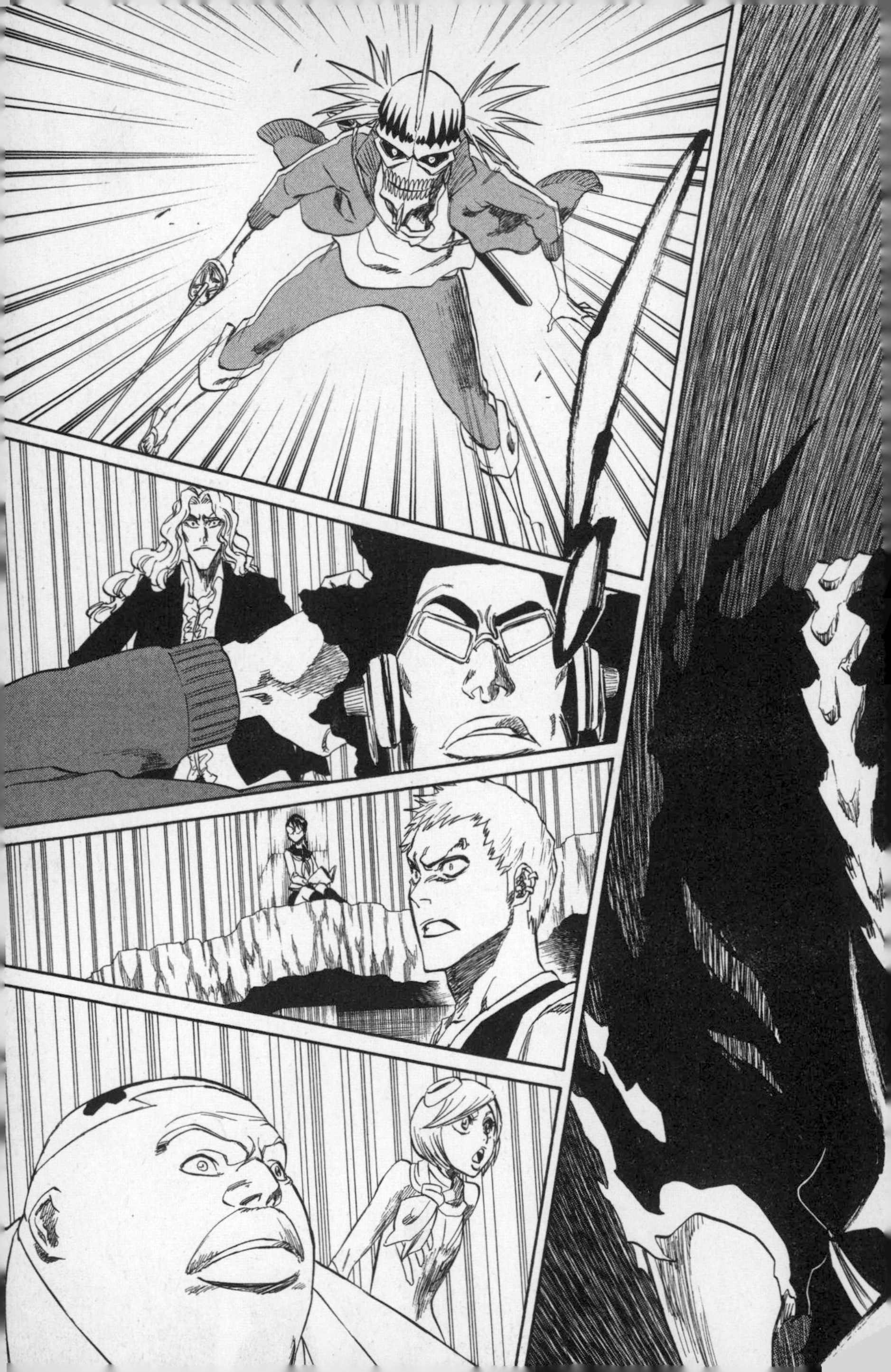

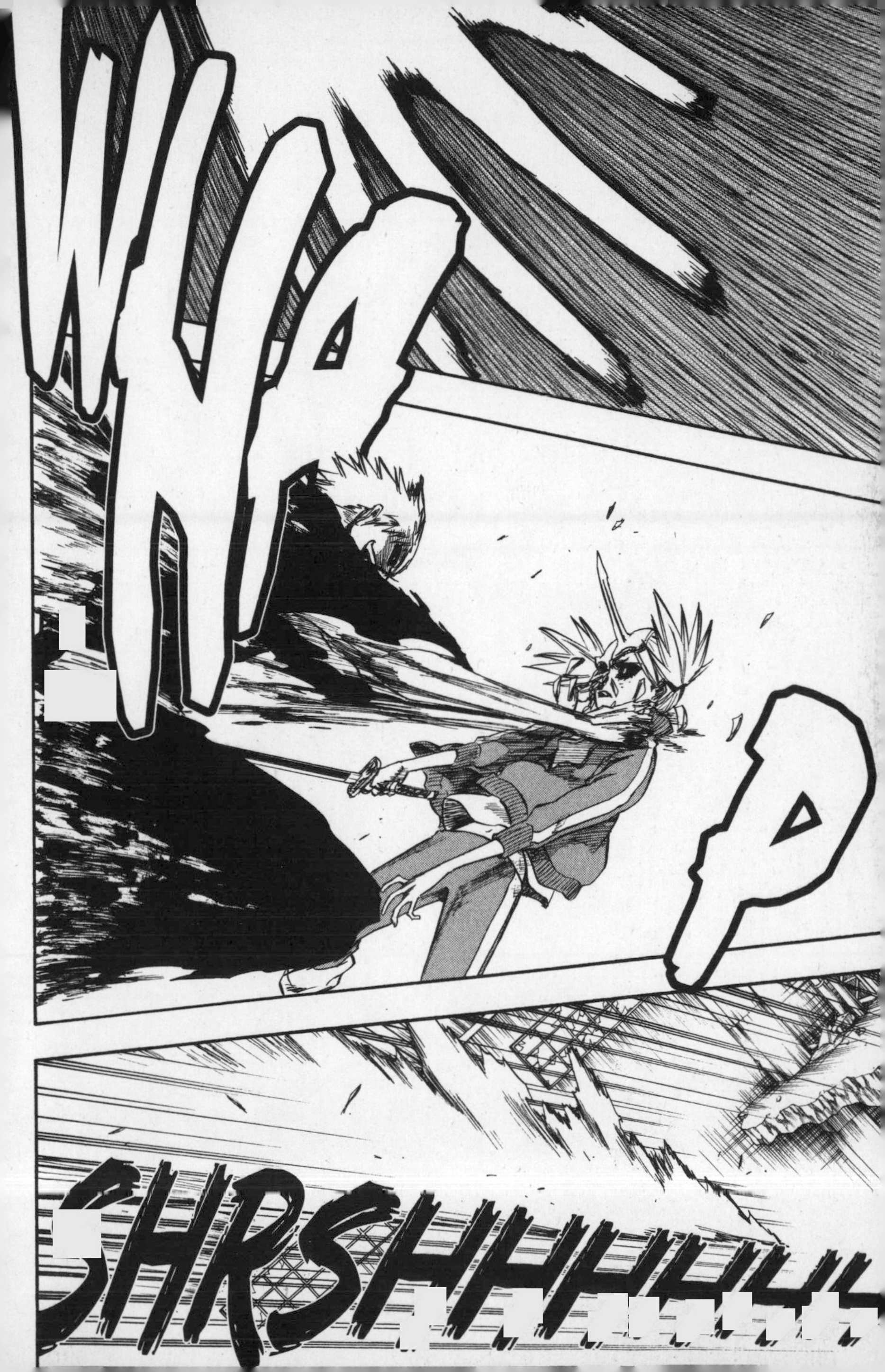
WHAP
SHRSHHHH

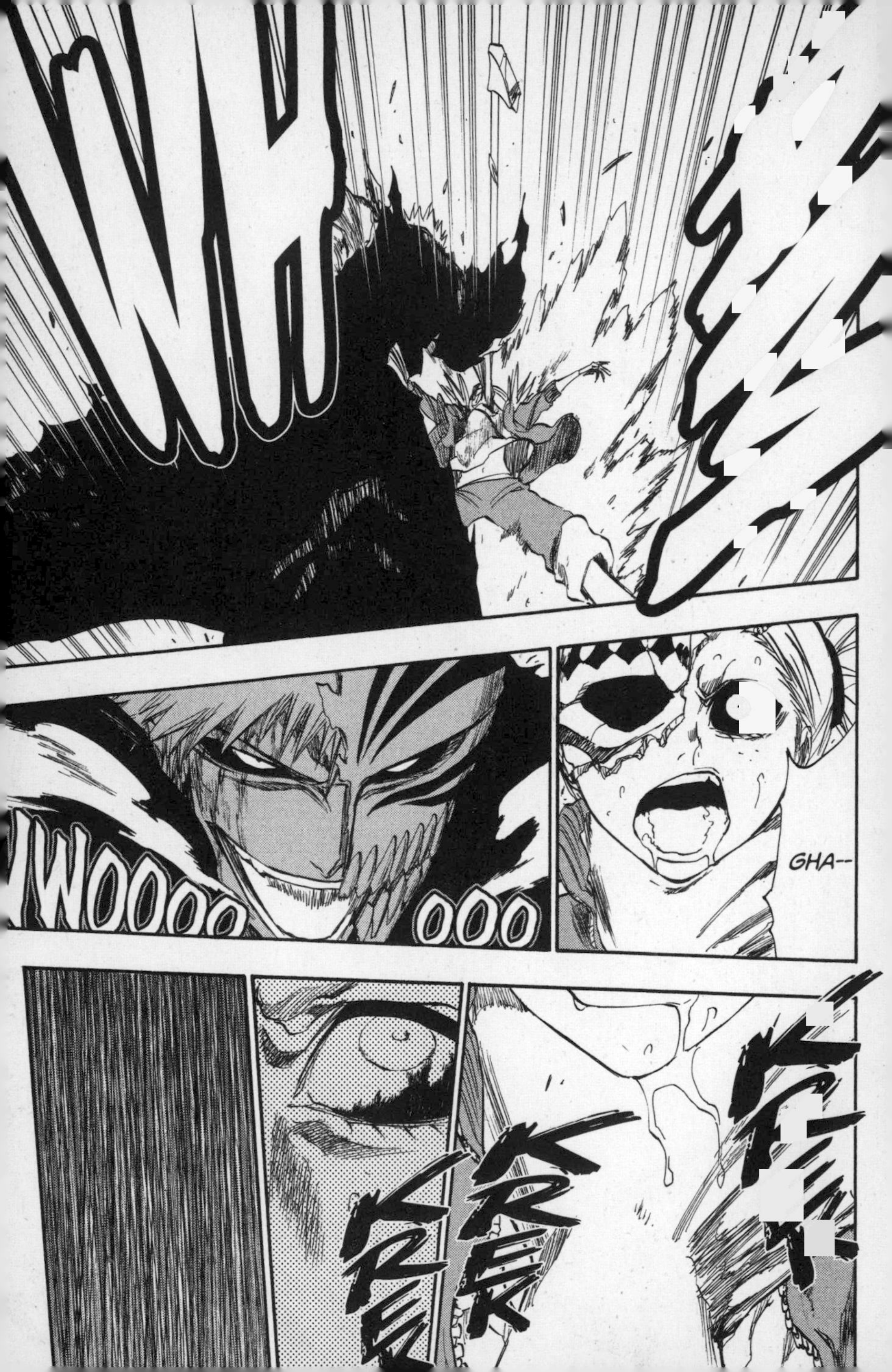
GHA--
WOOOO
OOO
KREK
KREK

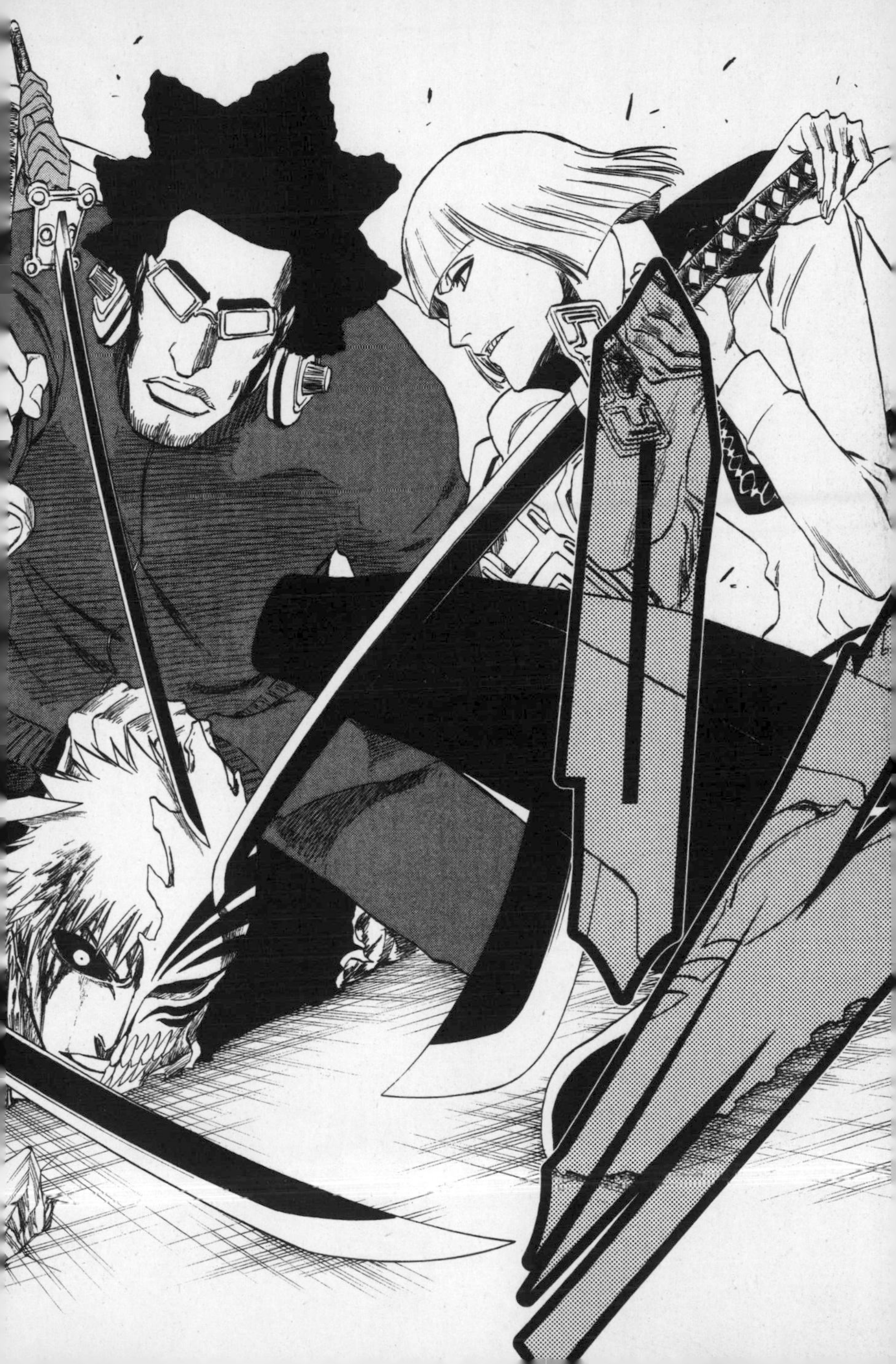

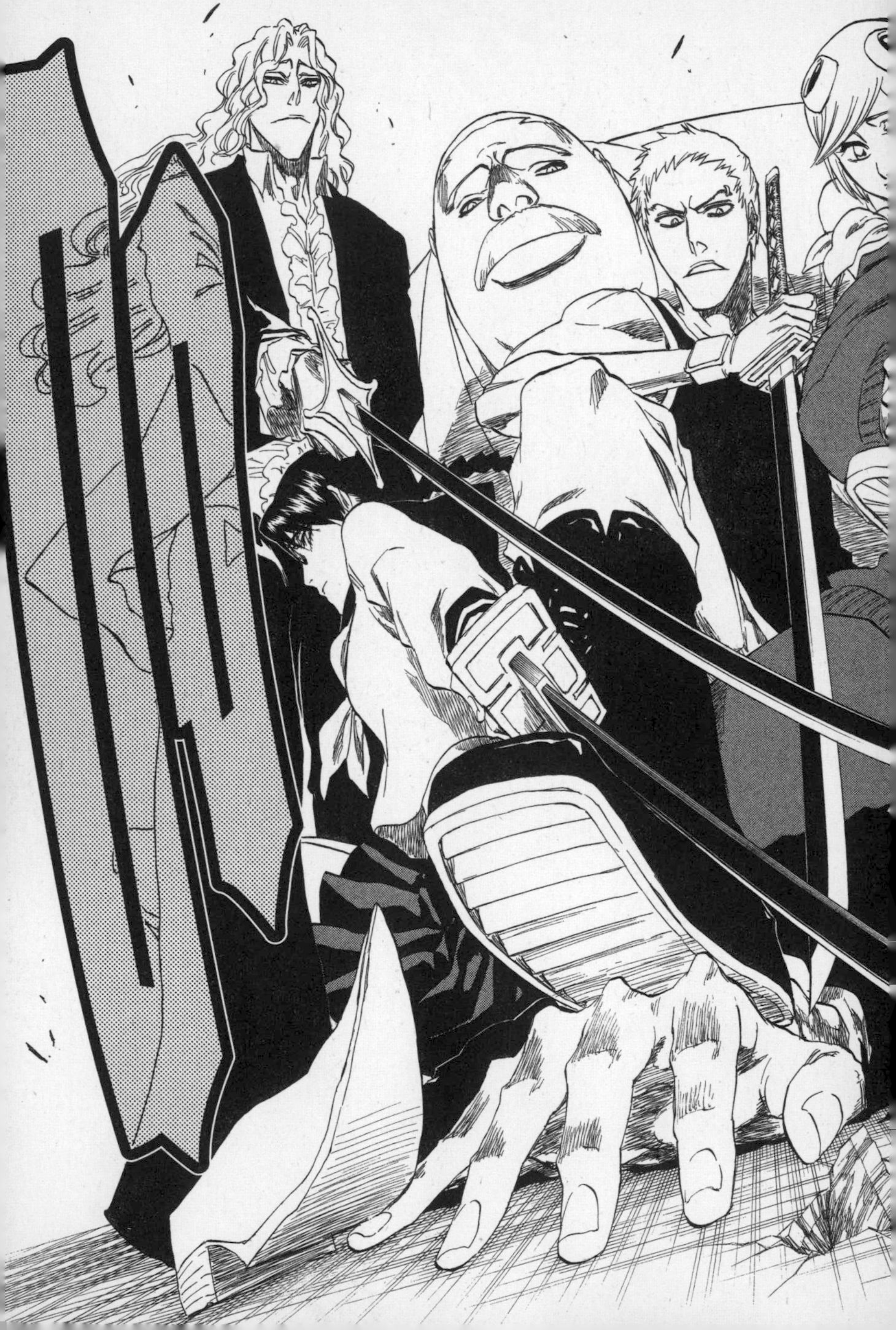

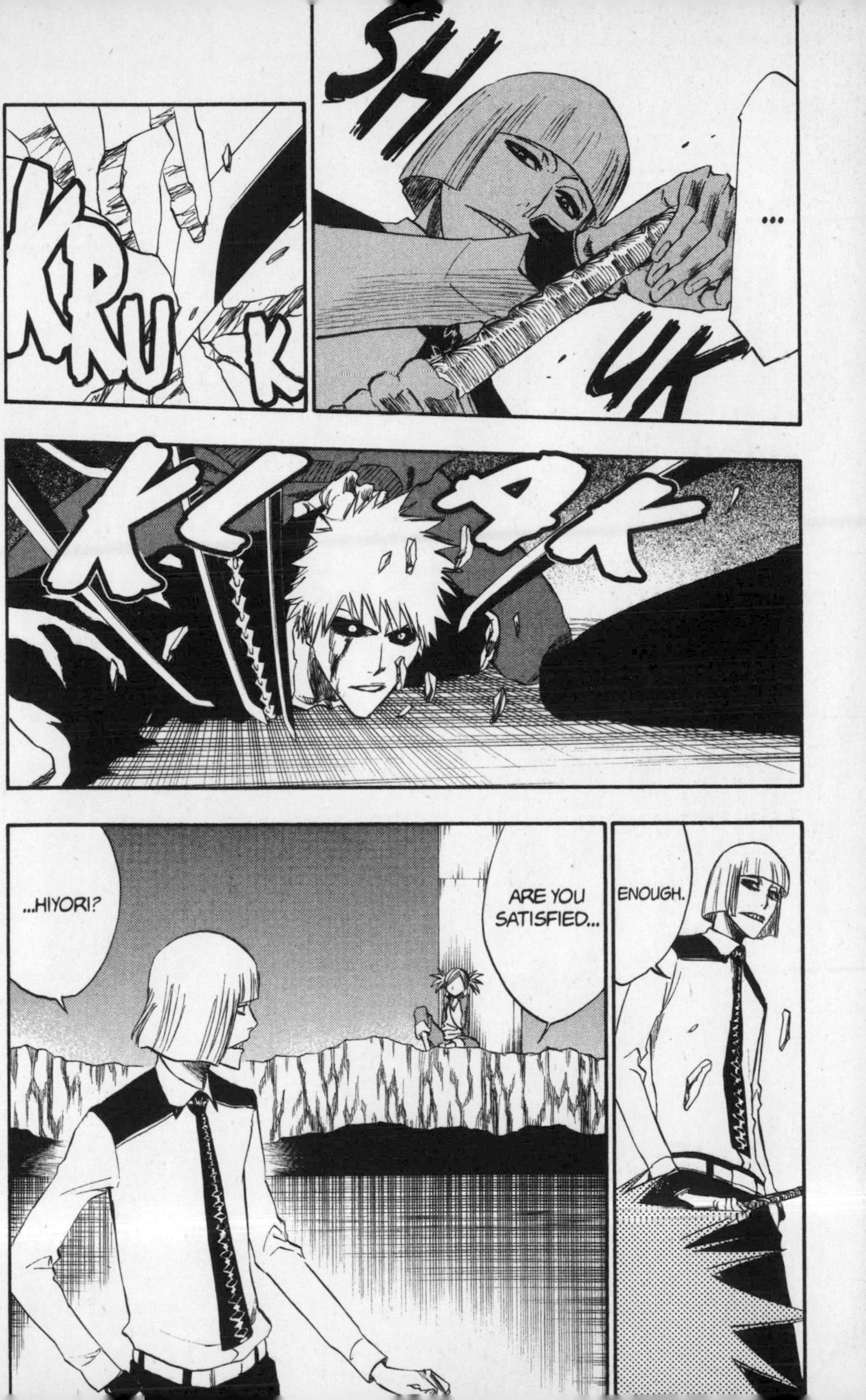
SHUK
...
KRUK
KLAK
ENOUGH.
ARE YOU SATISFIED...
...HIYORI?

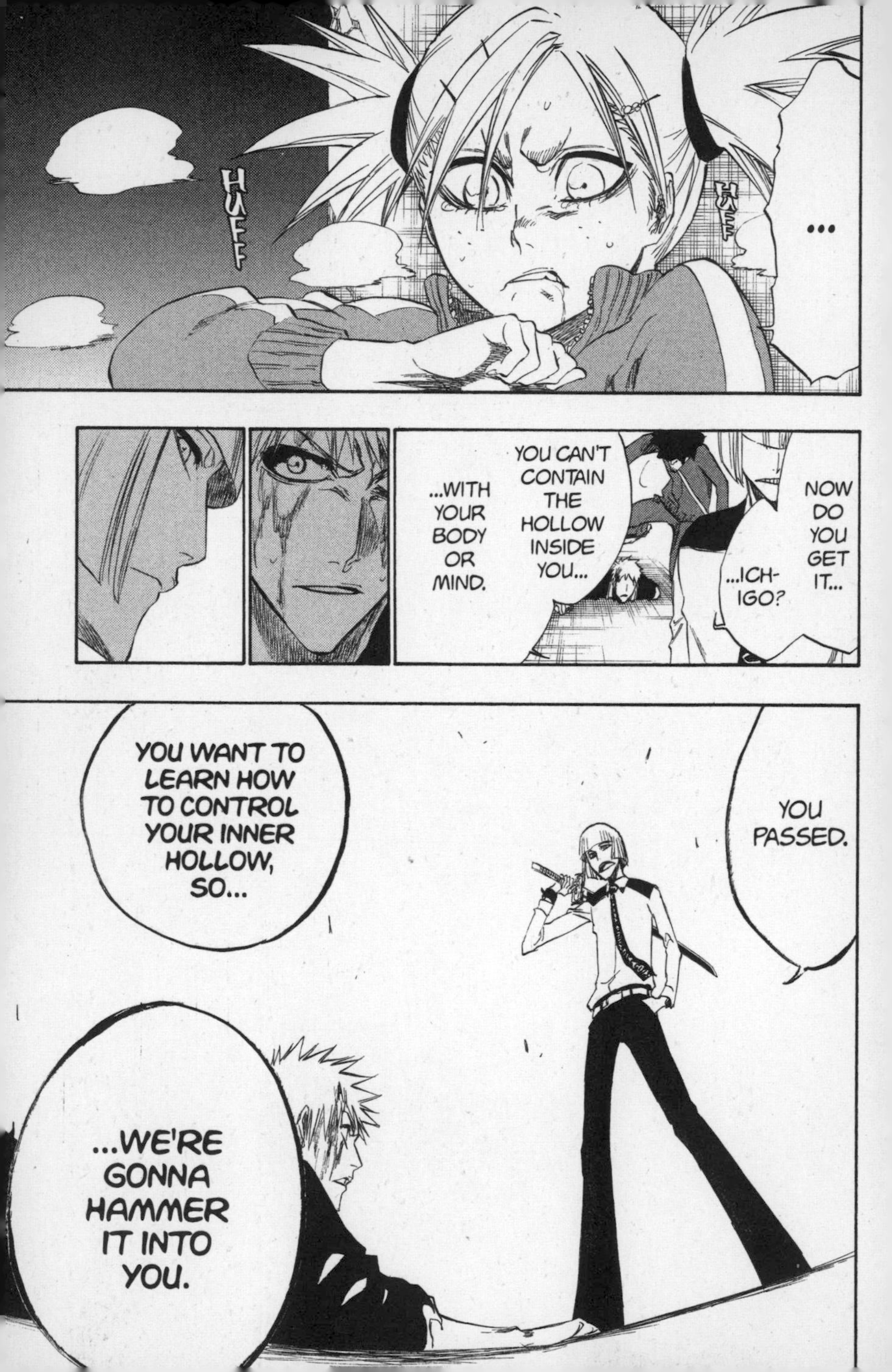
...
HUFF
HUFF
NOW DO YOU GET IT...
...ICHIGO?
YOU CAN'T CONTAIN THE HOLLOW INSIDE YOU...
...WITH YOUR BODY OR MIND.
YOU PASSED.
YOU WANT TO LEARN HOW TO CONTROL YOUR INNER HOLLOW, SO...
...WE'RE GONNA HAMMER IT INTO YOU.

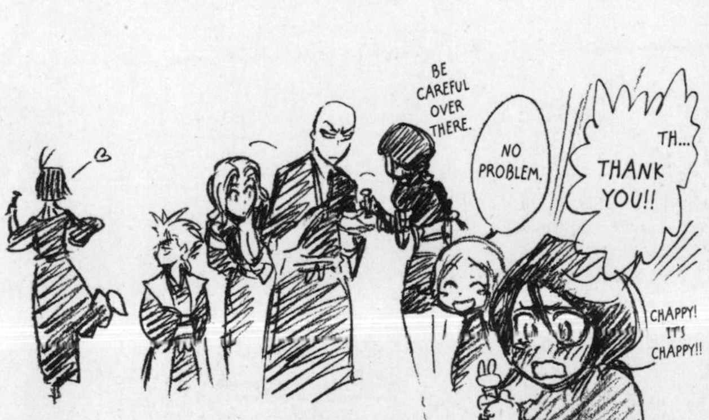
TH... THANK YOU!!
CHAPPY! IT'S CHAPPY!!
NO PROBLEM.
BE CAREFUL OVER THERE.

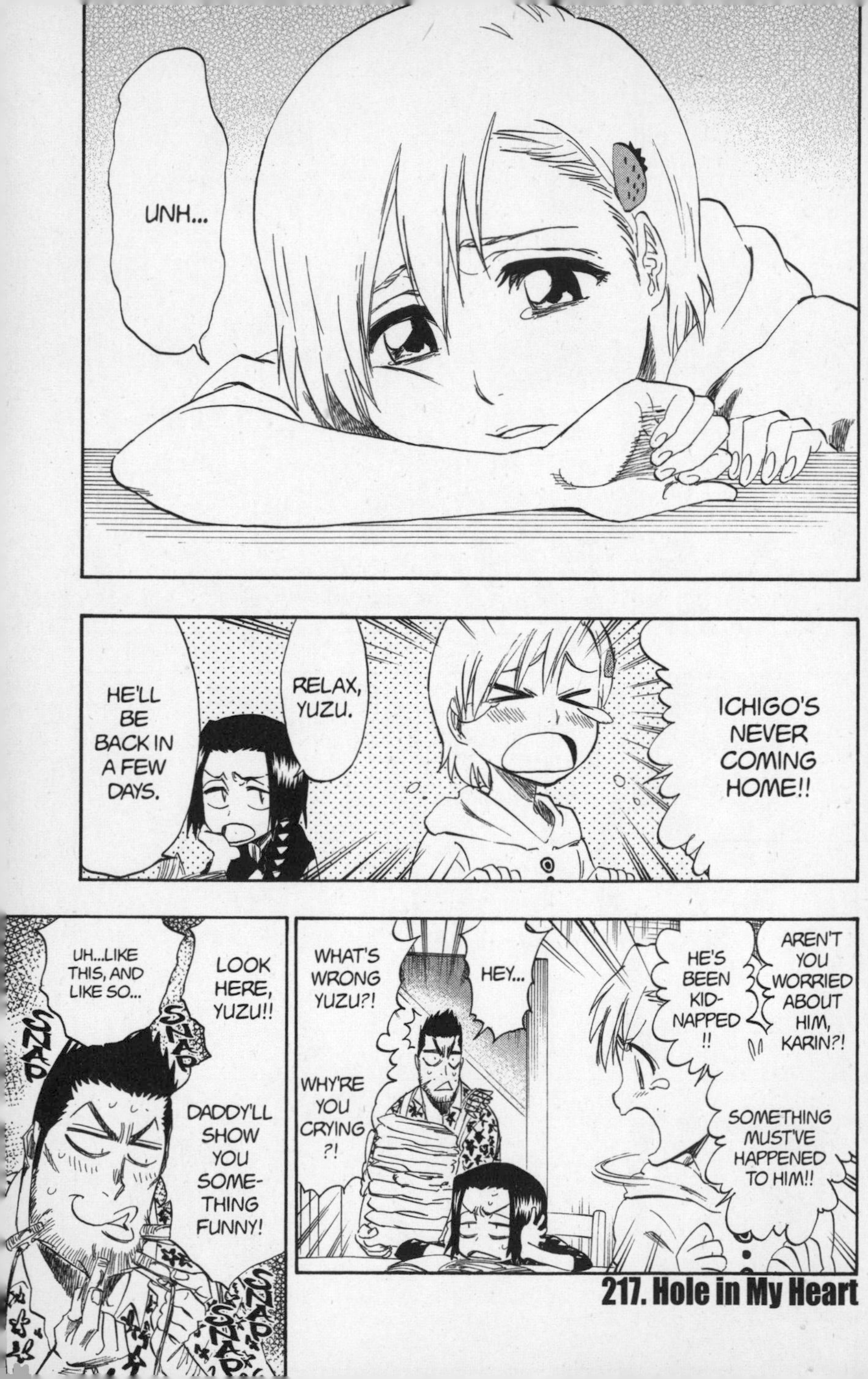
UNH...
ICHIGO'S NEVER COMING HOME!!
RELAX, YUZU.
HE'LL BE BACK IN A FEW DAYS.
AREN'T YOU WORRIED ABOUT HIM, KARIN?!
HE'S BEEN KID-NAPPED!!
SOMETHING MUST'VE HAPPENED TO HIM!!
HEY...
WHAT'S WRONG YUZU?!
WHY'RE YOU CRYING?!
LOOK HERE, YUZU!!
UH...LIKE THIS, AND LIKE SO...
SNAP
SNAP
DADDY'LL SHOW YOU SOME-THING FUNNY!
SNAP
SNAP

217. Hole in My Heart

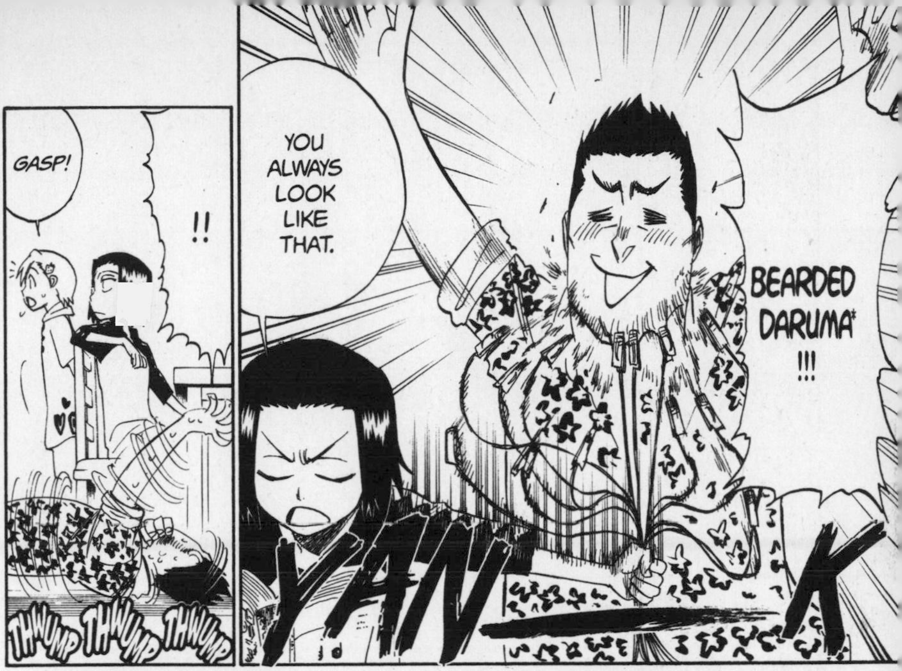
BEARDED DARUMA* !!!
YAN—K
YOU ALWAYS LOOK LIKE THAT.
GASP!
!!
THWUMP THWUMP THWUMP

*TRADITIONAL JAPANESE FIGURES REPRESENTING ZEN FOUNDER BODHIDHARMA.

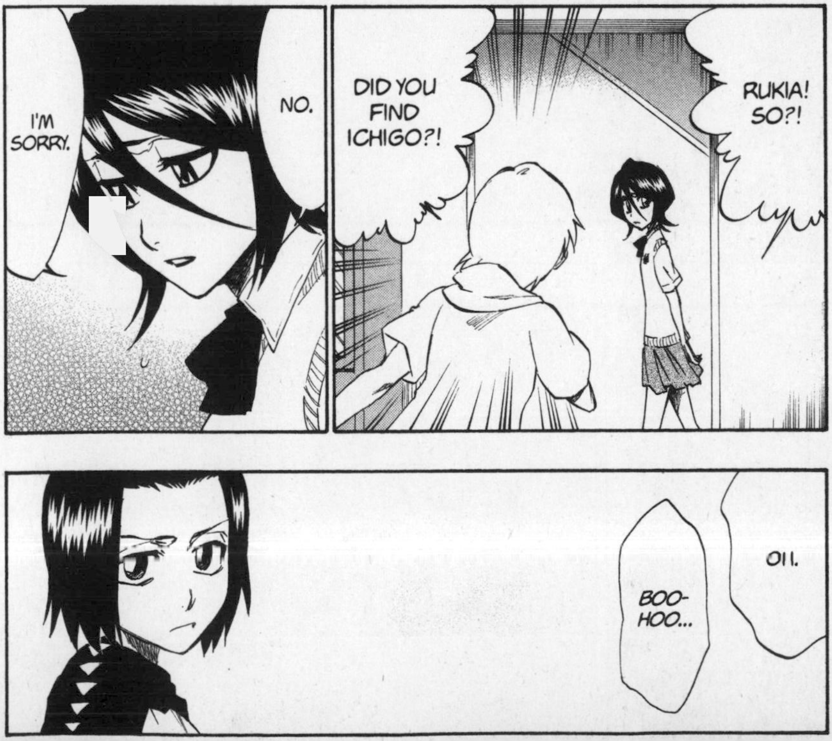
RUKIA! SO?!
DID YOU FIND ICHIGO?!
NO.
I'M SORRY.
OII.
BOO-HOO...

READ THIS WAY

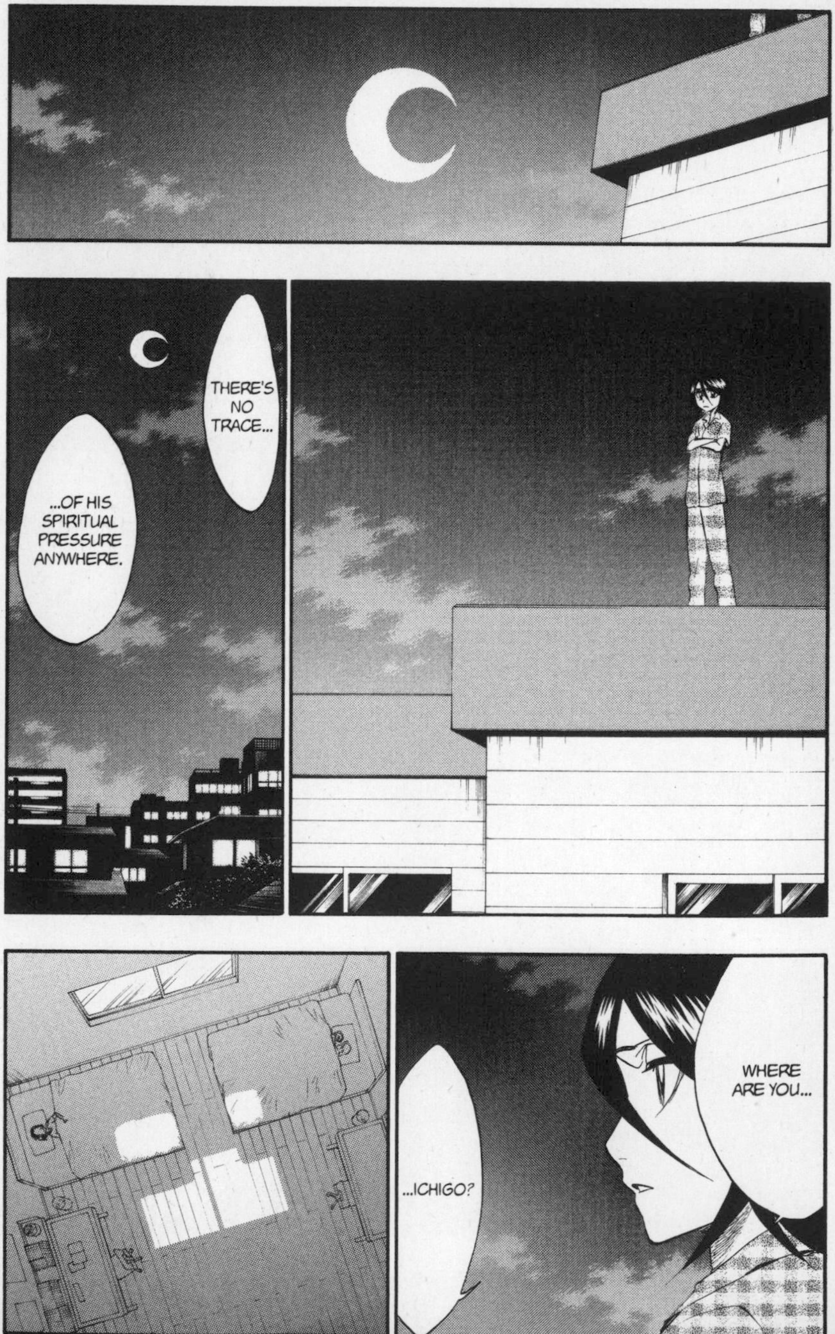
THERE'S NO TRACE...
...OF HIS SPIRITUAL PRESSURE ANYWHERE.
WHERE ARE YOU...
...ICHIGO?

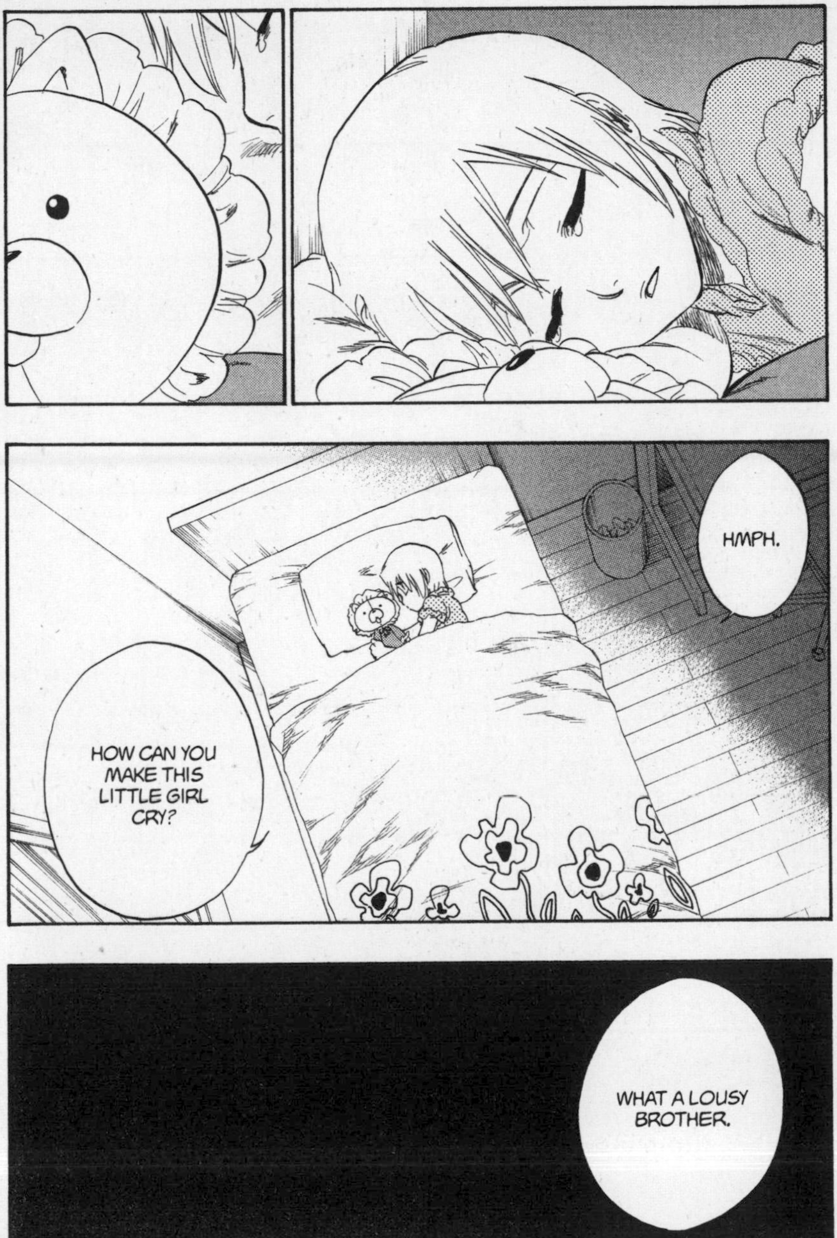
HMPH.
HOW CAN YOU MAKE THIS LITTLE GIRL CRY?
WHAT A LOUSY BROTHER.

BLEACH 217. Hole in My Heart

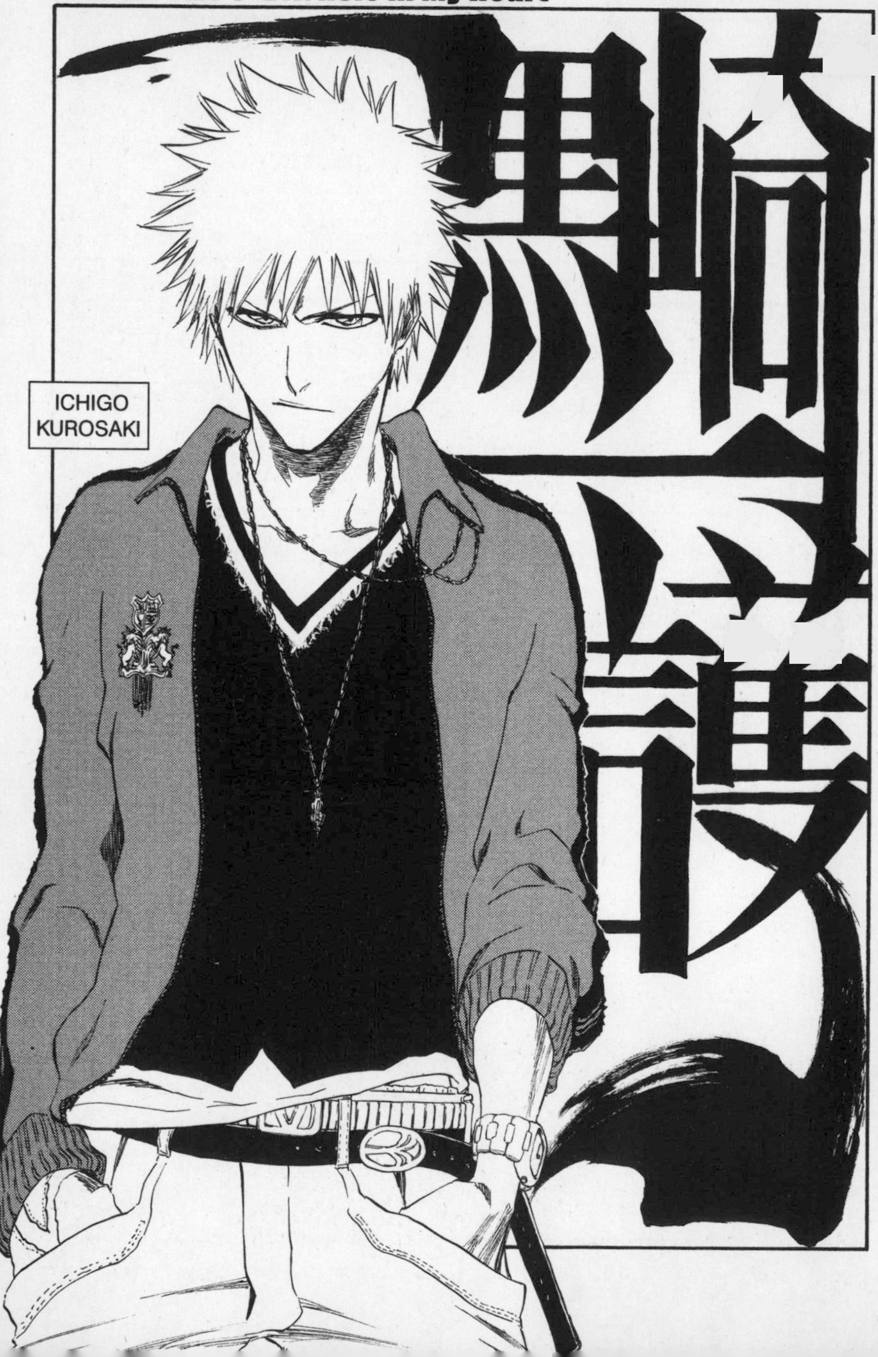
ICHIGO
KUROSAKI

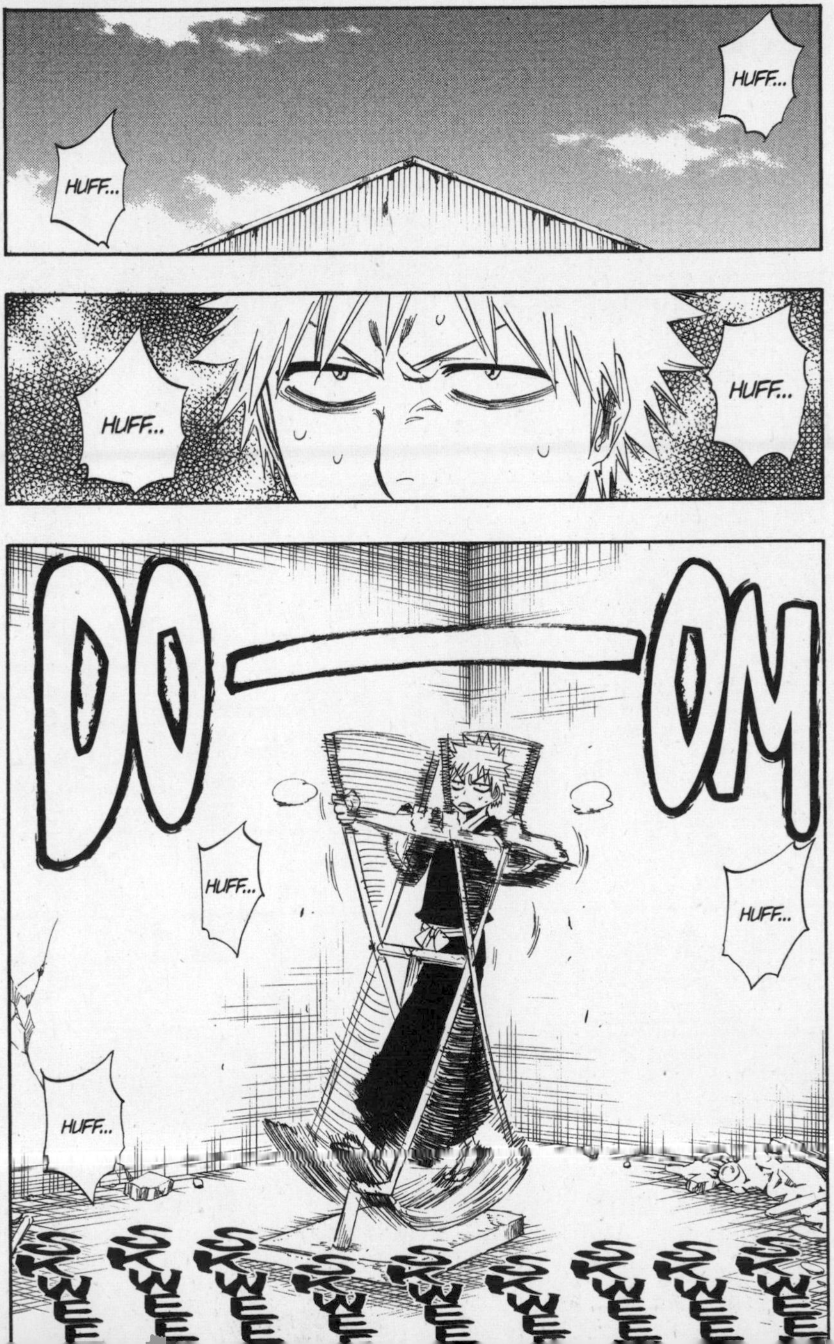
HUFF...
HUFF...
HUFF...
HUFF...
DO—OM
HUFF...
HUFF...
HUFF...
SKWEE SKWEE SKWEE SKWEE SKWEE SKWEE SKWEE SKWEE SKWEE

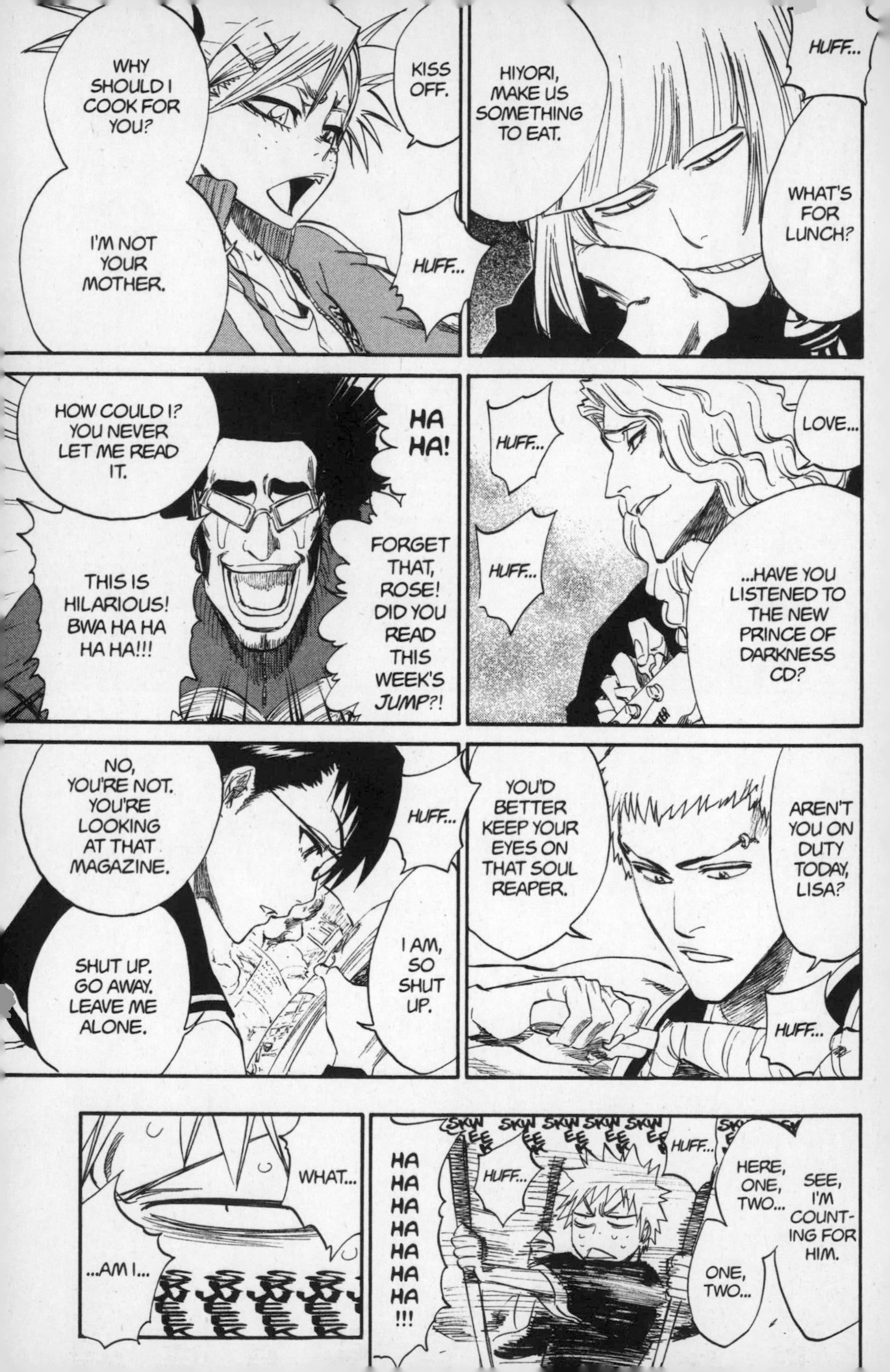
HUFF...
WHAT'S FOR LUNCH?
HIYORI, MAKE US SOMETHING TO EAT.
KISS OFF.
HUFF...
WHY SHOULD I COOK FOR YOU?
I'M NOT YOUR MOTHER.
LOVE...
HUFF...
HUFF...
...HAVE YOU LISTENED TO THE NEW PRINCE OF DARKNESS CD?
HA HA!
FORGET THAT, ROSE! DID YOU READ THIS WEEK'S JUMP?!
HOW COULD I? YOU NEVER LET ME READ IT.
THIS IS HILARIOUS! BWA HA HA HA HA!!!
AREN'T YOU ON DUTY TODAY, LISA?
YOU'D BETTER KEEP YOUR EYES ON THAT SOUL REAPER.
HUFF...
HUFF...
I AM, SO SHUT UP.
NO, YOU'RE NOT. YOU'RE LOOKING AT THAT MAGAZINE.
SHUT UP. GO AWAY. LEAVE ME ALONE.
SKWEEK SKWEEK SKWEEK SKWEEK SKWEEK SKWEEK
HUFF...
SEE, I'M COUNTING FOR HIM.
HERE, ONE, TWO...
HUFF...
ONE, TWO...
HA HA HA HA HA HA HA HA!!!
WHAT...
...AM I...
SKWEEK SKWEEK SKWEEK SKWEEK

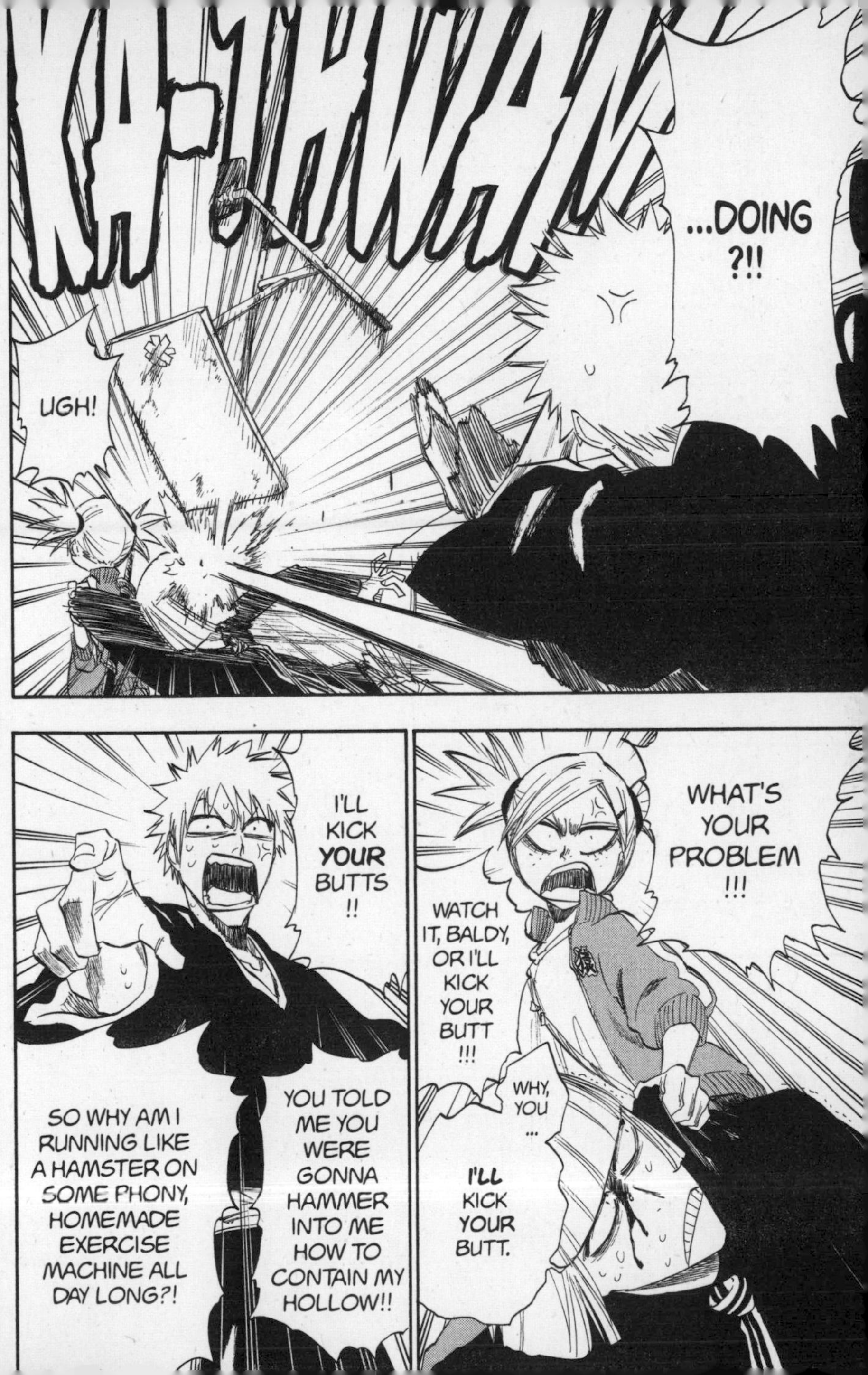
...DOING ?!!
UGH!
WHAT'S YOUR PROBLEM !!!
WATCH IT, BALDY, OR I'LL KICK YOUR BUTT !!!
WHY, YOU ...
I'LL KICK YOUR BUTT.
I'LL KICK YOUR BUTTS !!
YOU TOLD ME YOU WERE GONNA HAMMER INTO ME HOW TO CONTAIN MY HOLLOW!!
SO WHY AM I RUNNING LIKE A HAMSTER ON SOME PHONY, HOMEMADE EXERCISE MACHINE ALL DAY LONG?!

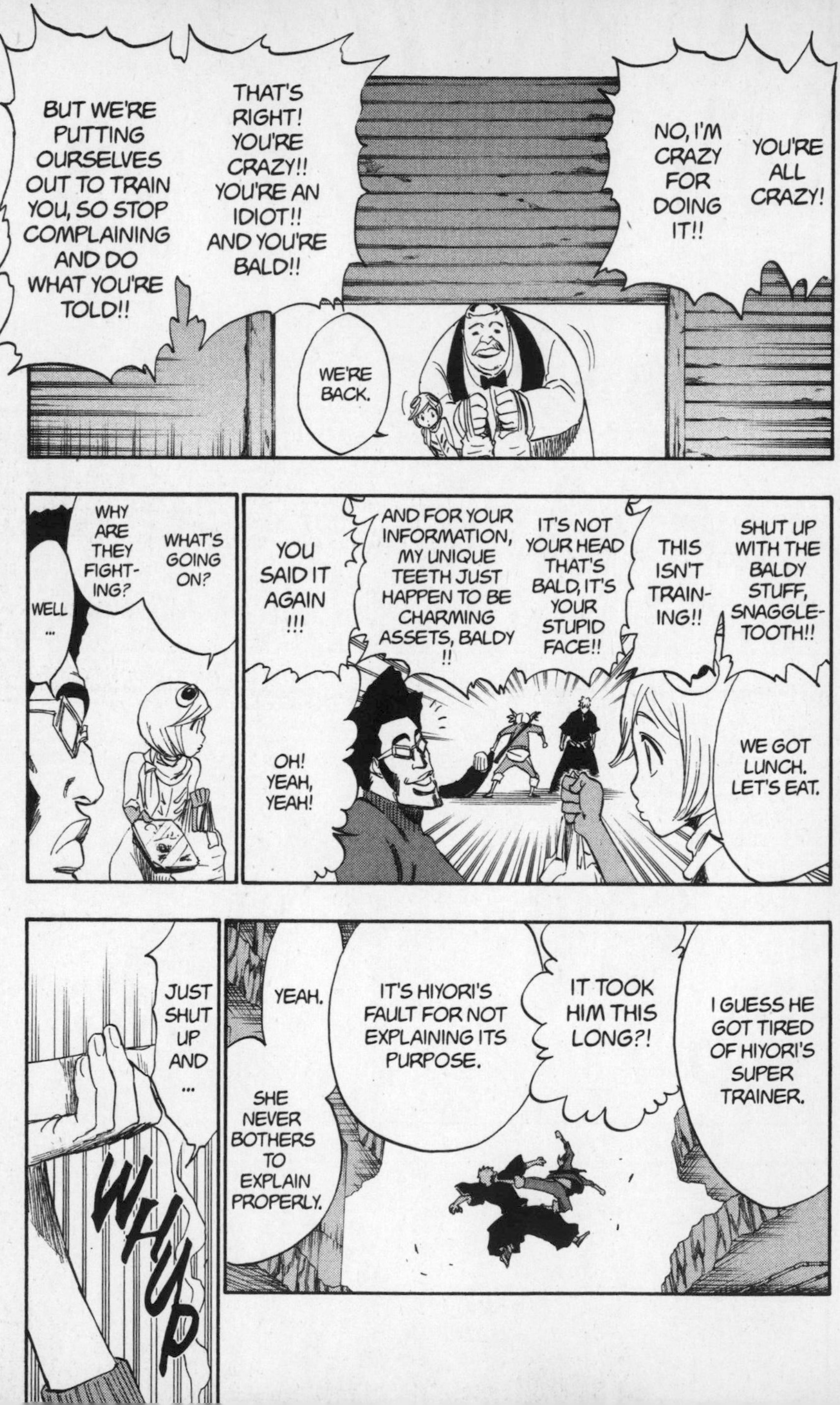

YOU'RE ALL CRAZY!
NO, I'M CRAZY FOR DOING IT!!
THAT'S RIGHT! YOU'RE CRAZY!! YOU'RE AN IDIOT!! AND YOU'RE BALD!!
BUT WE'RE PUTTING OURSELVES OUT TO TRAIN YOU, SO STOP COMPLAINING AND DO WHAT YOU'RE TOLD!!
WE'RE BACK.
SHUT UP WITH THE BALDY STUFF, SNAGGLE-TOOTH!!
THIS ISN'T TRAIN-ING!!
IT'S NOT YOUR HEAD THAT'S BALD, IT'S YOUR STUPID FACE!!
AND FOR YOUR INFORMATION, MY UNIQUE TEETH JUST HAPPEN TO BE CHARMING ASSETS, BALDY!!
YOU SAID IT AGAIN!!!
WE GOT LUNCH. LET'S EAT.
OH! YEAH, YEAH!
WHAT'S GOING ON?
WHY ARE THEY FIGHT-ING?
WELL ...
I GUESS HE GOT TIRED OF HIYORI'S SUPER TRAINER.
IT TOOK HIM THIS LONG?!
IT'S HIYORI'S FAULT FOR NOT EXPLAINING ITS PURPOSE.
YEAH.
SHE NEVER BOTHERS TO EXPLAIN PROPERLY.
JUST SHUT UP AND ...
WHUP

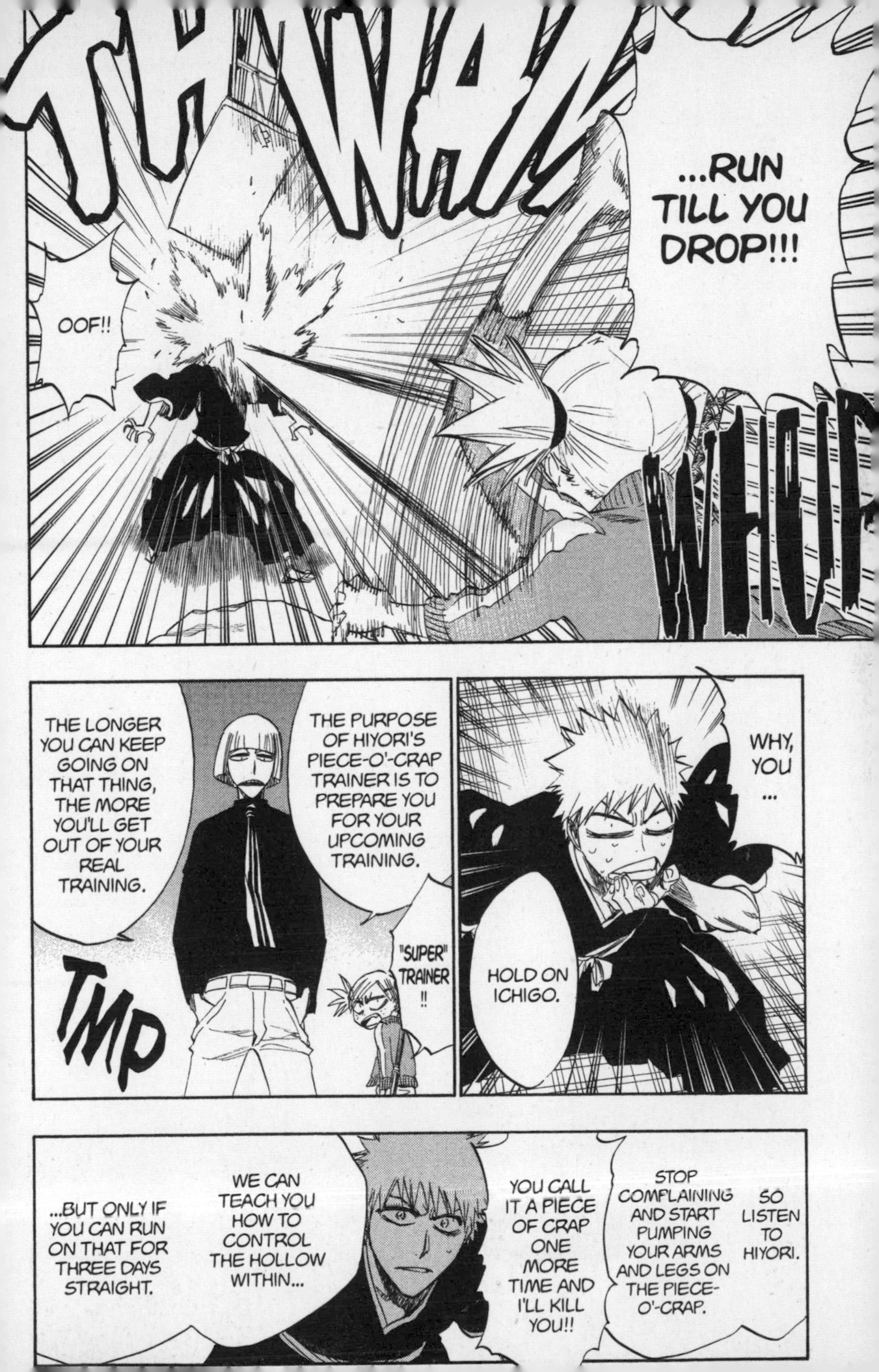
...RUN TILL YOU DROP!!!
OOF!!
WHY, YOU ...
HOLD ON ICHIGO.
THE PURPOSE OF HIYORI'S PIECE-O'-CRAP TRAINER IS TO PREPARE YOU FOR YOUR UPCOMING TRAINING.
THE LONGER YOU CAN KEEP GOING ON THAT THING, THE MORE YOU'LL GET OUT OF YOUR REAL TRAINING.
"SUPER" TRAINER !!
TMP
SO LISTEN TO HIYORI.
STOP COMPLAINING AND START PUMPING YOUR ARMS AND LEGS ON THE PIECE-O'-CRAP.
YOU CALL IT A PIECE OF CRAP ONE MORE TIME AND I'LL KILL YOU!!
WE CAN TEACH YOU HOW TO CONTROL THE HOLLOW WITHIN...
...BUT ONLY IF YOU CAN RUN ON THAT FOR THREE DAYS STRAIGHT.

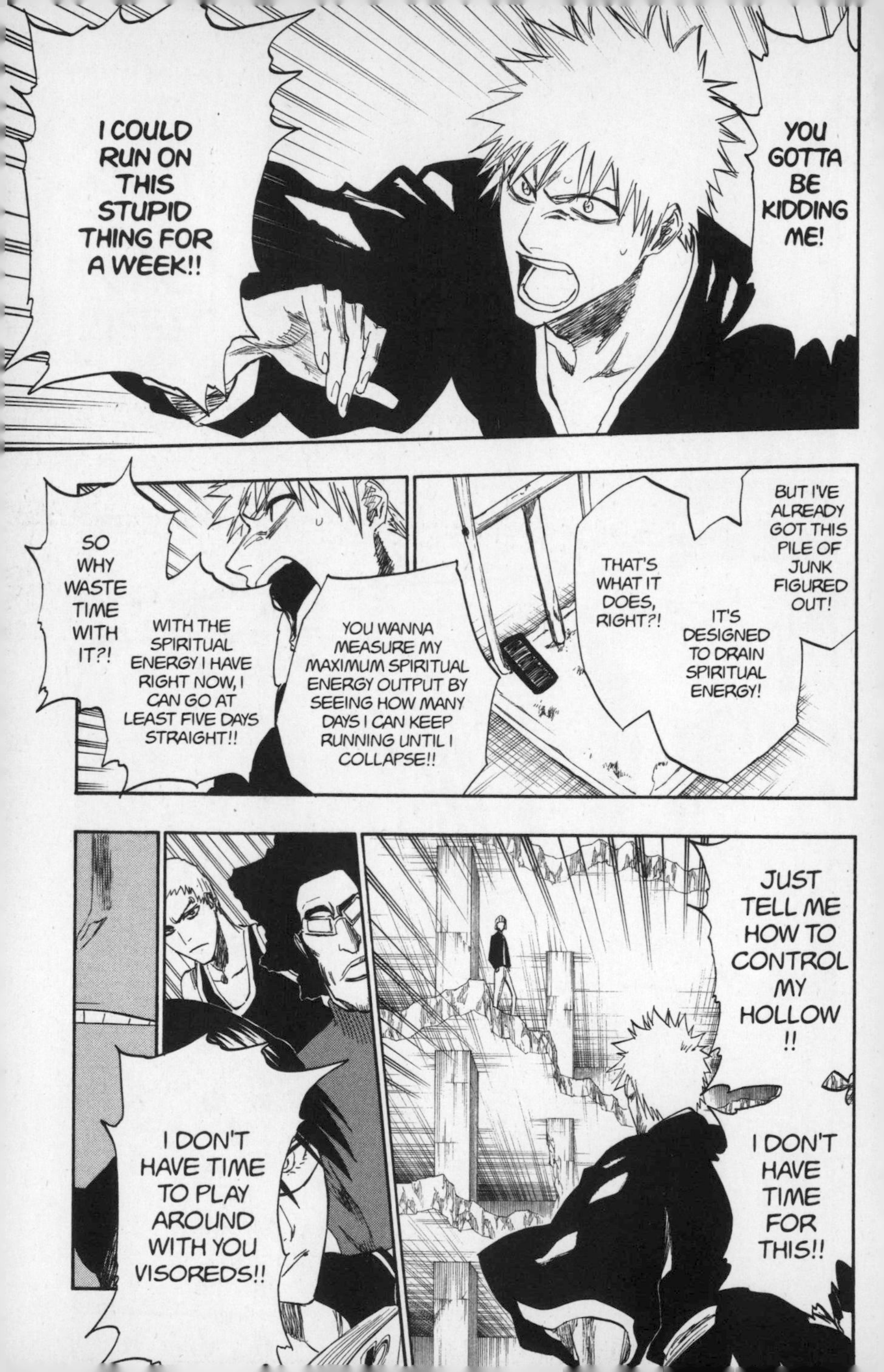
YOU GOTTA BE KIDDING ME!
I COULD RUN ON THIS STUPID THING FOR A WEEK!!
BUT I'VE ALREADY GOT THIS PILE OF JUNK FIGURED OUT!
IT'S DESIGNED TO DRAIN SPIRITUAL ENERGY!
THAT'S WHAT IT DOES, RIGHT?!
YOU WANNA MEASURE MY MAXIMUM SPIRITUAL ENERGY OUTPUT BY SEEING HOW MANY DAYS I CAN KEEP RUNNING UNTIL I COLLAPSE!!
WITH THE SPIRITUAL ENERGY I HAVE RIGHT NOW, I CAN GO AT LEAST FIVE DAYS STRAIGHT!!
SO WHY WASTE TIME WITH IT?!
JUST TELL ME HOW TO CONTROL MY HOLLOW!!
I DON'T HAVE TIME FOR THIS!!
I DON'T HAVE TIME TO PLAY AROUND WITH YOU VISOREDS!!

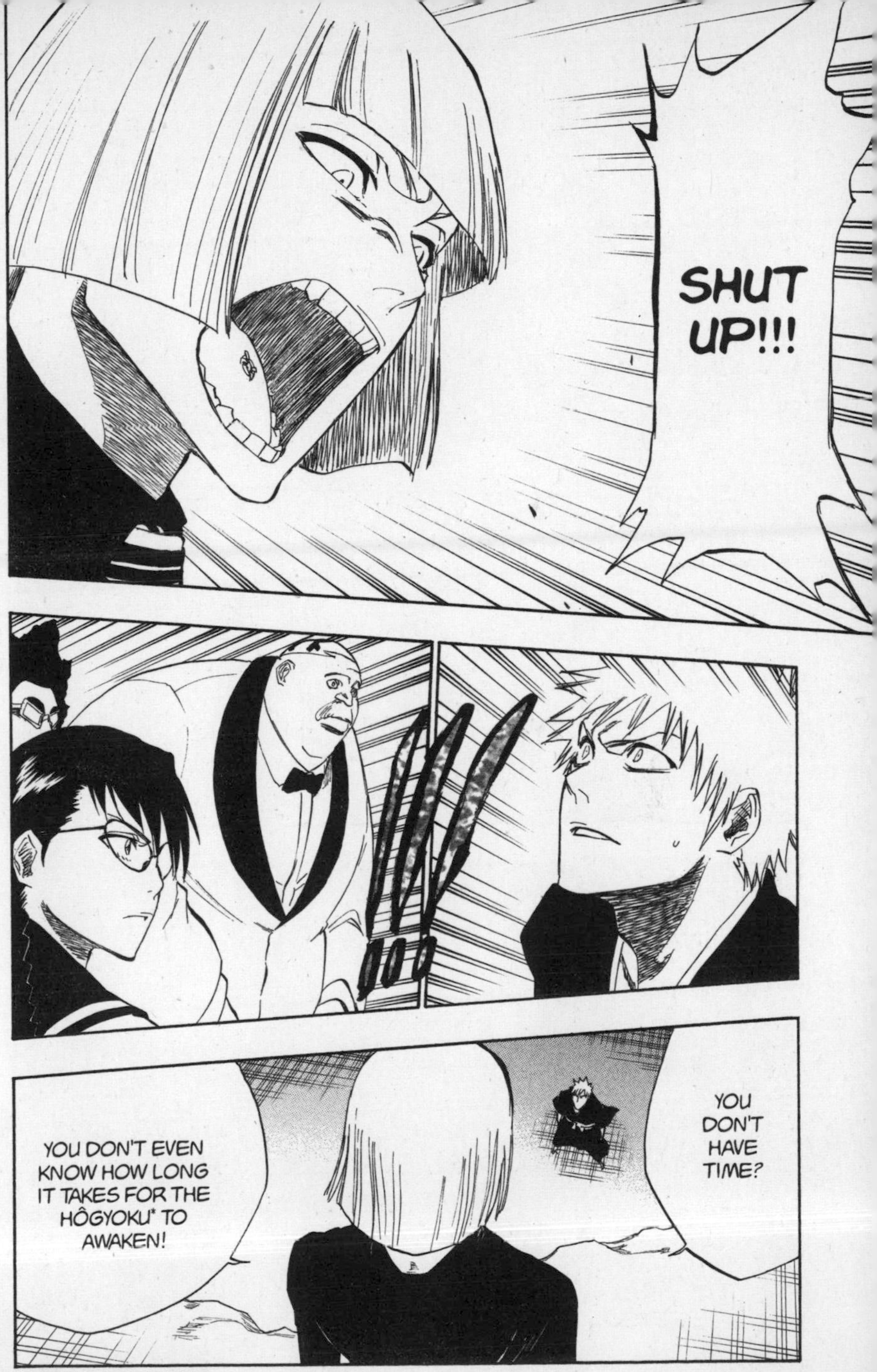
SHUT UP!!!
YOU DON'T HAVE TIME?
YOU DON'T EVEN KNOW HOW LONG IT TAKES FOR THE HÔGYOKU* TO AWAKEN!

*BREAK DOWN SPHERE

READ THIS WAY

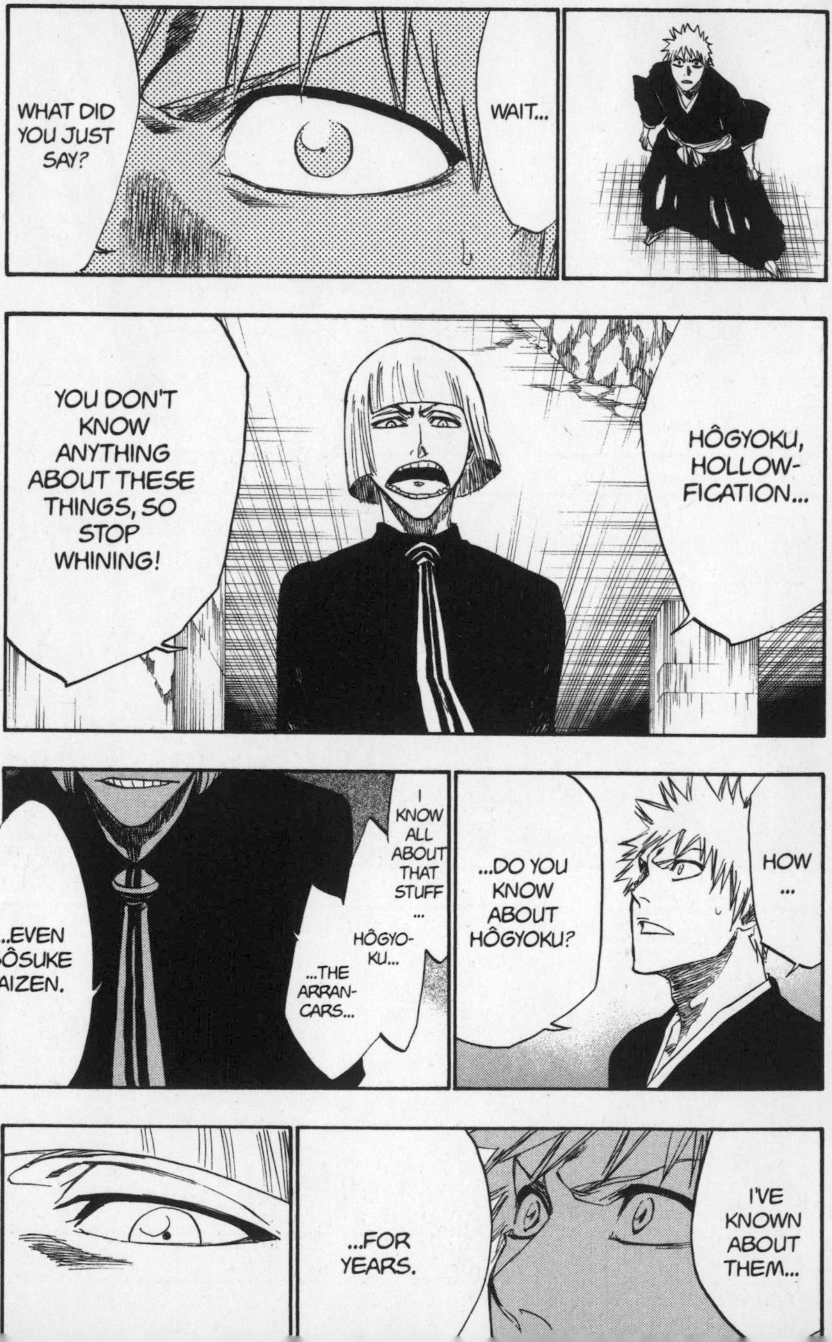

WAIT...
WHAT DID YOU JUST SAY?
HÔGYOKU, HOLLOW-FICATION...
YOU DON'T KNOW ANYTHING ABOUT THESE THINGS, SO STOP WHINING!
HOW ...
...DO YOU KNOW ABOUT HÔGYOKU?
I KNOW ALL ABOUT THAT STUFF ...
HÔGYO-KU...
...THE ARRAN-CARS...
...EVEN SÔSUKE AIZEN.
I'VE KNOWN ABOUT THEM...
...FOR YEARS.

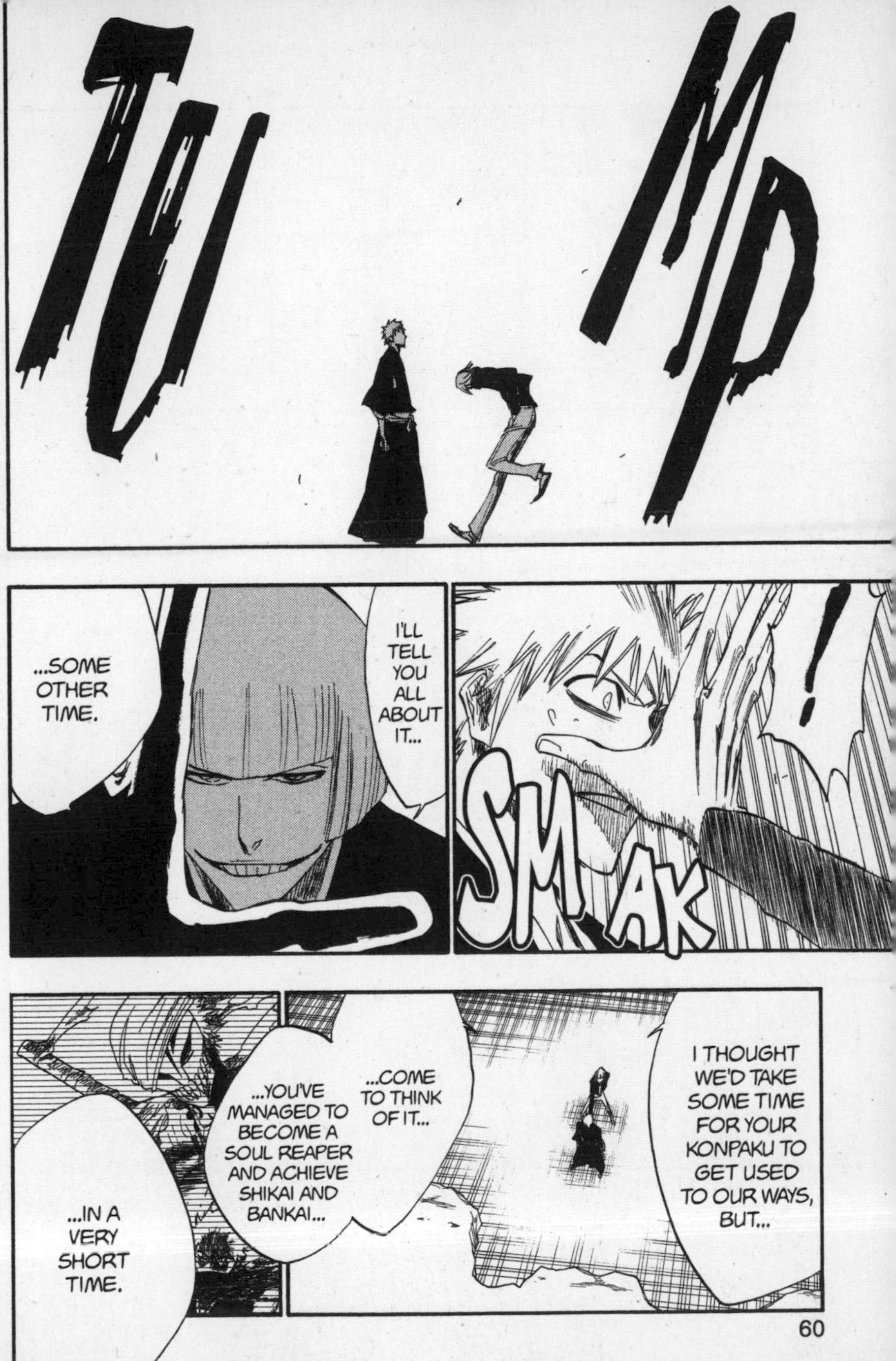
TUMP
!
SMAK
I'LL TELL YOU ALL ABOUT IT...
...SOME OTHER TIME.
I THOUGHT WE'D TAKE SOME TIME FOR YOUR KONPAKU TO GET USED TO OUR WAYS, BUT...
...COME TO THINK OF IT...
...YOU'VE MANAGED TO BECOME A SOUL REAPER AND ACHIEVE SHIKAI AND BANKAI...
...IN A VERY SHORT TIME.

READ THIS WAY

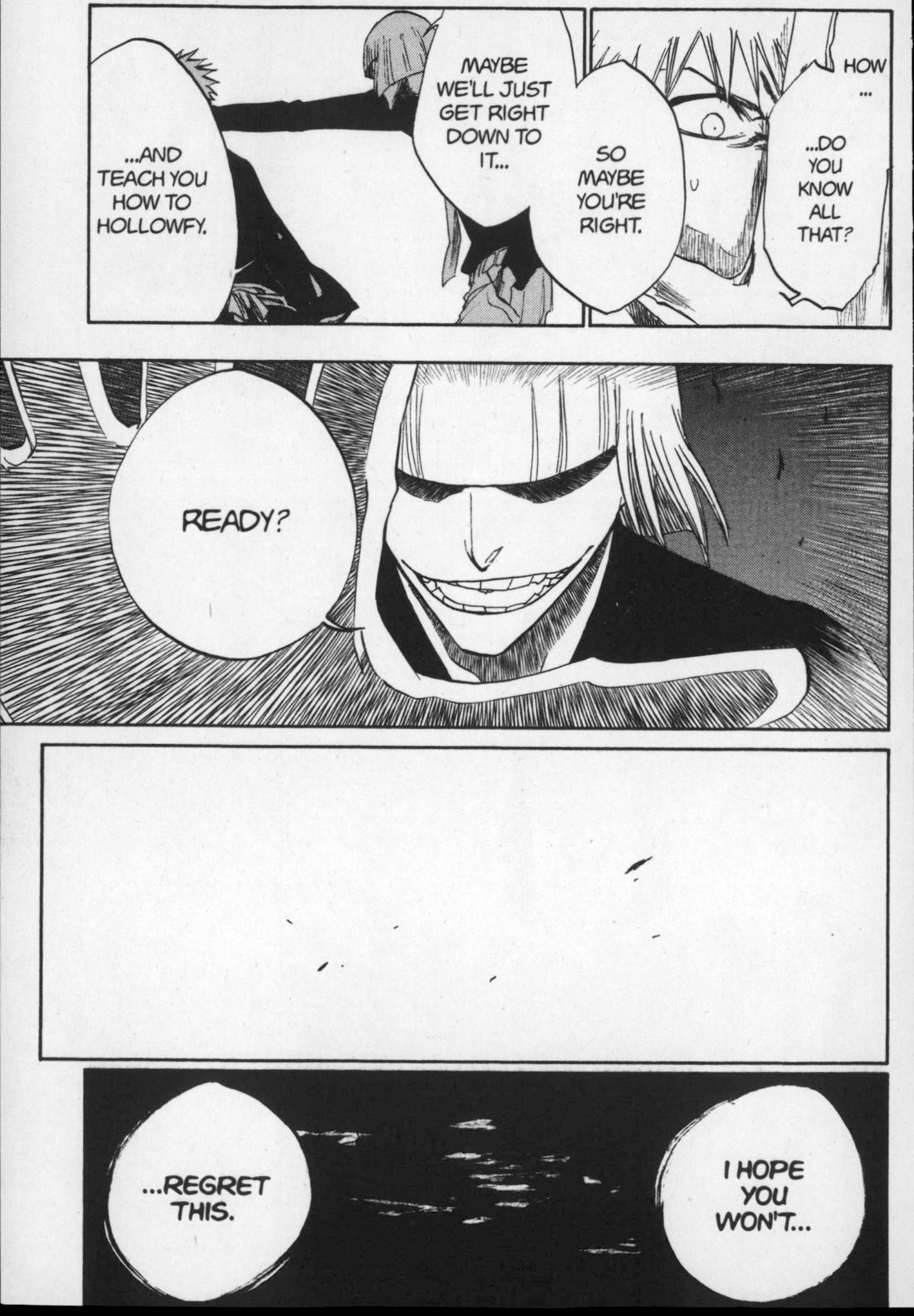
HOW ...
...DO YOU KNOW ALL THAT?
SO MAYBE YOU'RE RIGHT.
MAYBE WE'LL JUST GET RIGHT DOWN TO IT...
...AND TEACH YOU HOW TO HOLLOWFY.
READY?
I HOPE YOU WON'T...
...REGRET THIS.

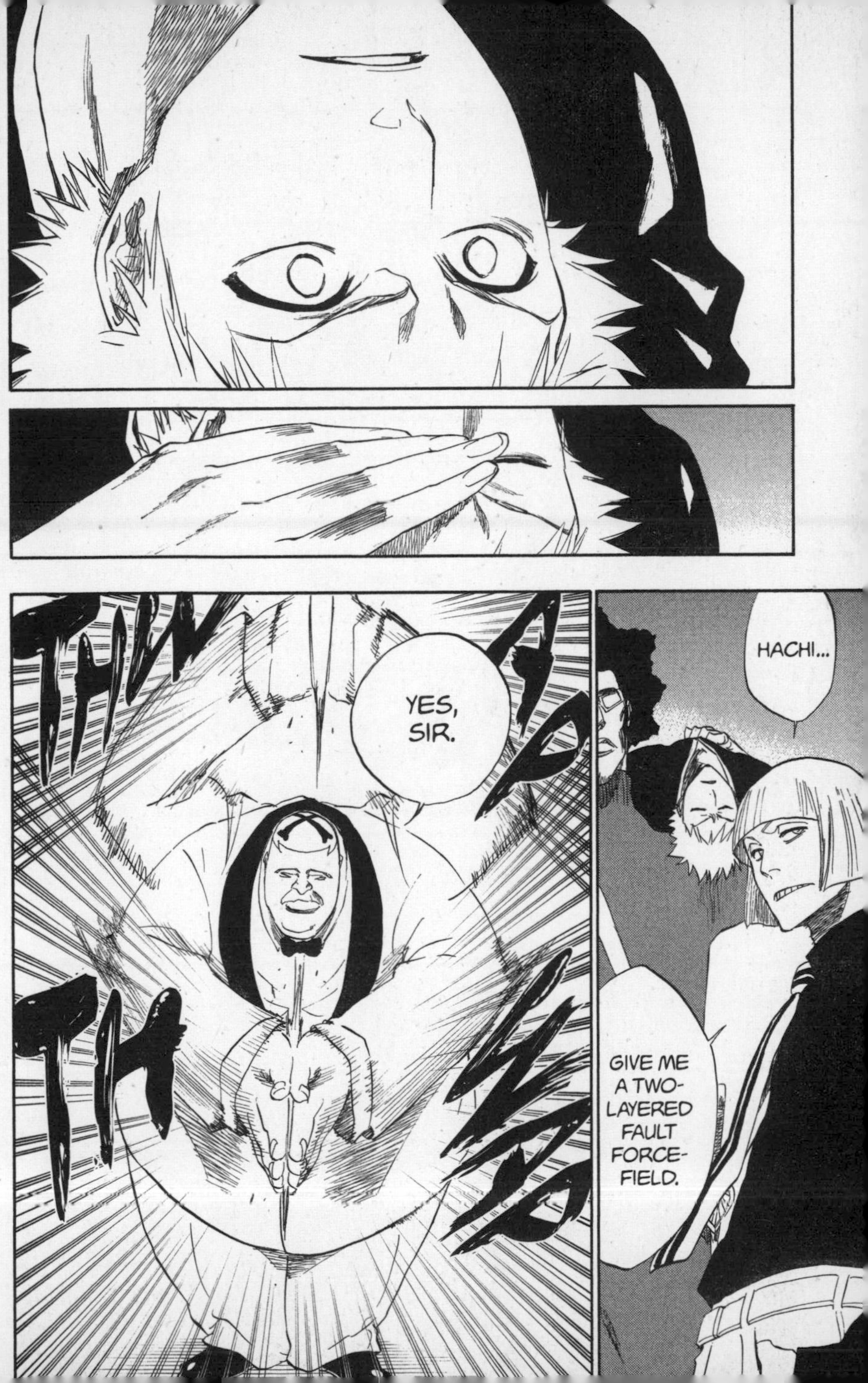
HACHI...
GIVE ME A TWO-LAYERED FAULT FORCE-FIELD.
YES, SIR.

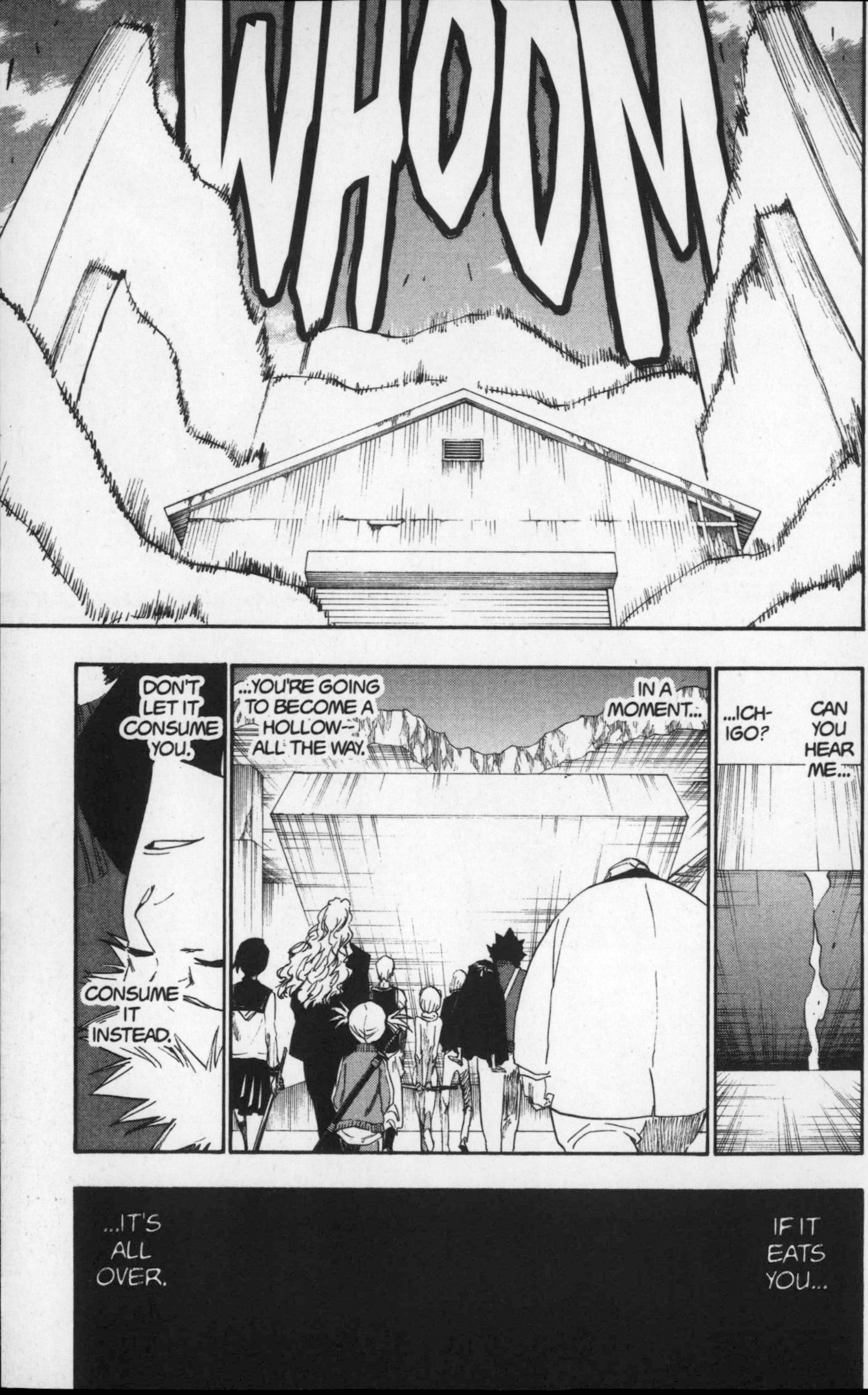
WHOOM
CAN YOU HEAR ME...
...ICH-IGO?
IN A MOMENT...
...YOU'RE GOING TO BECOME A HOLLOW--ALL THE WAY.
DON'T LET IT CONSUME YOU.
CONSUME IT INSTEAD.
IF IT EATS YOU...
...IT'S ALL OVER.

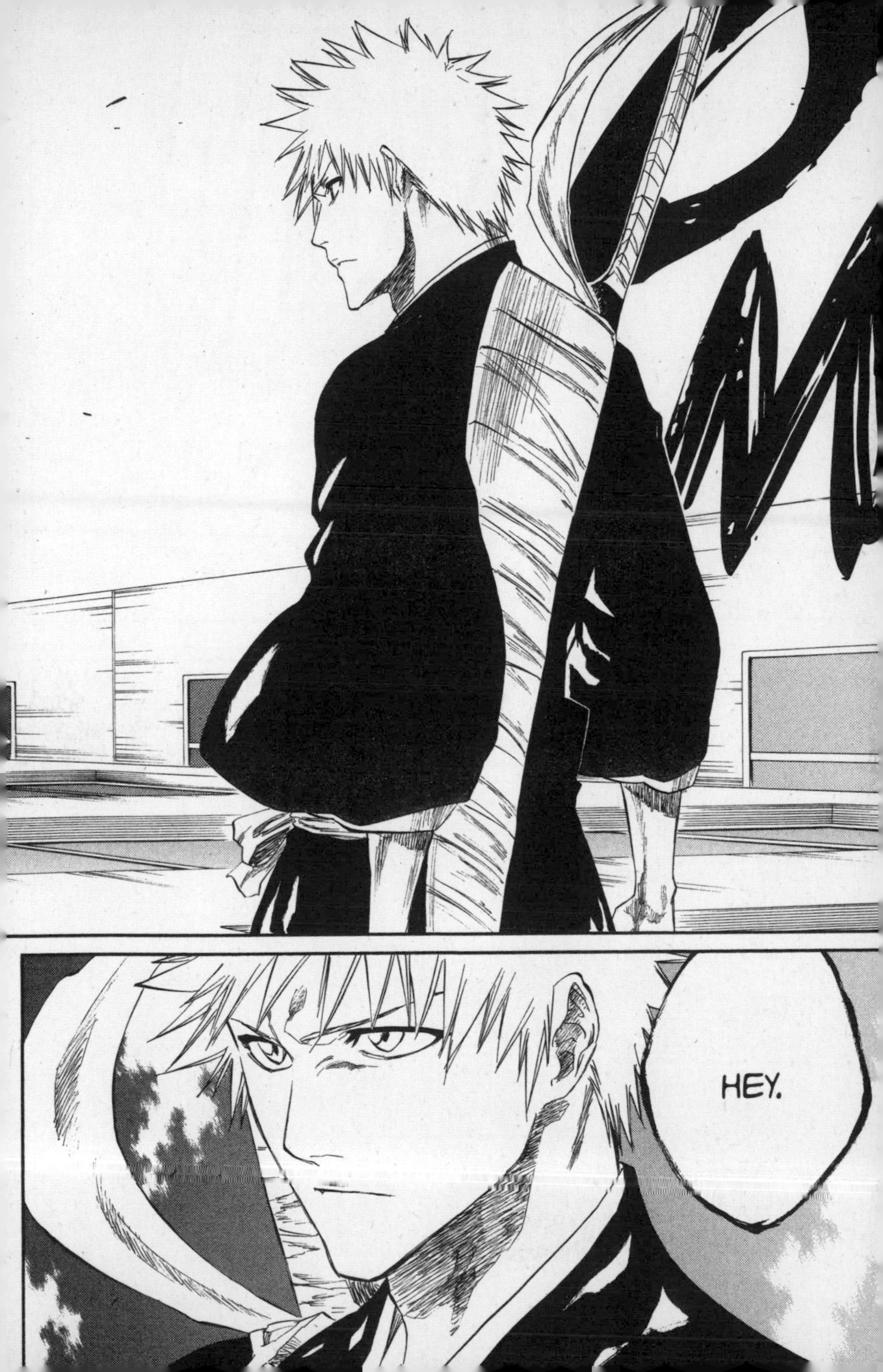
HEY.

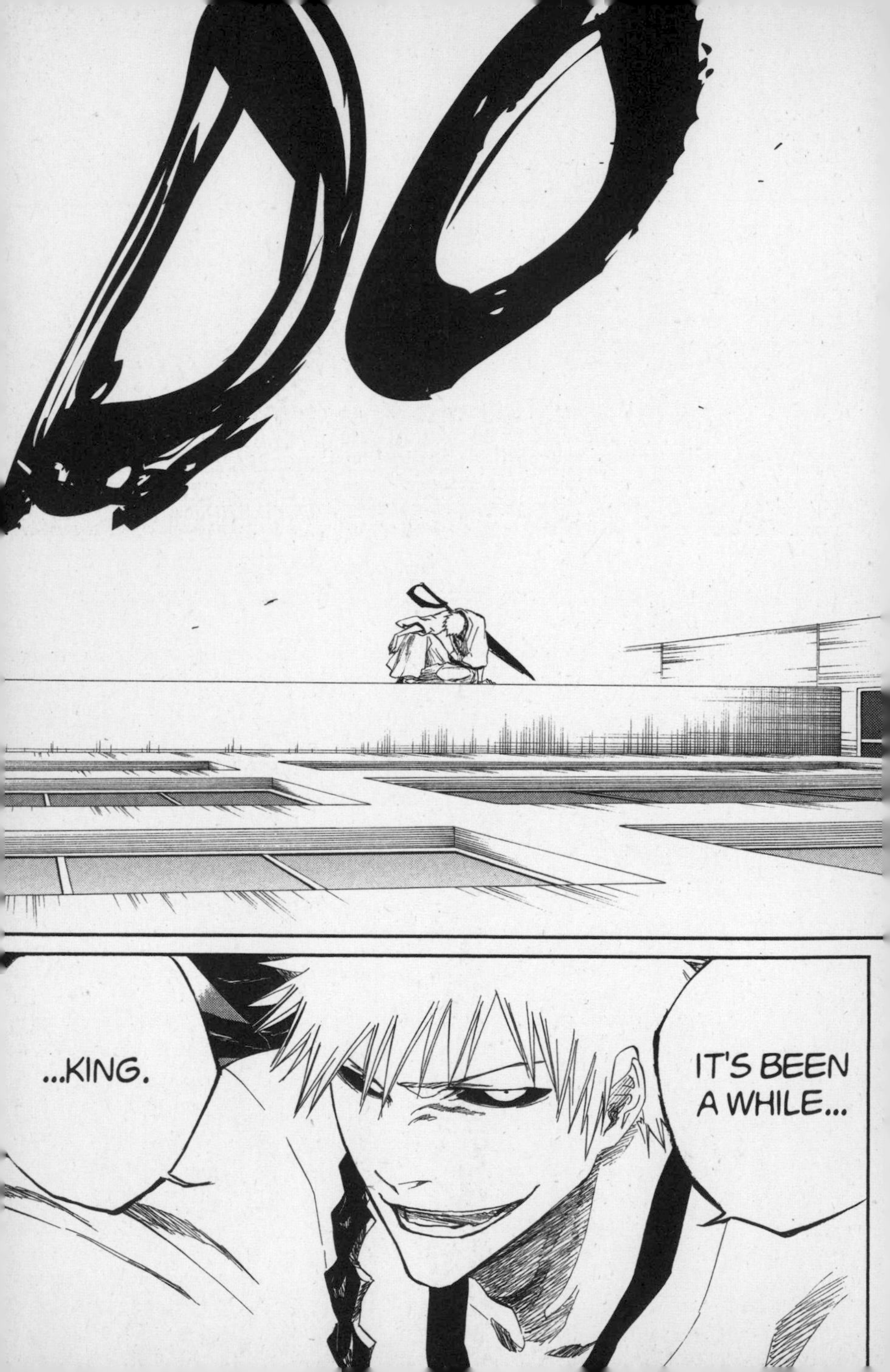
DO
IT'S BEEN A WHILE...
...KING.

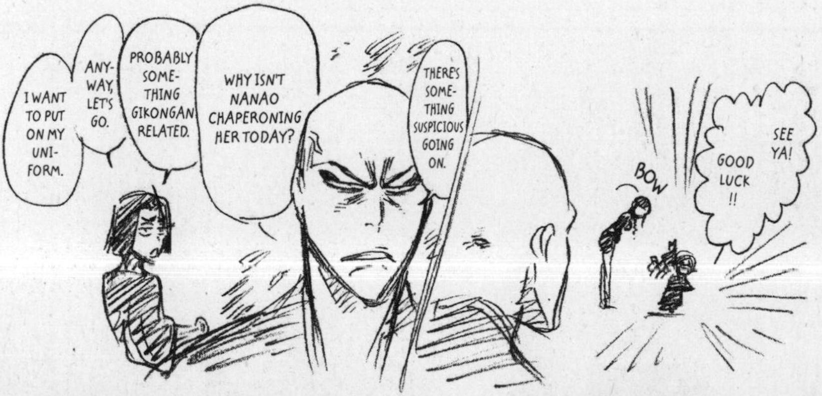
SEE YA!
GOOD LUCK !!
BOW
THERE'S SOME-THING SUSPICIOUS GOING ON.
WHY ISN'T NANAO CHAPERONING HER TODAY?
PROBABLY SOME-THING GIKONGAN RELATED.
ANY-WAY, LET'S GO.
I WANT TO PUT ON MY UNI-FORM.

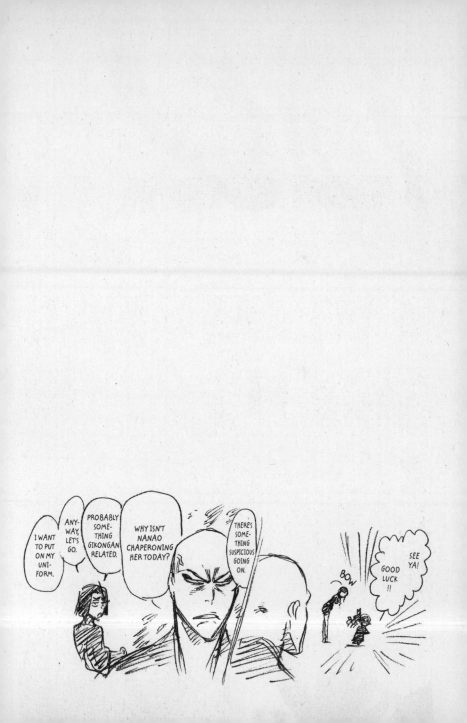

218. Dark Side of the Universe 3

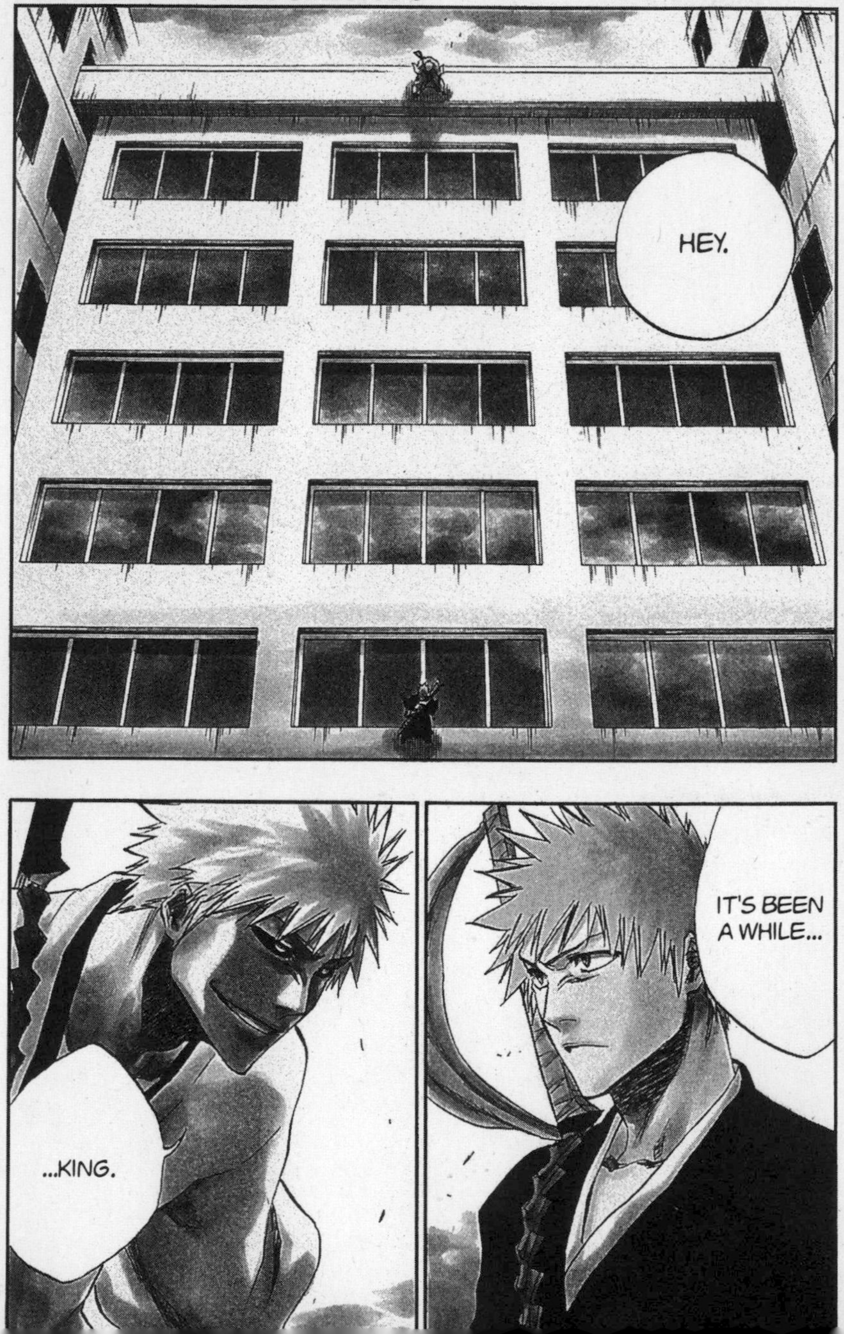
HEY.
IT'S BEEN A WHILE...
...KING.

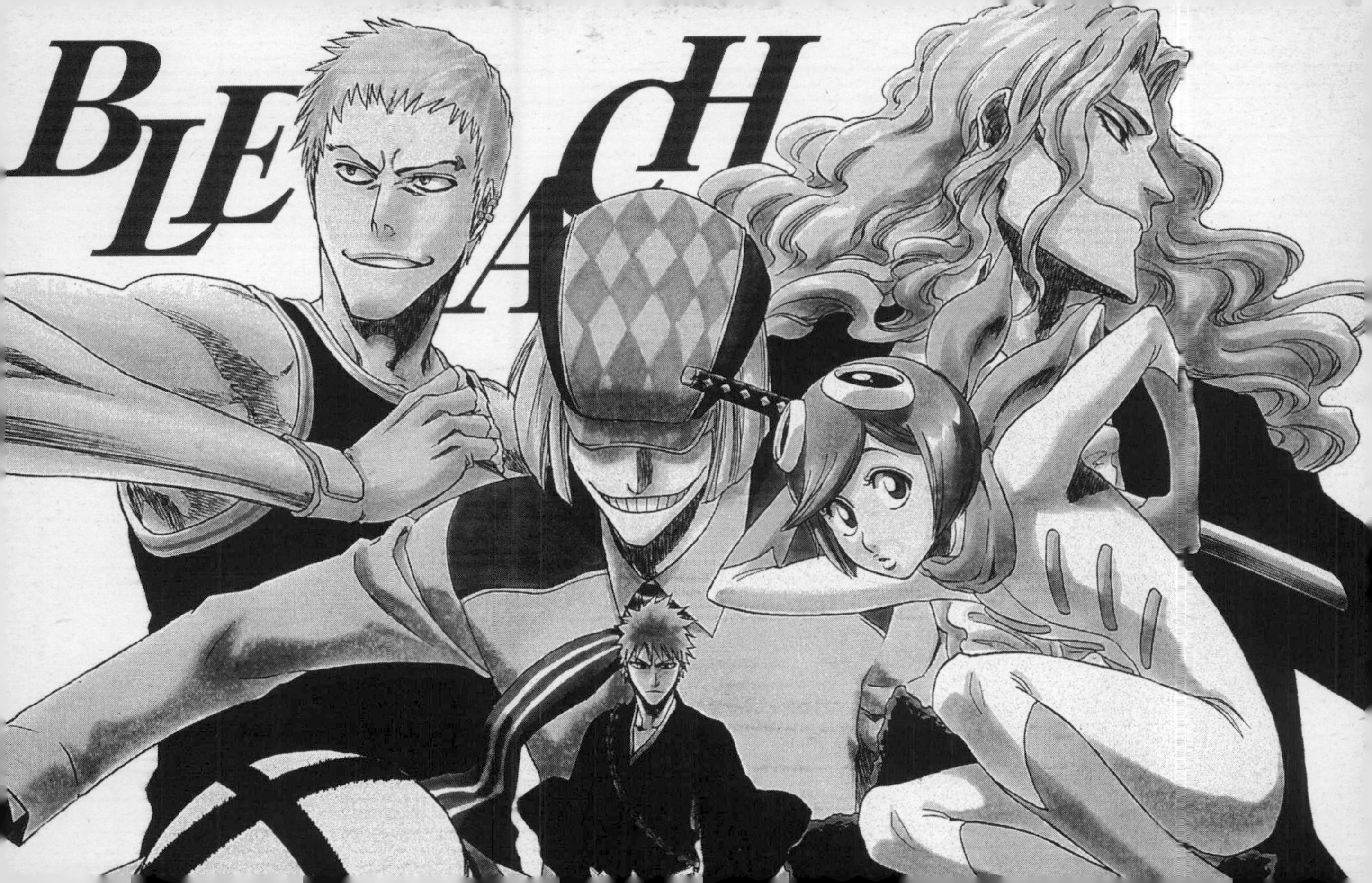
BLEACH

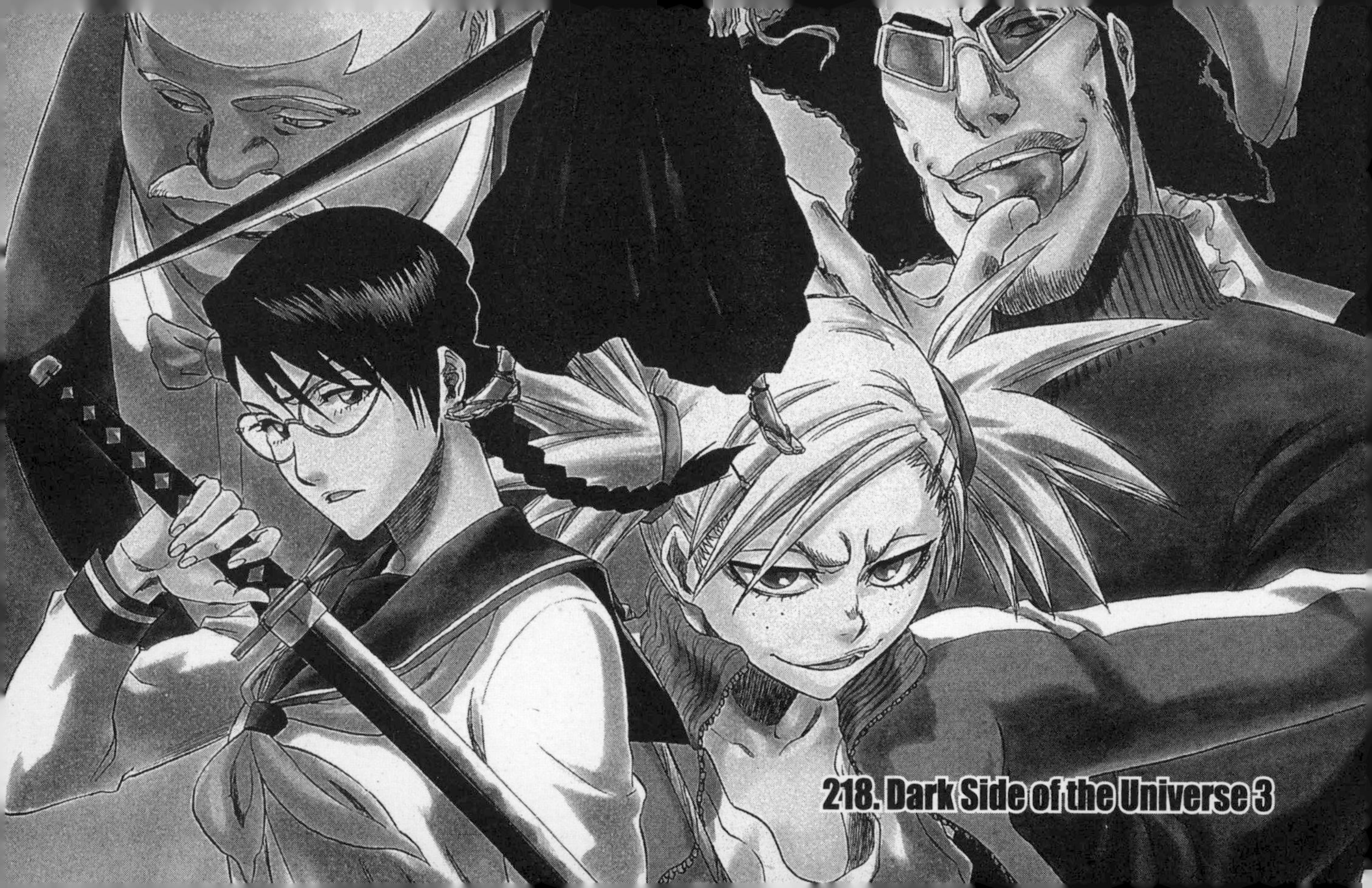
218. Dark Side of the Universe 3

BLEACH

ブリーチ

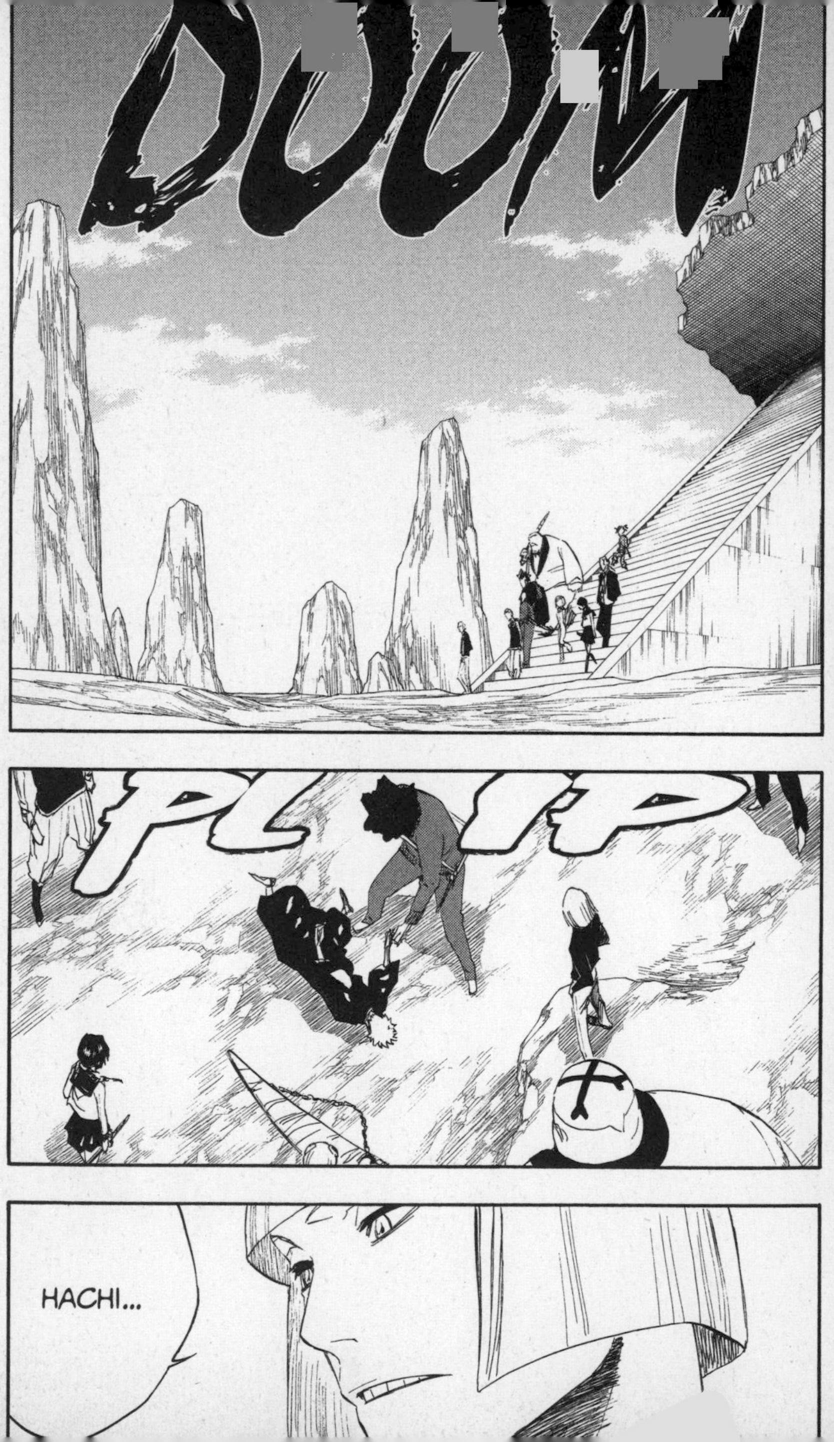
DOOM
HACHI...

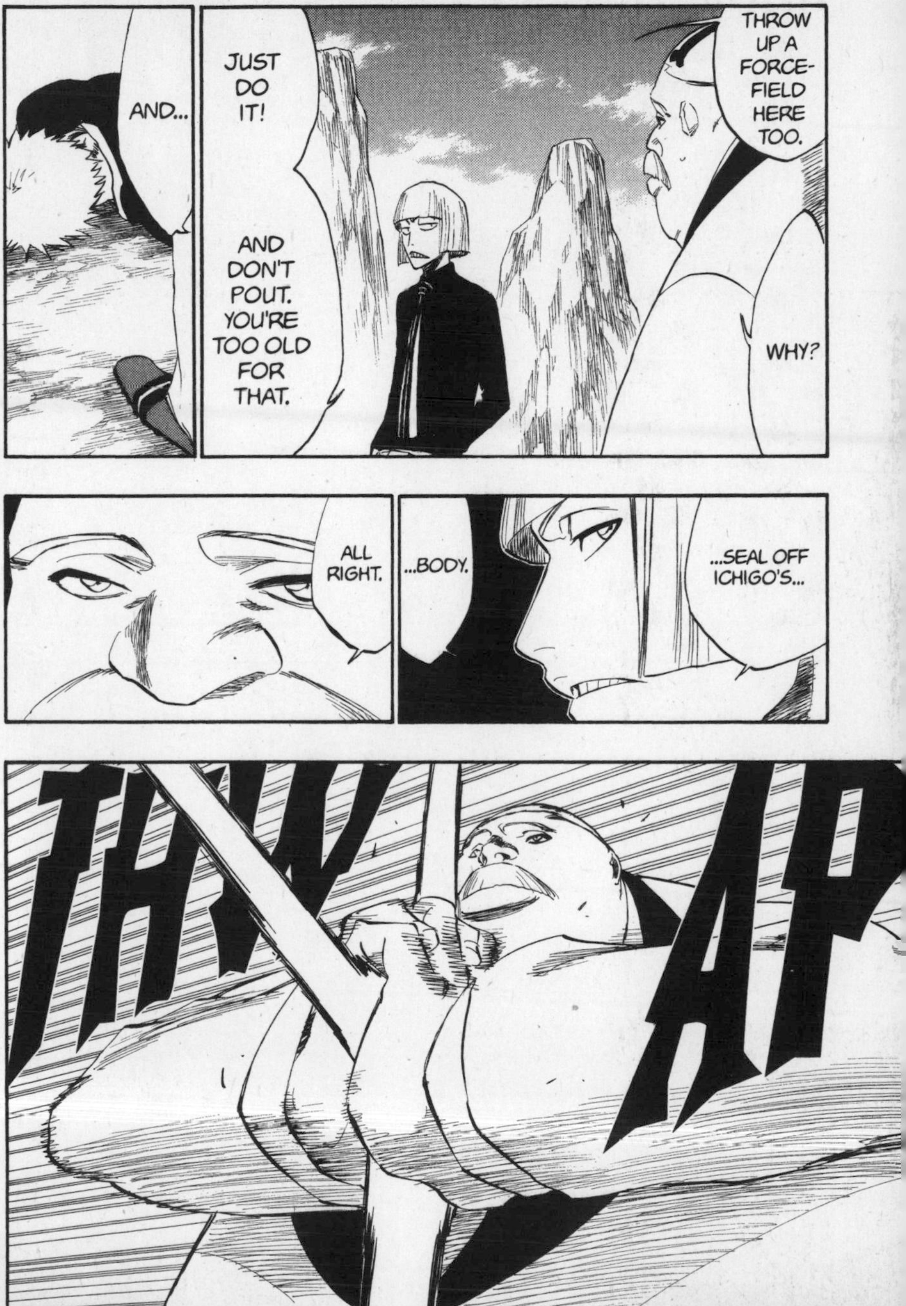
THROW UP A FORCE-FIELD HERE TOO.
WHY?
JUST DO IT!
AND DON'T POUT. YOU'RE TOO OLD FOR THAT.
AND...
...SEAL OFF ICHIGO'S...
...BODY.
ALL RIGHT.
THWAP

READ THIS WAY

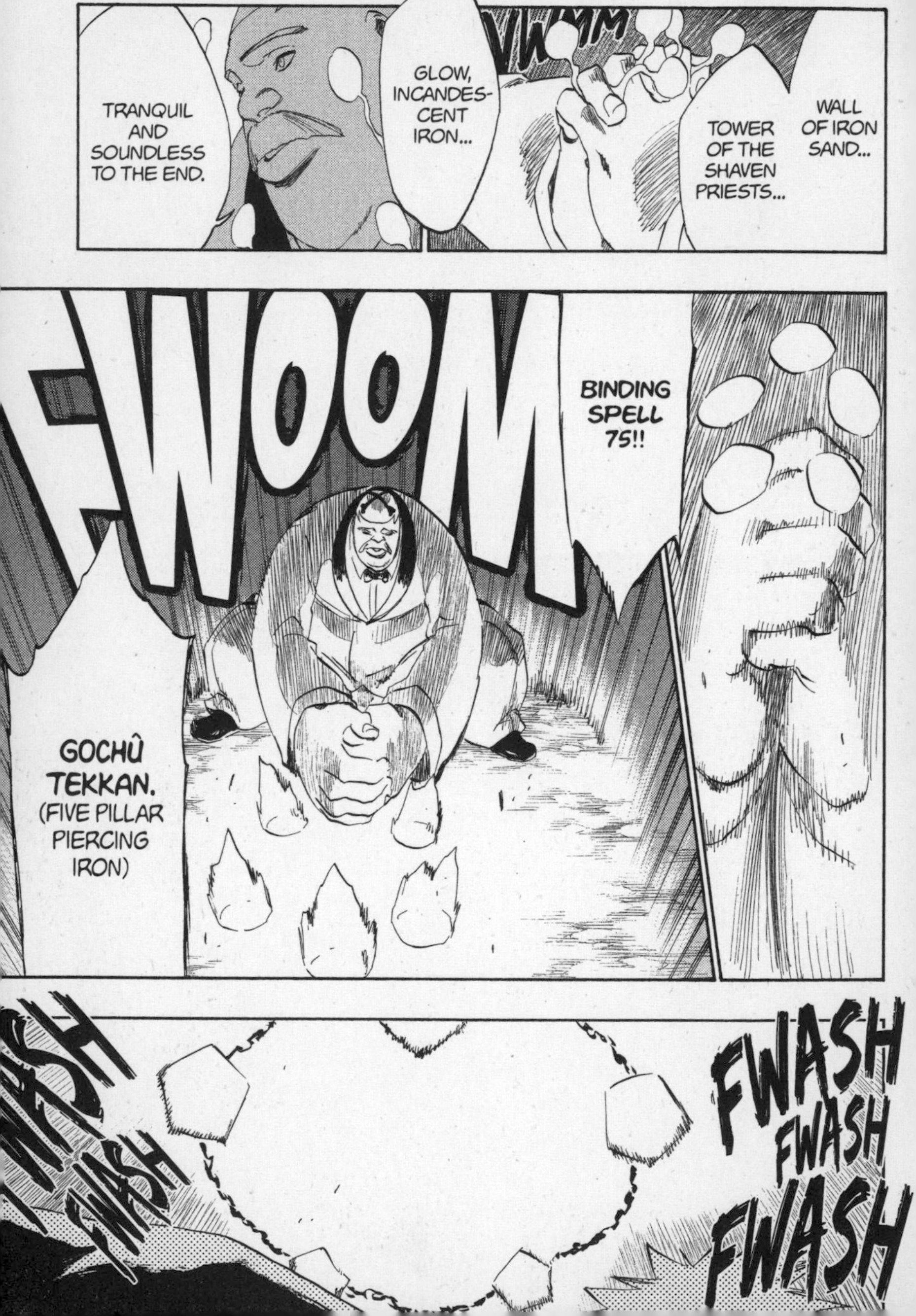
WALL OF IRON SAND...
TOWER OF THE SHAVEN PRIESTS...
VWMM
GLOW, INCANDES-CENT IRON...
TRANQUIL AND SOUNDLESS TO THE END.
WOOM
BINDING SPELL 75!!
GOCHÛ TEKKAN. (FIVE PILLAR PIERCING IRON)
FWASH FWASH FWASH
FWASH

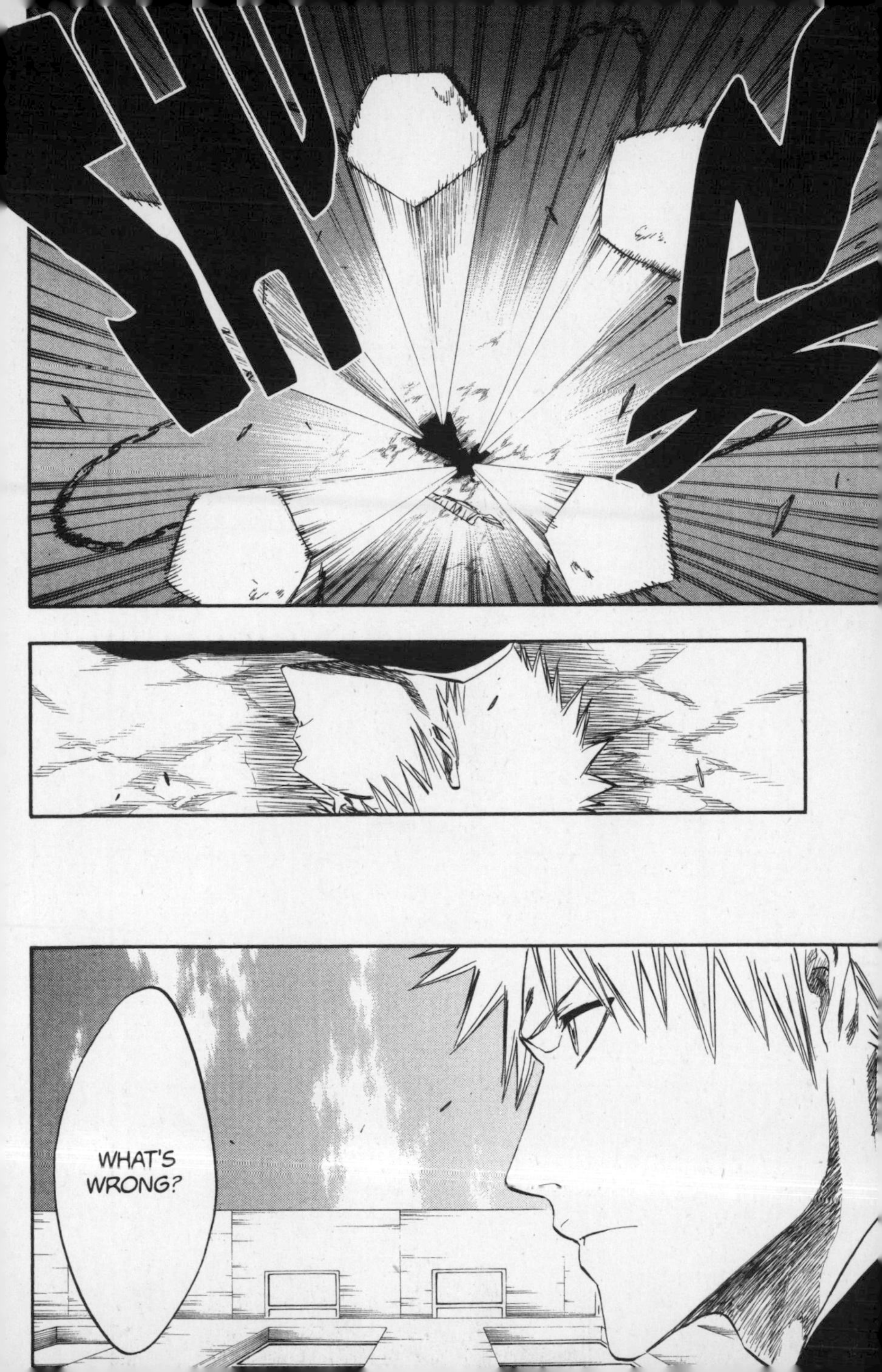
WHAT'S WRONG?

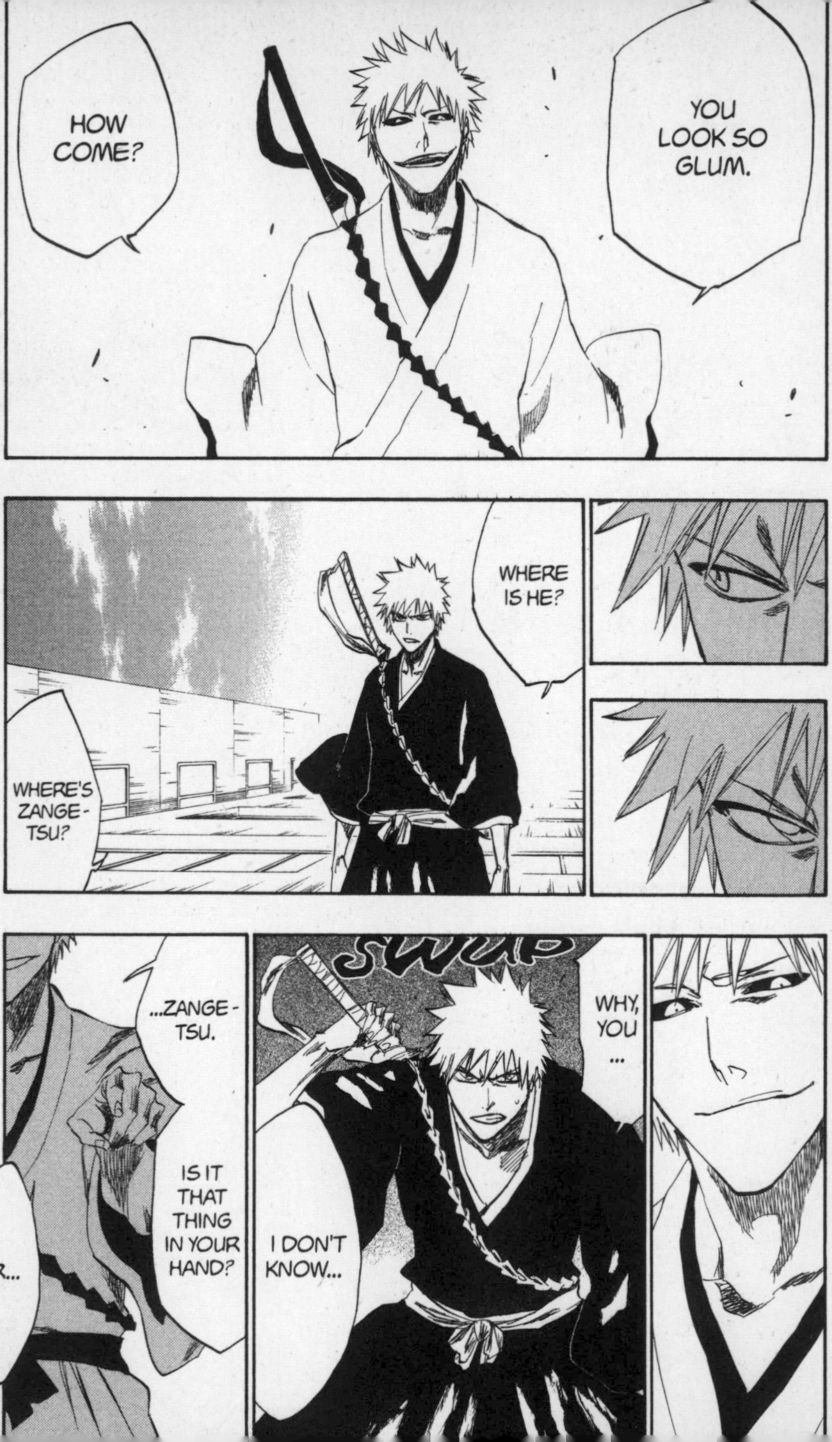
YOU LOOK SO GLUM.
HOW COME?
WHERE IS HE?
WHERE'S ZANGE-TSU?
WHY, YOU ...
SWUP
I DON'T KNOW...
...ZANGE-TSU.
IS IT THAT THING IN YOUR HAND?
OR...

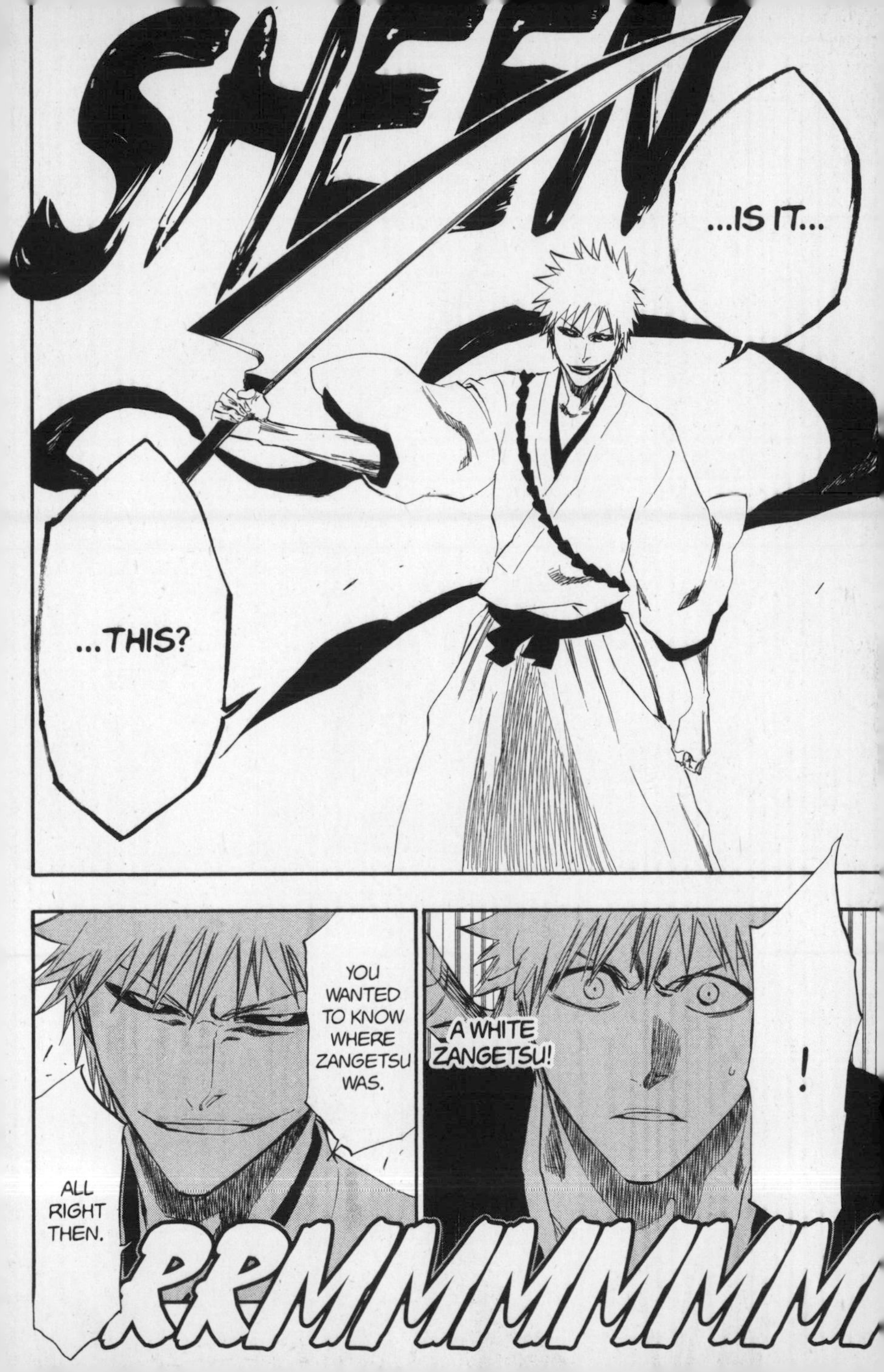
SHEEN
...IS IT...
...THIS?
!
A WHITE ZANGETSU!
YOU WANTED TO KNOW WHERE ZANGETSU WAS.
ALL RIGHT THEN.
REMMMMMMMM

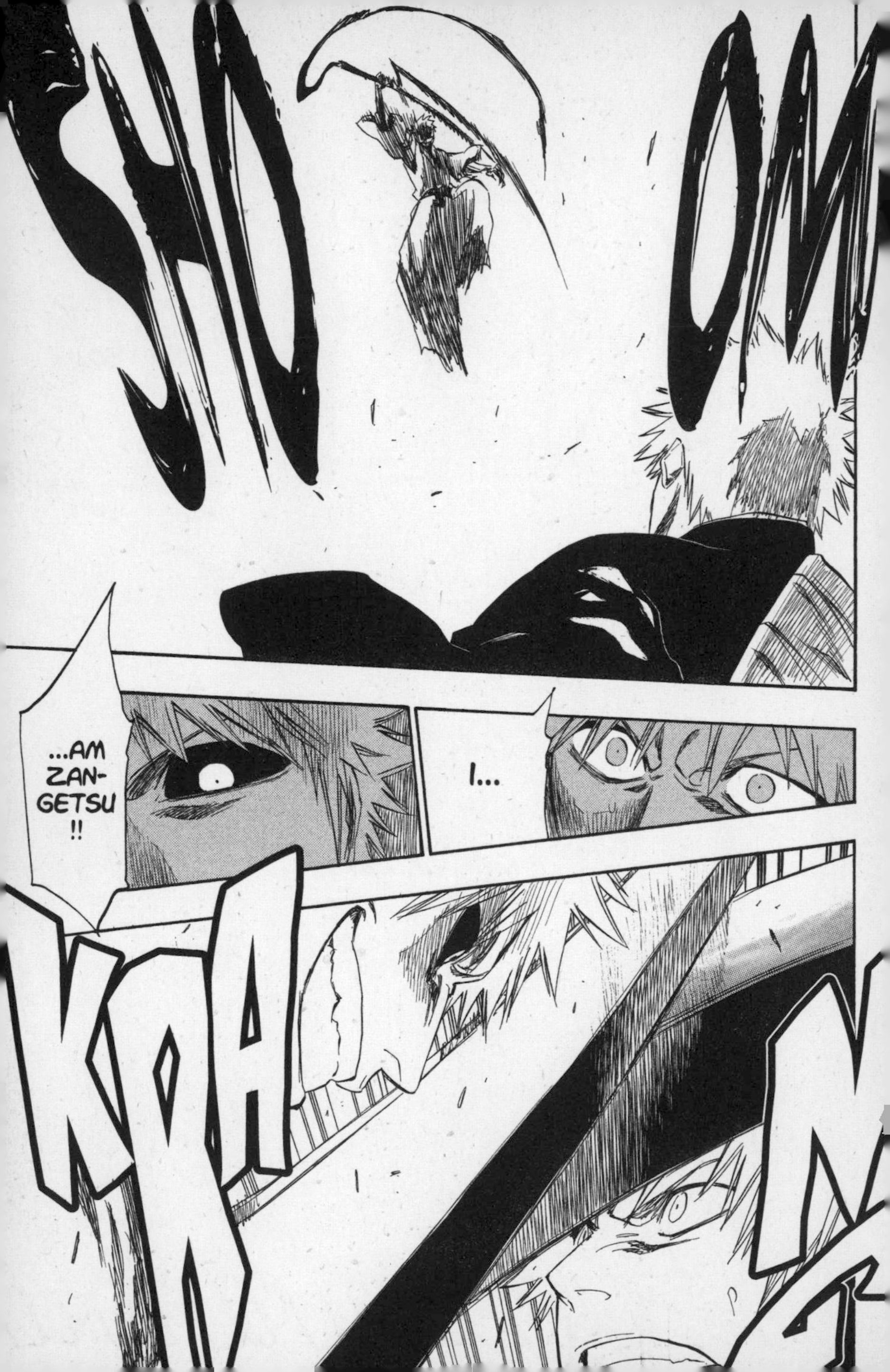
I...
...AM ZANGETSU!!

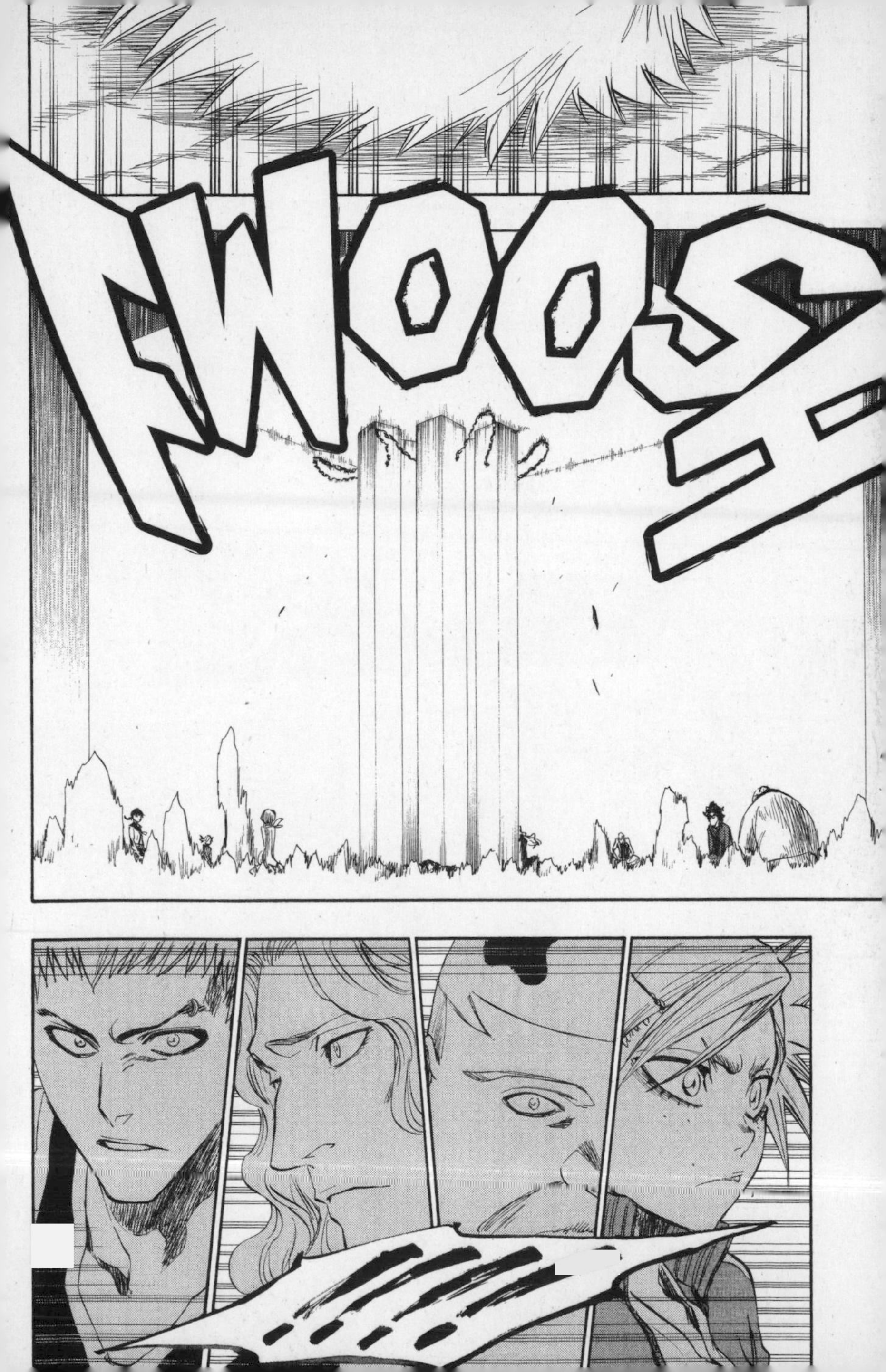
FWOOSH
...!!

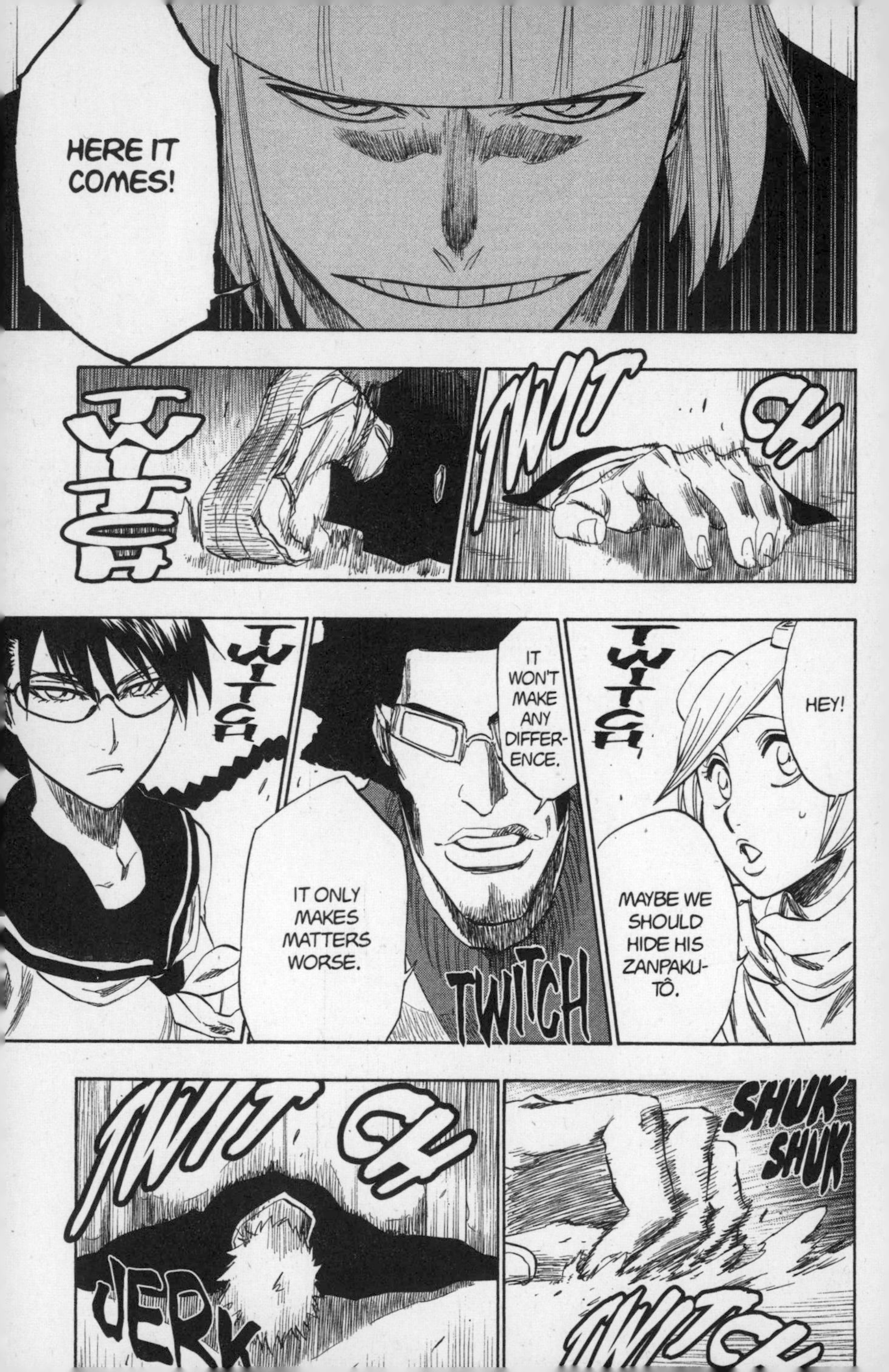
HERE IT COMES!
TWITCH
TWITCH
HEY!
MAYBE WE SHOULD HIDE HIS ZANPAKU-TÔ.
TWITCH
IT WON'T MAKE ANY DIFFERENCE.
IT ONLY MAKES MATTERS WORSE.
TWITCH
TWITCH
SHUK SHUK
TWITCH
TWITCH
JERK

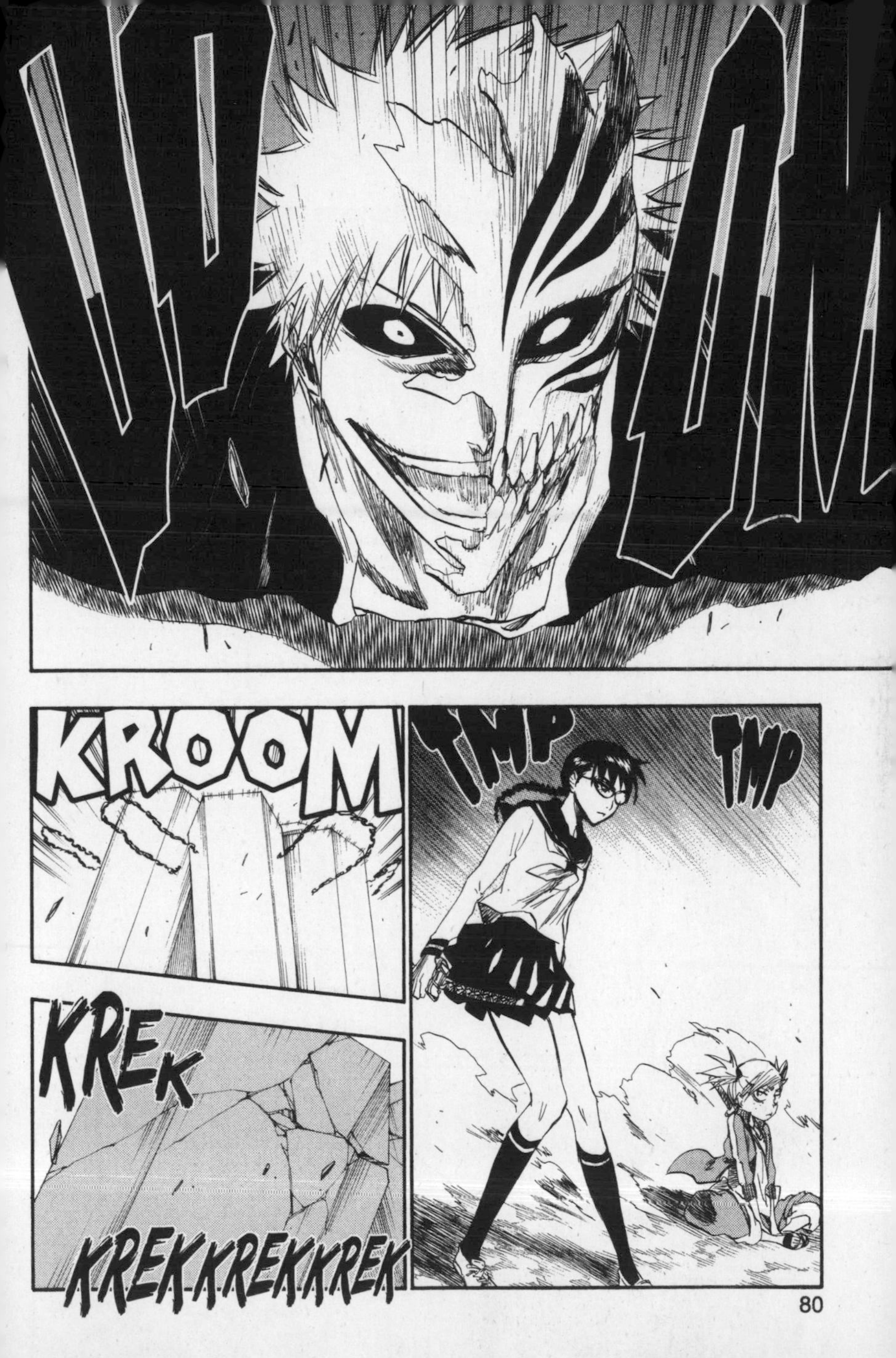
TMP
TMP
KROOM
KREK
KREK KREK KREK

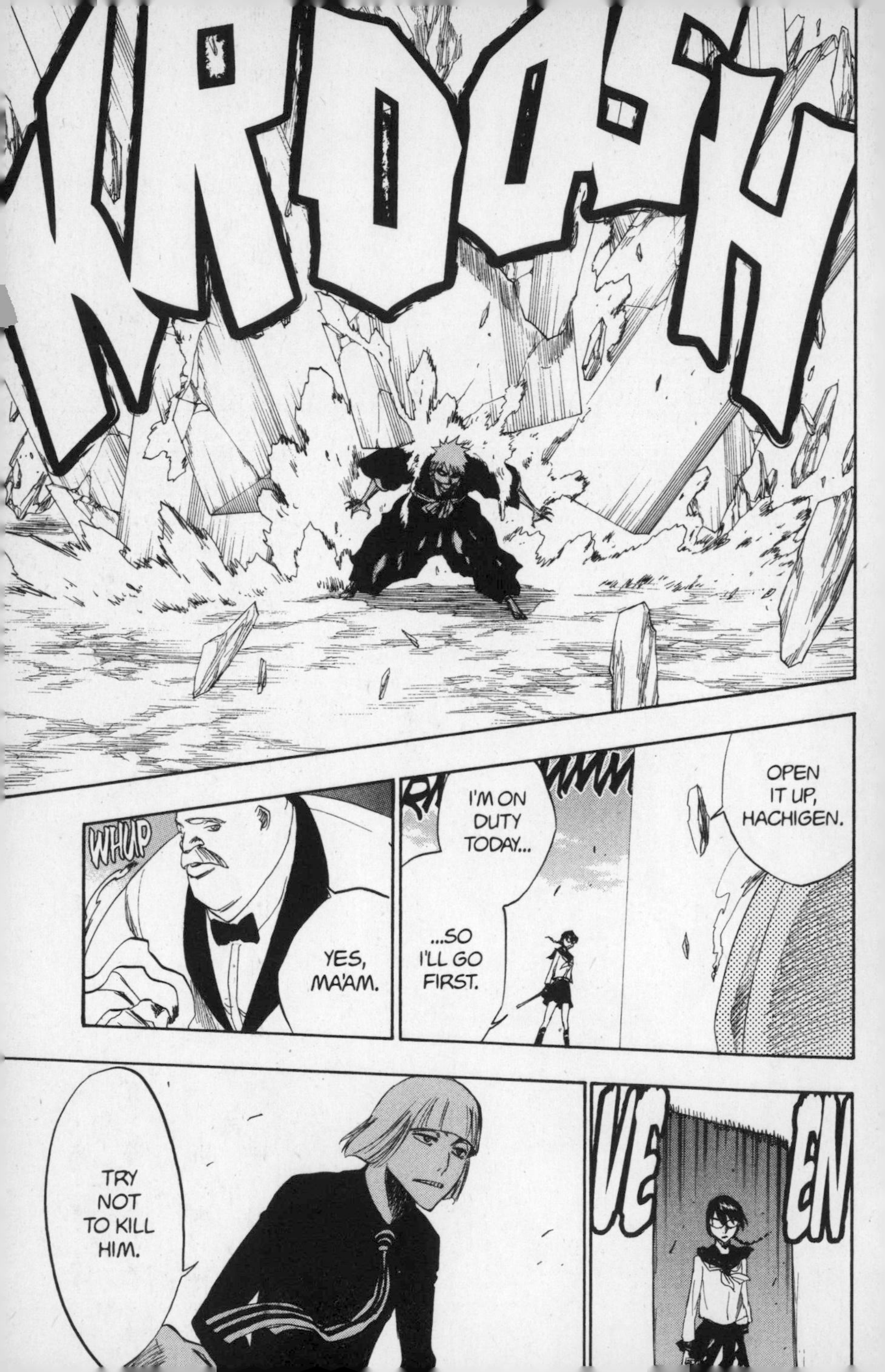
OPEN IT UP, HACHIGEN.
I'M ON DUTY TODAY...
...SO I'LL GO FIRST.
WHUP
YES, MA'AM.
TRY NOT TO KILL HIM.

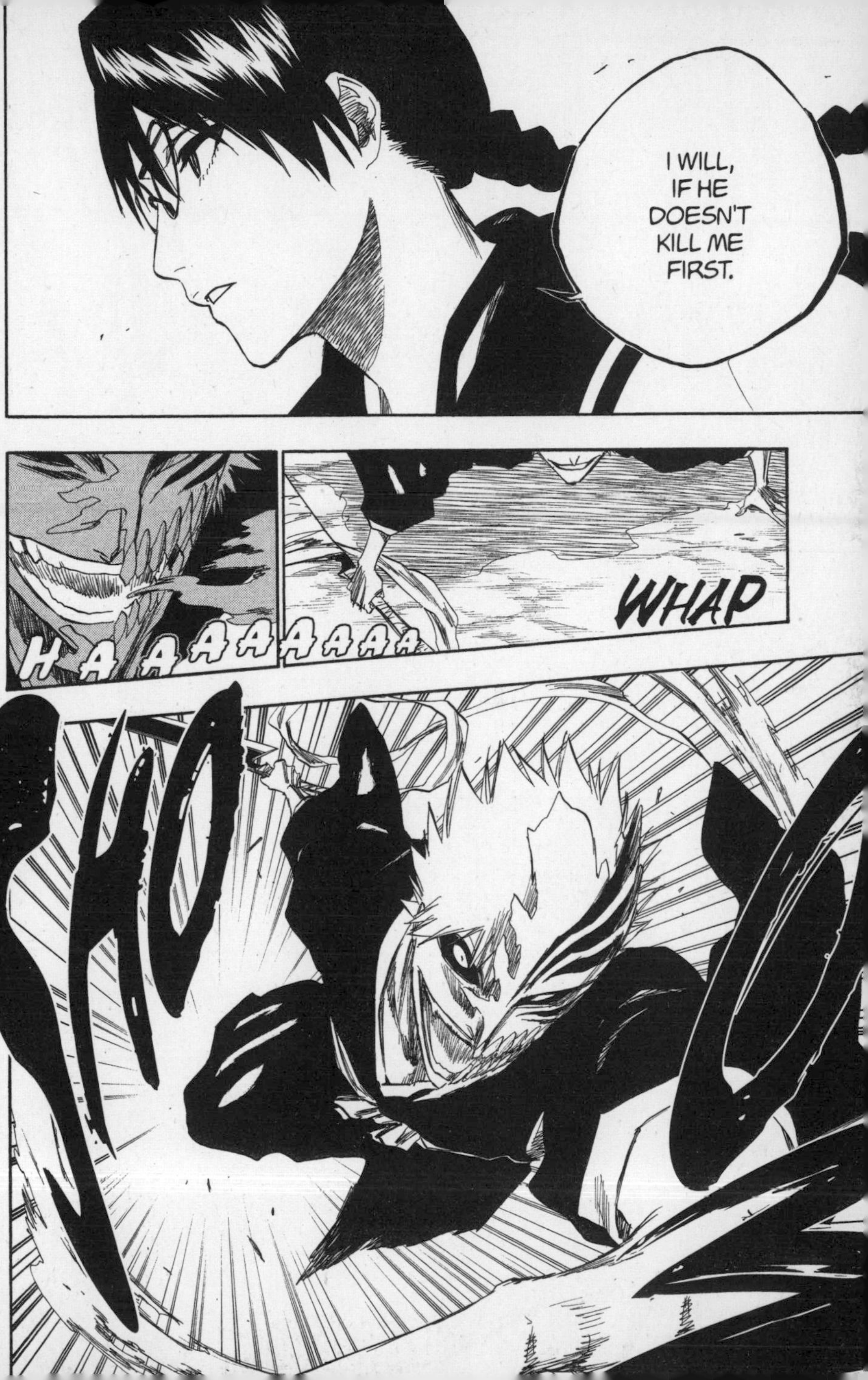
I WILL, IF HE DOESN'T KILL ME FIRST.
WHAP
HAAAAAAAA

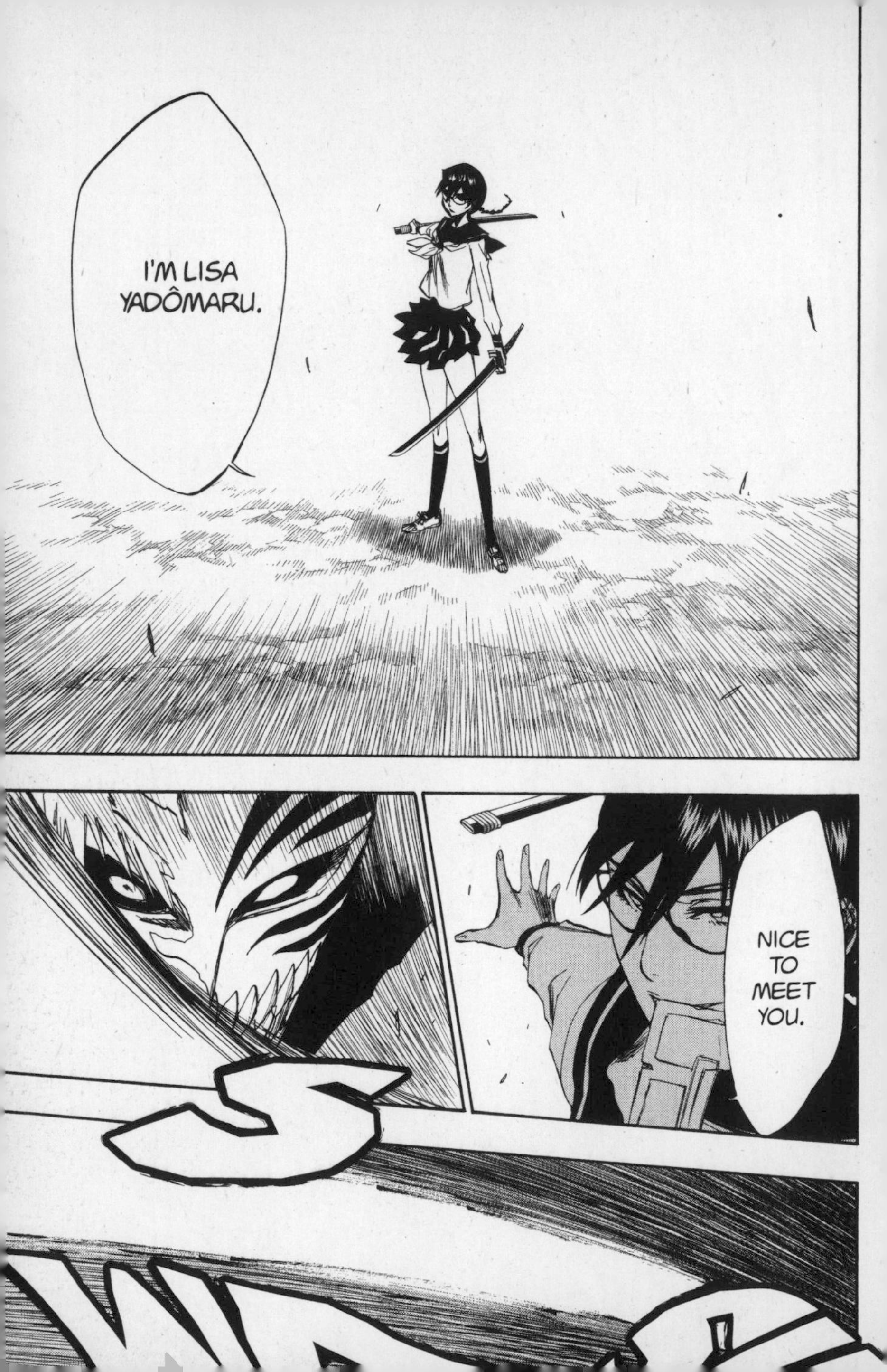
I'M LISA YADÔMARU.
NICE TO MEET YOU.

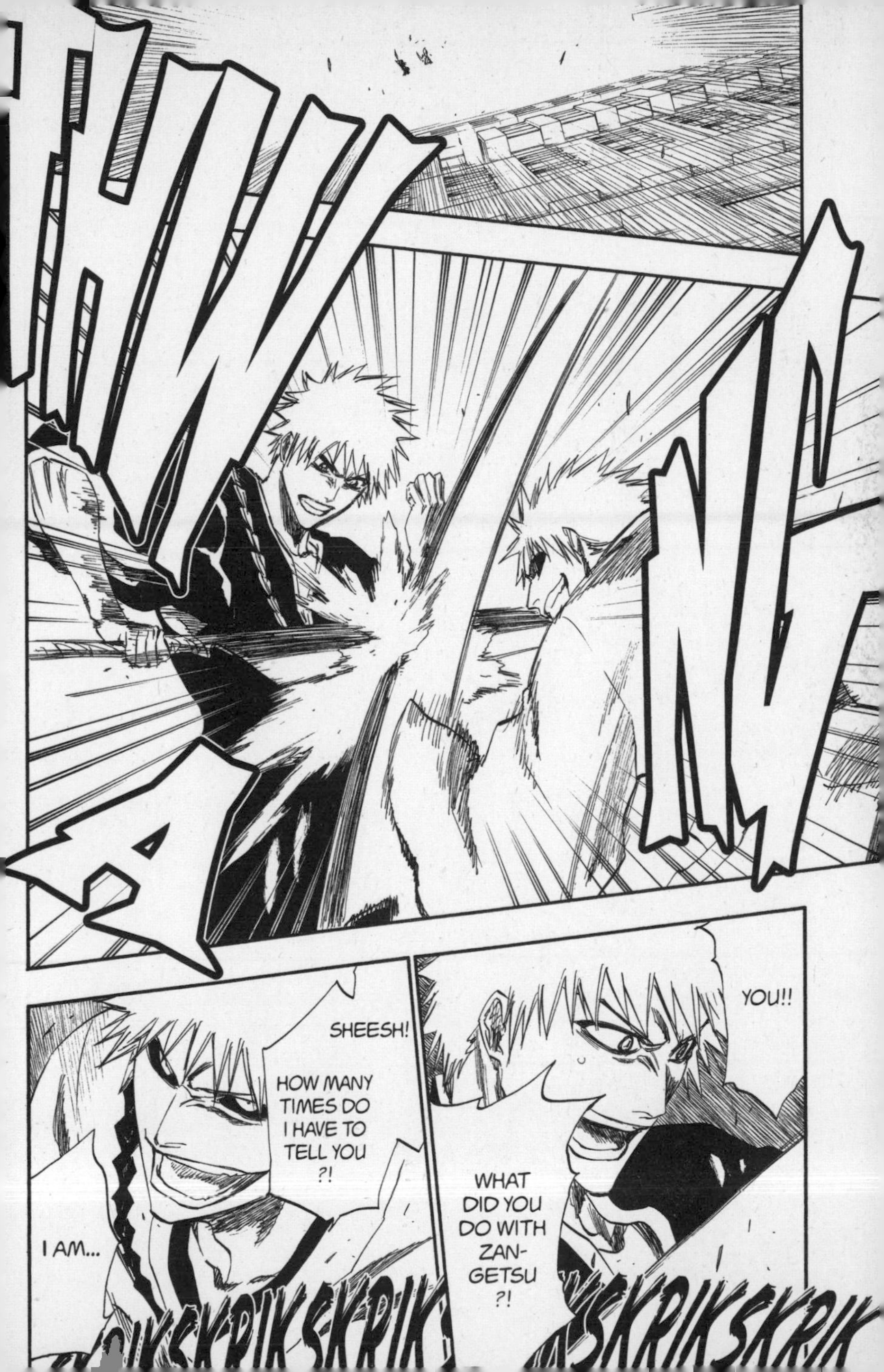
YOU!!
WHAT DID YOU DO WITH ZAN-GETSU ?!
SKRIK SKRIK
SHEESH!
HOW MANY TIMES DO I HAVE TO TELL YOU ?!
I AM...
SKRIK SKRIK SKRIK

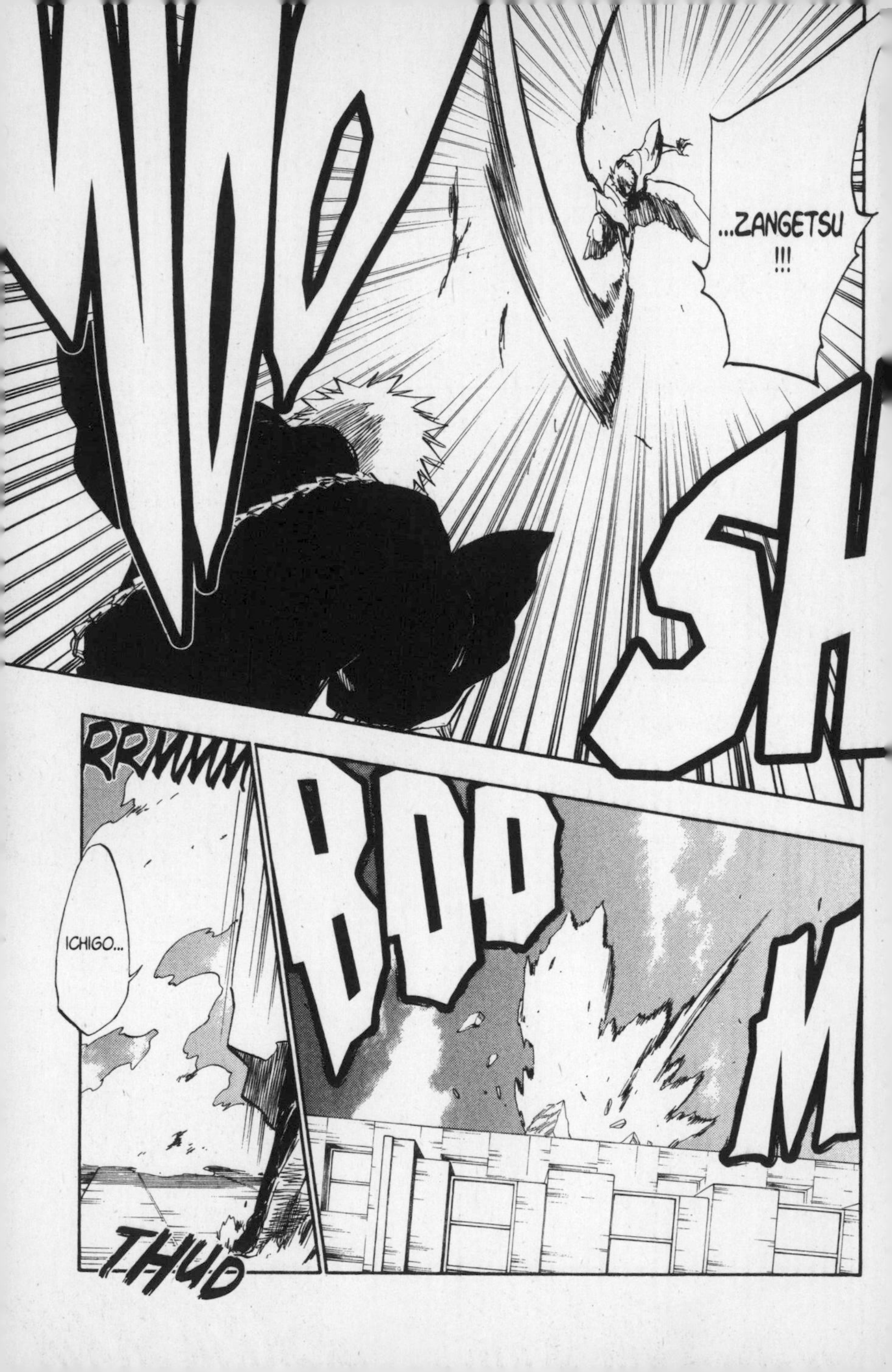
...ZANGETSU!!!
BOOM
RRMMMM
ICHIGO...
THUD

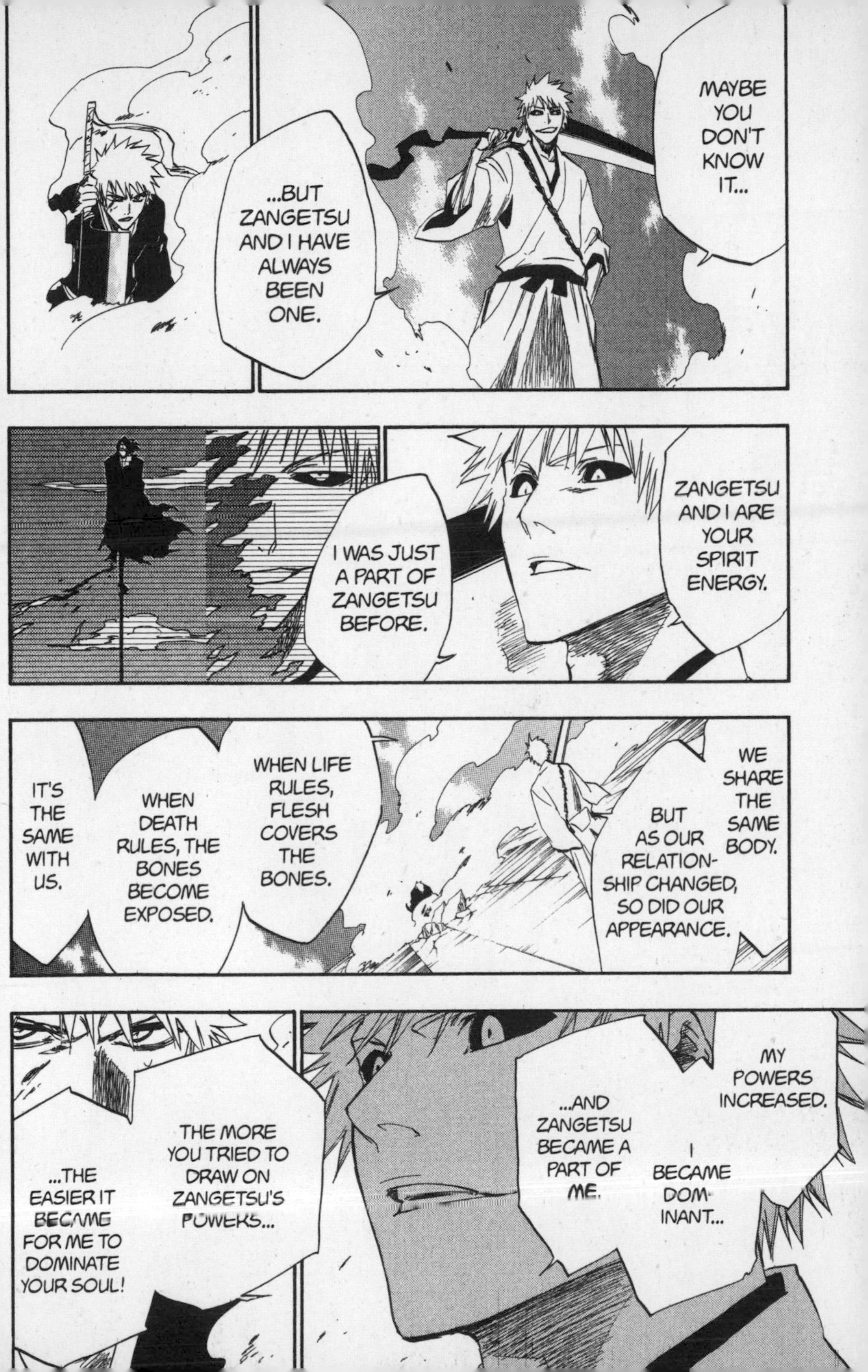
MAYBE YOU DON'T KNOW IT...
...BUT ZANGETSU AND I HAVE ALWAYS BEEN ONE.
ZANGETSU AND I ARE YOUR SPIRIT ENERGY.
I WAS JUST A PART OF ZANGETSU BEFORE.
WE SHARE THE SAME BODY.
BUT AS OUR RELATION-SHIP CHANGED, SO DID OUR APPEARANCE.
WHEN LIFE RULES, FLESH COVERS THE BONES.
WHEN DEATH RULES, THE BONES BECOME EXPOSED.
IT'S THE SAME WITH US.
MY POWERS INCREASED.
I BECAME DOM-INANT...
...AND ZANGETSU BECAME A PART OF ME.
THE MORE YOU TRIED TO DRAW ON ZANGETSU'S POWERS...
...THE EASIER IT BECAME FOR ME TO DOMINATE YOUR SOUL!

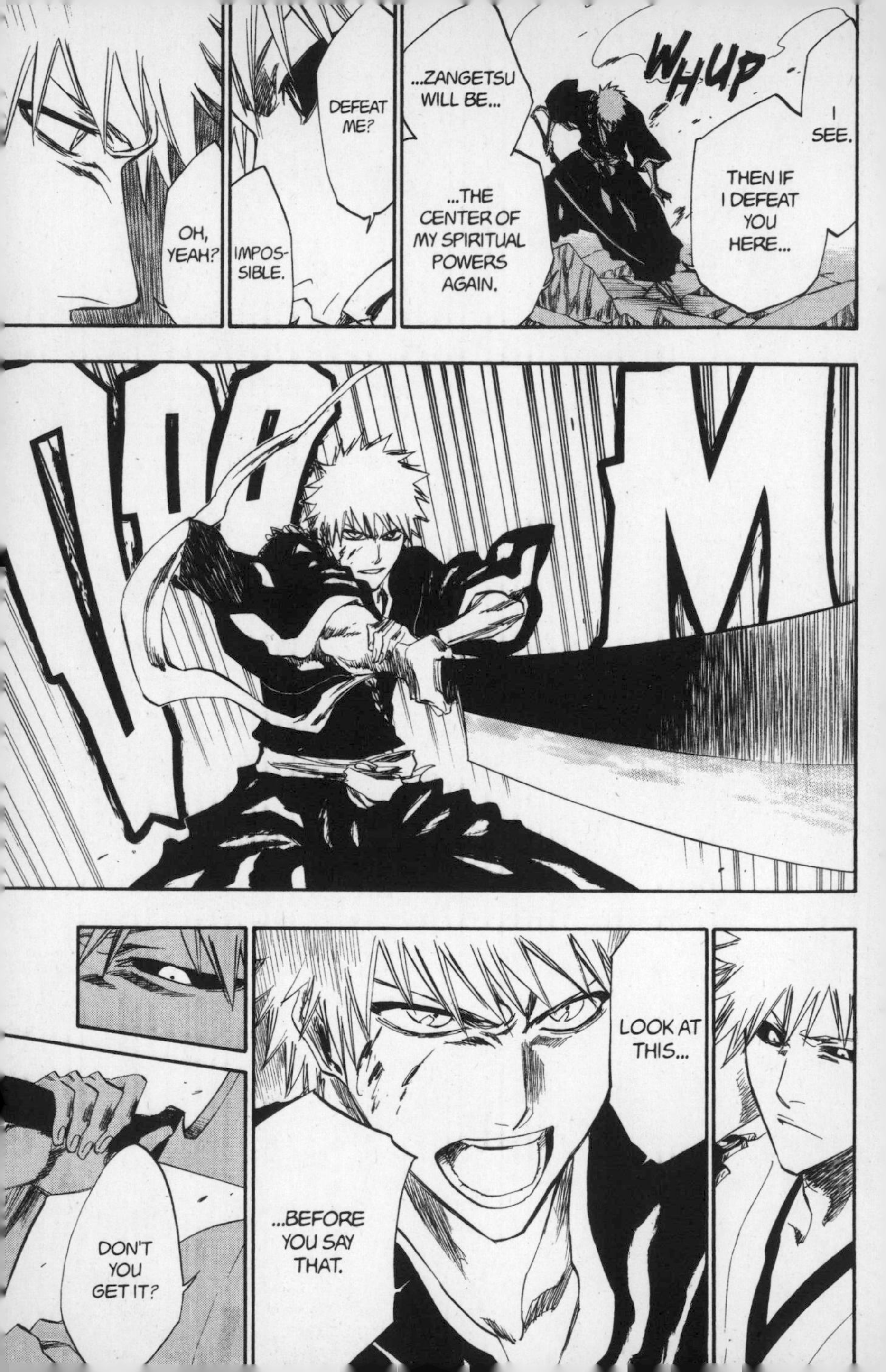
WHUP
I SEE.
THEN IF I DEFEAT YOU HERE...
...ZANGETSU WILL BE...
...THE CENTER OF MY SPIRITUAL POWERS AGAIN.
DEFEAT ME?
IMPOSSIBLE.
OH, YEAH?
LOOK AT THIS...
...BEFORE YOU SAY THAT.
DON'T YOU GET IT?

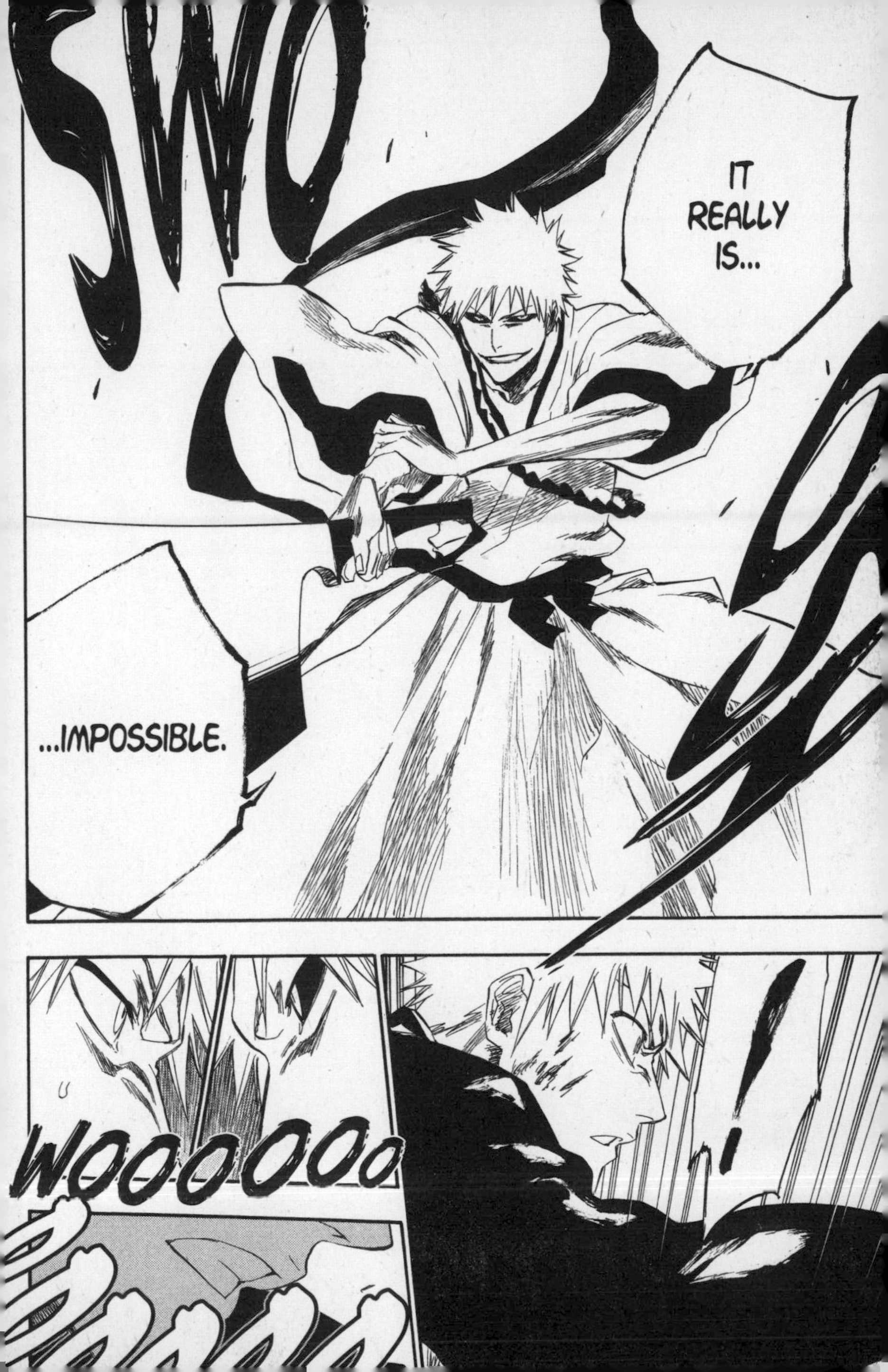

IT REALLY IS...
...IMPOSSIBLE.
SWO
!
WOOOOOO

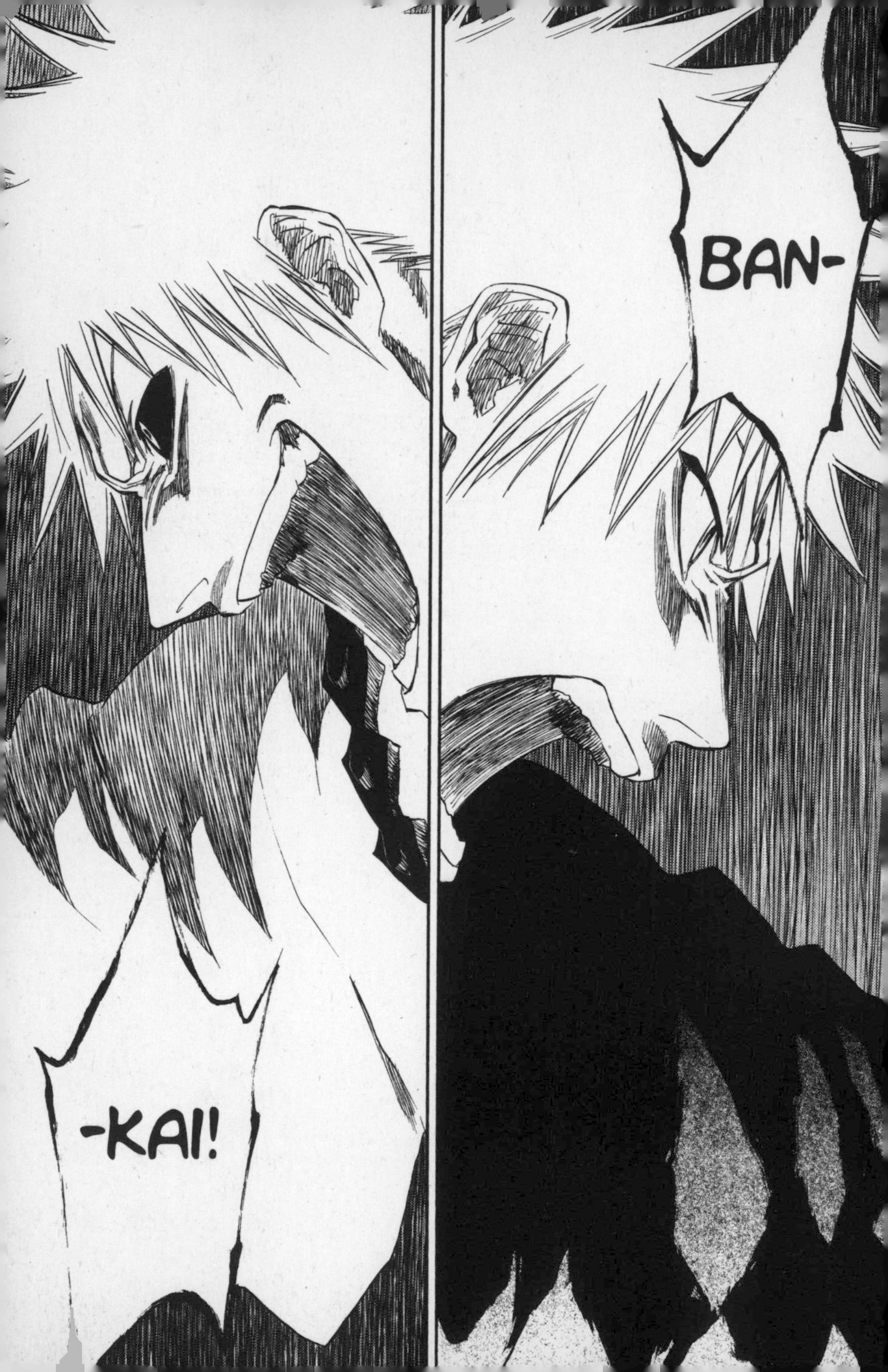
BAN-
-KAI!

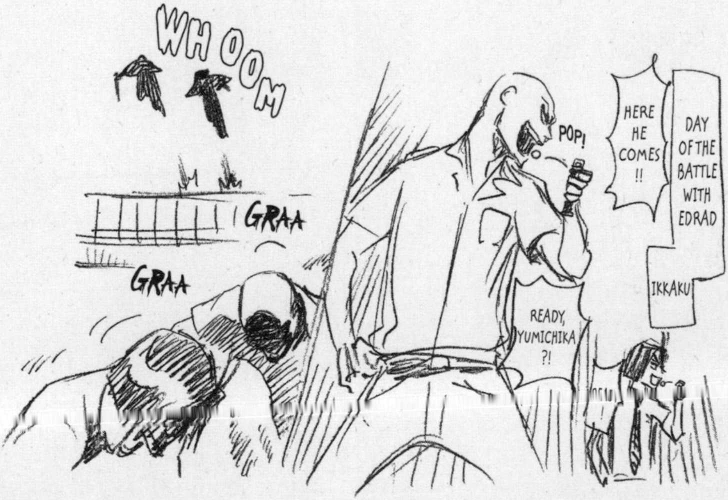
DAY OF THE BATTLE WITH EDRAD
IKKAKU
HERE HE COMES!!
POP!
READY, YUMICHIKA?!
WHOOM
GRAA
GRAA

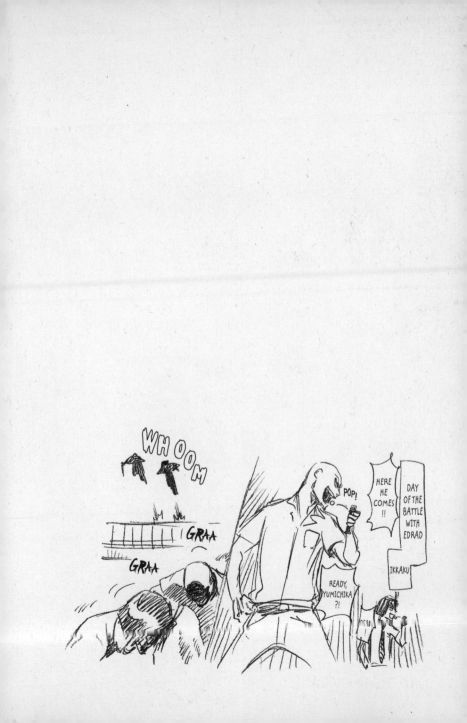

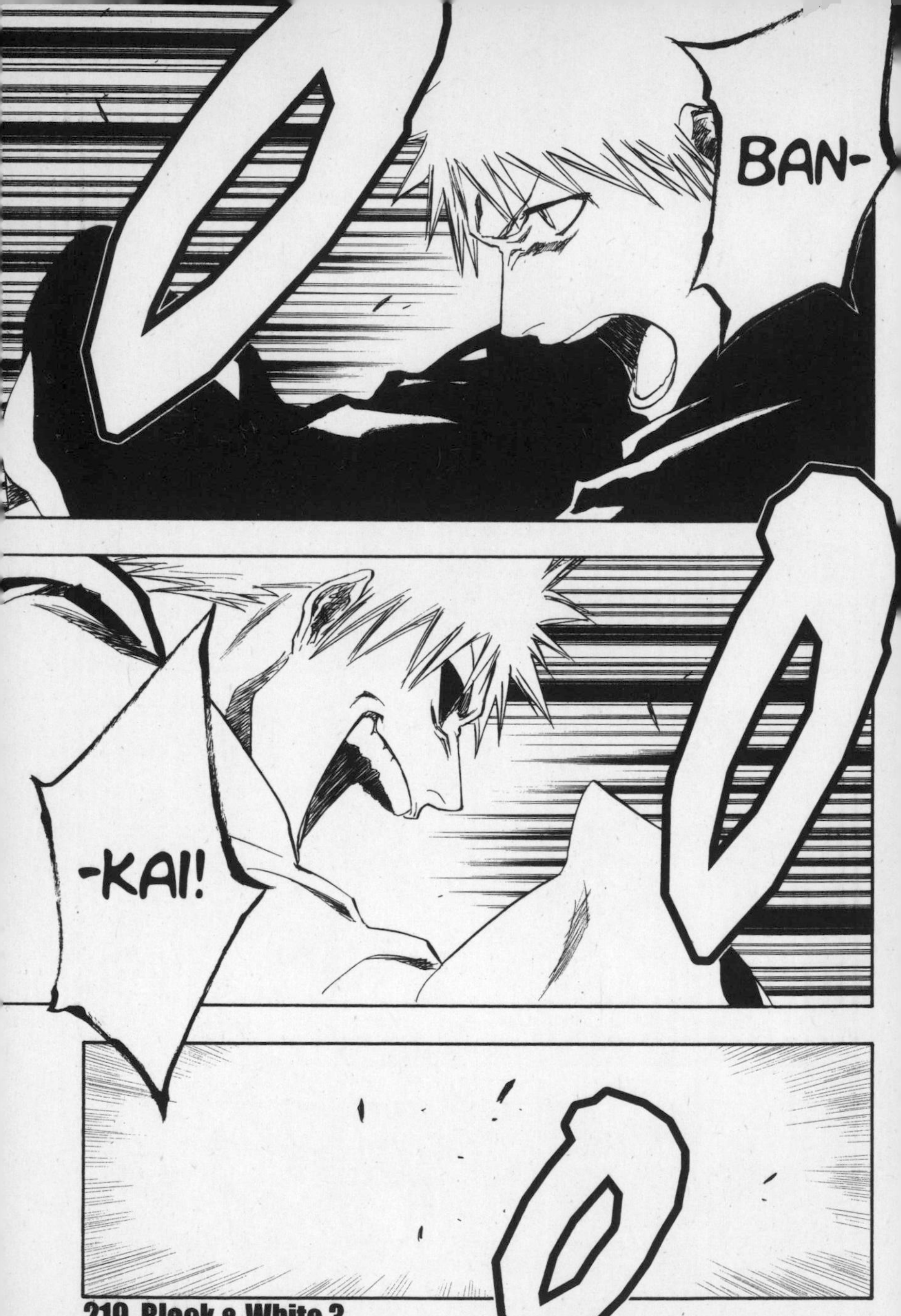
BAN-
-KAI!

219. Black & White 3

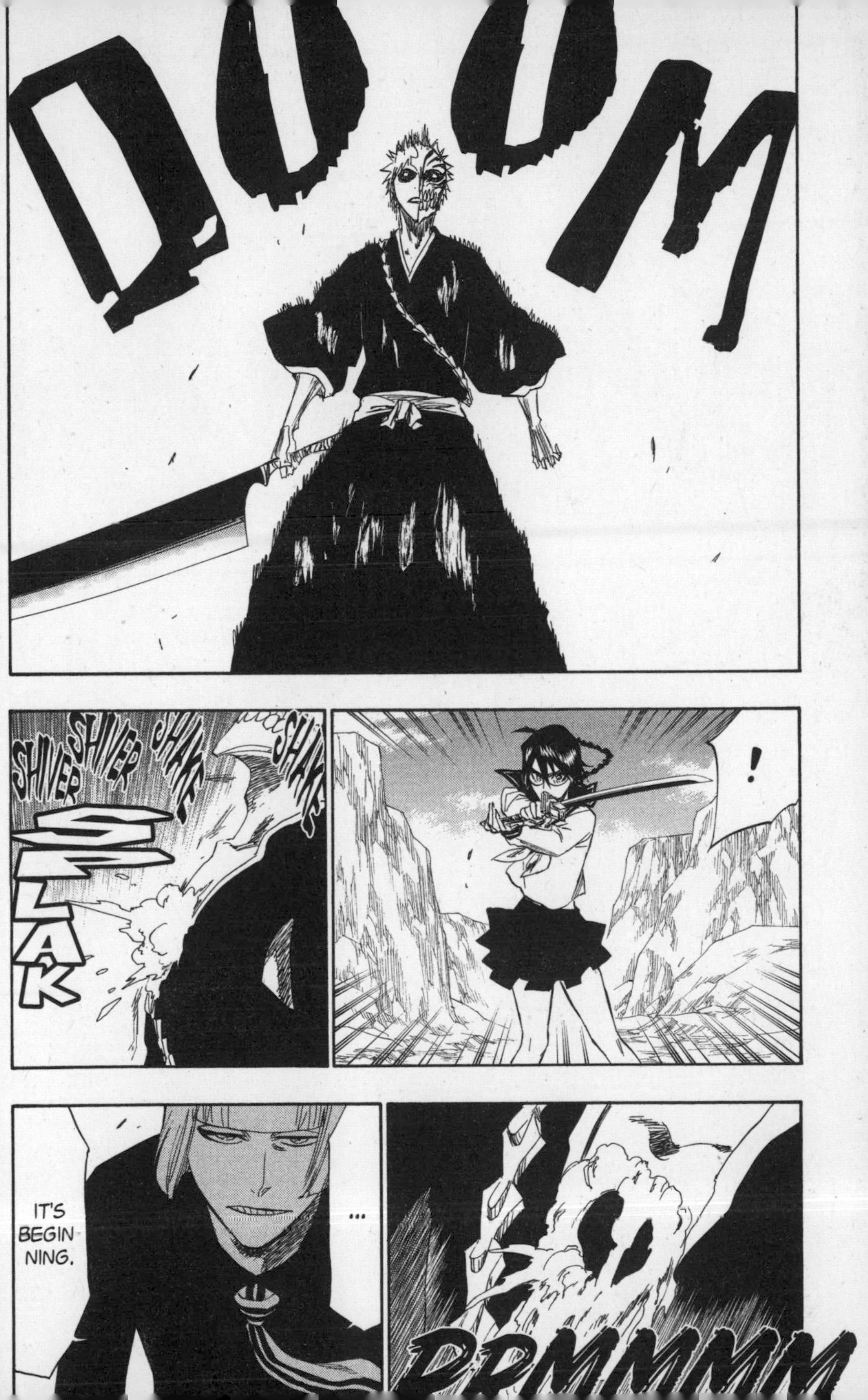
DOOM
!
SHIVER SHIVER
SHAKE SHAKE
SPLAK
DDMMMM
...
IT'S BEGINNING.

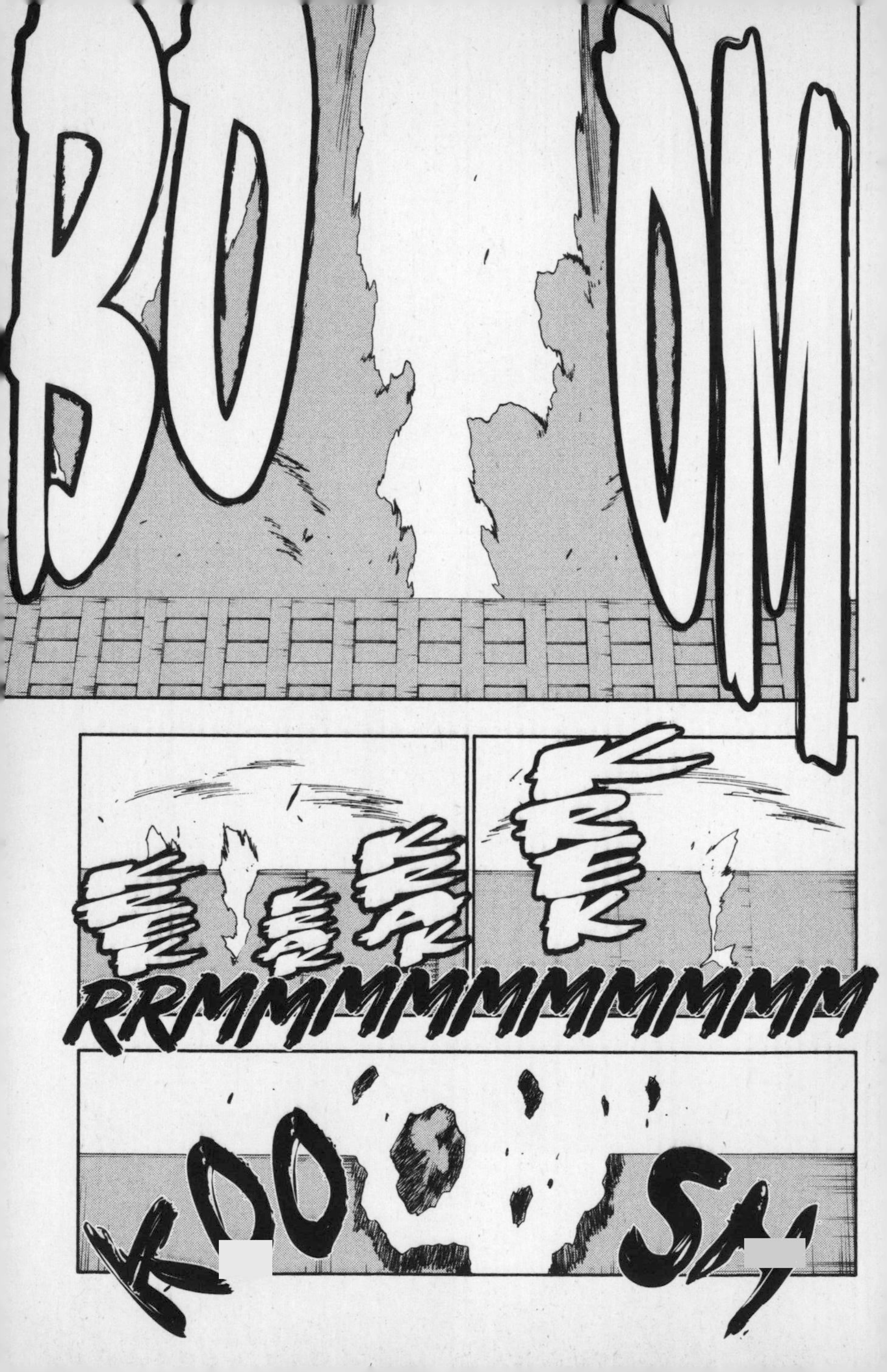
BOOM
RRMMMMMMMMMMMM
KOOSH

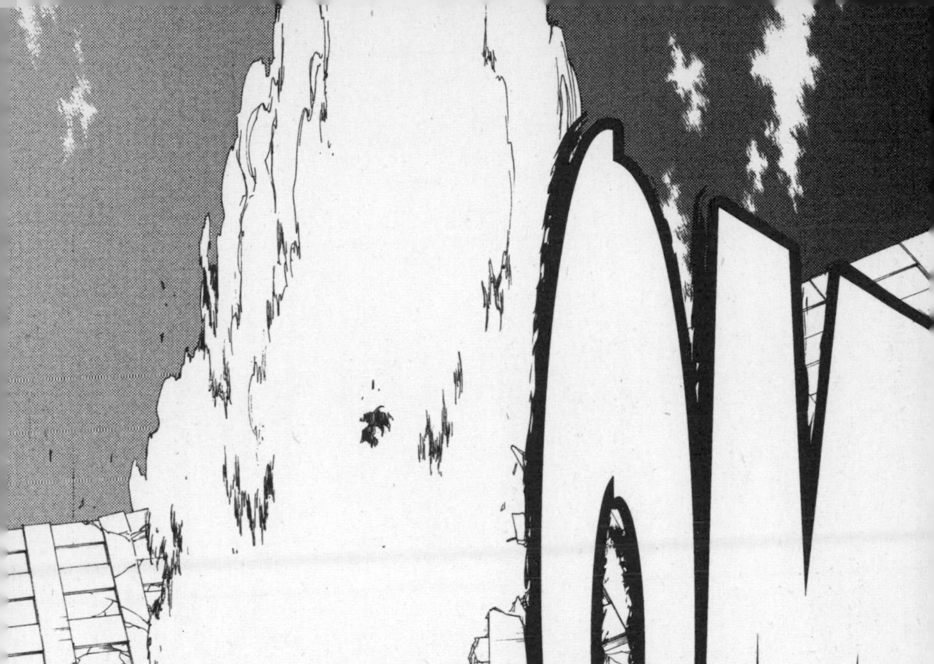

Black & White 3

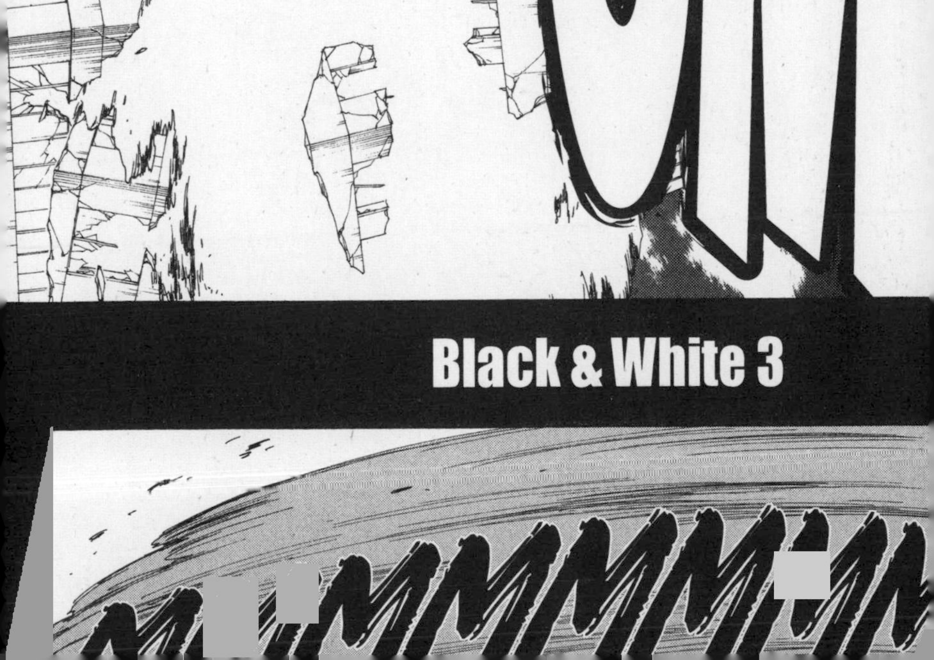

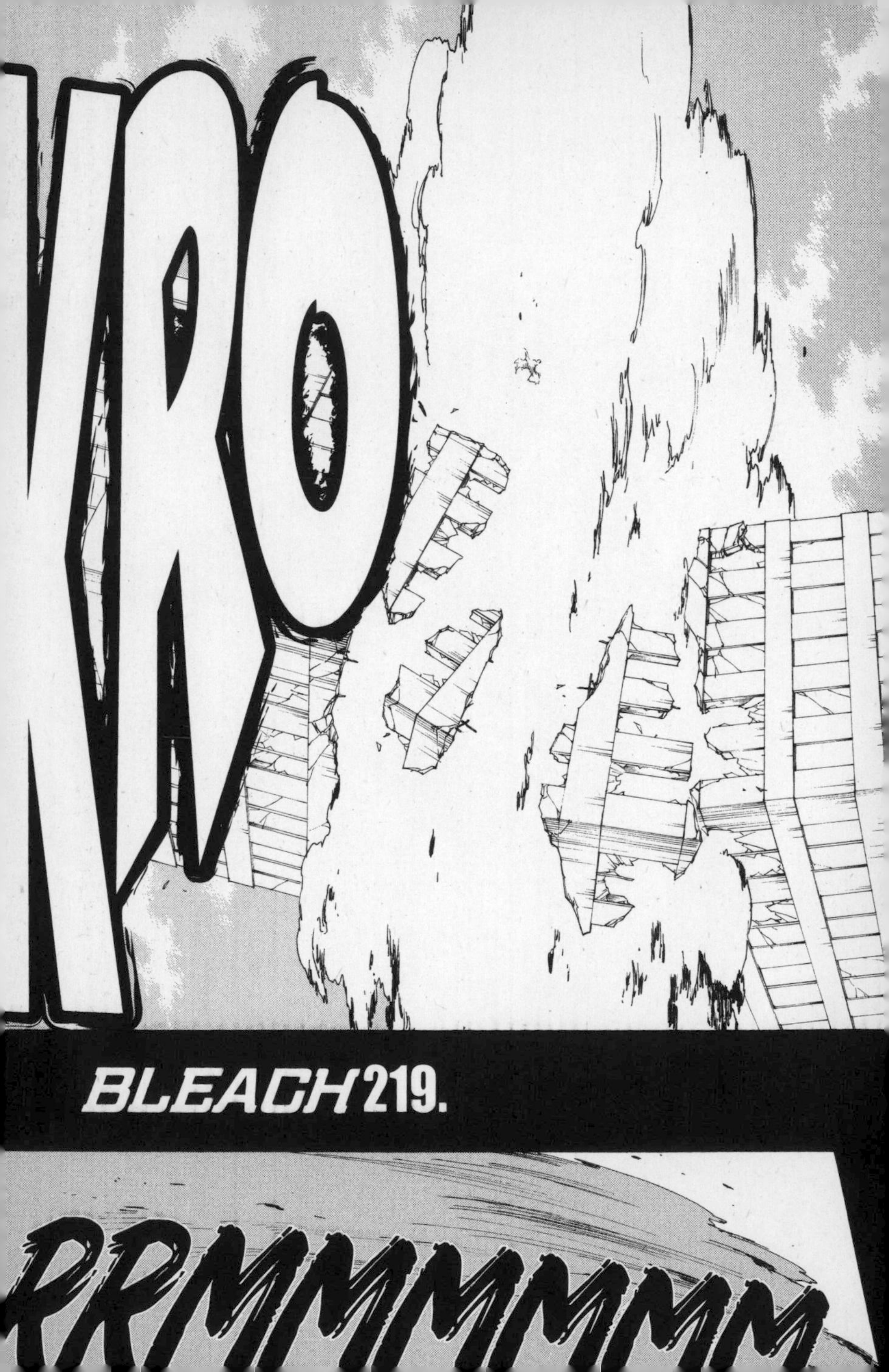
BLEACH 219.
RRMMMMMM

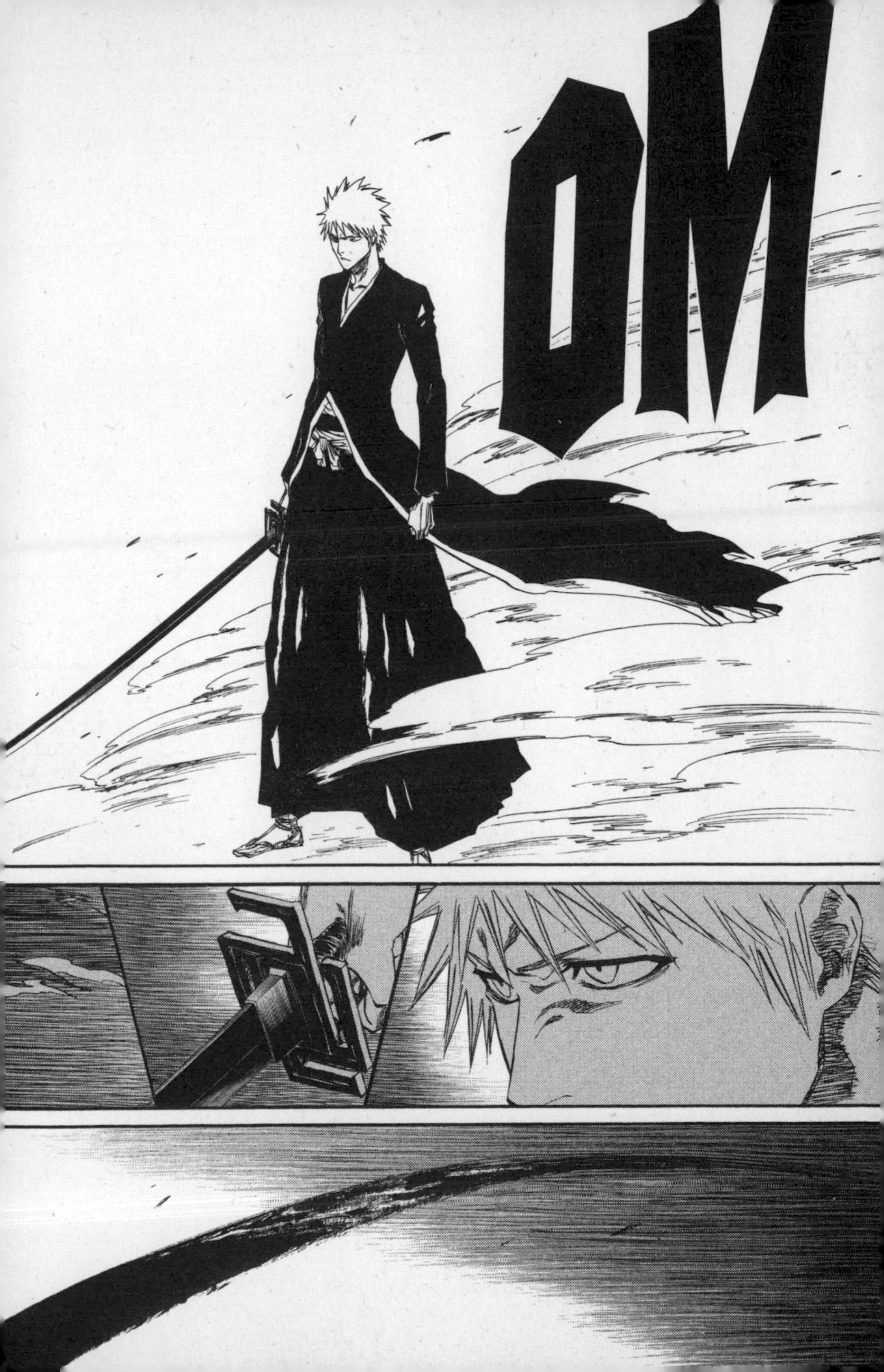

OM

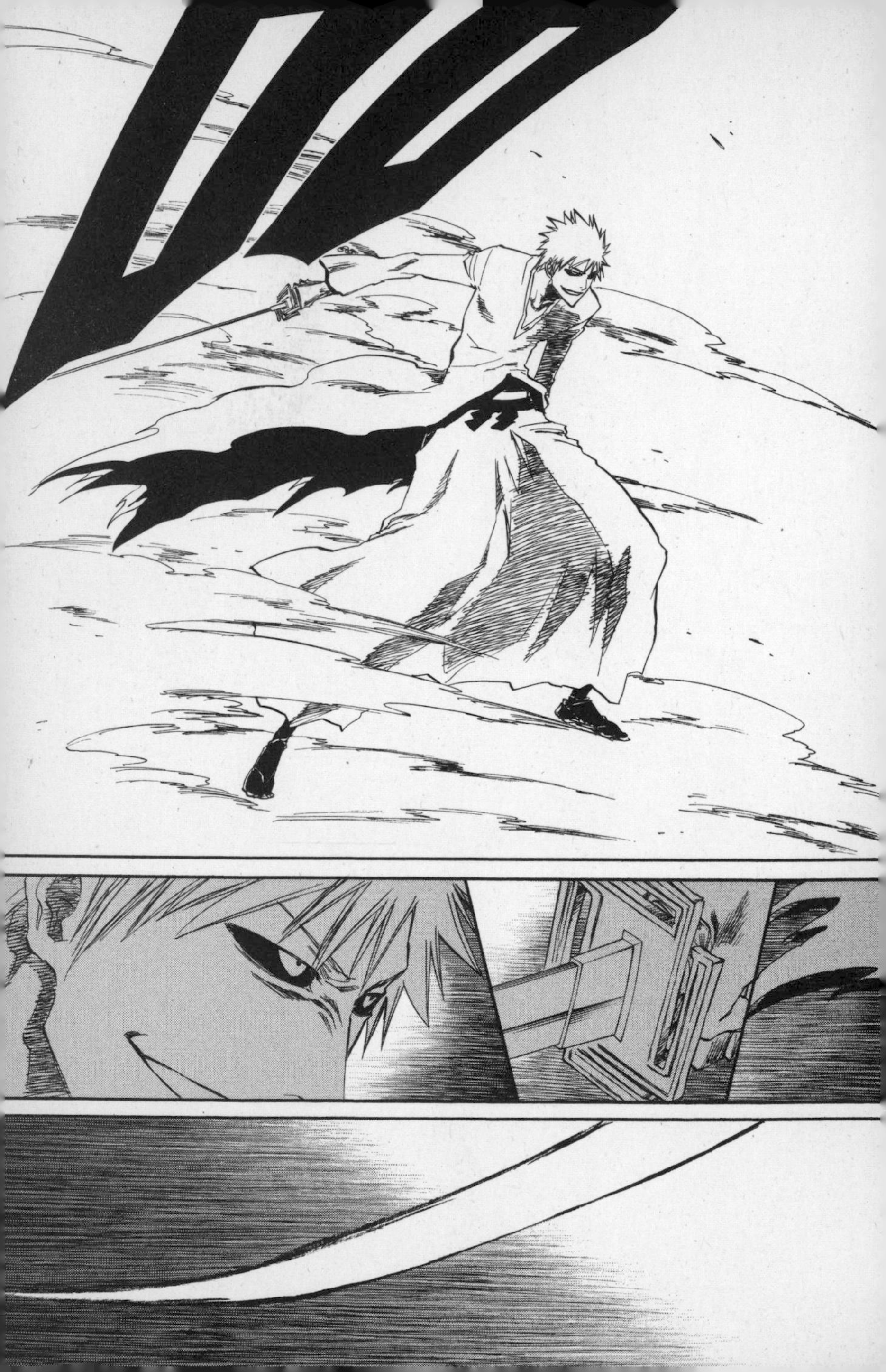

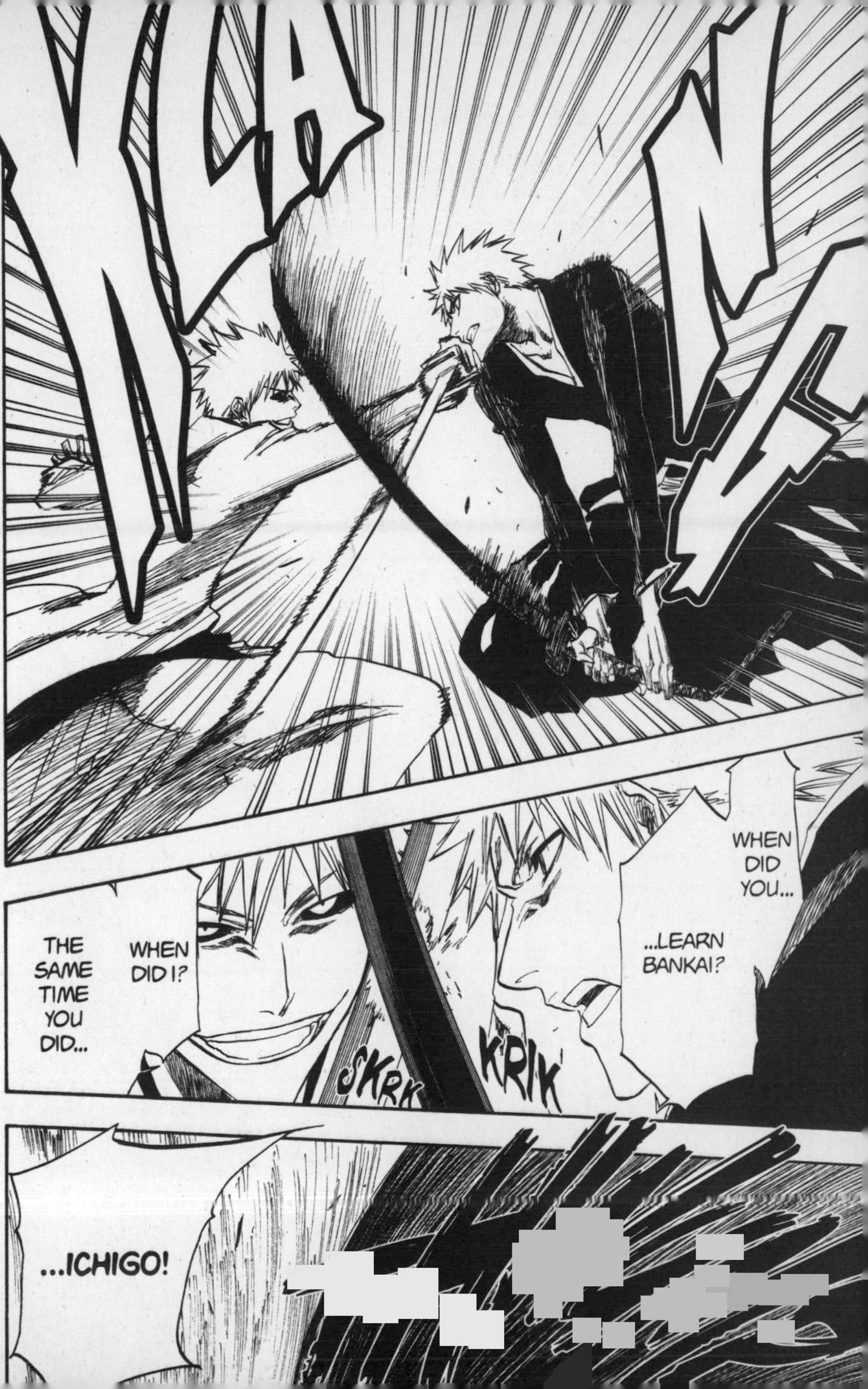
WHEN DID YOU...
...LEARN BANKAI?
KRIK
WHEN DID I?
THE SAME TIME YOU DID...
SKRK
...ICHIGO!

READ THIS WAY

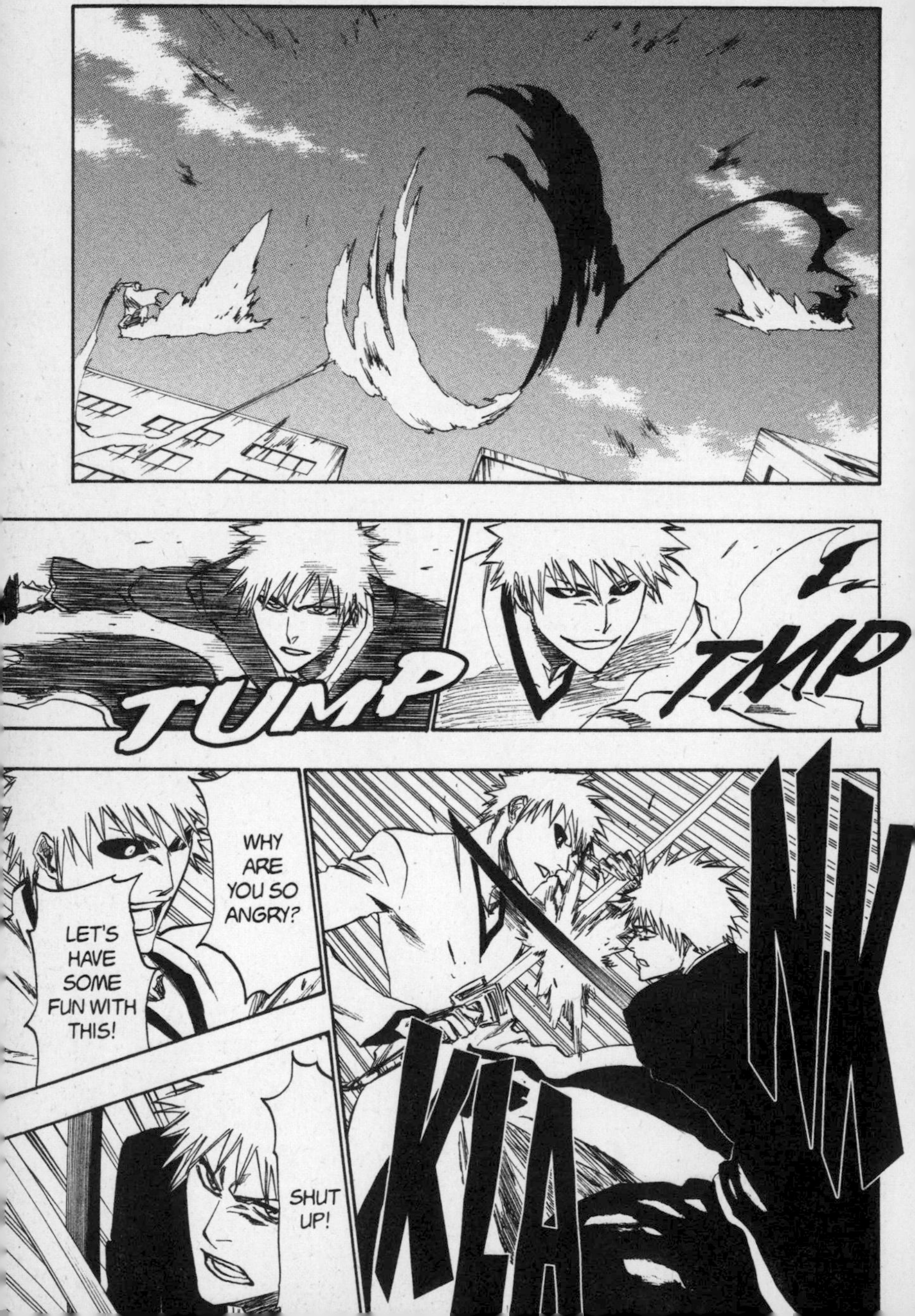
TMP
TUMP
KLANNK
WHY ARE YOU SO ANGRY?
LET'S HAVE SOME FUN WITH THIS!
SHUT UP!

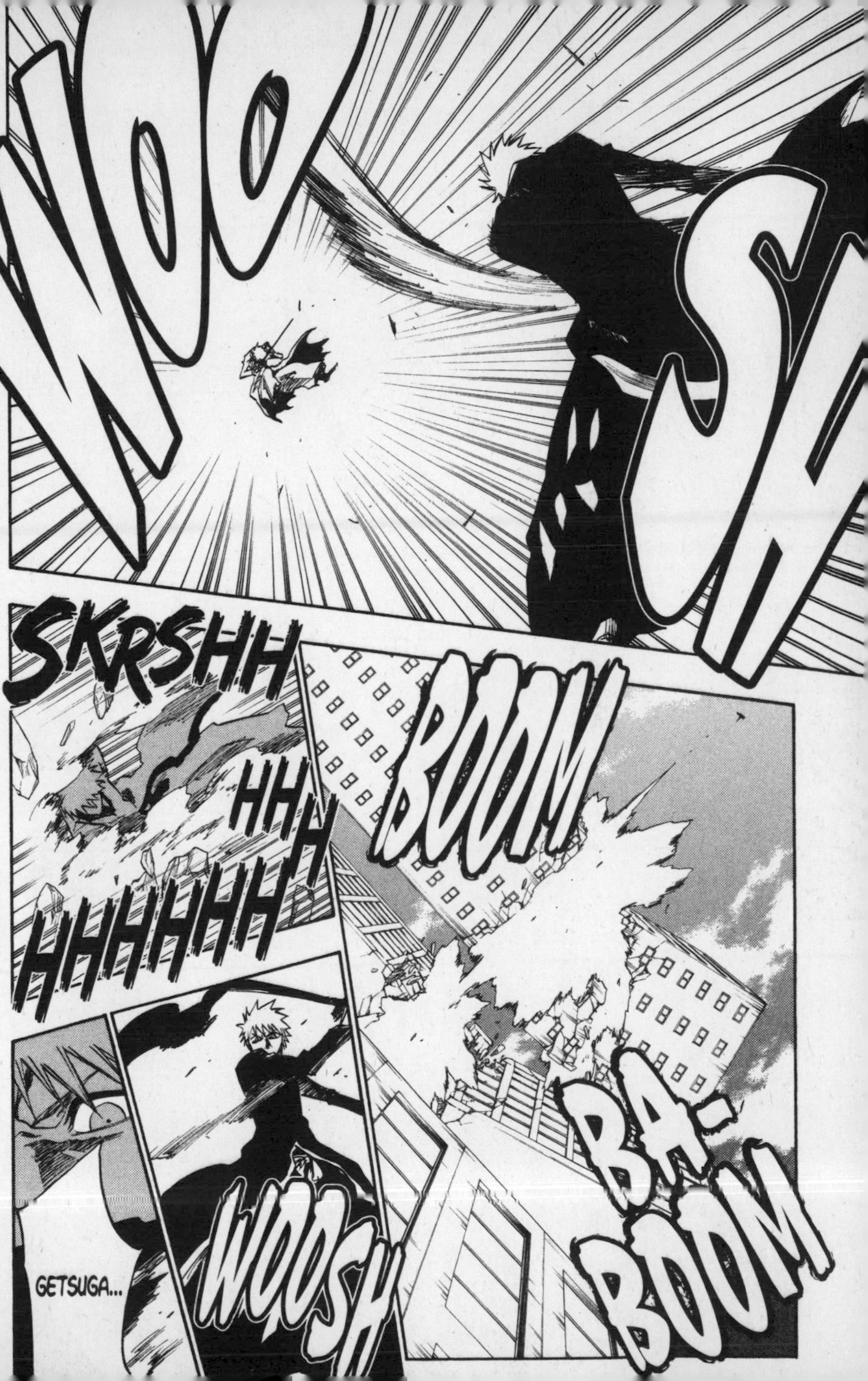
WOOOSH
BOOM
SKRSHHHHHHHHHHH
BA-BOOM
WOOSH
GETSUGA...

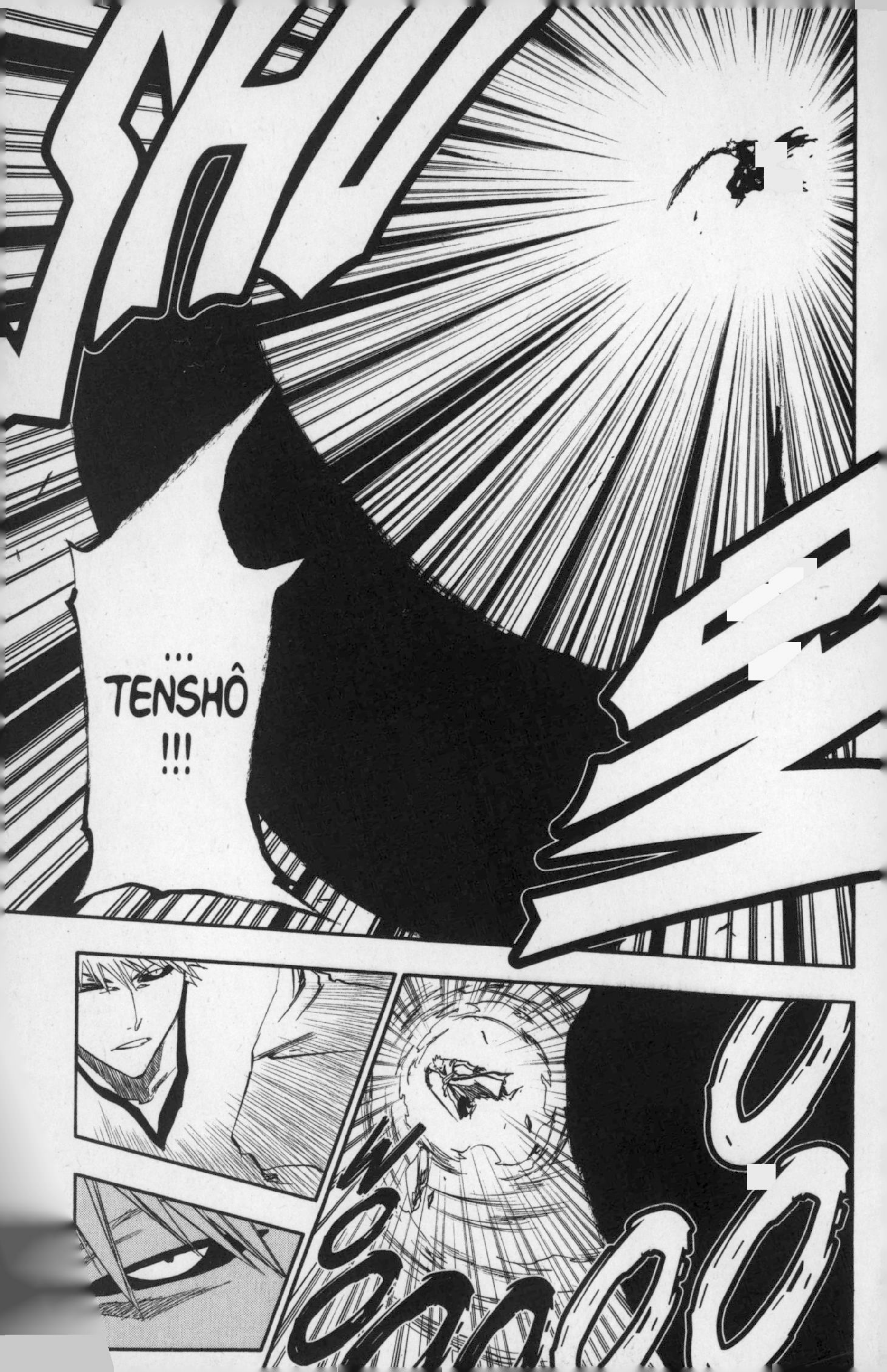
... TENSHÔ !!!

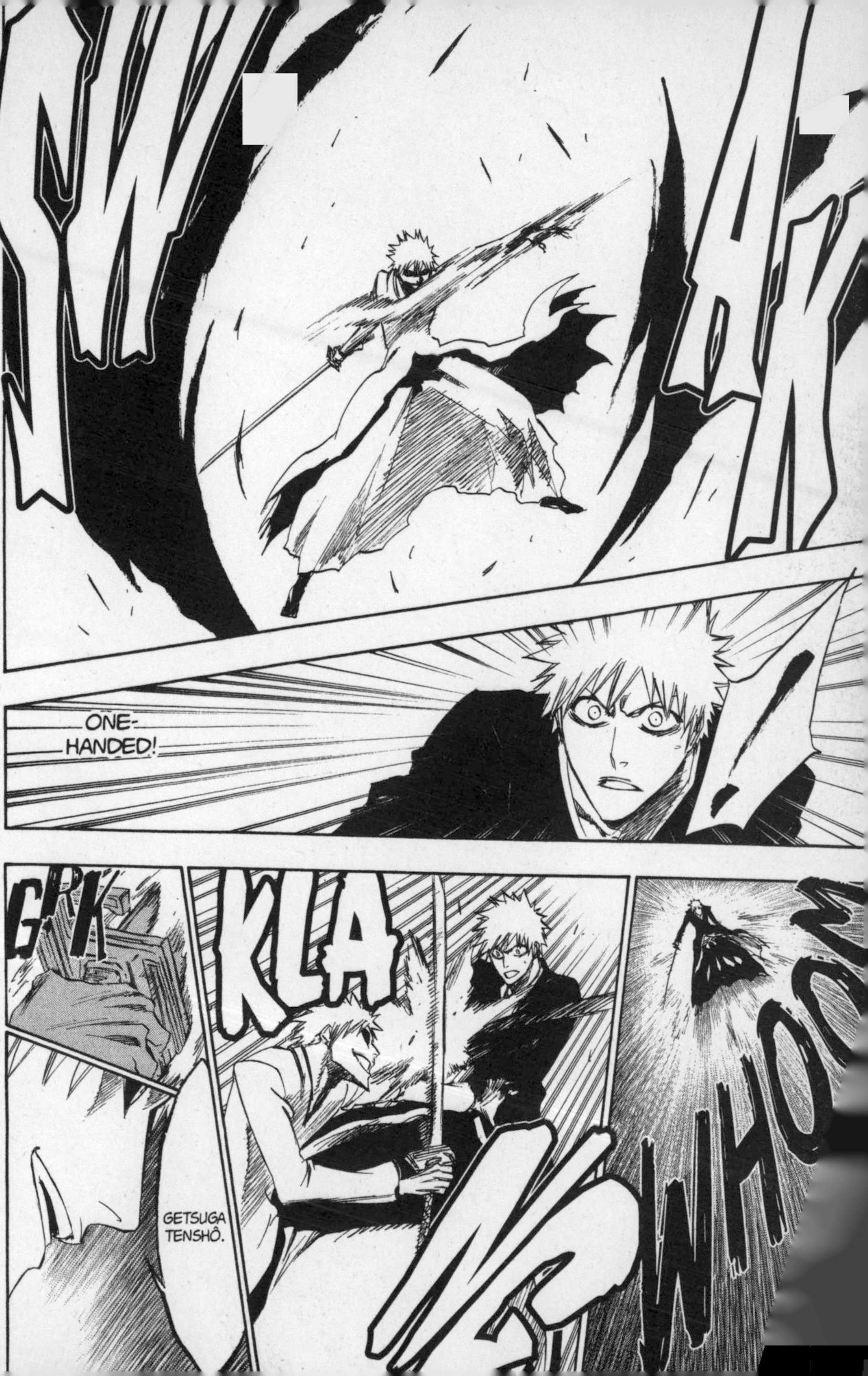
ONE-HANDED!
KLA
GETSUGA TENSHÔ.
G'RK

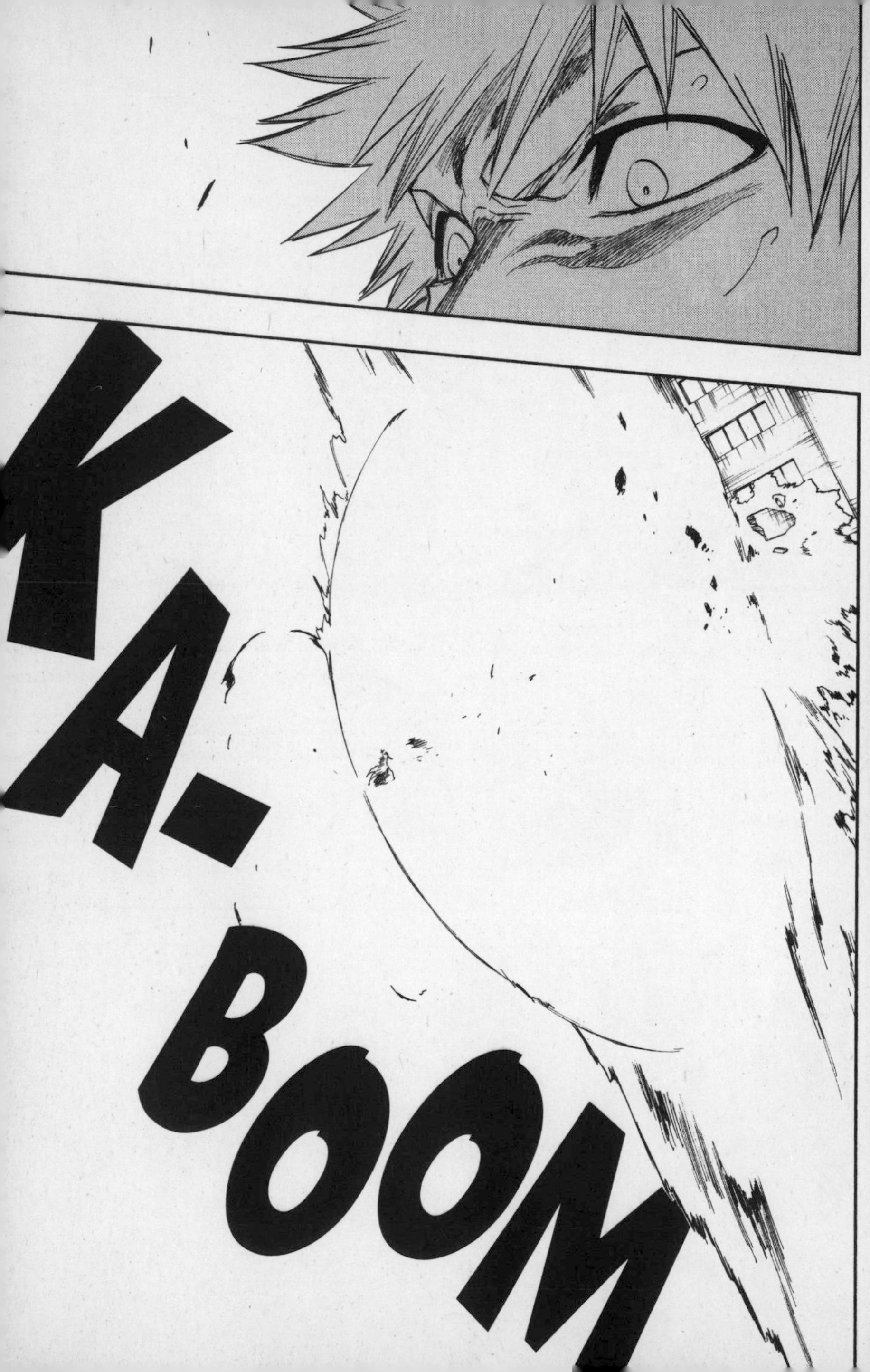
KA-BOOM

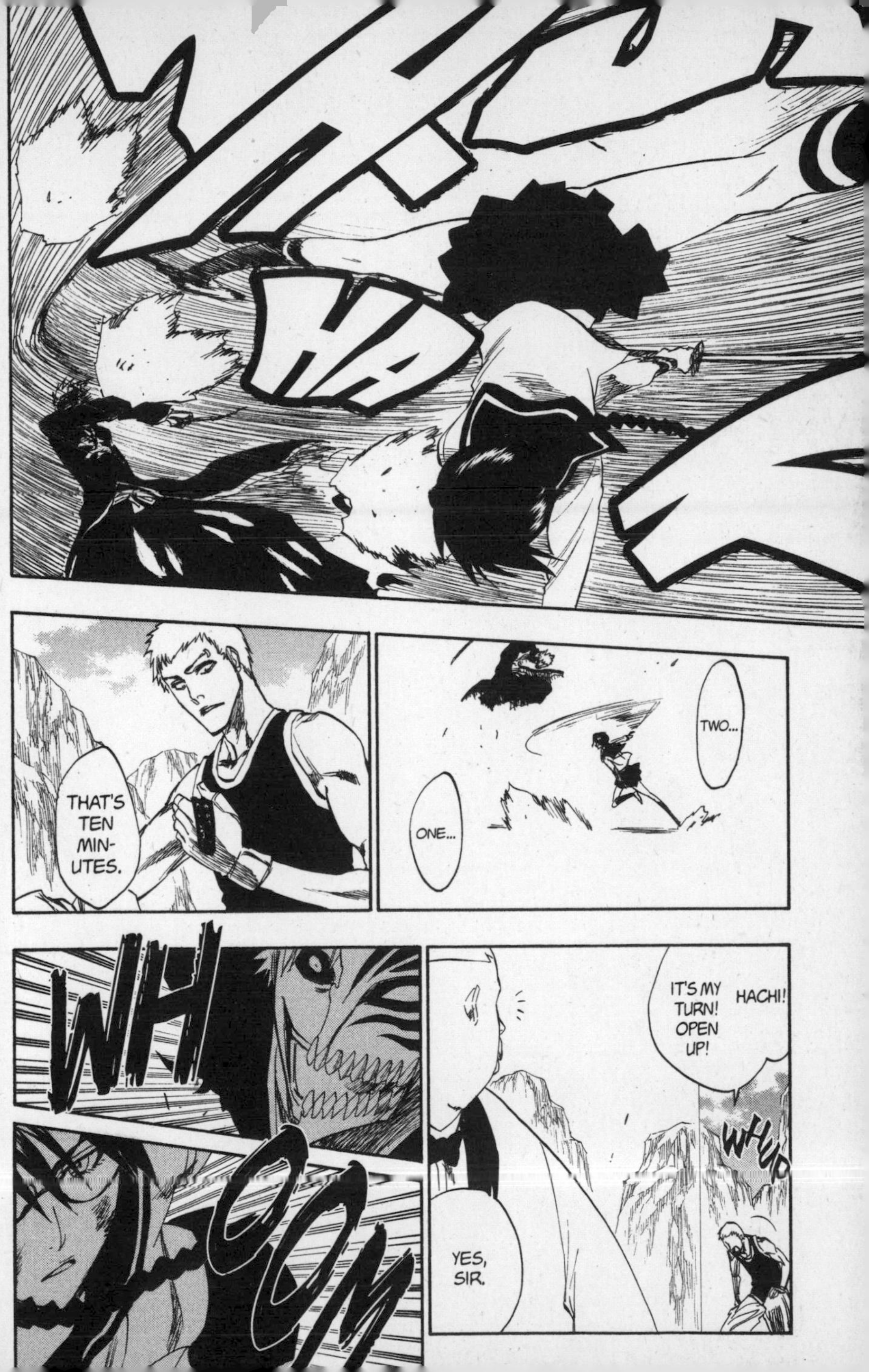
TWO...
ONE...
THAT'S TEN MIN- UTES.
HACHI!
IT'S MY TURN! OPEN UP!
WHUP
YES, SIR.
WHOOM

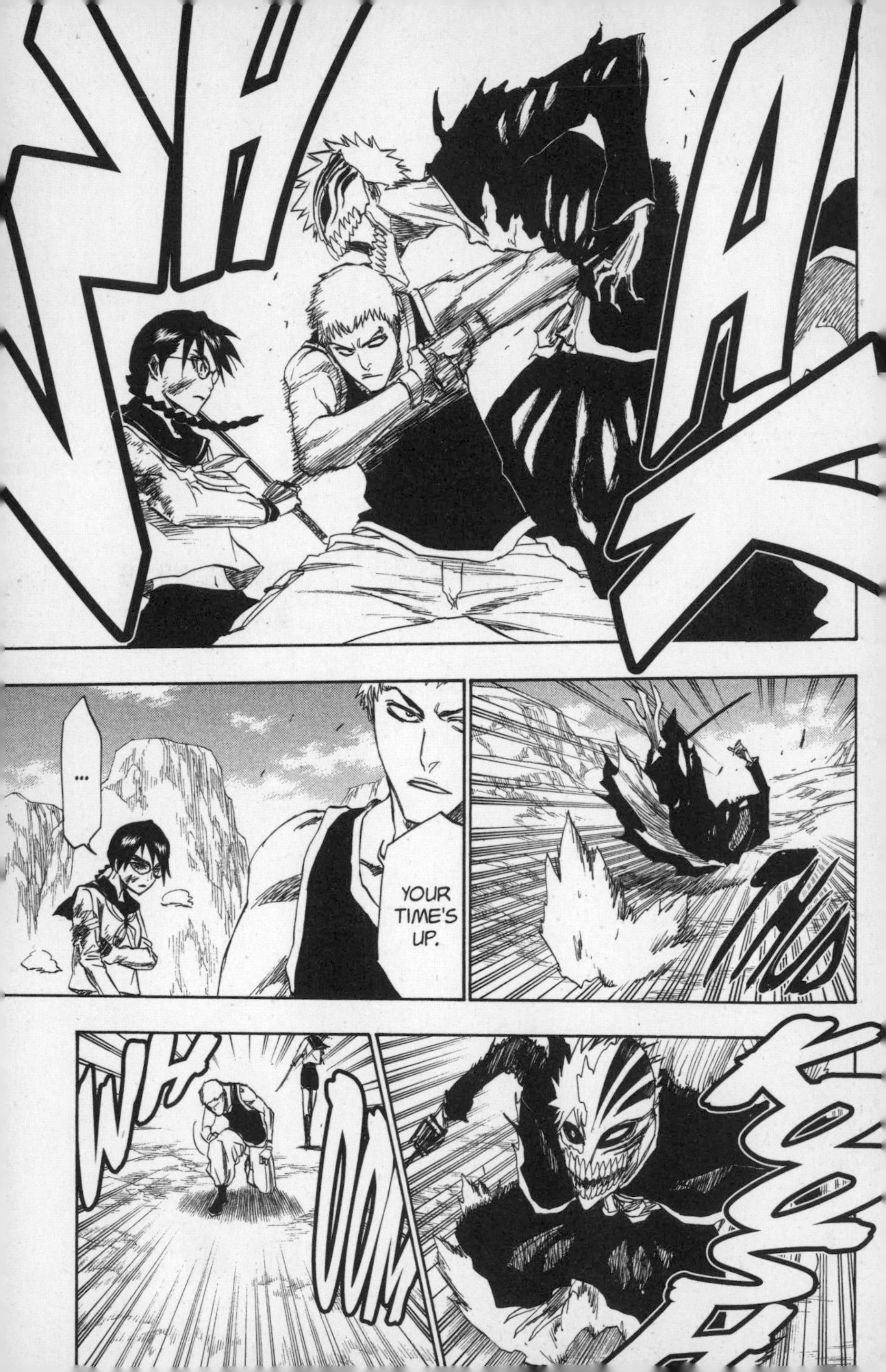
...
YOUR TIME'S UP.

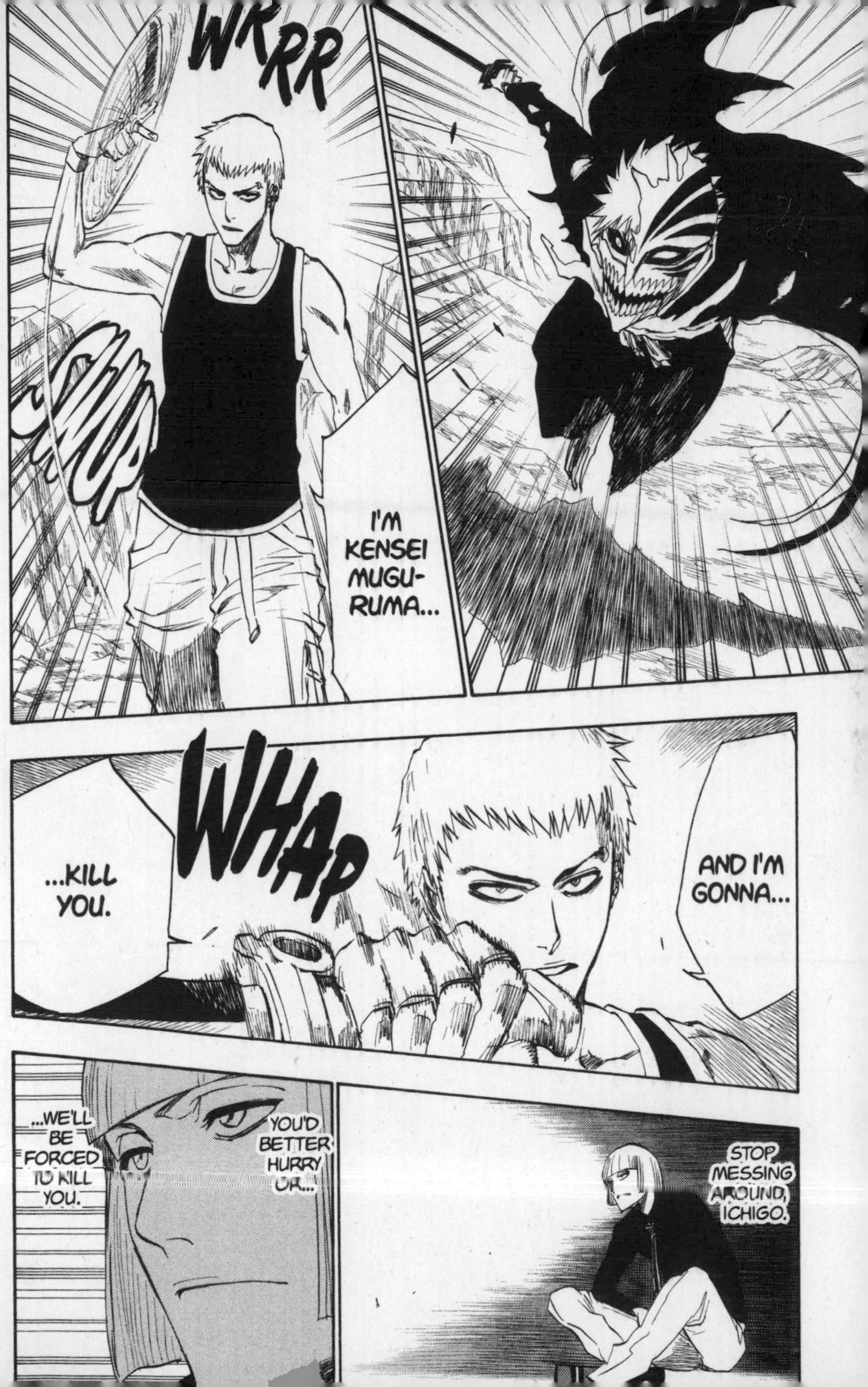
WRRR
SHUP
I'M KENSEI MUGURUMA...
AND I'M GONNA...
WHAP
...KILL YOU.
STOP MESSING AROUND, ICHIGO.
YOU'D BETTER HURRY UP...
...WE'LL BE FORCED TO KILL YOU.

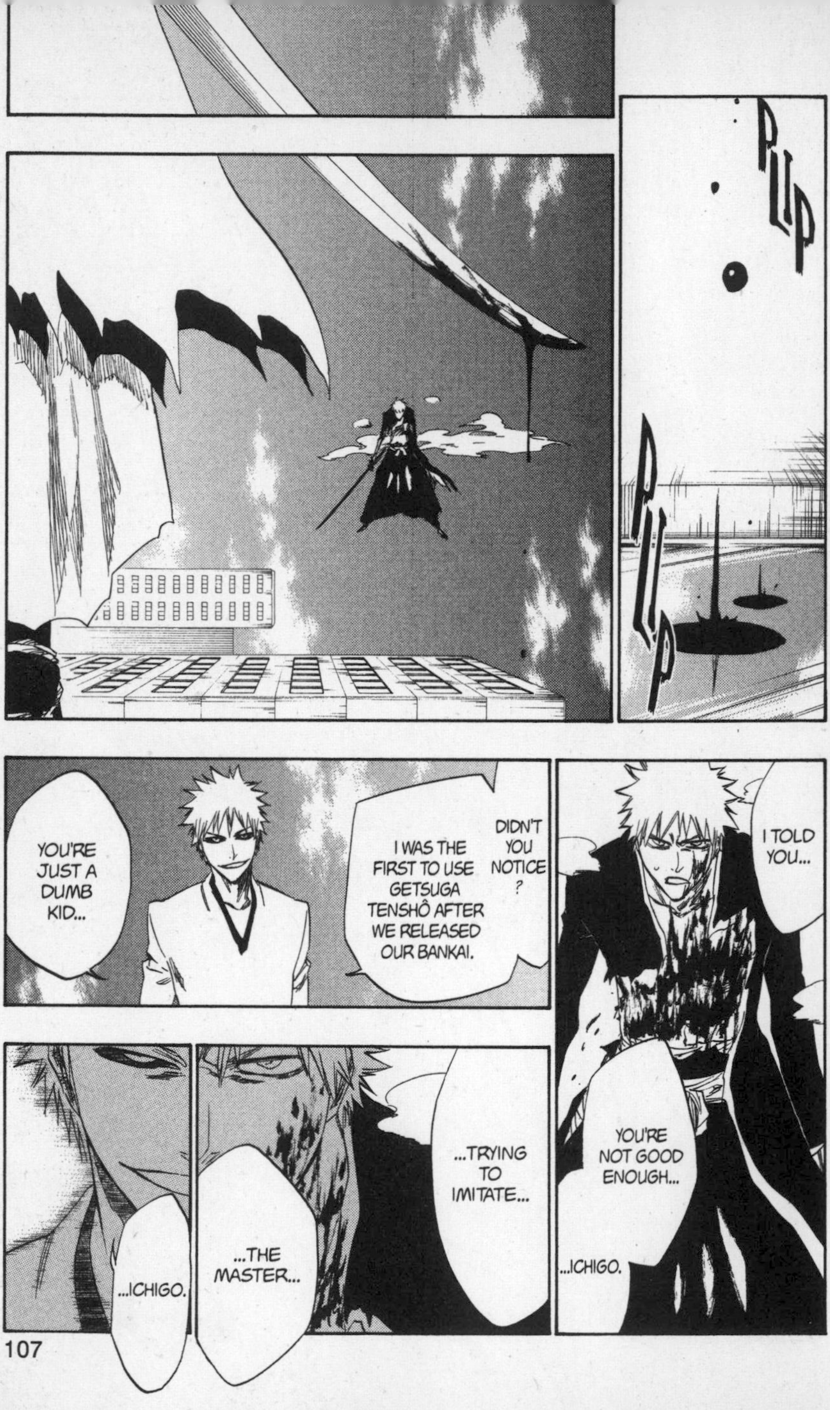
PLIP
PLIP
I TOLD YOU...
YOU'RE NOT GOOD ENOUGH...
...ICHIGO.
DIDN'T YOU NOTICE?
I WAS THE FIRST TO USE GETSUGA TENSHÔ AFTER WE RELEASED OUR BANKAI.
YOU'RE JUST A DUMB KID...
...TRYING TO IMITATE...
...THE MASTER...
...ICHIGO.

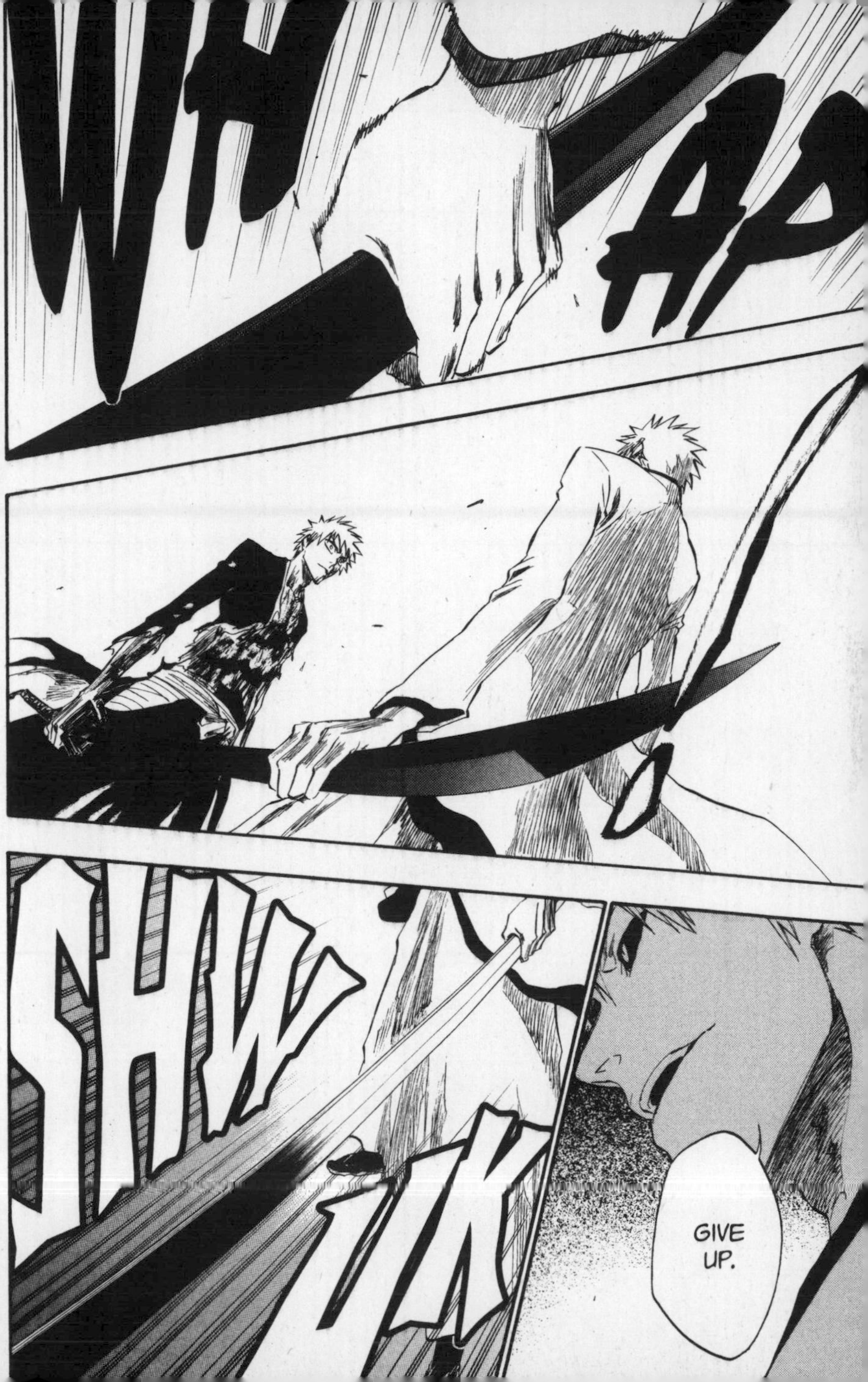
WHAP
GIVE UP.

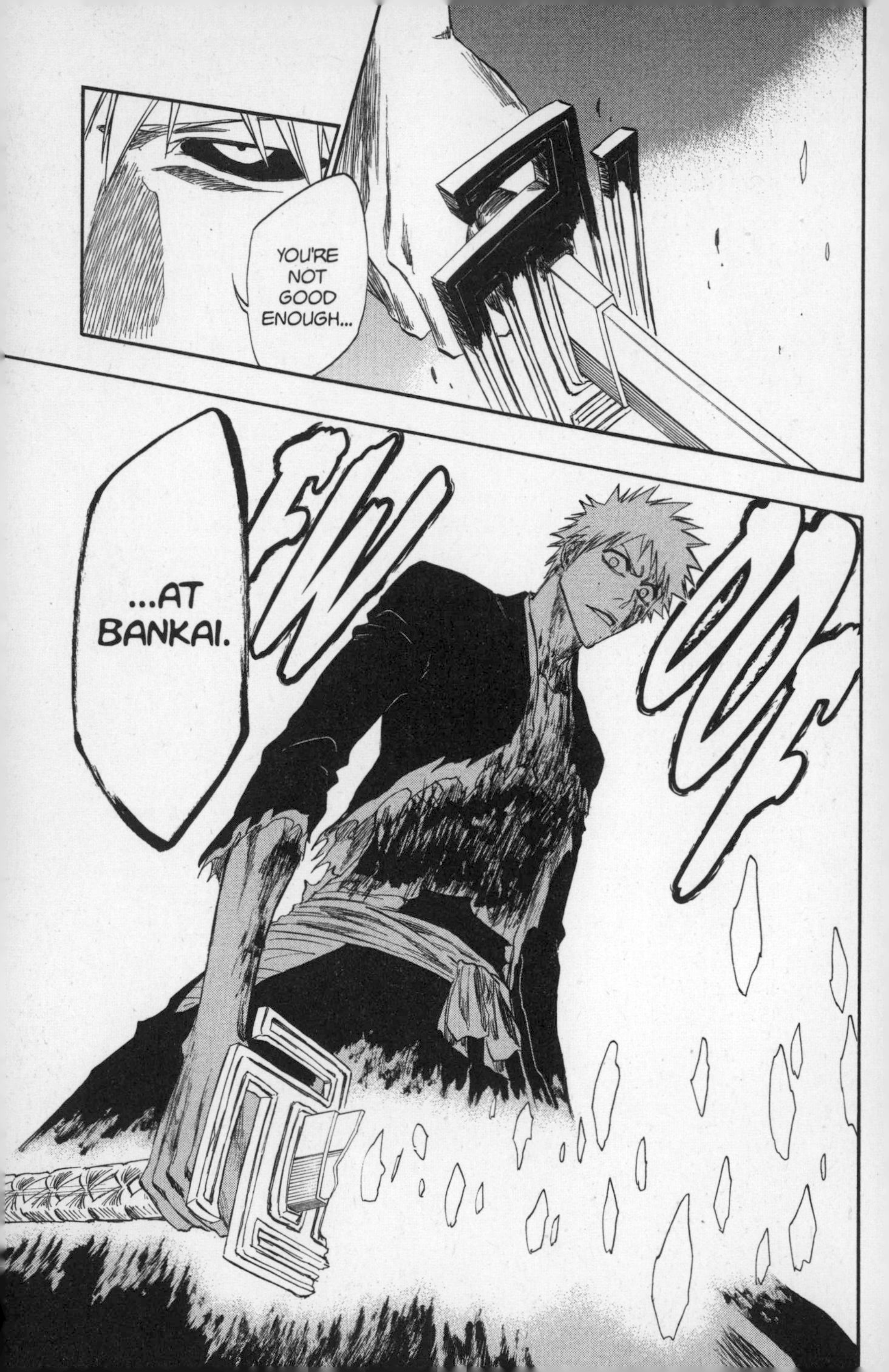
YOU'RE NOT GOOD ENOUGH...
...AT BANKAI.

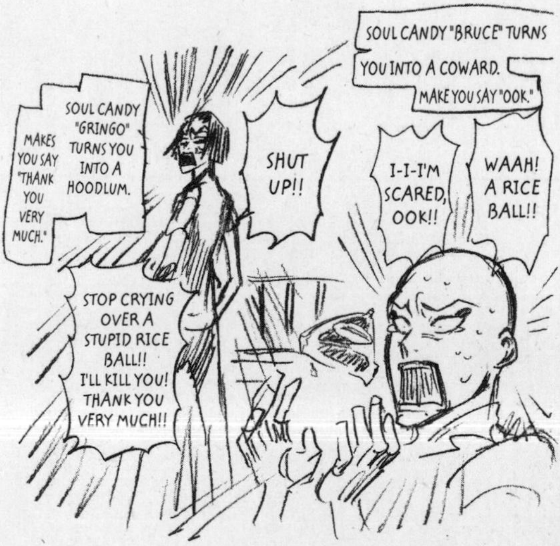
SOUL CANDY "BRUCE" TURNS YOU INTO A COWARD.
MAKE YOU SAY "OOK."
WAAH! A RICE BALL!!
I-I-I'M SCARED, OOK!!
SHUT UP!!
SOUL CANDY "GRINGO" TURNS YOU INTO A HOODLUM.
MAKES YOU SAY "THANK YOU VERY MUCH."
STOP CRYING OVER A STUPID RICE BALL!! I'LL KILL YOU! THANK YOU VERY MUCH!!

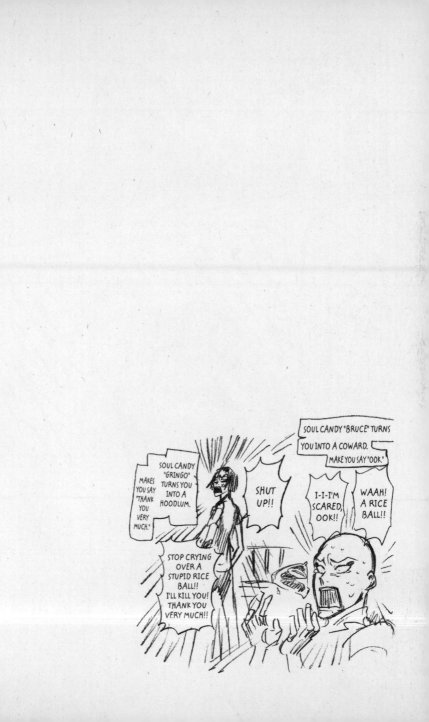

220. King & His Horse

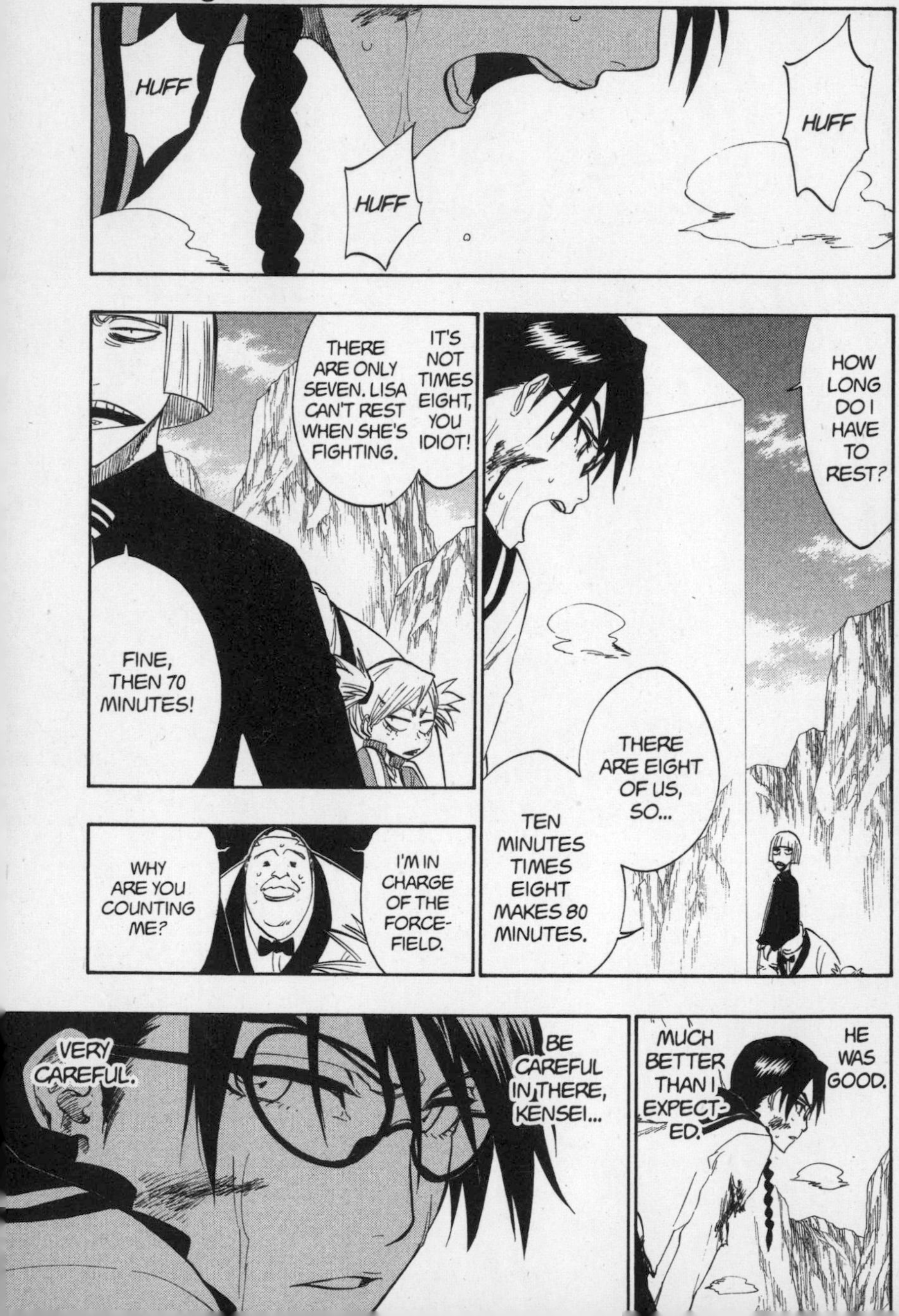
HUFF
HUFF
HUFF
HOW LONG DO I HAVE TO REST?
THERE ARE EIGHT OF US, SO...
TEN MINUTES TIMES EIGHT MAKES 80 MINUTES.
IT'S NOT TIMES EIGHT, YOU IDIOT!
THERE ARE ONLY SEVEN. LISA CAN'T REST WHEN SHE'S FIGHTING.
FINE, THEN 70 MINUTES!
I'M IN CHARGE OF THE FORCE-FIELD.
WHY ARE YOU COUNTING ME?
HE WAS GOOD.
MUCH BETTER THAN I EXPECT-ED.
BE CAREFUL IN THERE, KENSEI...
VERY CAREFUL.

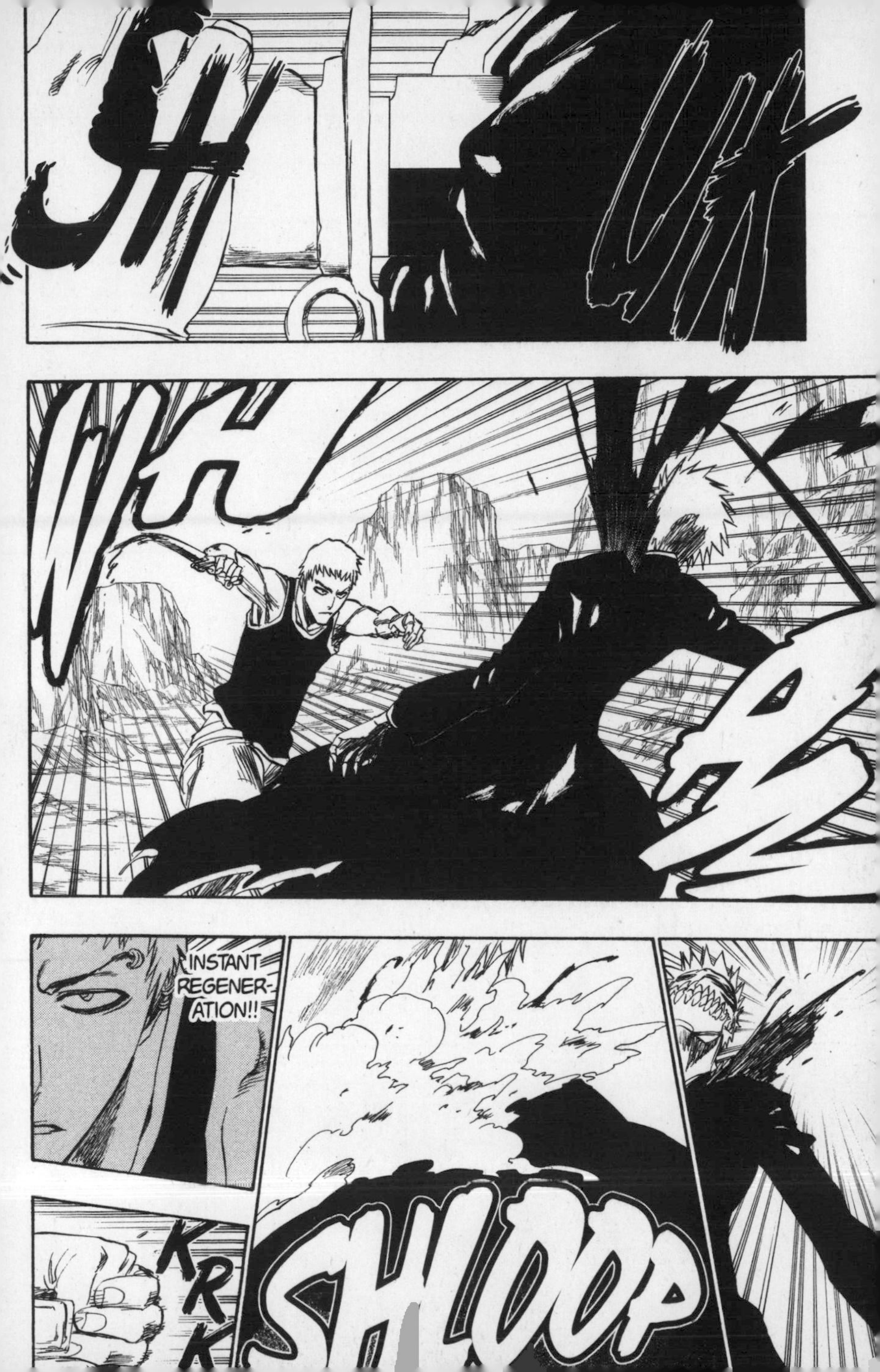
SHOOP
INSTANT REGENER-ATION!!
KRK

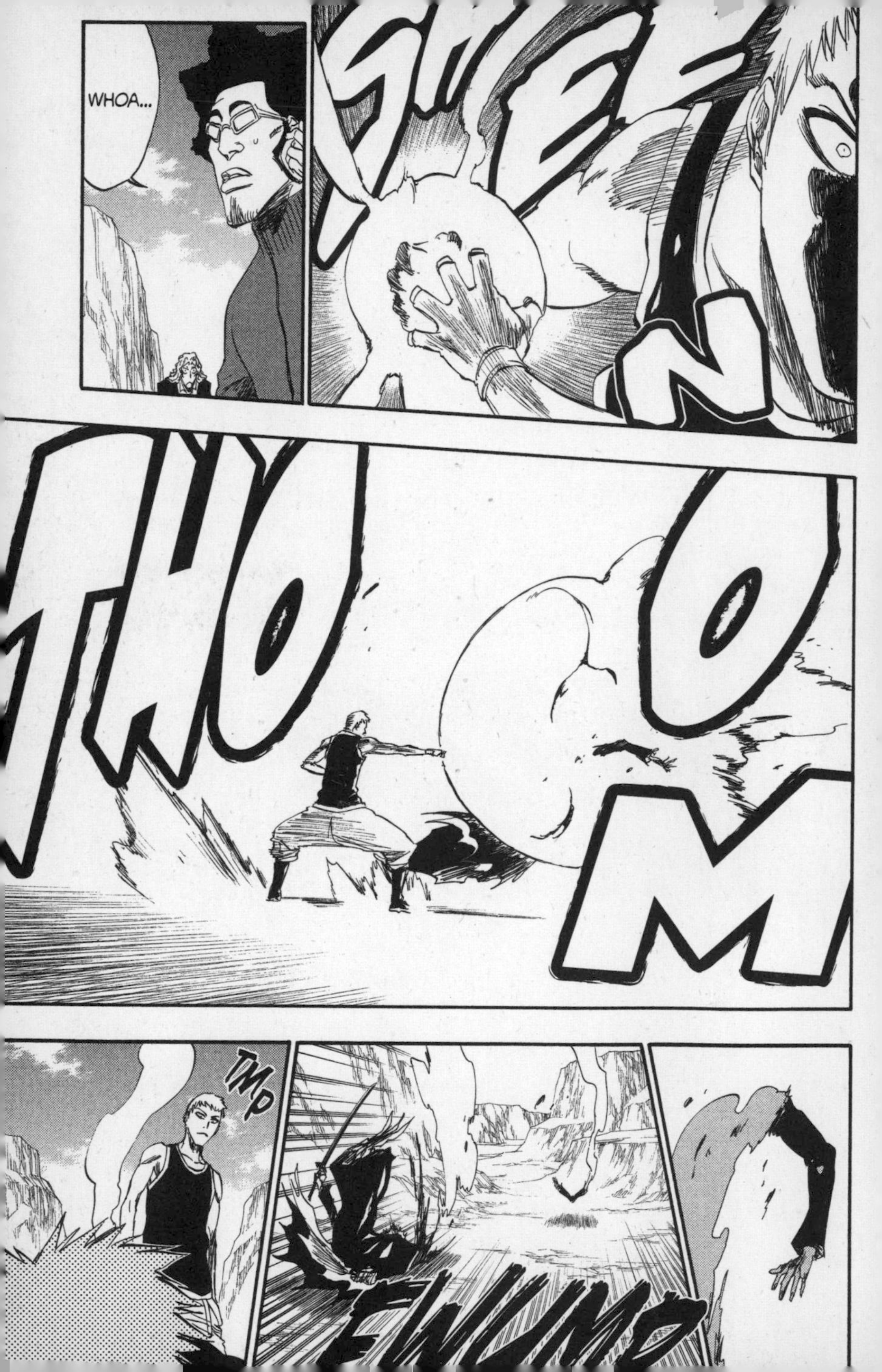
WHOA...
THOOM
TMP

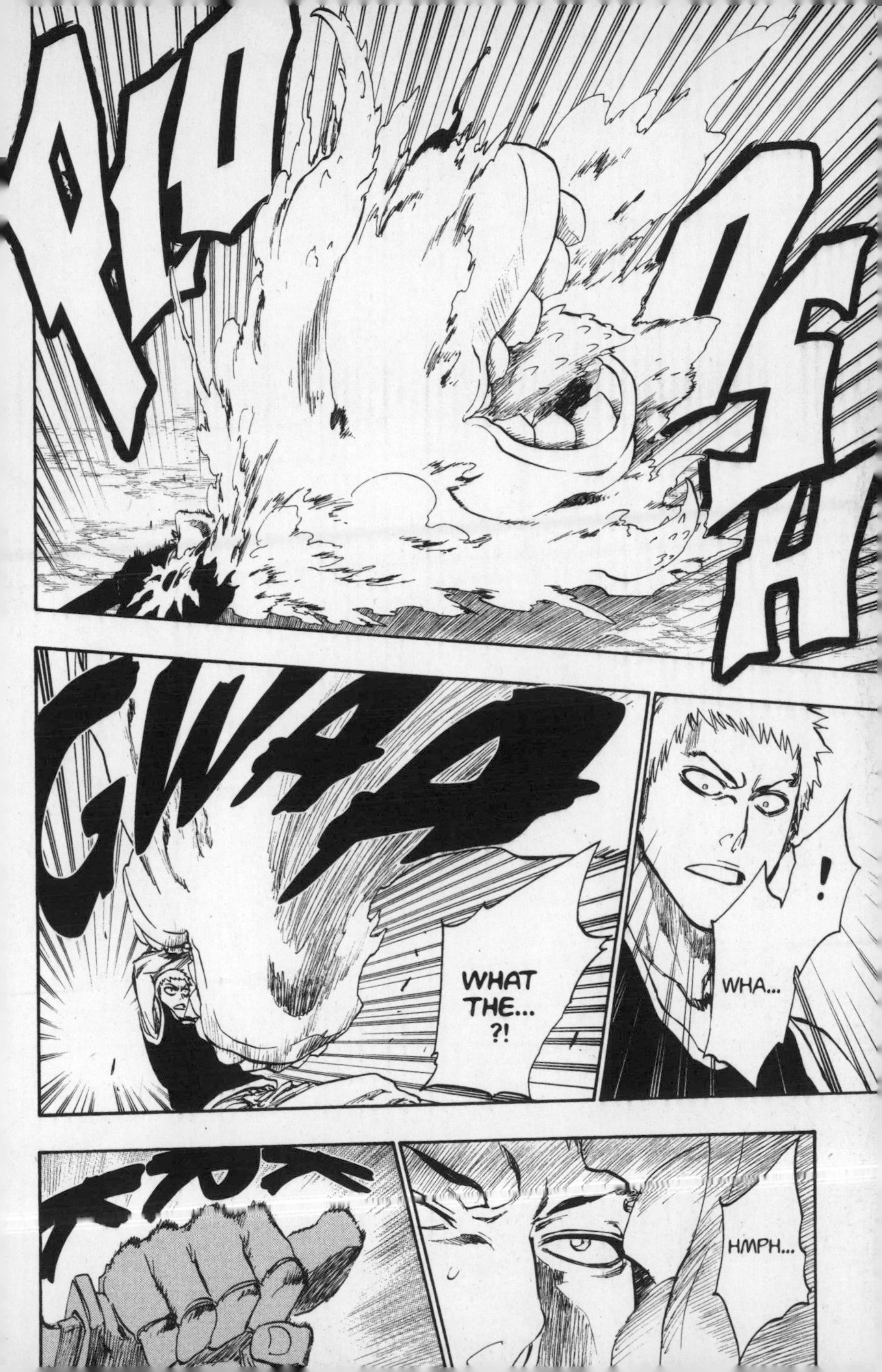
!
WHA...
WHAT THE... ?!
HMPH...

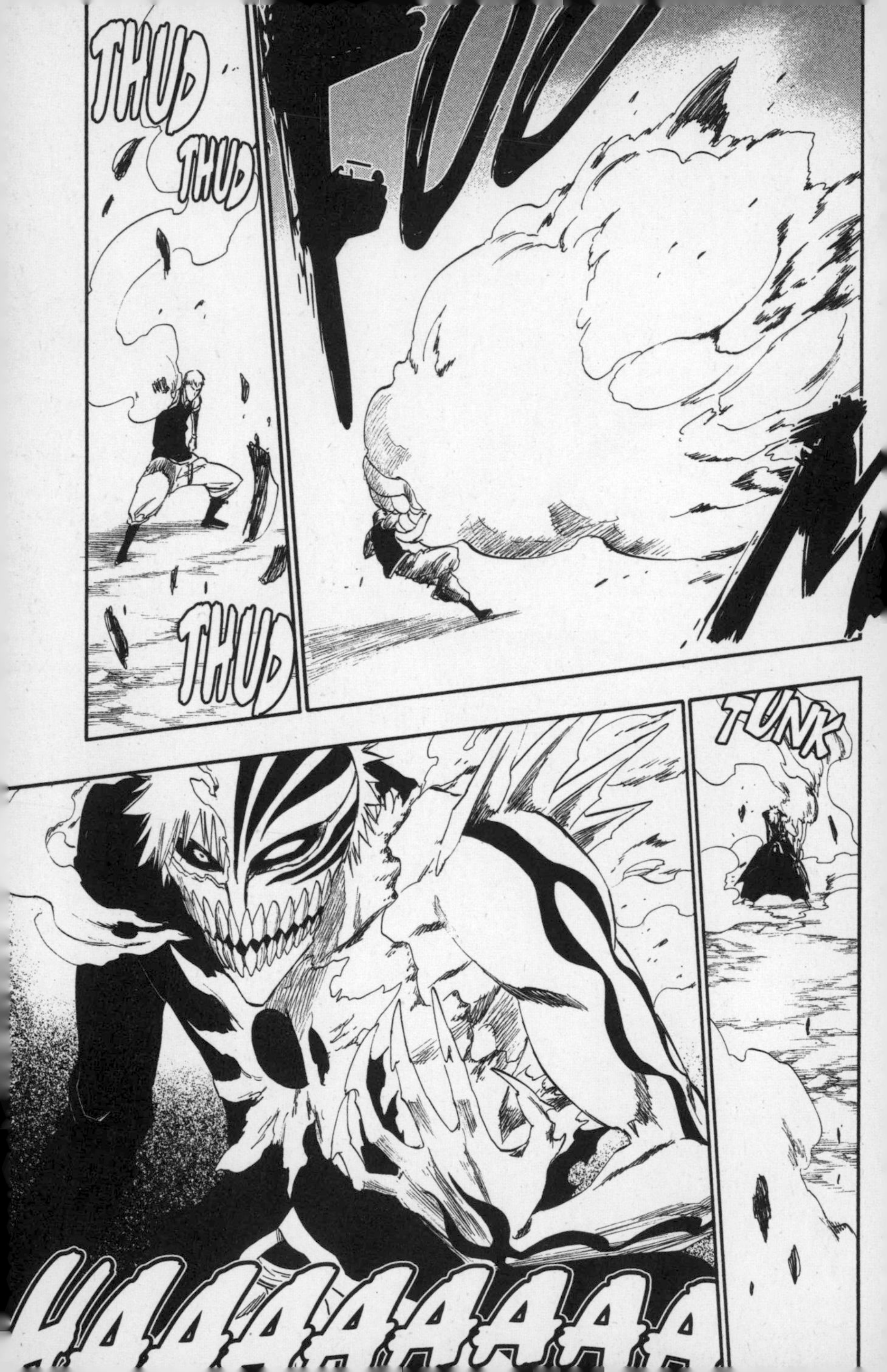
THUD
THUD
THUD
TUNK

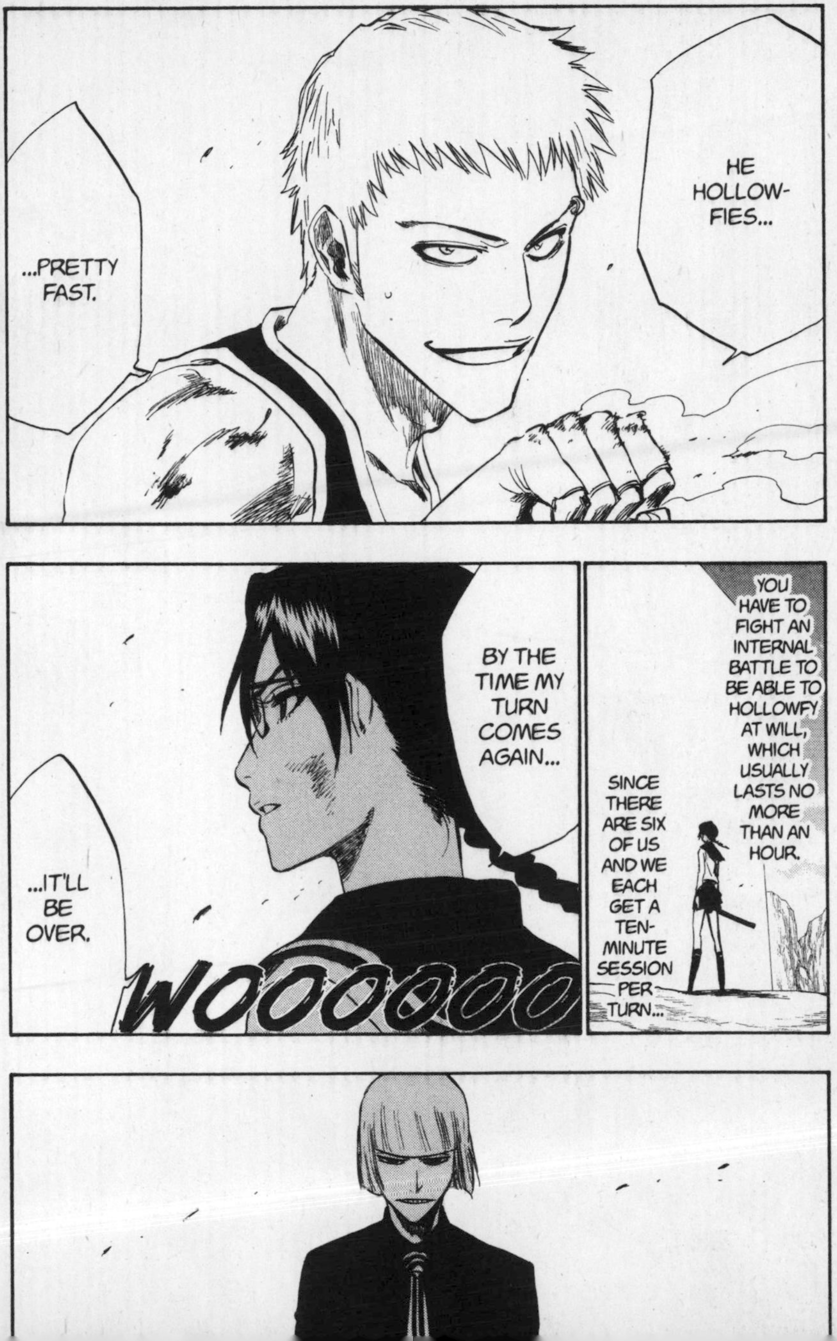
HE HOLLOW-FIES...
...PRETTY FAST.
YOU HAVE TO FIGHT AN INTERNAL BATTLE TO BE ABLE TO HOLLOWFY AT WILL, WHICH USUALLY LASTS NO MORE THAN AN HOUR.
SINCE THERE ARE SIX OF US AND WE EACH GET A TEN-MINUTE SESSION PER TURN...
BY THE TIME MY TURN COMES AGAIN...
...IT'LL BE OVER.
WOOOOOO

BLEACH 220. King & His Horse

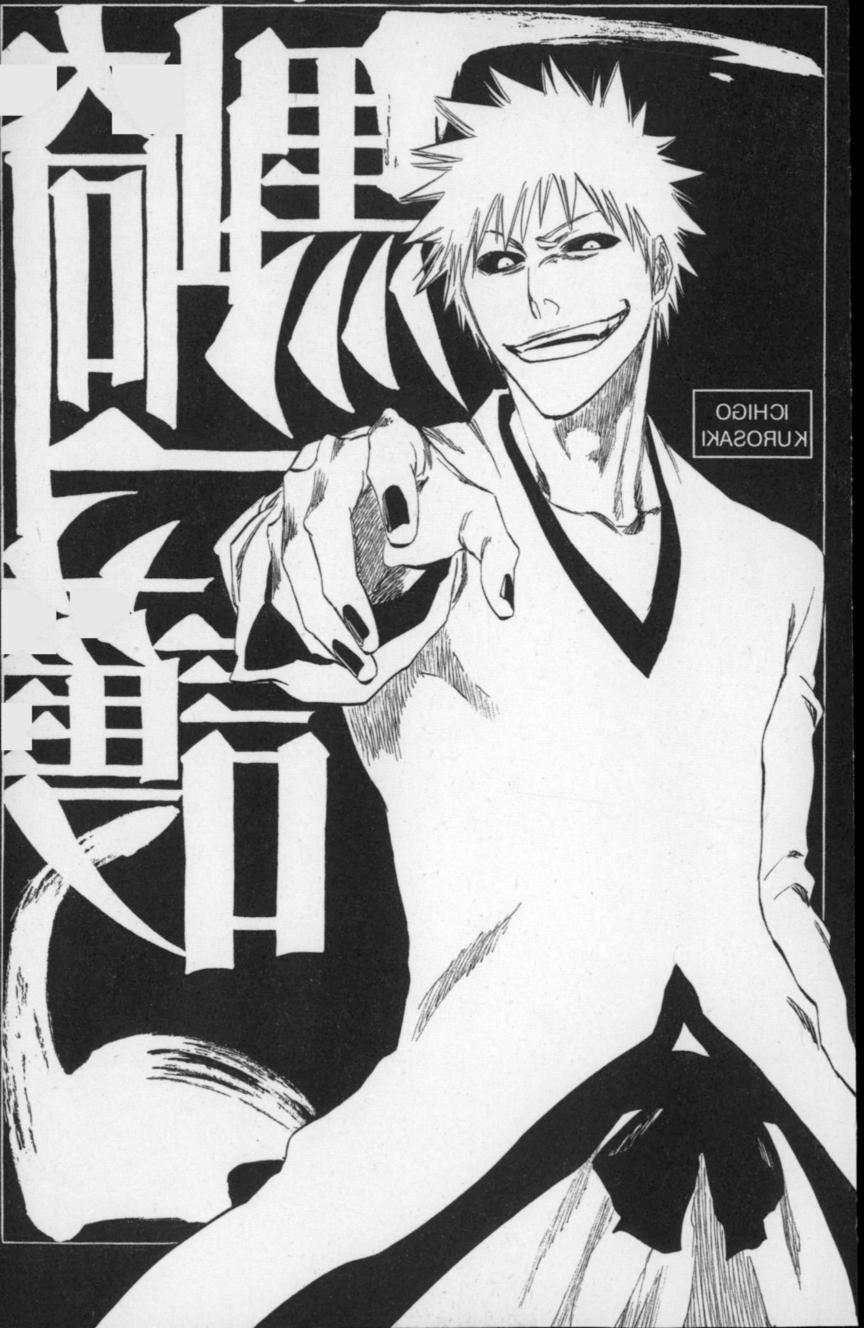
ICHIGO KUROSAKI

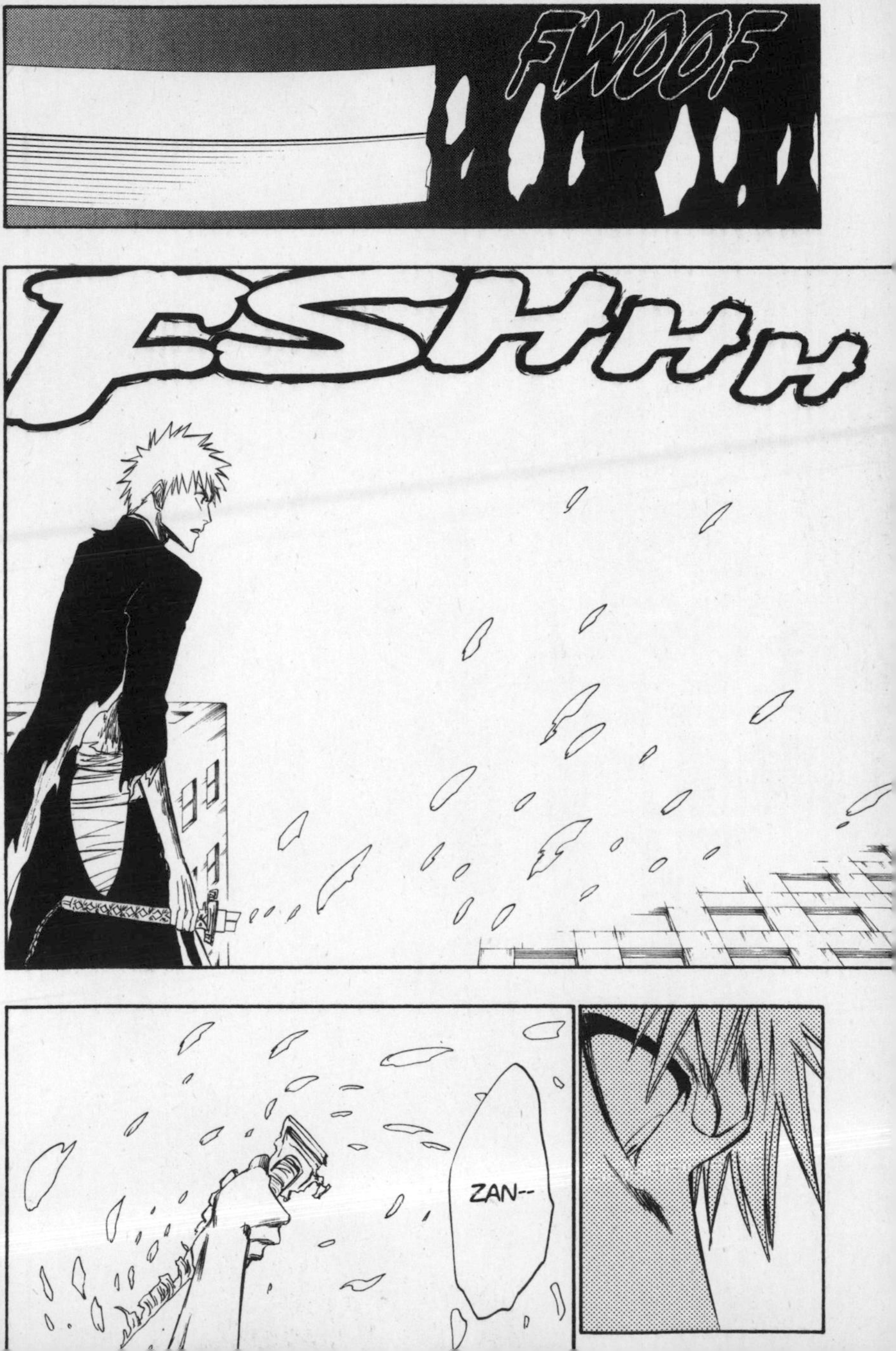
FWOOF
FSHH
ZAN--

READ THIS WAY

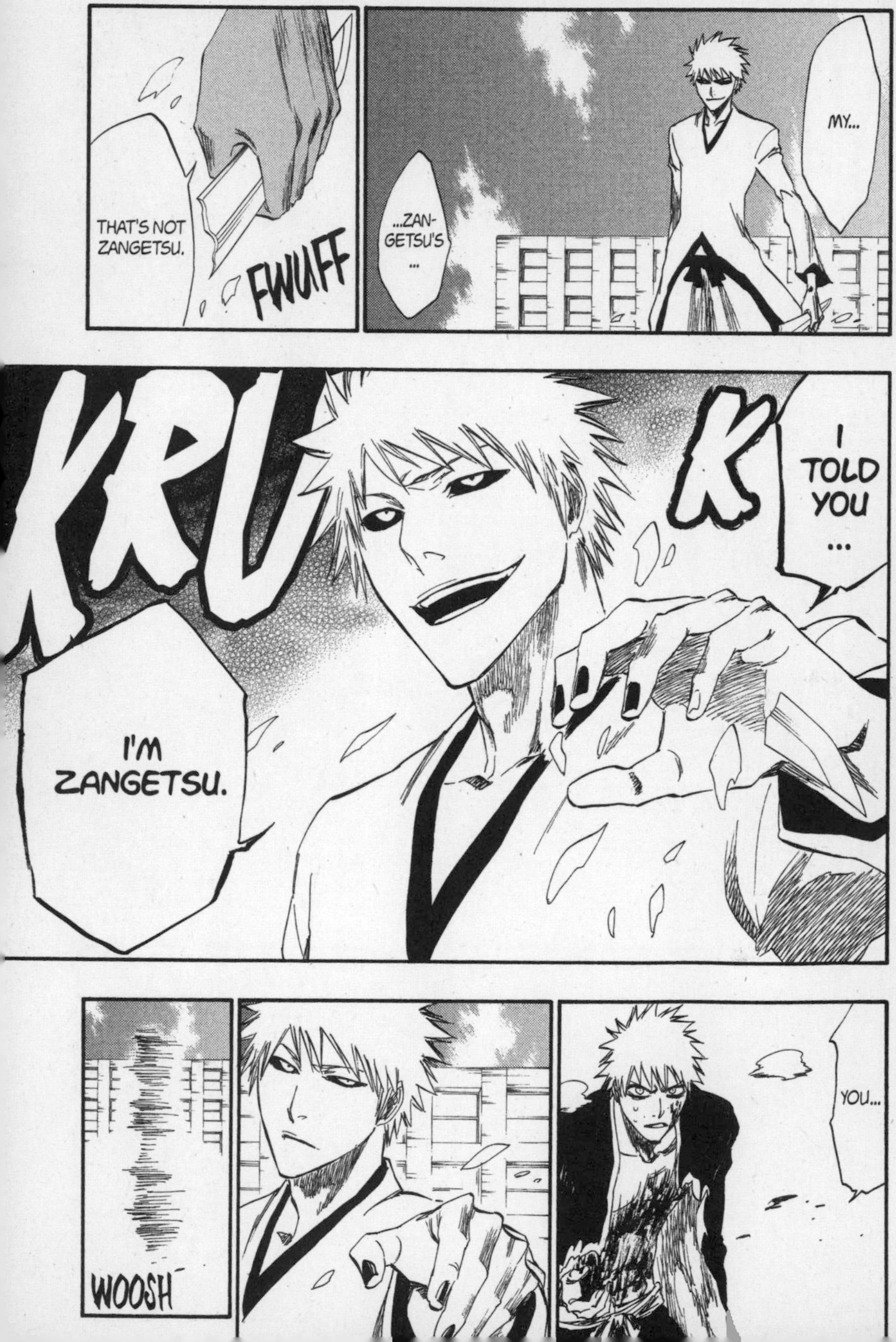
MY...
...ZAN-GETSU'S ...
THAT'S NOT ZANGETSU.
FWUFF
KRU K
I TOLD YOU ...
I'M ZANGETSU.
YOU...
WOOSH

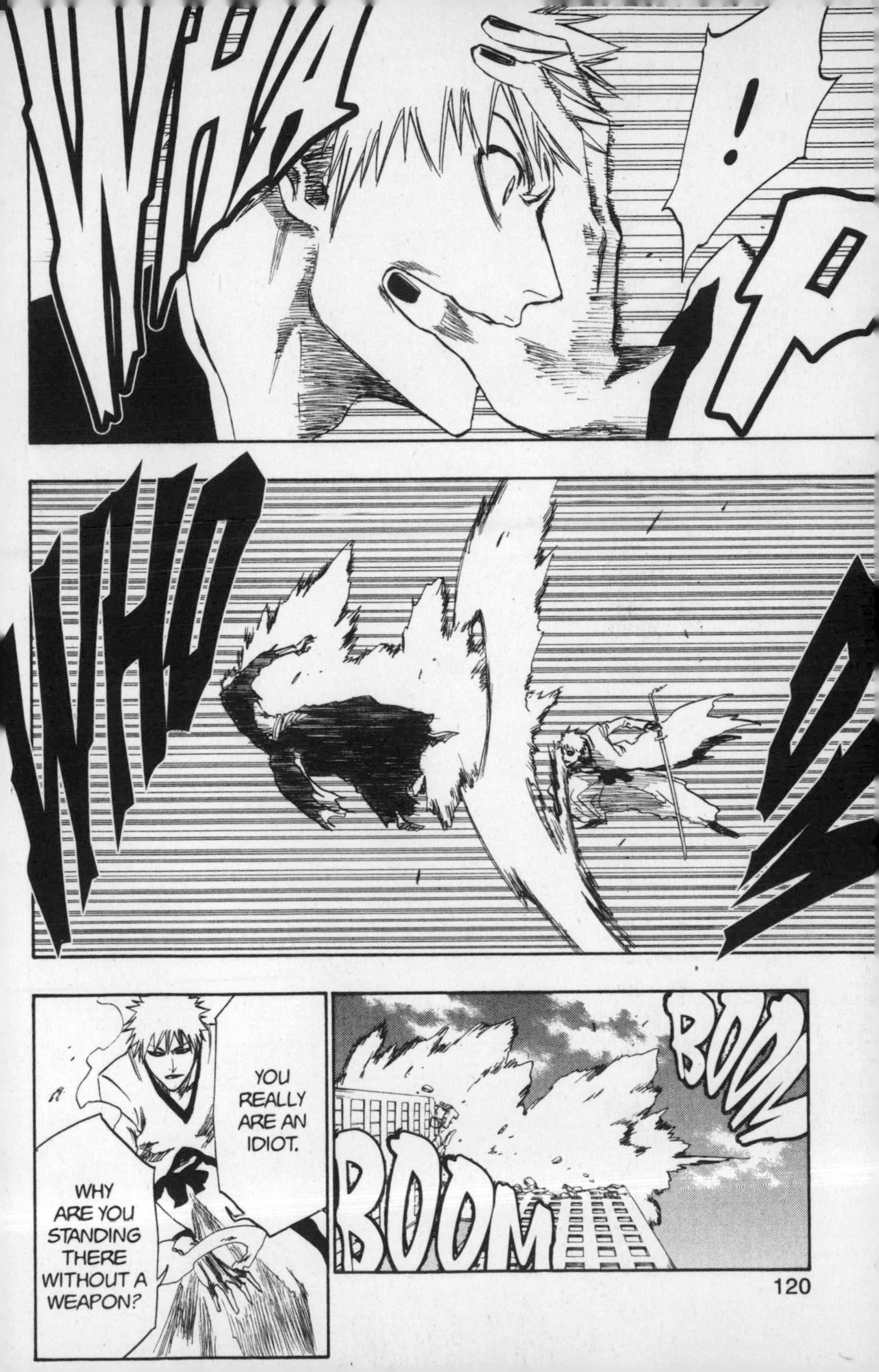
!
BOOM
YOU REALLY ARE AN IDIOT.
WHY ARE YOU STANDING THERE WITHOUT A WEAPON?

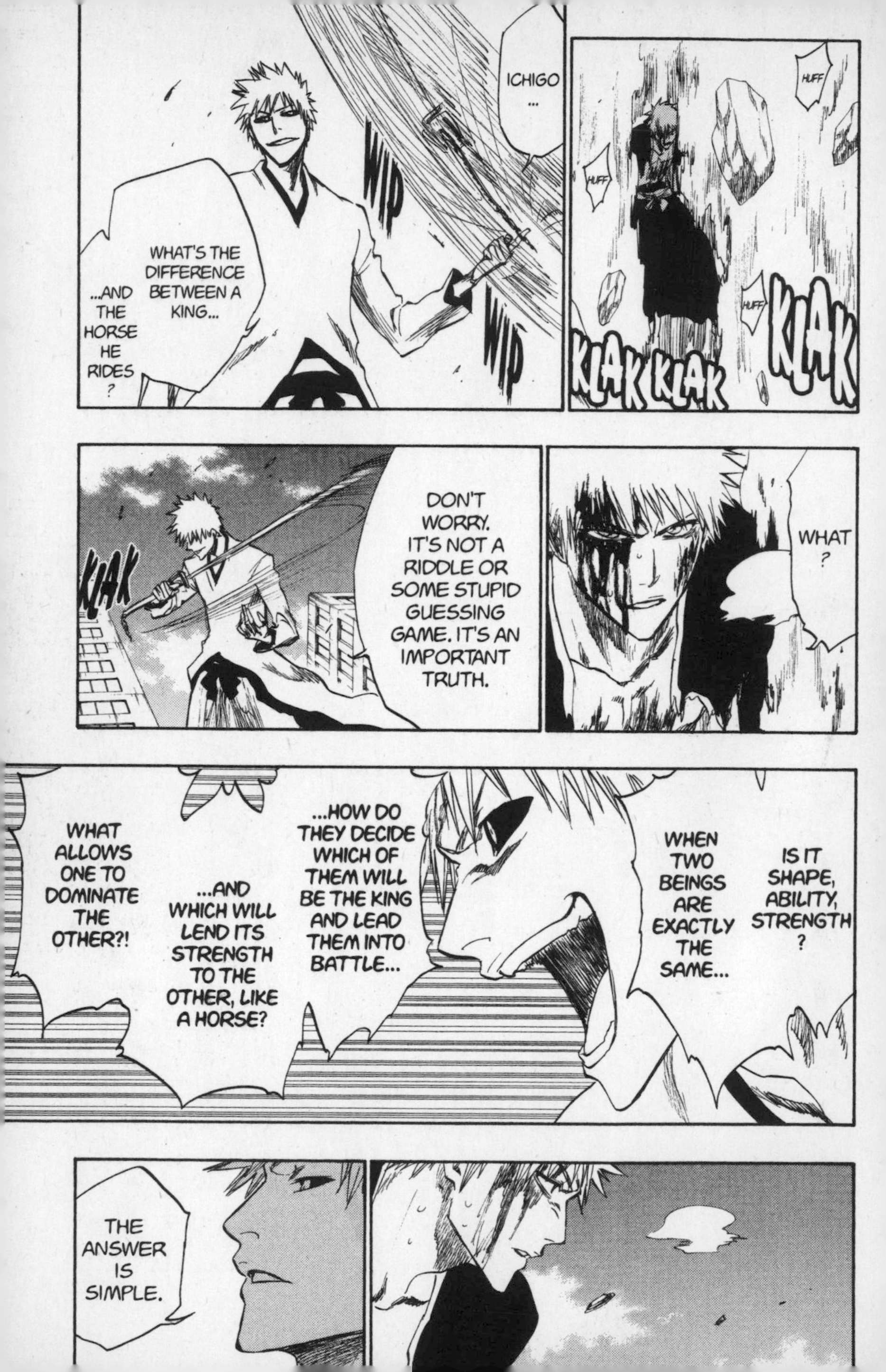
HUFF
HUFF
HUFF
KLAK
KLAK KLAK
ICHIGO ...
WHIP
WHIP
WHAT'S THE DIFFERENCE BETWEEN A KING...
...AND THE HORSE HE RIDES?
WHAT?
DON'T WORRY. IT'S NOT A RIDDLE OR SOME STUPID GUESSING GAME. IT'S AN IMPORTANT TRUTH.
KLAK
IS IT SHAPE, ABILITY, STRENGTH?
WHEN TWO BEINGS ARE EXACTLY THE SAME...
...HOW DO THEY DECIDE WHICH OF THEM WILL BE THE KING AND LEAD THEM INTO BATTLE...
...AND WHICH WILL LEND ITS STRENGTH TO THE OTHER, LIKE A HORSE?
WHAT ALLOWS ONE TO DOMINATE THE OTHER?!
THE ANSWER IS SIMPLE.

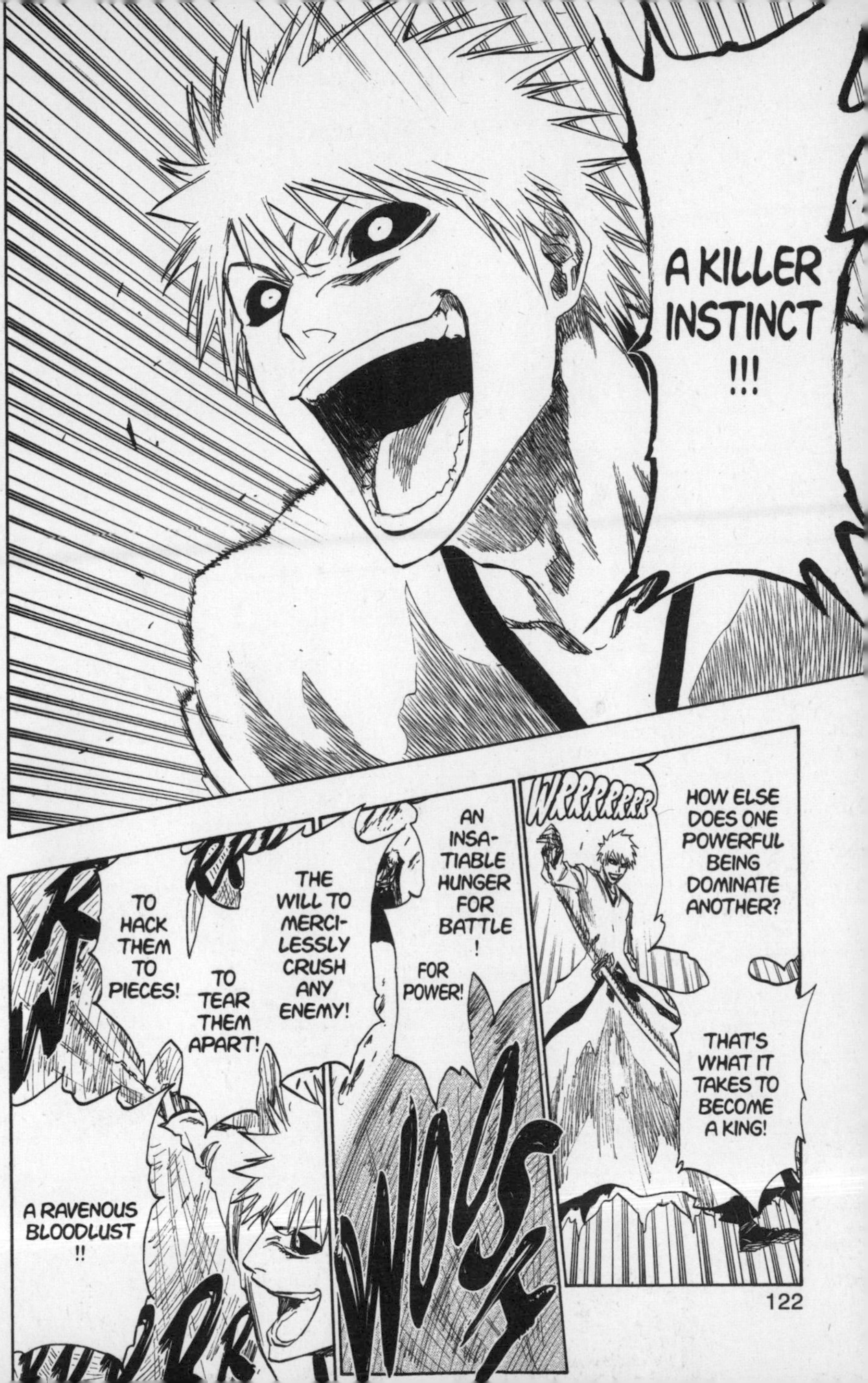
A KILLER INSTINCT !!!
WRRRRRRRR
HOW ELSE DOES ONE POWERFUL BEING DOMINATE ANOTHER?
THAT'S WHAT IT TAKES TO BECOME A KING!
AN INSATIABLE HUNGER FOR BATTLE!
FOR POWER!
THE WILL TO MERCILESSLY CRUSH ANY ENEMY!
TO TEAR THEM APART!
TO HACK THEM TO PIECES!
A RAVENOUS BLOODLUST !!

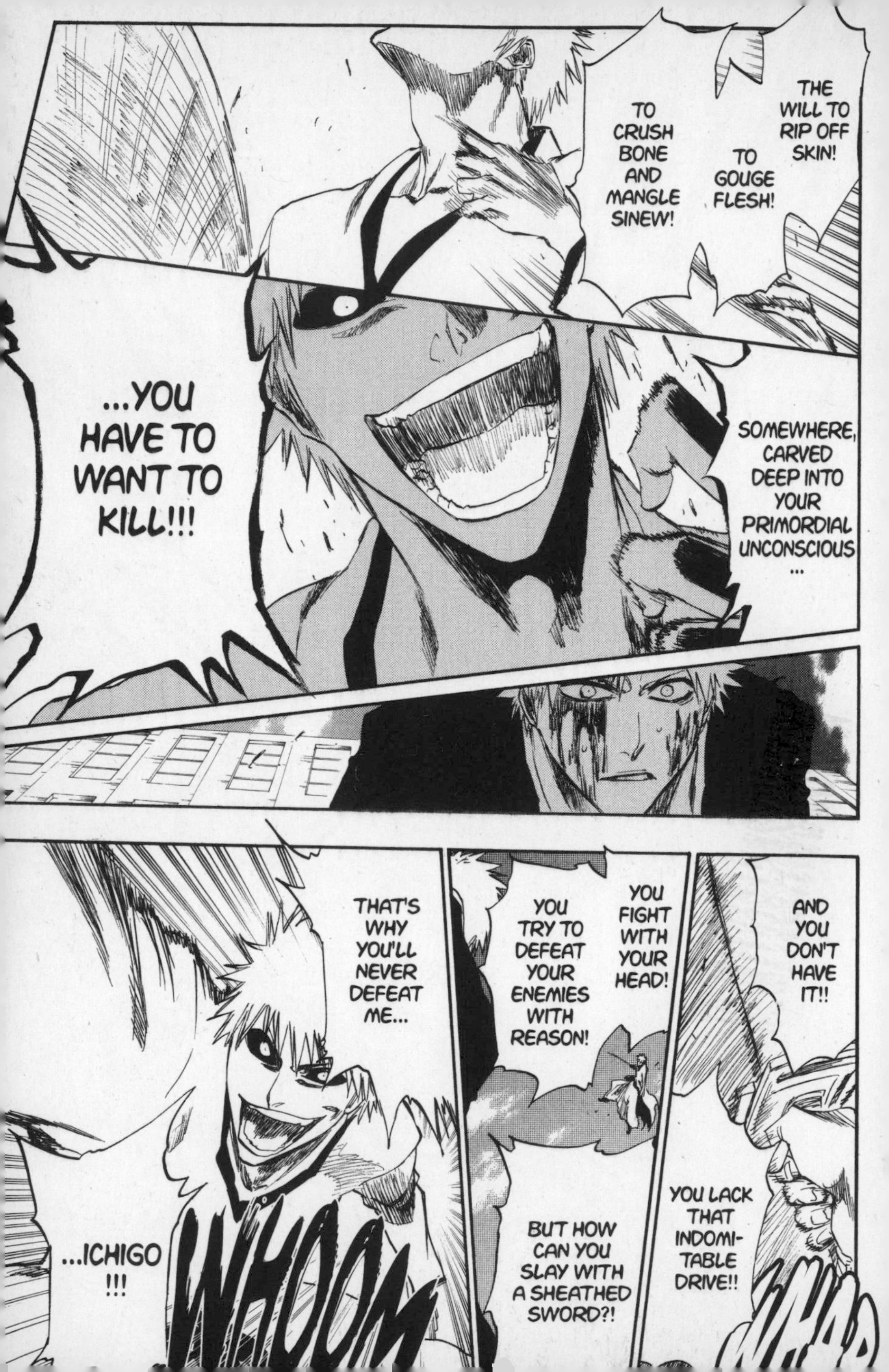
THE WILL TO RIP OFF SKIN!
TO GOUGE FLESH!
TO CRUSH BONE AND MANGLE SINEW!
SOMEWHERE, CARVED DEEP INTO YOUR PRIMORDIAL UNCONSCIOUS...
...YOU HAVE TO WANT TO KILL!!!
AND YOU DON'T HAVE IT!!
YOU LACK THAT INDOMITABLE DRIVE!!
WHAP
YOU FIGHT WITH YOUR HEAD!
YOU TRY TO DEFEAT YOUR ENEMIES WITH REASON!
BUT HOW CAN YOU SLAY WITH A SHEATHED SWORD?!
THAT'S WHY YOU'LL NEVER DEFEAT ME...
...ICHIGO!!!
WHOOM

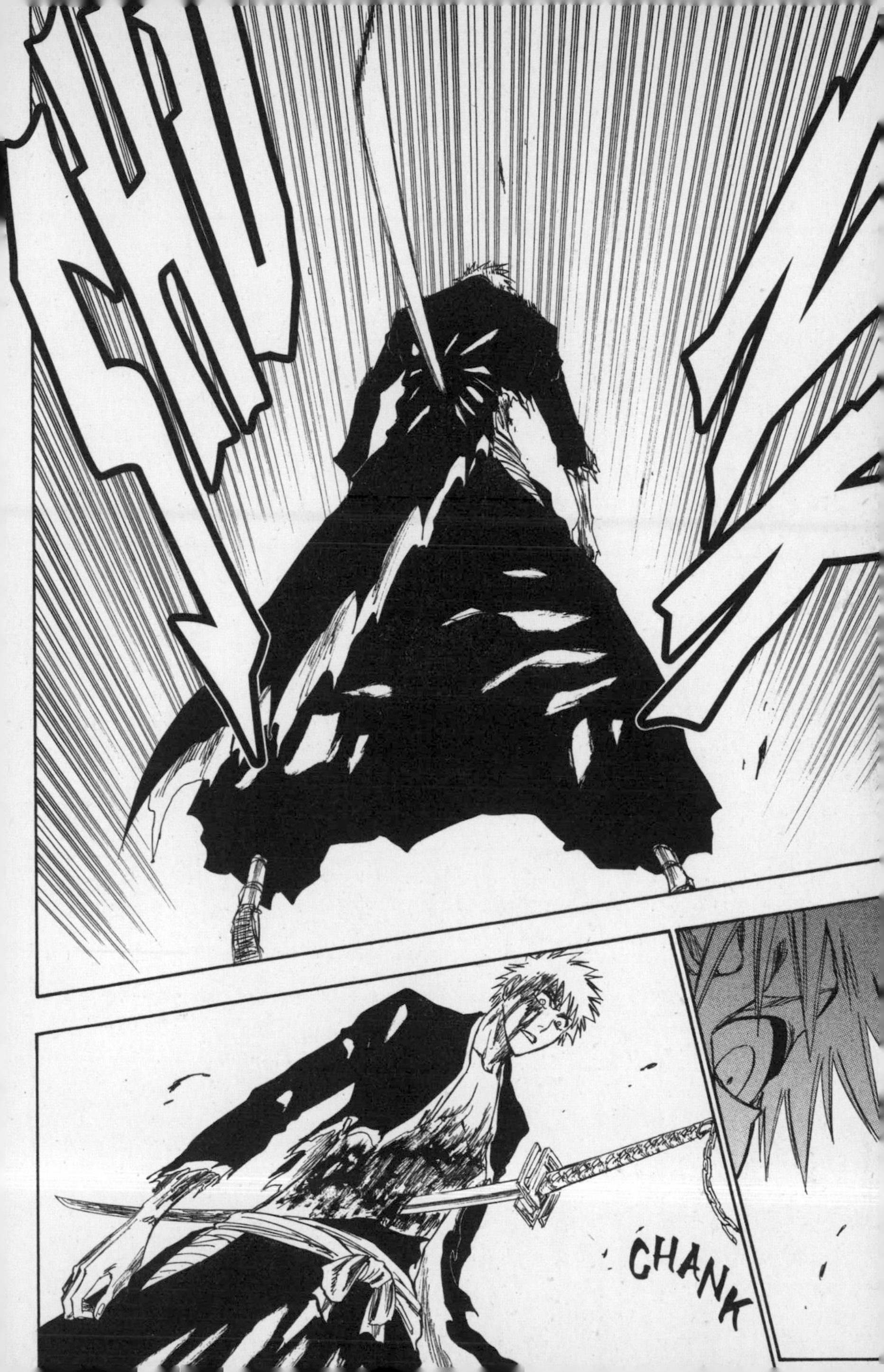
CHANK

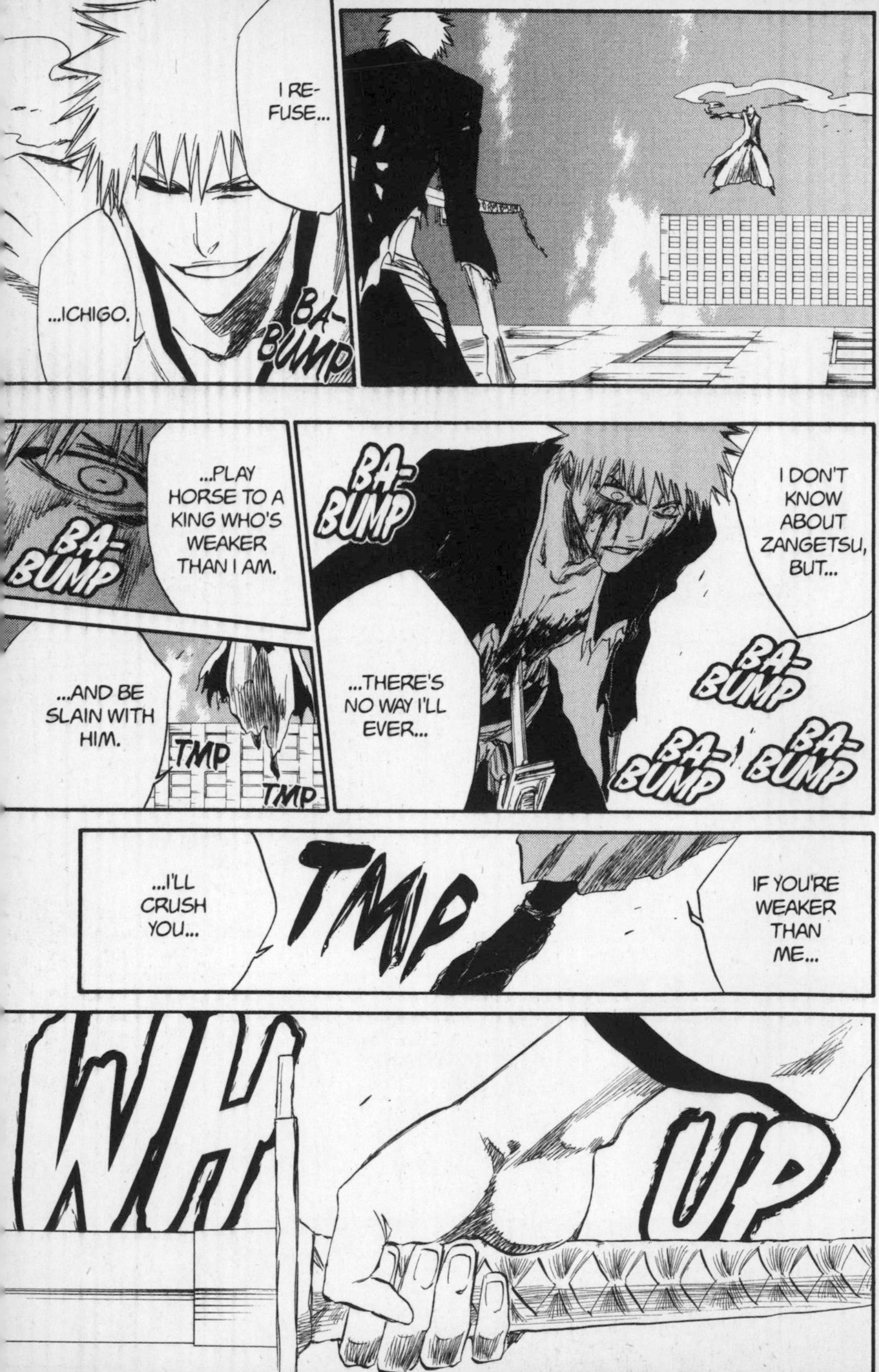
I RE-FUSE...
...ICHIGO.
BA-BUMP
I DON'T KNOW ABOUT ZANGETSU, BUT...
BA-BUMP
...THERE'S NO WAY I'LL EVER...
BA-BUMP
BA-BUMP
BA-BUMP
...PLAY HORSE TO A KING WHO'S WEAKER THAN I AM.
BA-BUMP
...AND BE SLAIN WITH HIM.
TMP
TMP
IF YOU'RE WEAKER THAN ME...
TMP
...I'LL CRUSH YOU...
WHUP

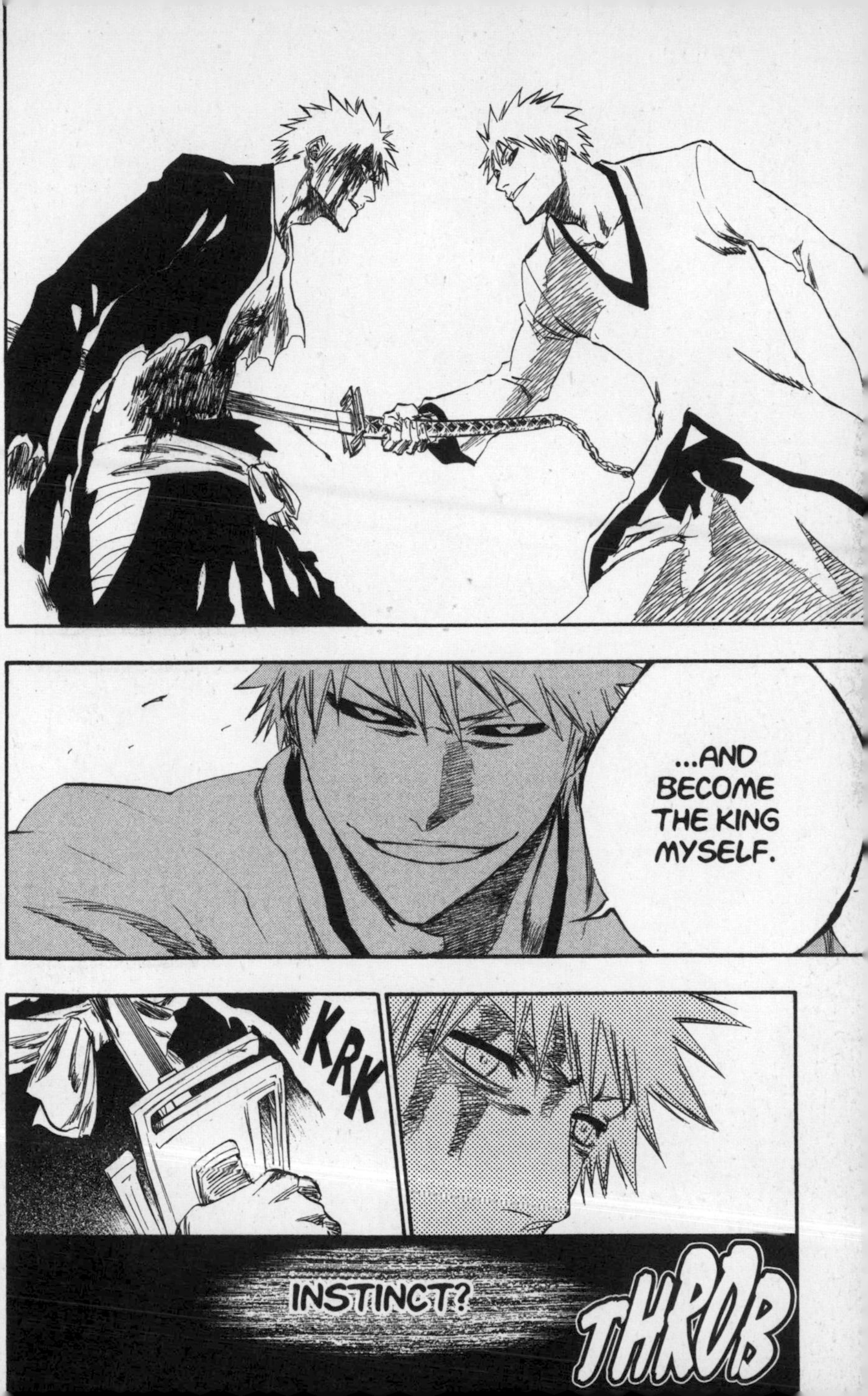
...AND BECOME THE KING MYSELF.
KRK
INSTINCT?
THROB

READ THIS WAY

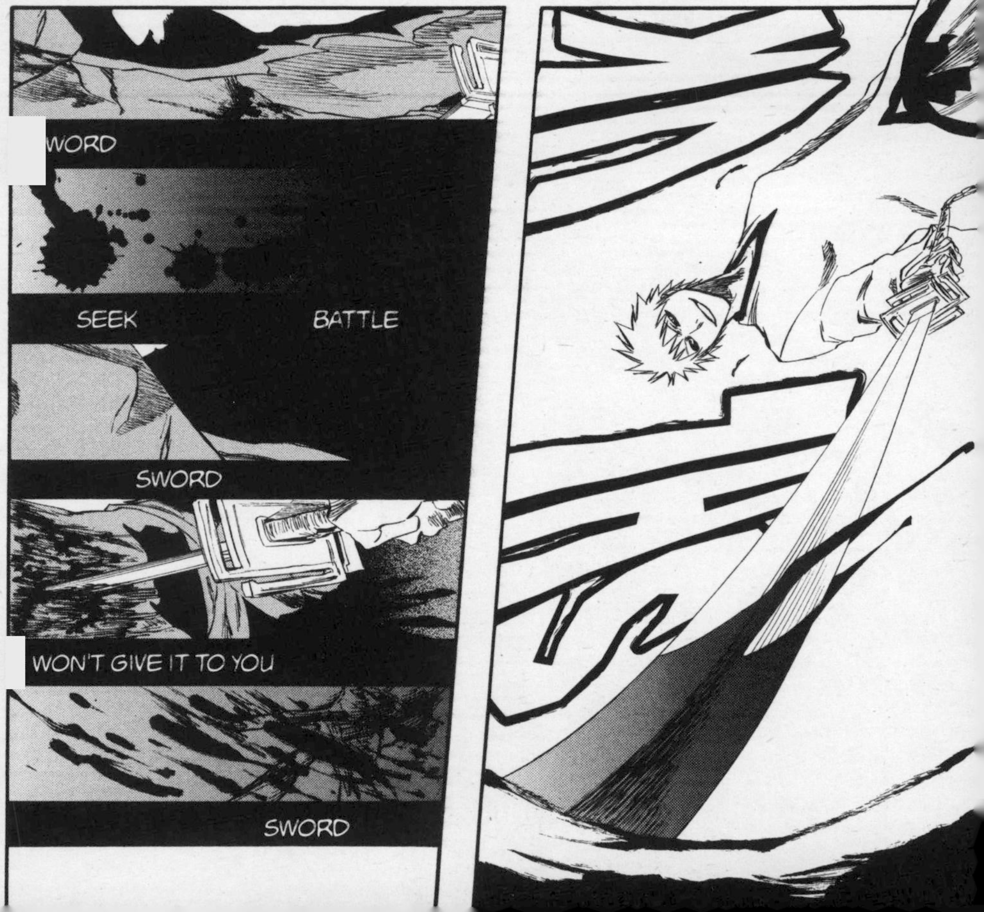
WORD
SEEK
BATTLE
SWORD
WON'T GIVE IT TO YOU
SWORD

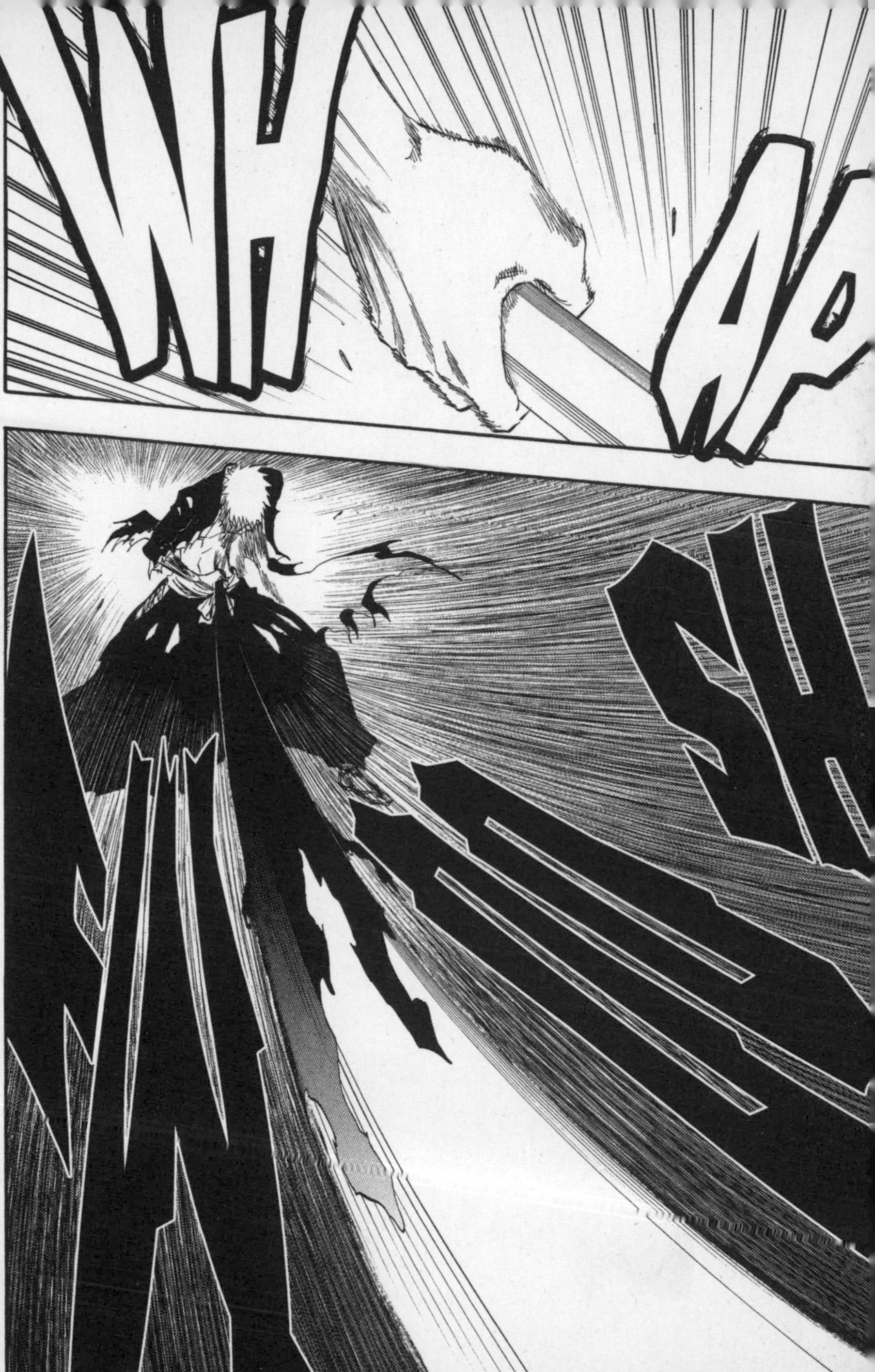
WHAP
SH

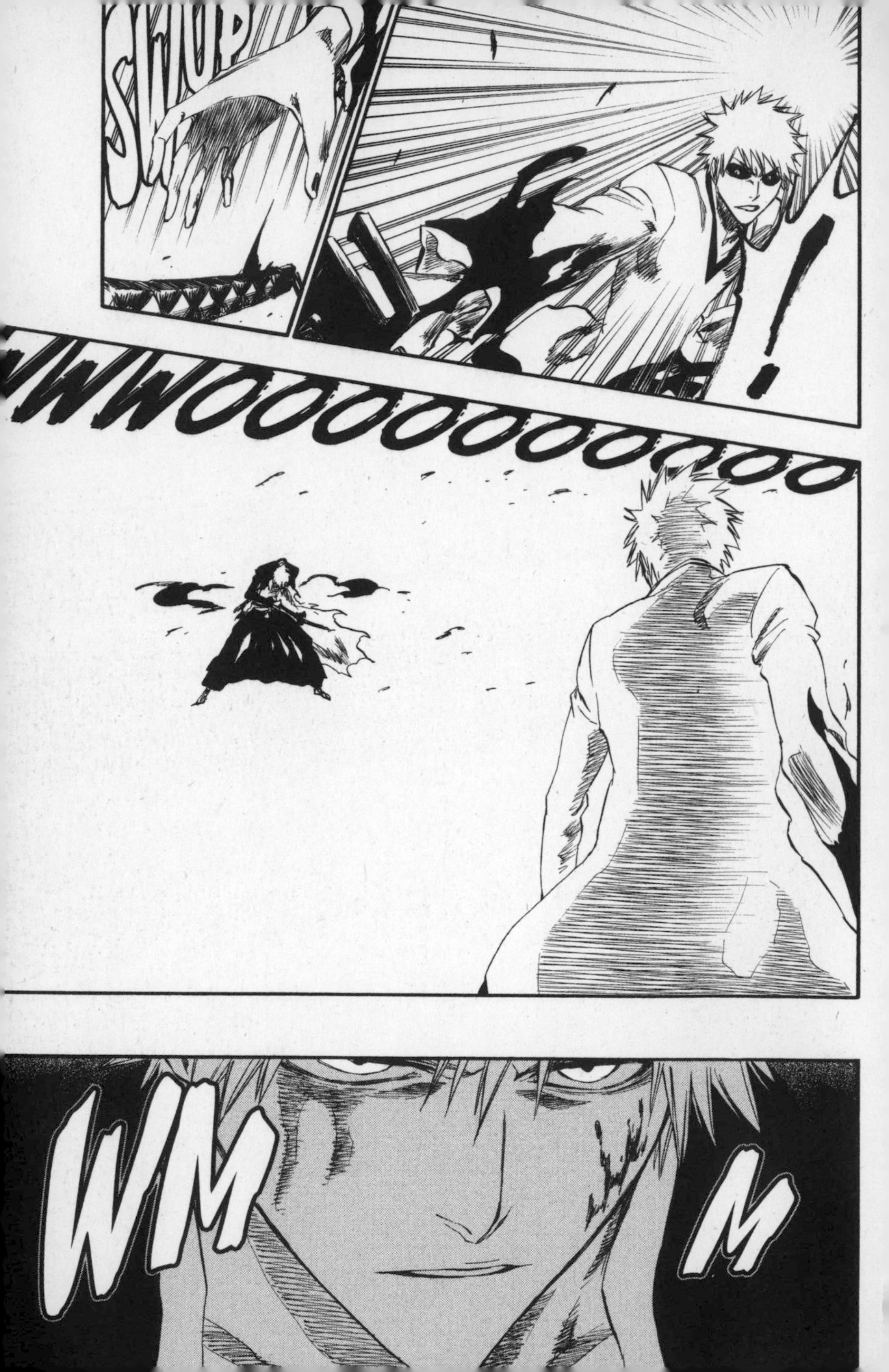

!
SHUP
WWWOOOOOOOOOO
WM
M

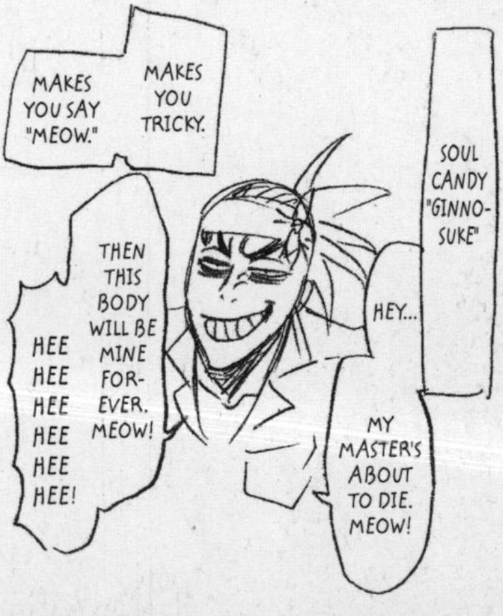
SOUL CANDY "GINNO-SUKE"
MAKES YOU TRICKY.
MAKES YOU SAY "MEOW."
HEY...
MY MASTER'S ABOUT TO DIE. MEOW!
THEN THIS BODY WILL BE MINE FOREVER. MEOW!
HEE HEE HEE HEE HEE HEE!

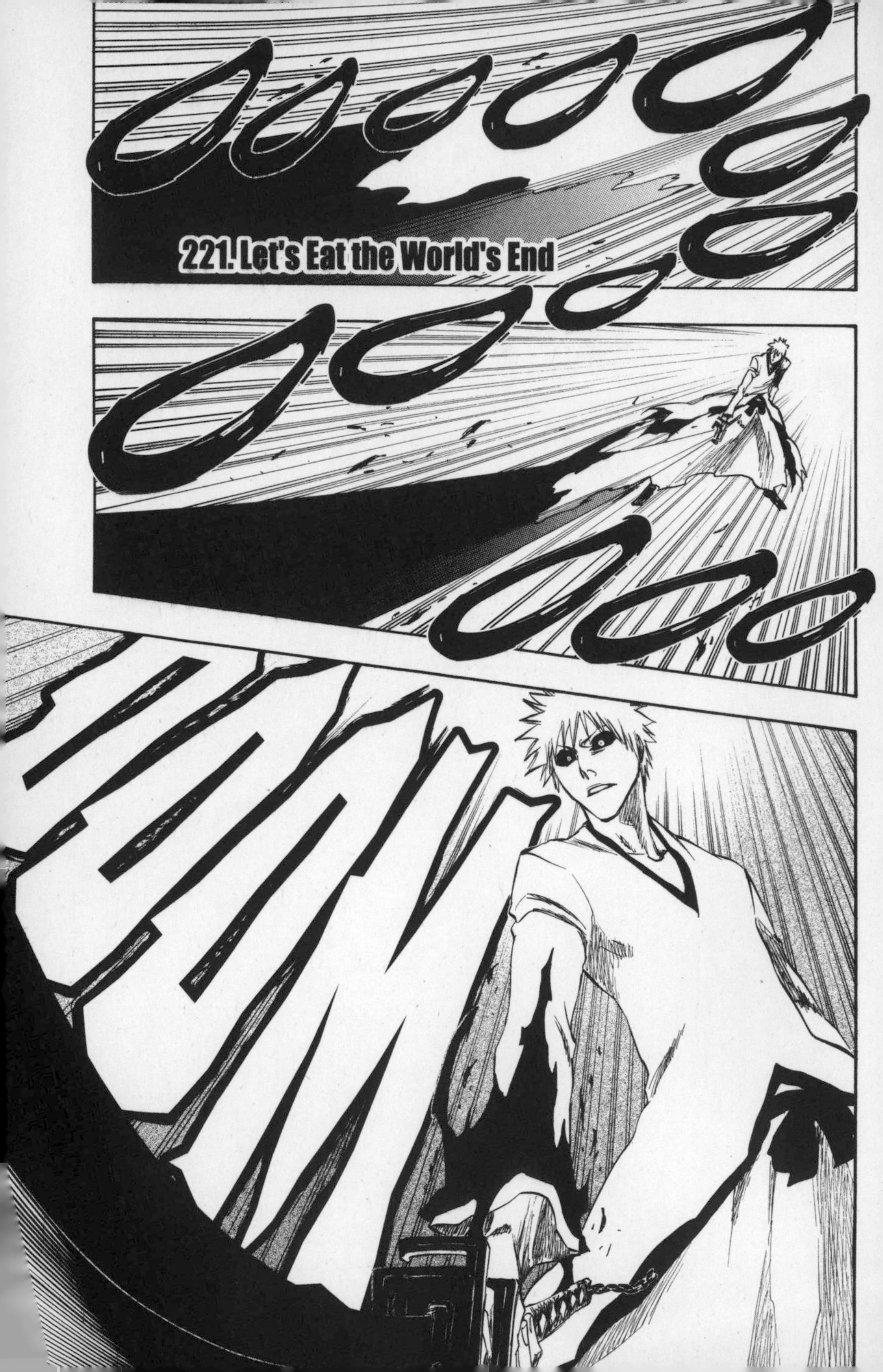
221. Let's Eat the World's End

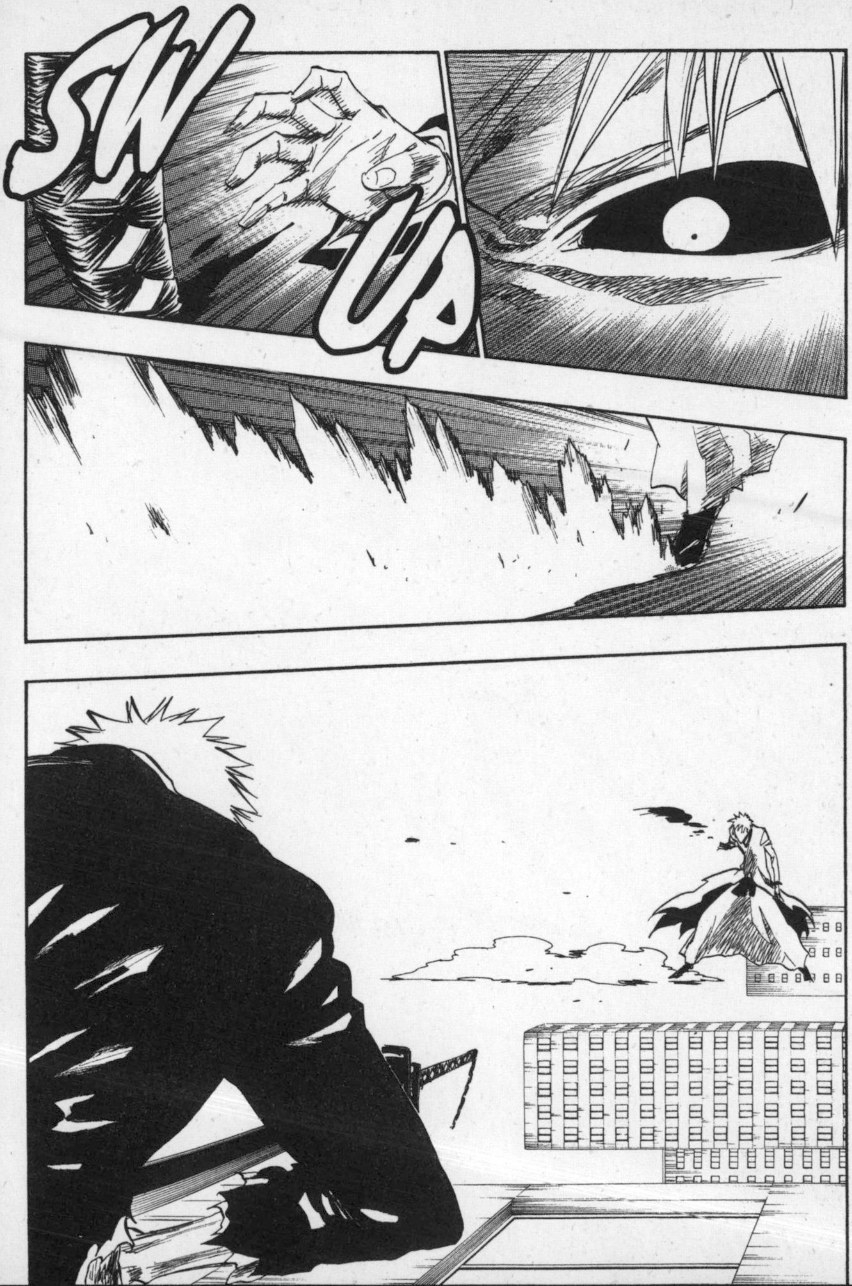
SWUP

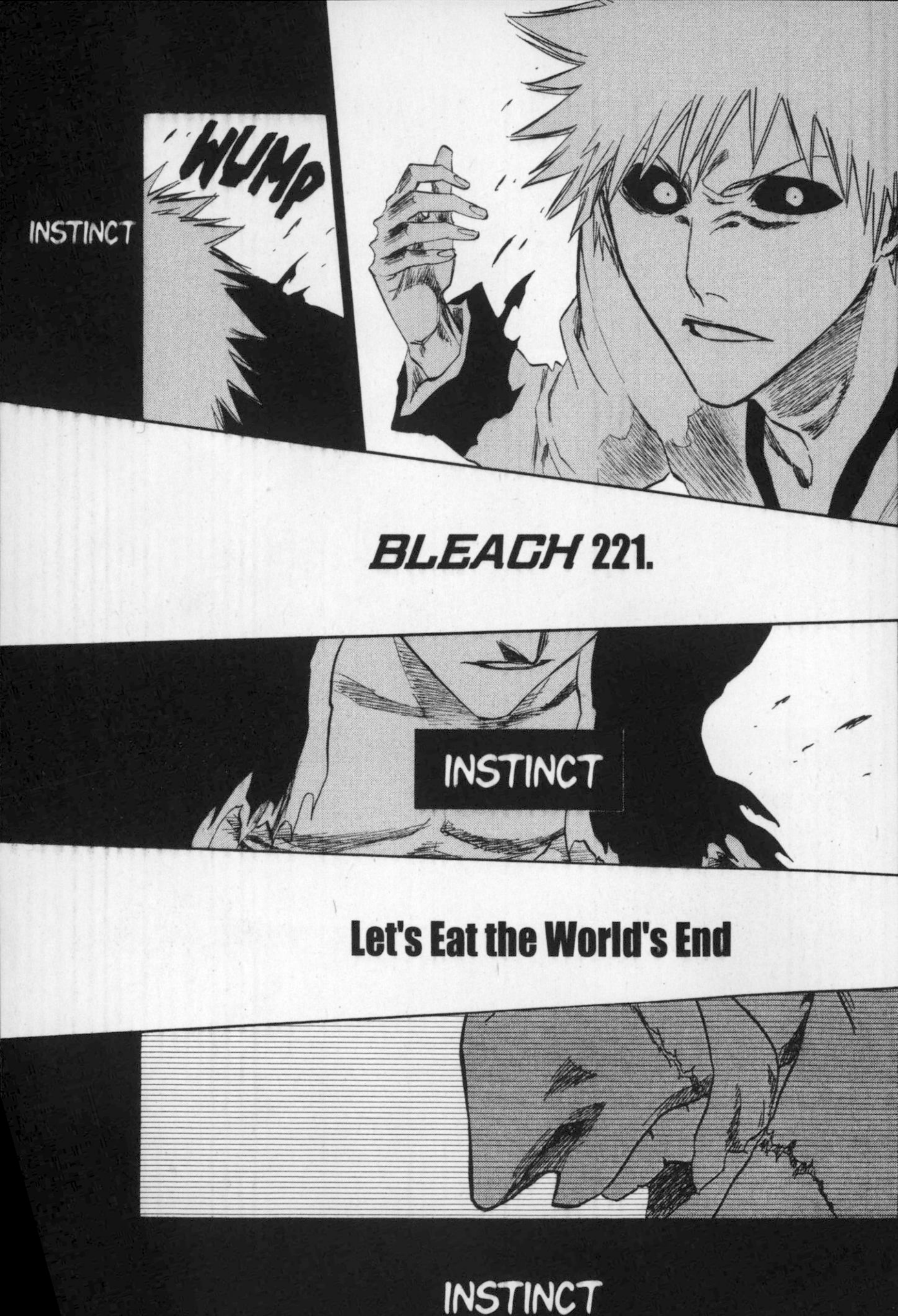
WUMP
INSTINCT
BLEACH 221.
INSTINCT
Let's Eat the World's End
INSTINCT

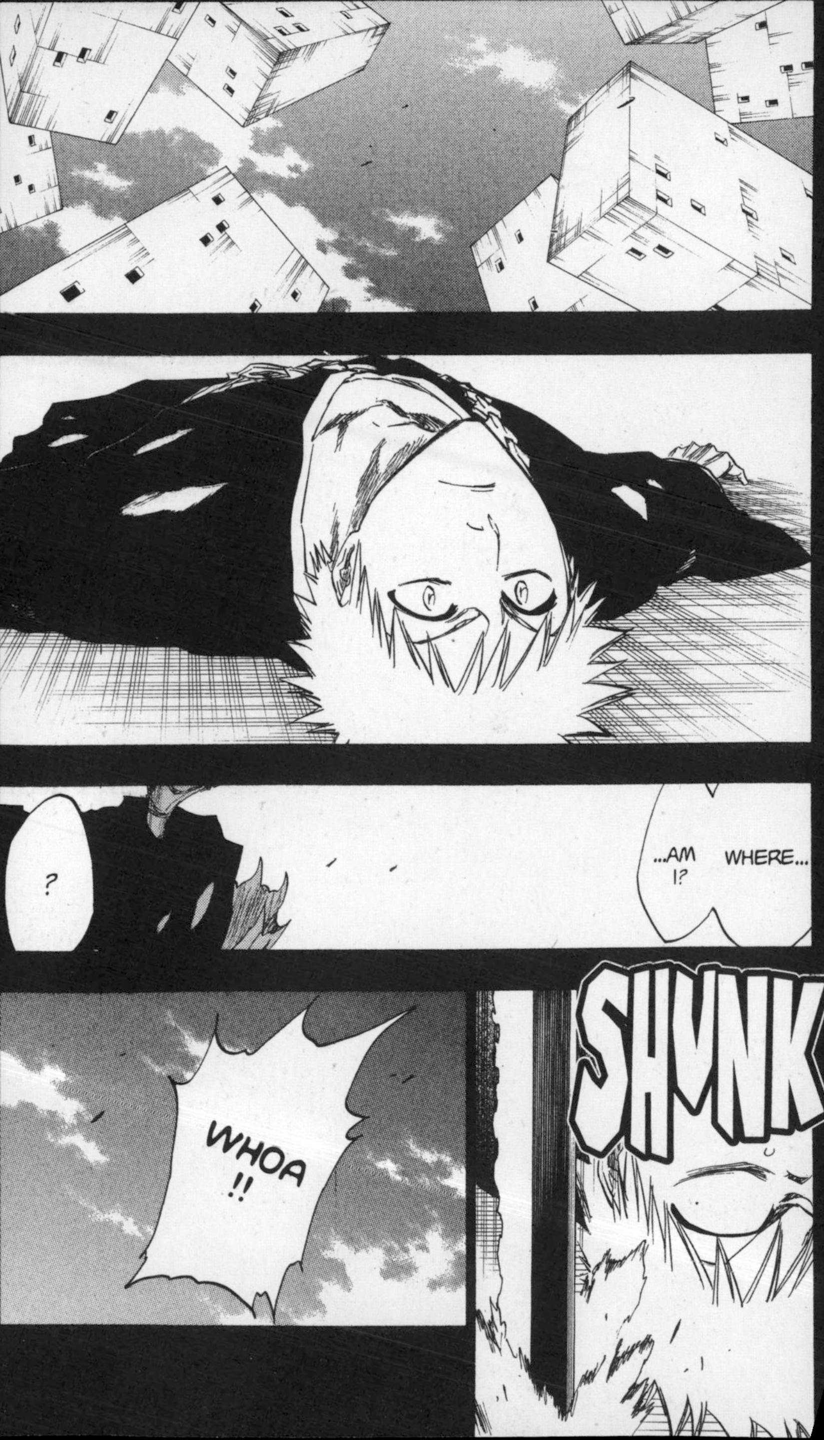
WHERE... ...AM I?
?
SHUNK
WHOA!!

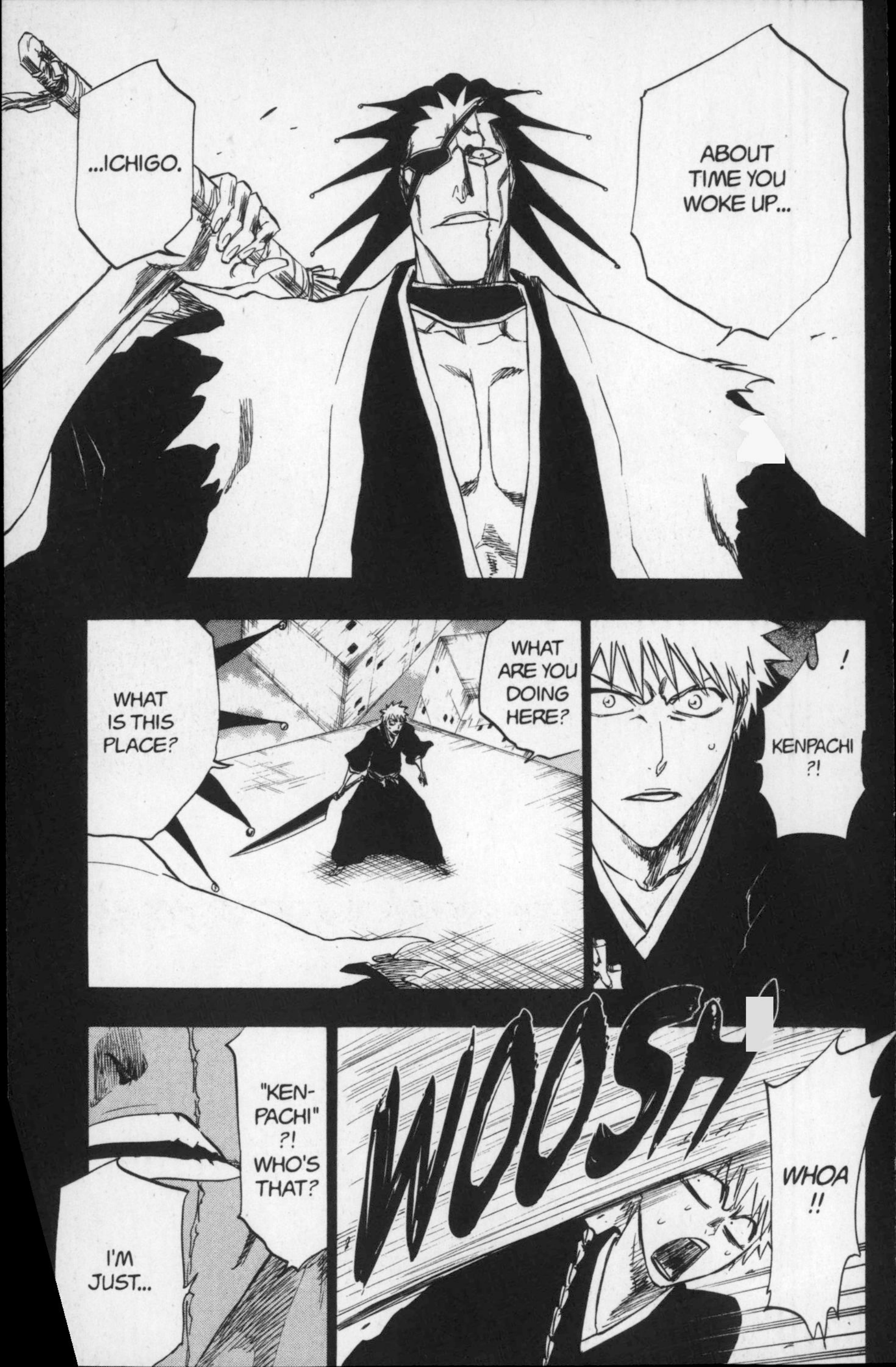
ABOUT TIME YOU WOKE UP...
...ICHIGO.
!
KENPACHI ?!
WHAT ARE YOU DOING HERE?
WHAT IS THIS PLACE?
WOOSH
WHOA !!
"KEN-PACHI" ?! WHO'S THAT?
I'M JUST...

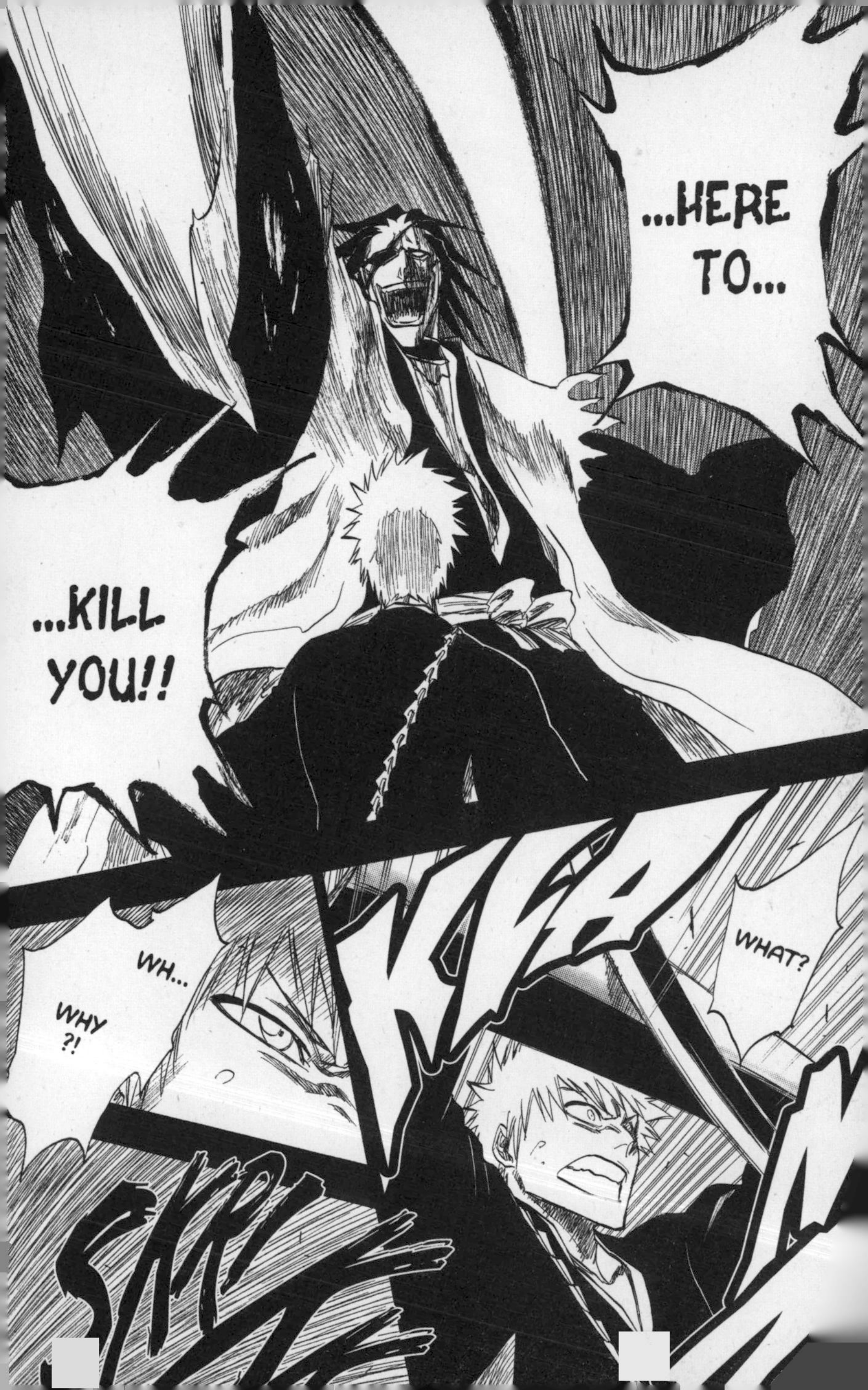
...HERE TO...
...KILL YOU!!
WHAT?
WH...
WHY ?!

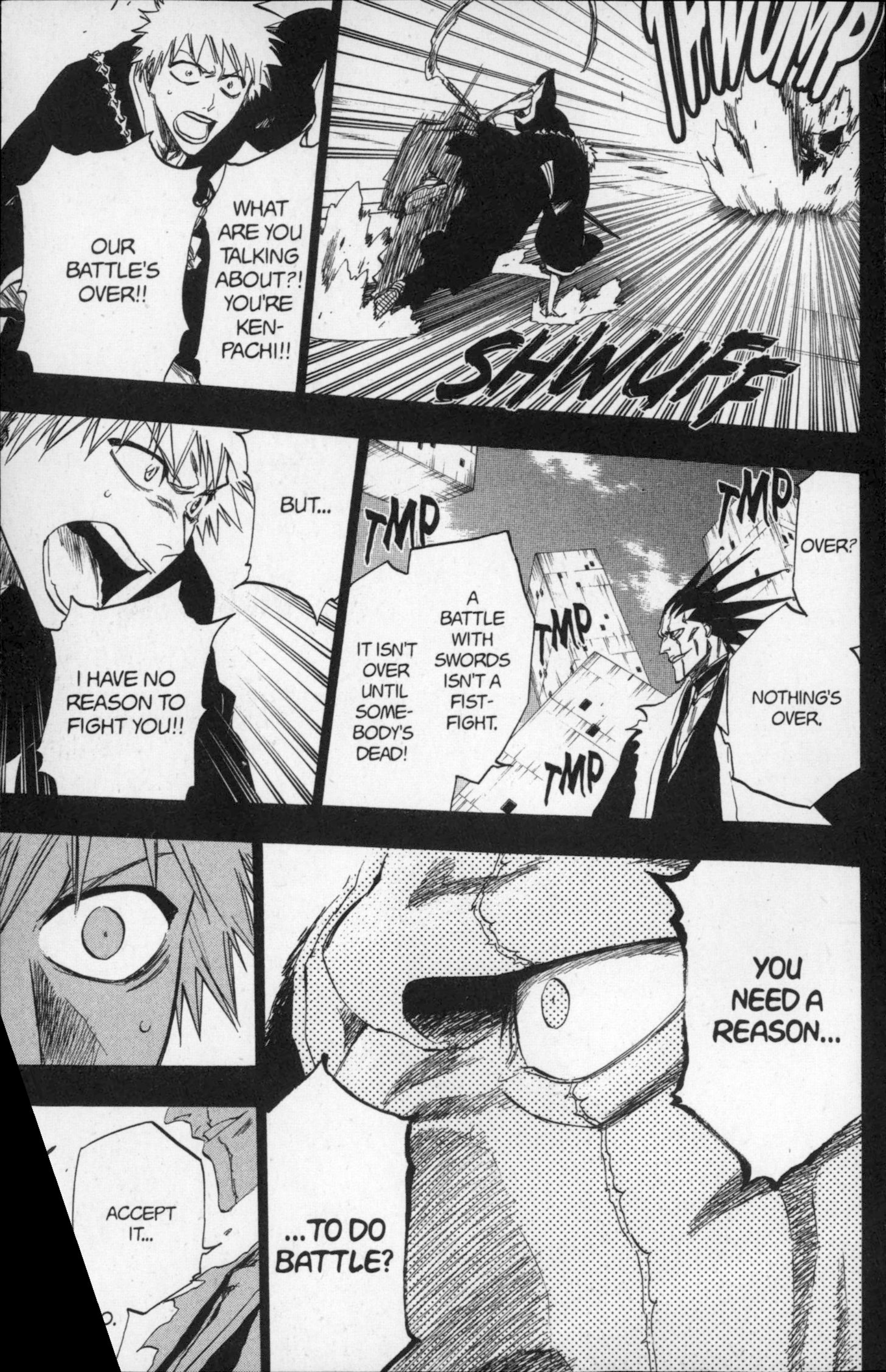
TWUMP
SHWUFF
WHAT ARE YOU TALKING ABOUT?! YOU'RE KEN-PACHI!!
OUR BATTLE'S OVER!!
TMP
OVER?
NOTHING'S OVER.
A BATTLE WITH SWORDS ISN'T A FIST-FIGHT.
IT ISN'T OVER UNTIL SOME-BODY'S DEAD!
TMP
TMP
TMP
BUT...
I HAVE NO REASON TO FIGHT YOU!!
YOU NEED A REASON...
...TO DO BATTLE?
ACCEPT IT...

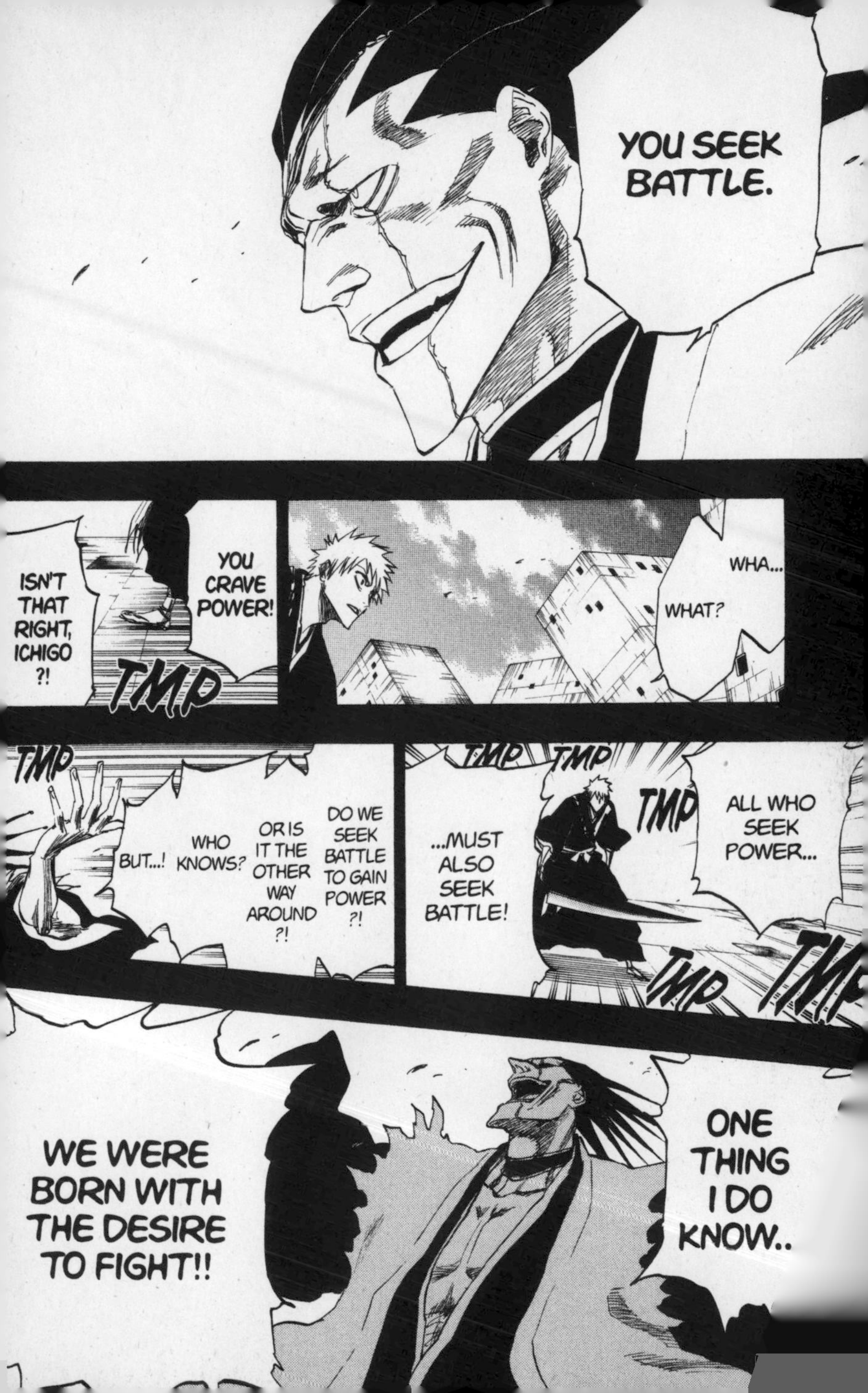
YOU SEEK BATTLE.
WHA...
WHAT?
YOU CRAVE POWER!
ISN'T THAT RIGHT, ICHIGO?!
TMP
TMP
TMP
TMP
ALL WHO SEEK POWER...
...MUST ALSO SEEK BATTLE!
TMP
TMP
TMP
DO WE SEEK BATTLE TO GAIN POWER?!
OR IS IT THE OTHER WAY AROUND?!
WHO KNOWS?
BUT...!
ONE THING I DO KNOW..
WE WERE BORN WITH THE DESIRE TO FIGHT!!

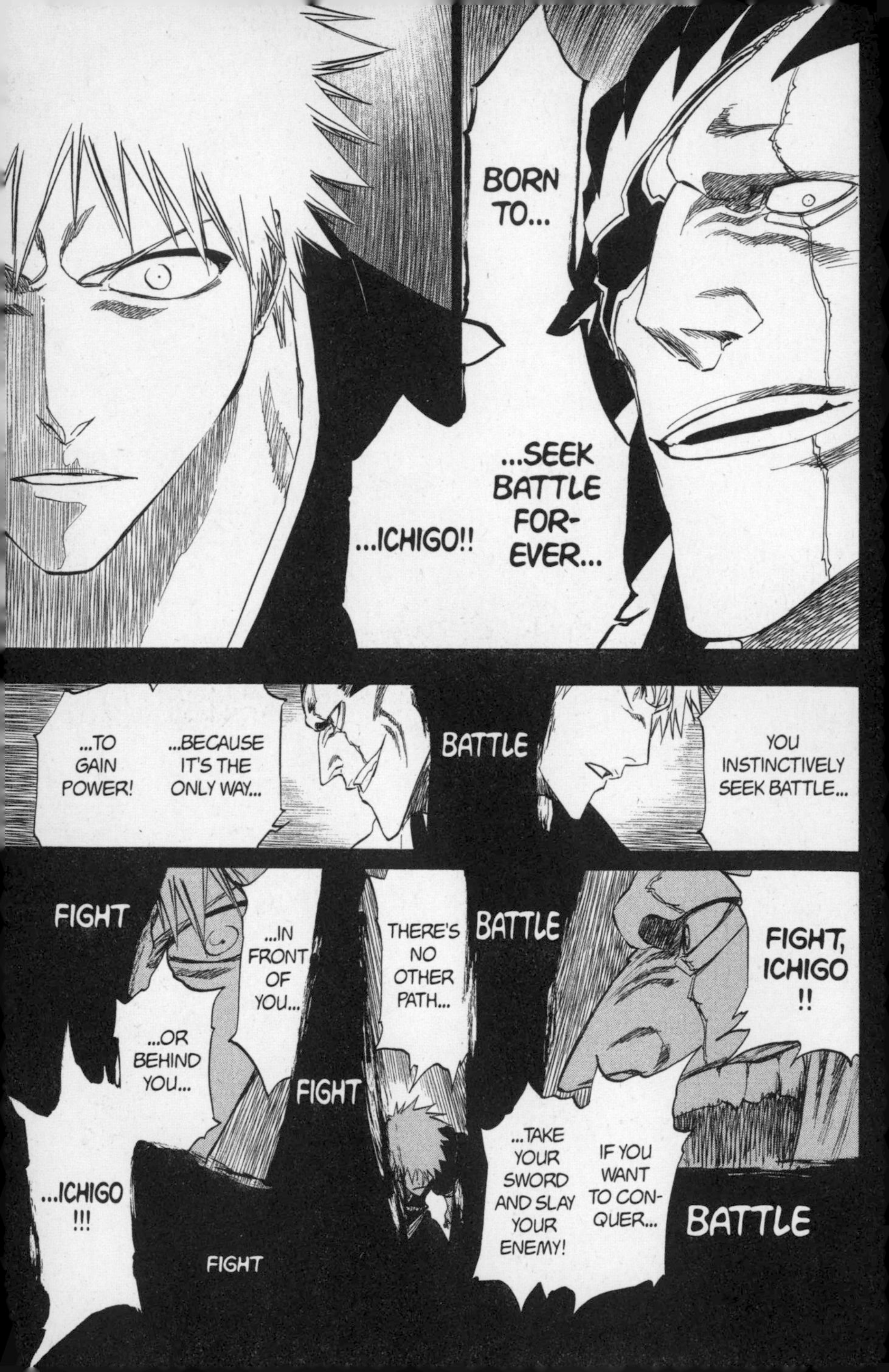
BORN TO...
...SEEK BATTLE FOR-EVER...
...ICHIGO!!
YOU INSTINCTIVELY SEEK BATTLE...
BATTLE
...BECAUSE IT'S THE ONLY WAY...
...TO GAIN POWER!
FIGHT, ICHIGO!!
BATTLE
IF YOU WANT TO CON-QUER...
...TAKE YOUR SWORD AND SLAY YOUR ENEMY!
BATTLE
THERE'S NO OTHER PATH...
FIGHT
...IN FRONT OF YOU...
FIGHT
...OR BEHIND YOU...
...ICHIGO!!!
FIGHT

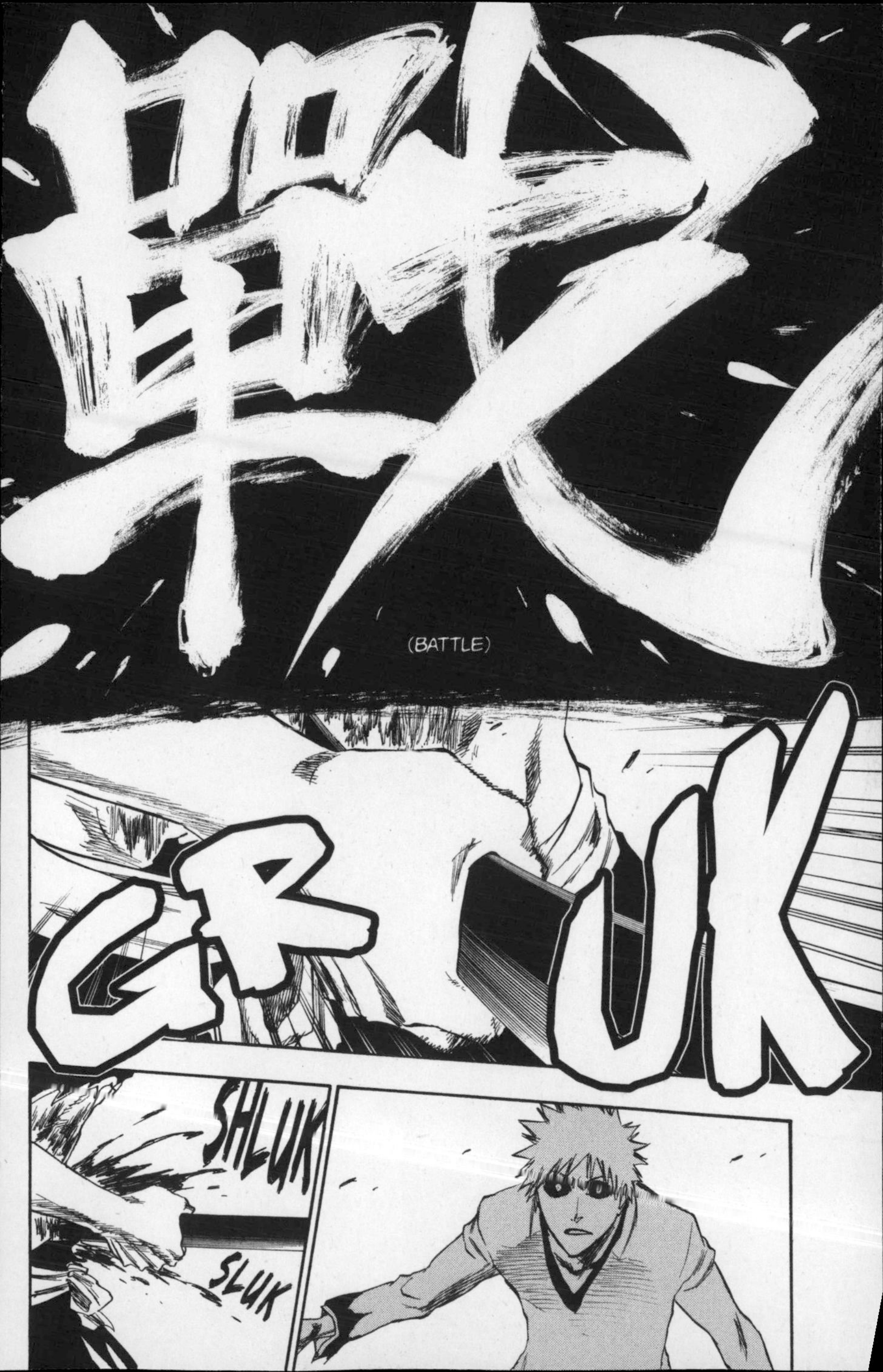
戦
(BATTLE)
GRUK
SHLUK
SLUK

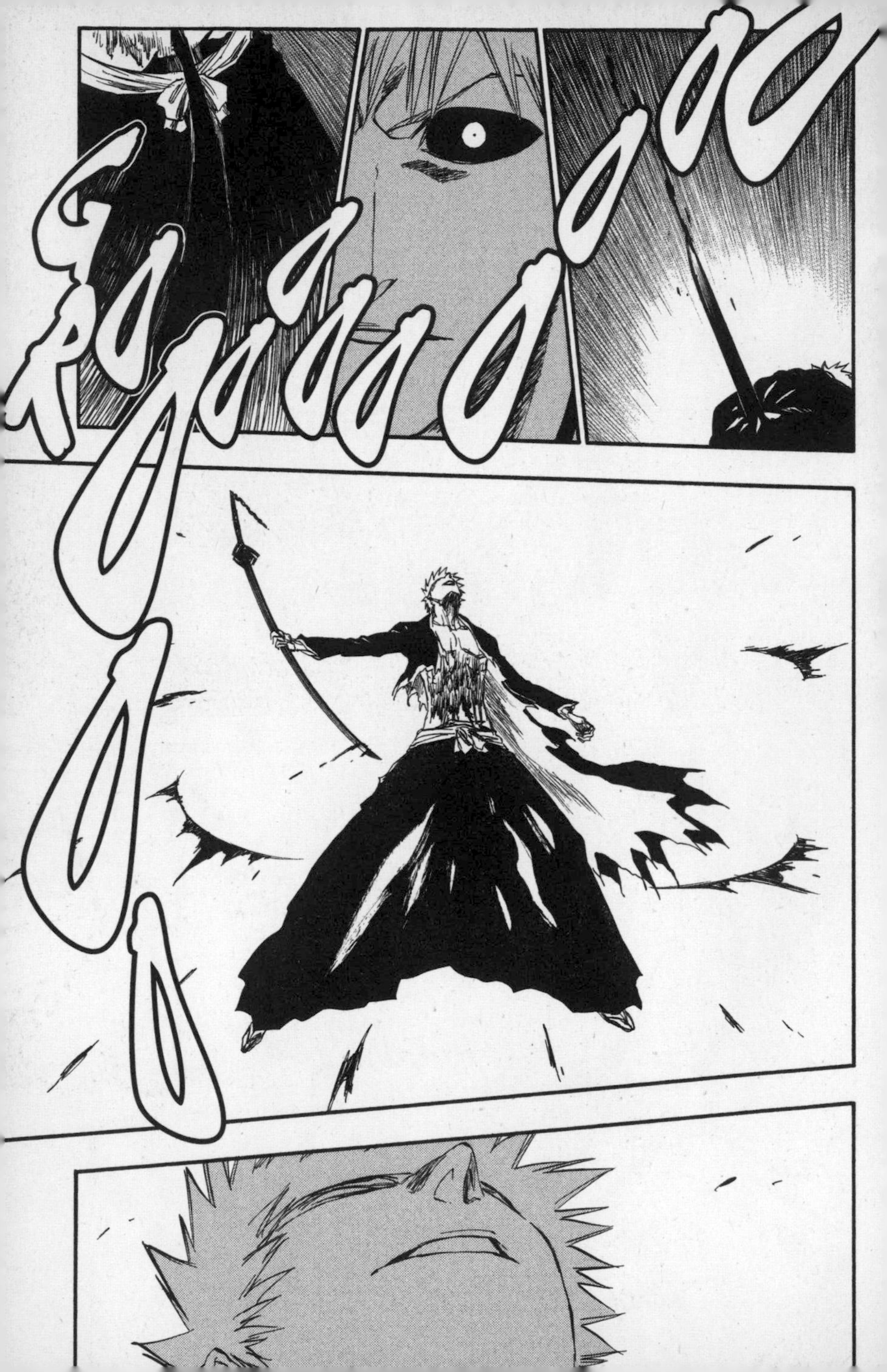

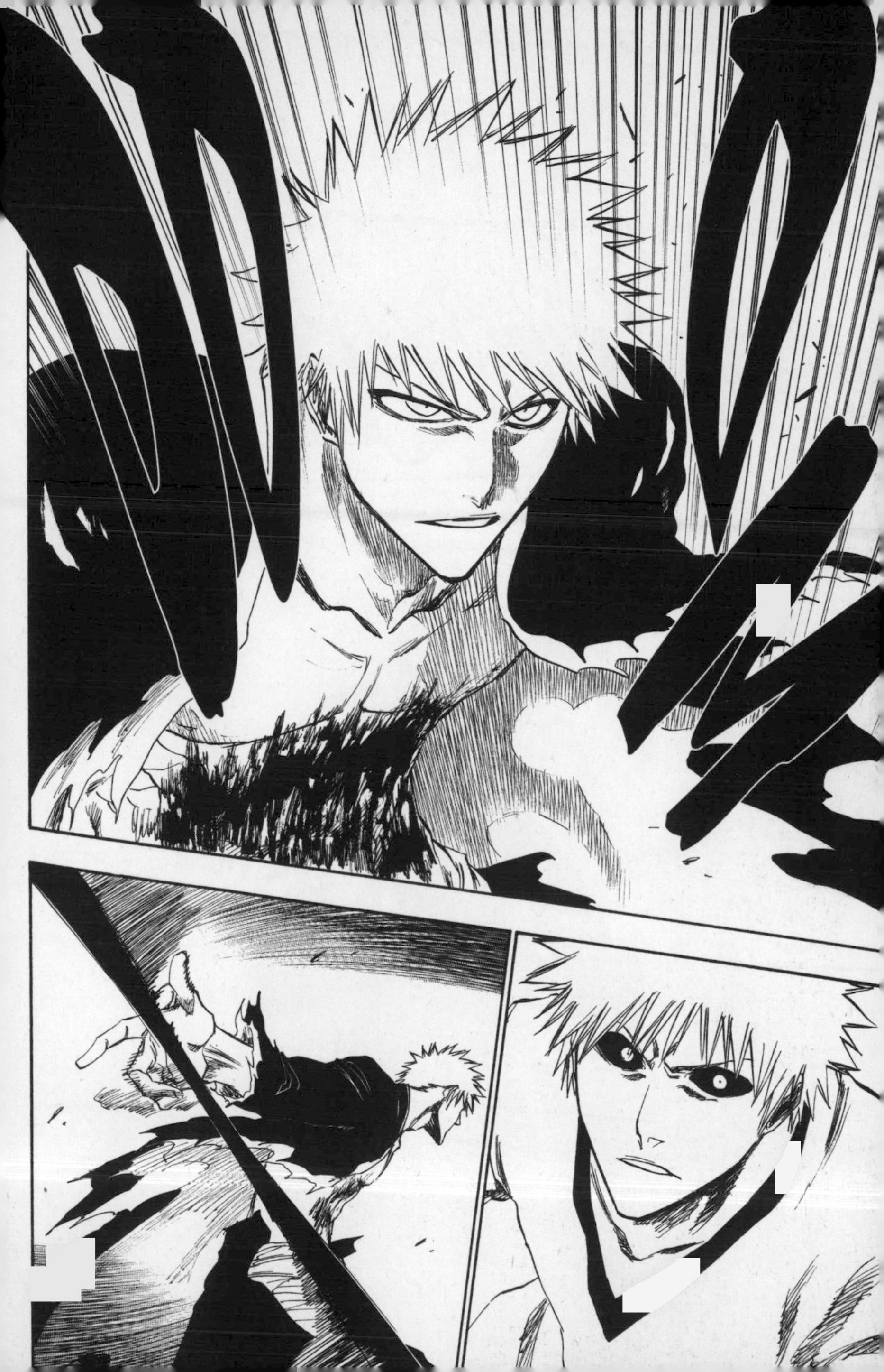

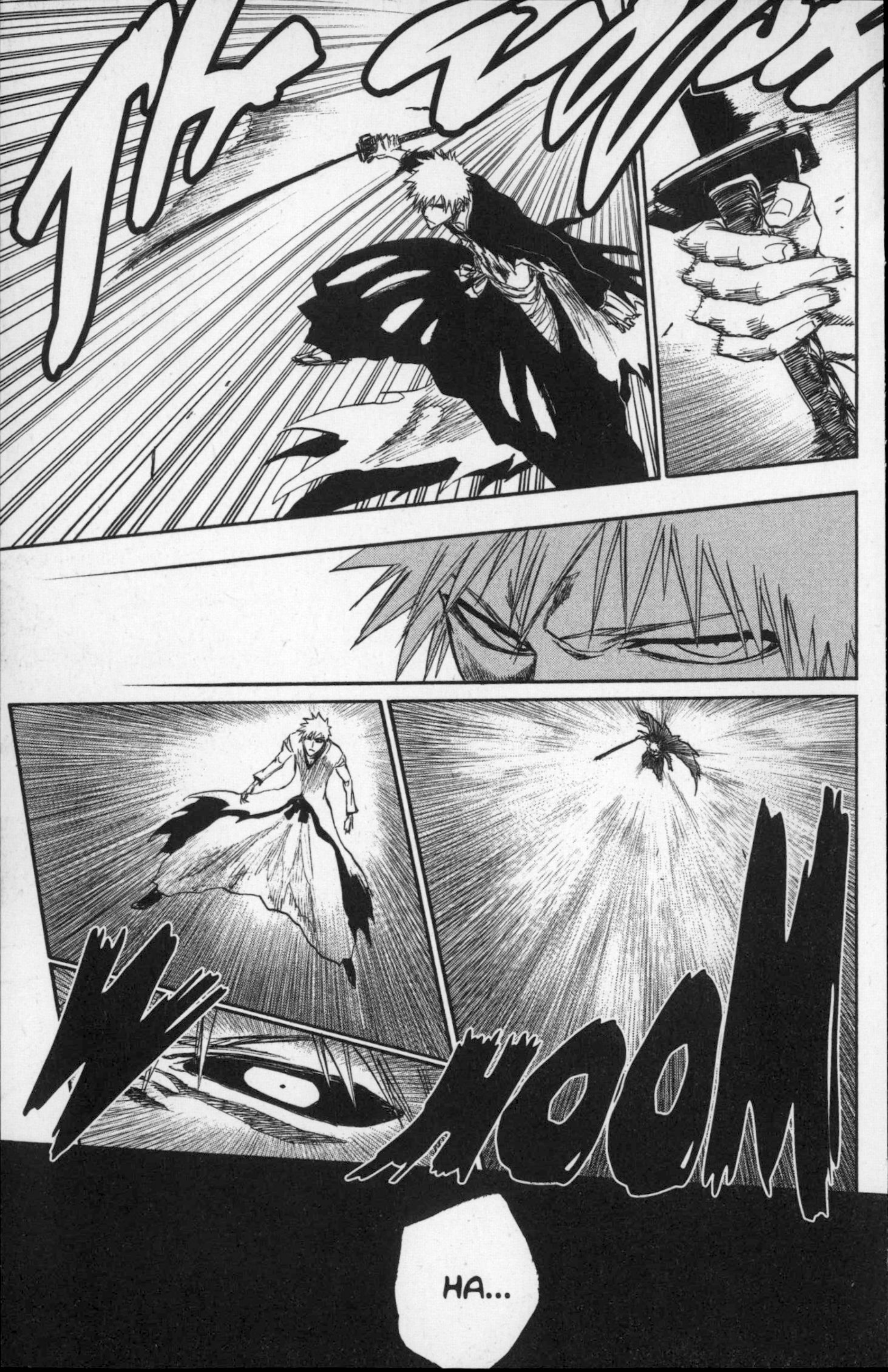
HA...

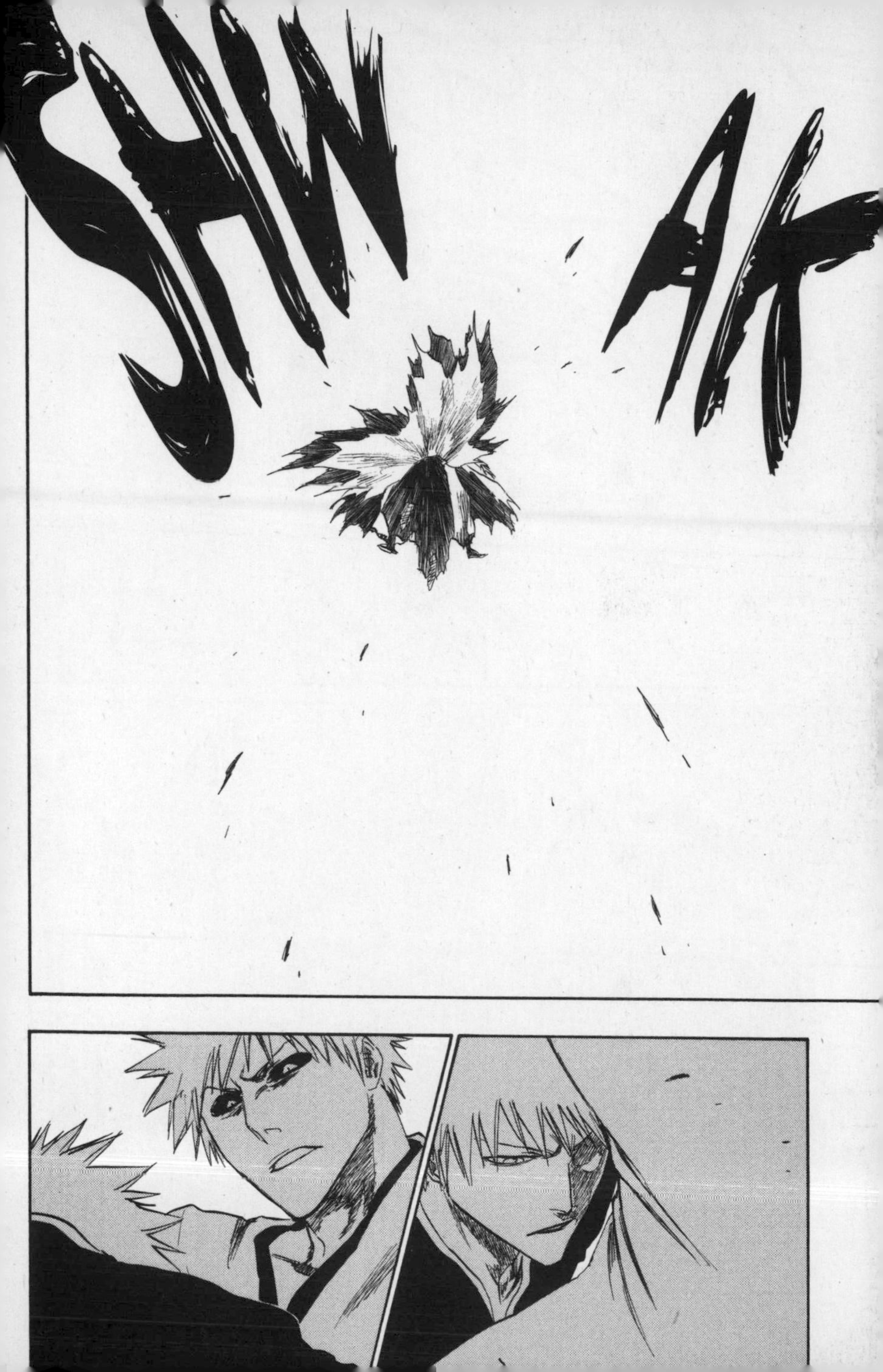
SHWAK

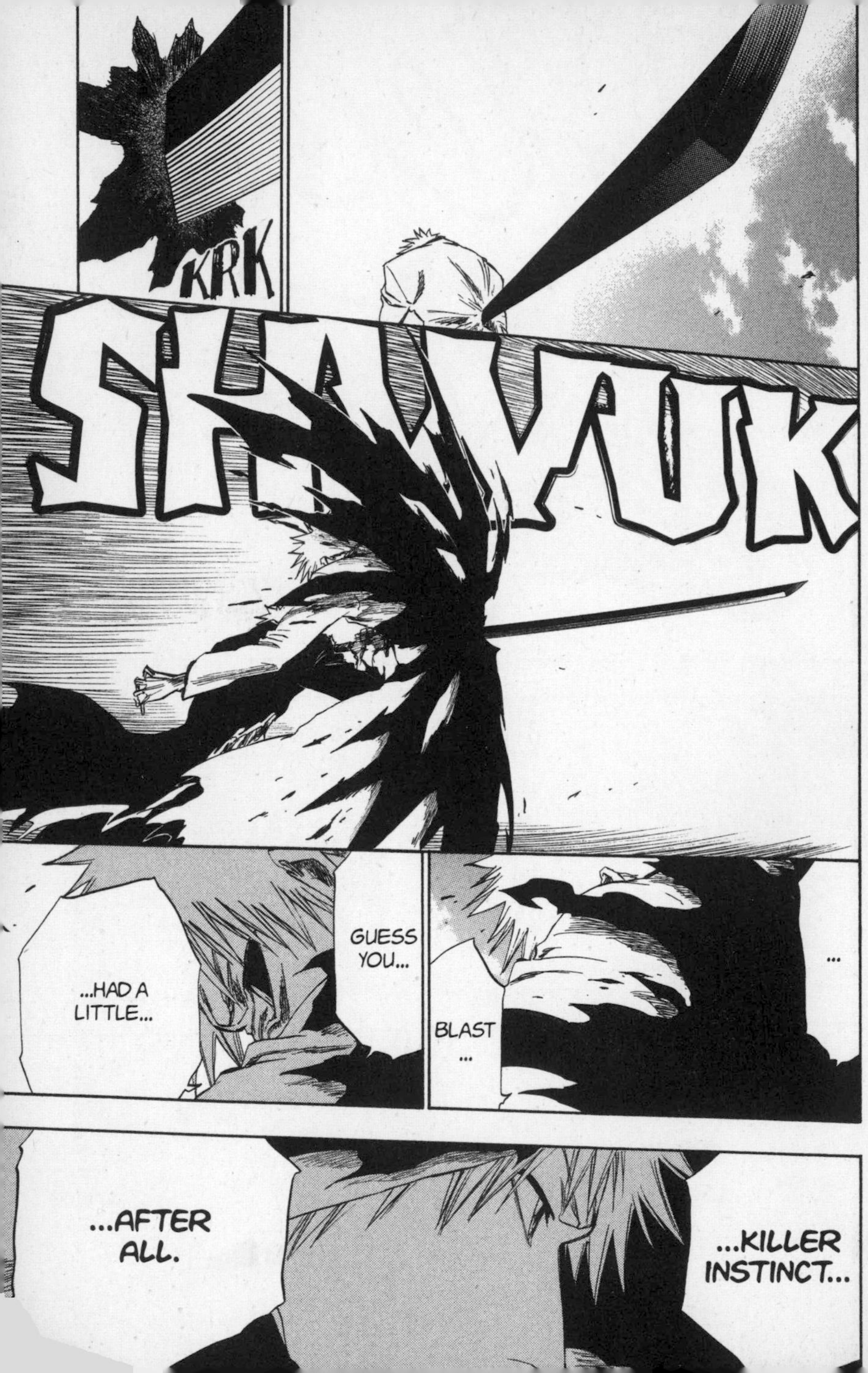
KRK
SHUVUK
...
BLAST ...
GUESS YOU...
...HAD A LITTLE...
...KILLER INSTINCT...
...AFTER ALL.

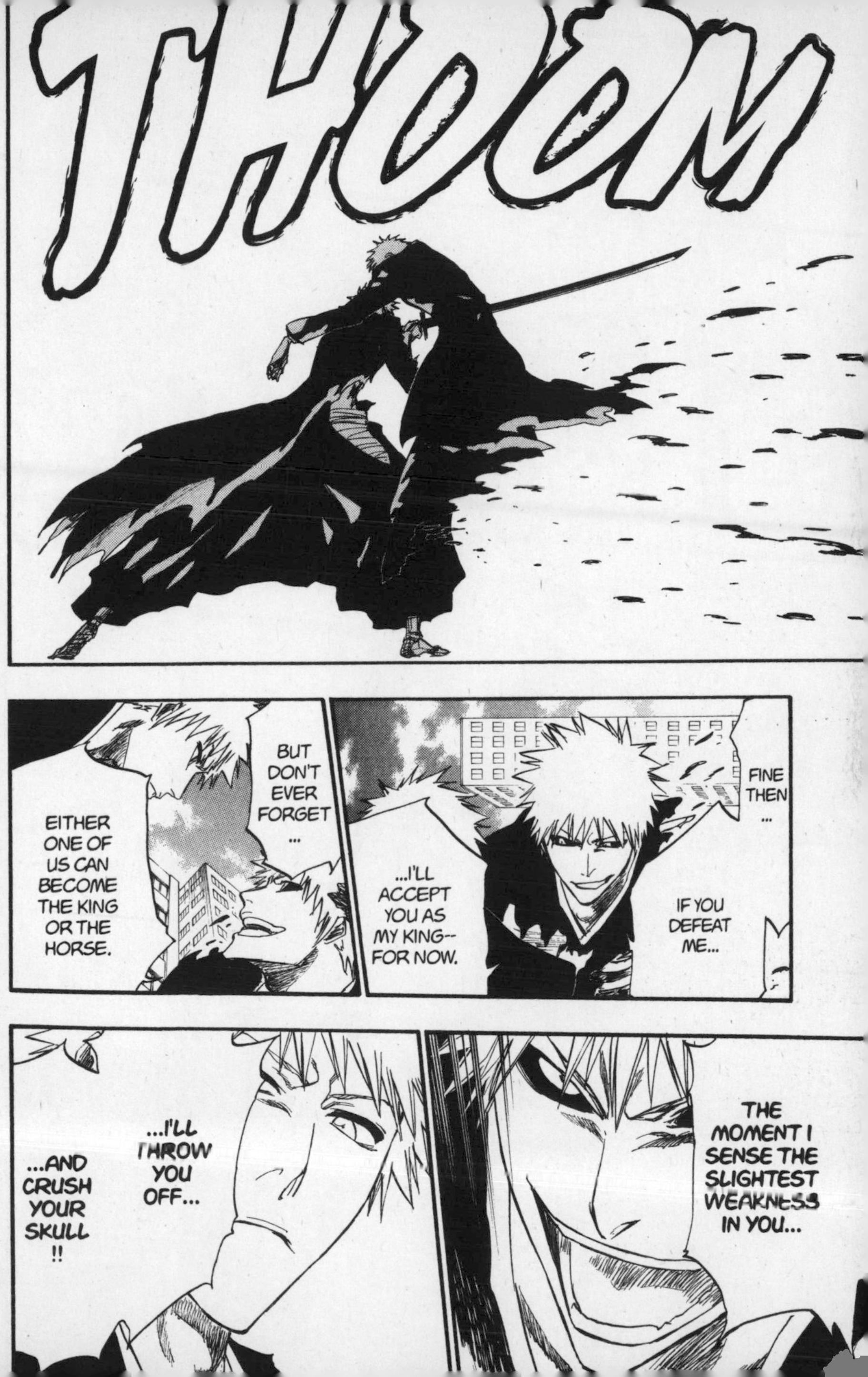
THOOM
FINE THEN ...
IF YOU DEFEAT ME...
...I'LL ACCEPT YOU AS MY KING-- FOR NOW.
BUT DON'T EVER FORGET ...
EITHER ONE OF US CAN BECOME THE KING OR THE HORSE.
THE MOMENT I SENSE THE SLIGHTEST WEAKNESS IN YOU...
...I'LL THROW YOU OFF...
...AND CRUSH YOUR SKULL !!

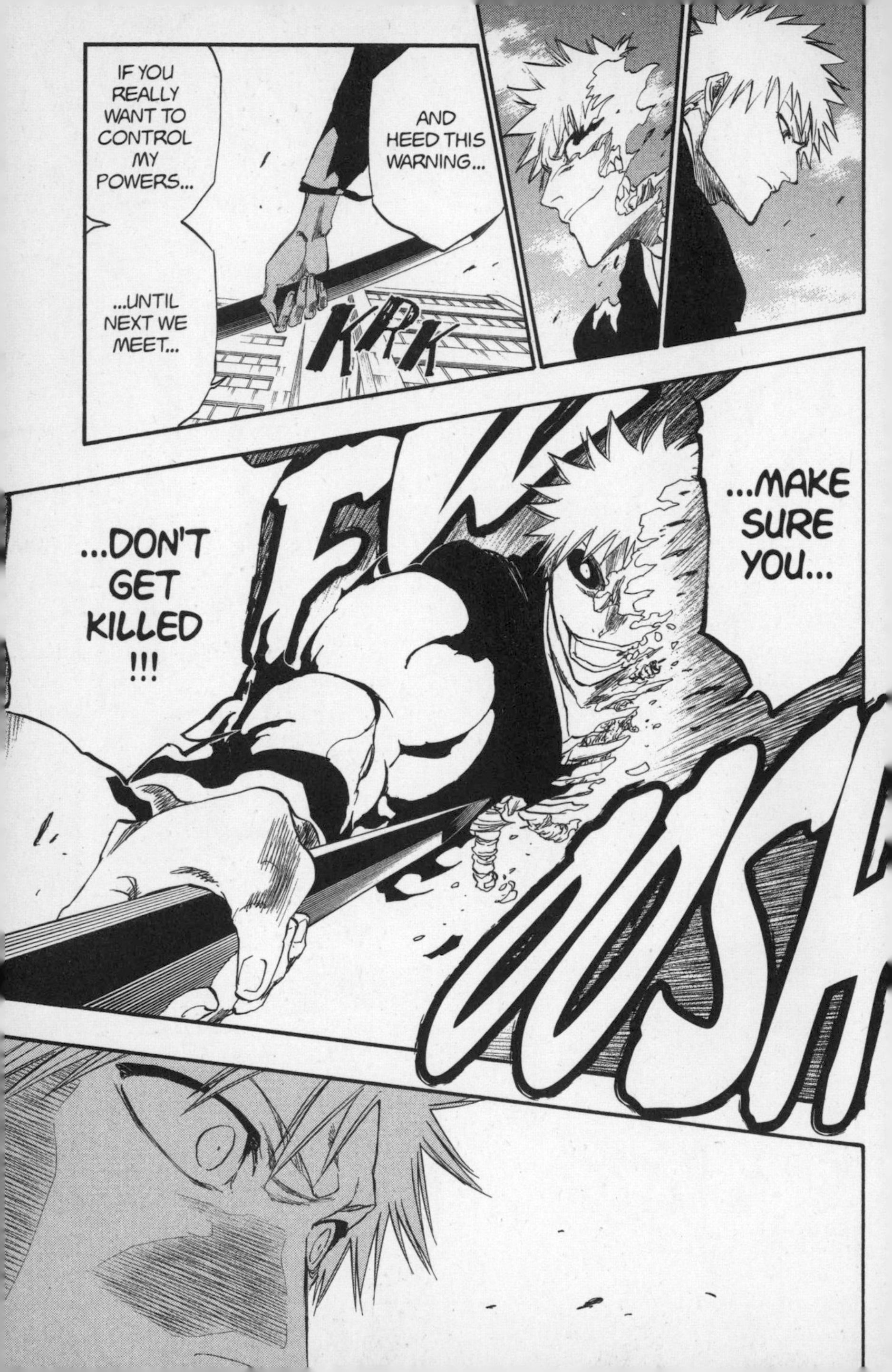
IF YOU REALLY WANT TO CONTROL MY POWERS...
AND HEED THIS WARNING...
KRK
...UNTIL NEXT WE MEET...
...MAKE SURE YOU...
...DON'T GET KILLED!!!

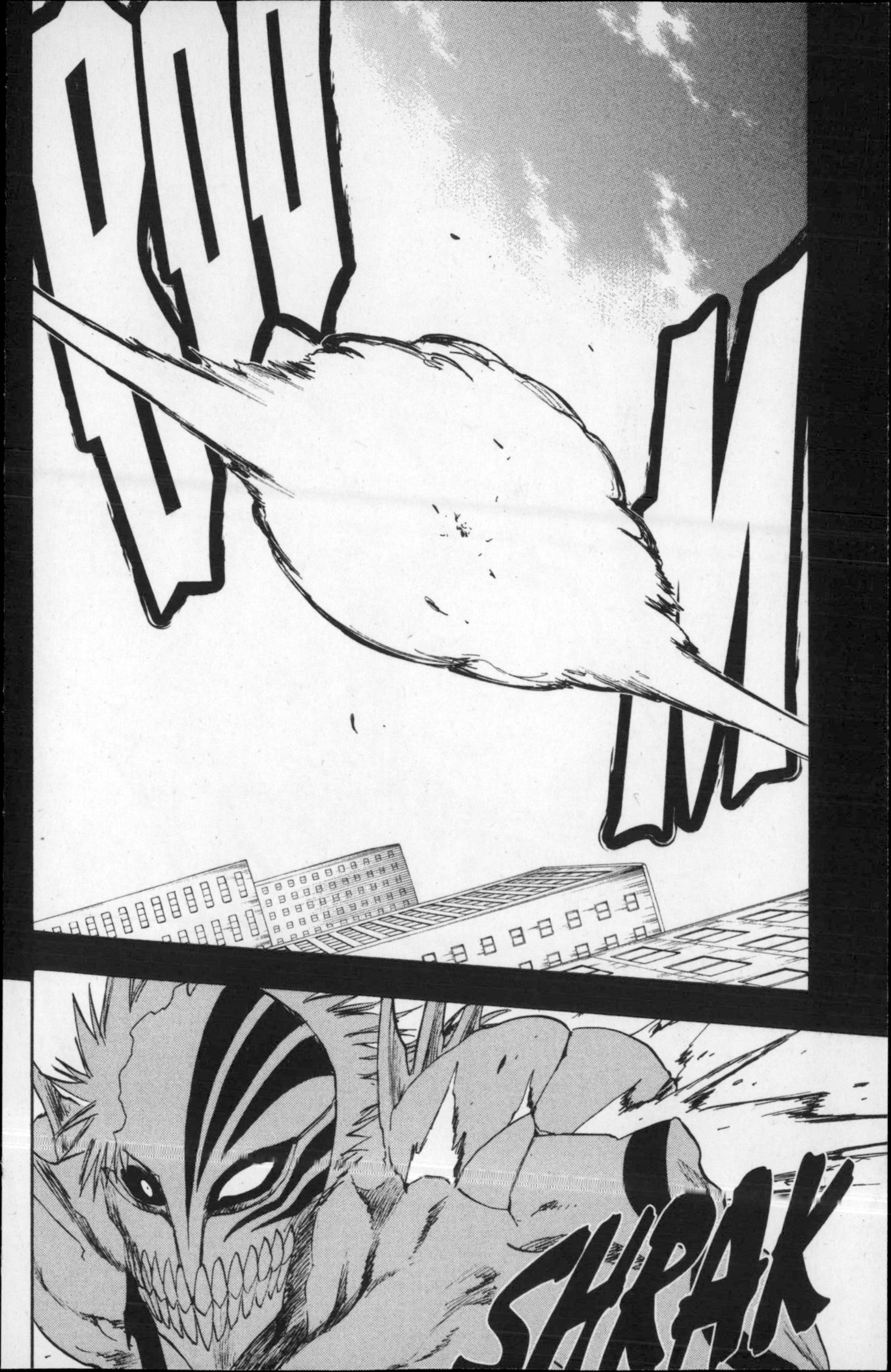
SHRAK

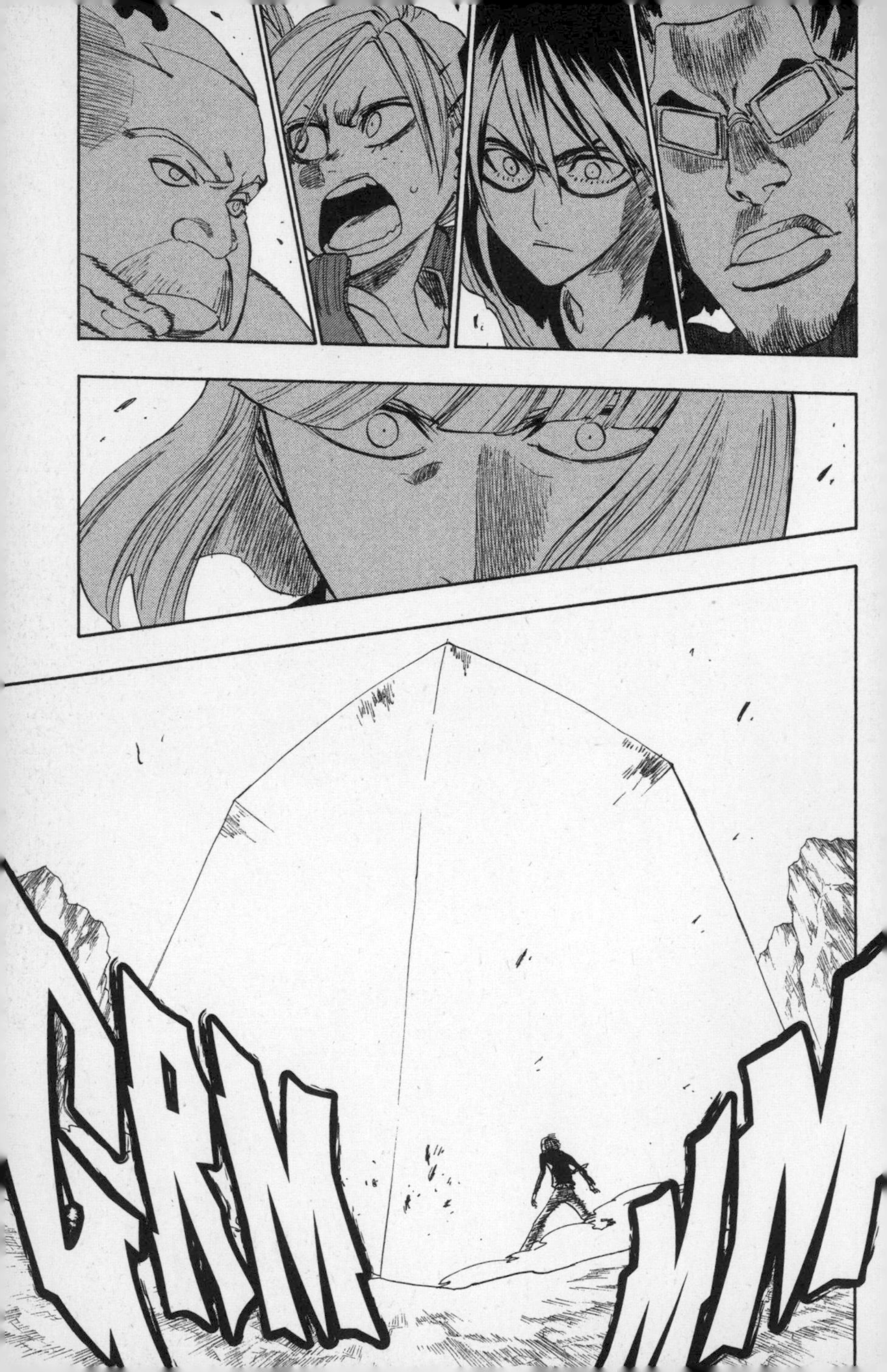

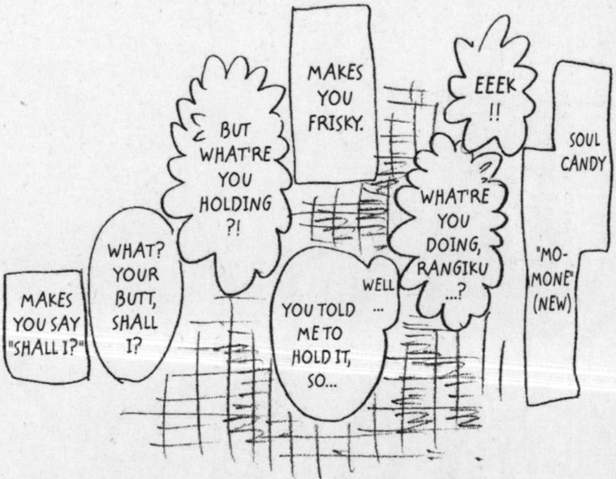
SOUL CANDY
"MO-MONE" (NEW)
EEEK!!
MAKES YOU FRISKY.
BUT WHAT'RE YOU HOLDING?!
WHAT'RE YOU DOING, RANGIKU...?
WELL...
YOU TOLD ME TO HOLD IT, SO...
WHAT? YOUR BUTT, SHALL I?
MAKES YOU SAY "SHALL I?"
CENSORED

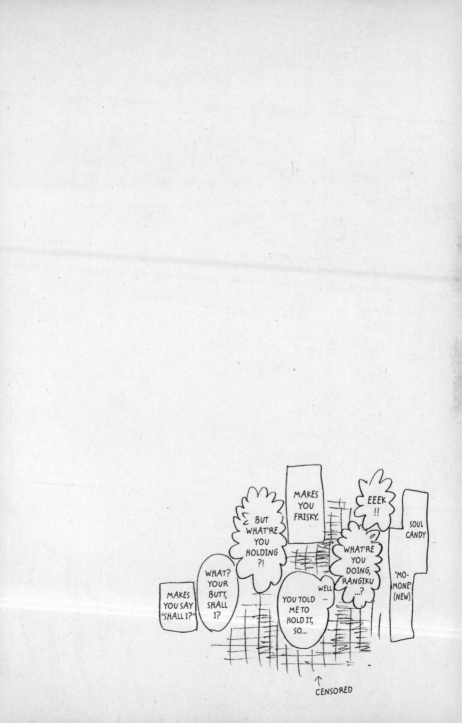

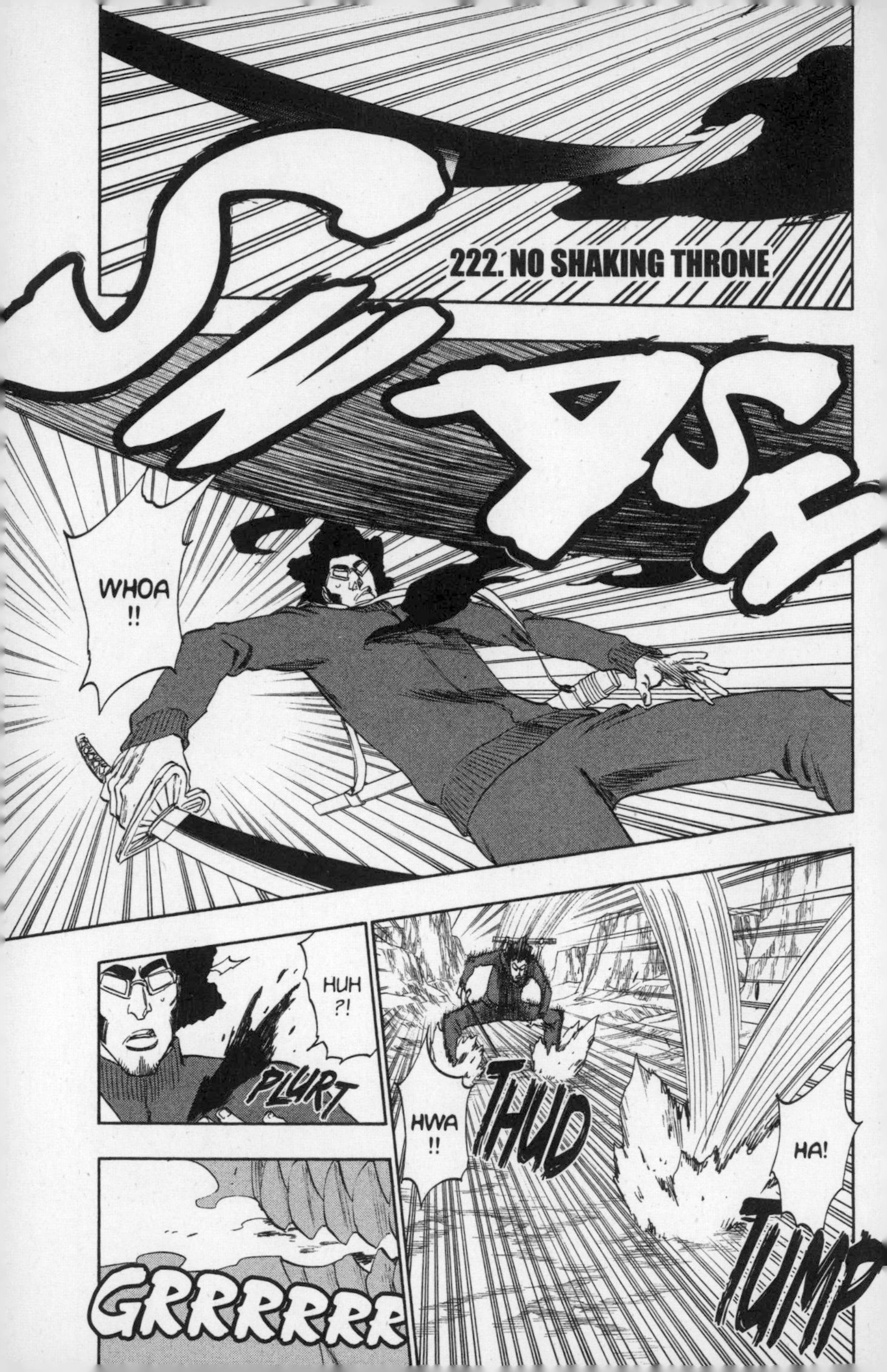
222. NO SHAKING THRONE
SWASH
WHOA !!
THUD
HWA !!
HA!
TUMP
HUH ?!
PLURT
GRRRRRRR

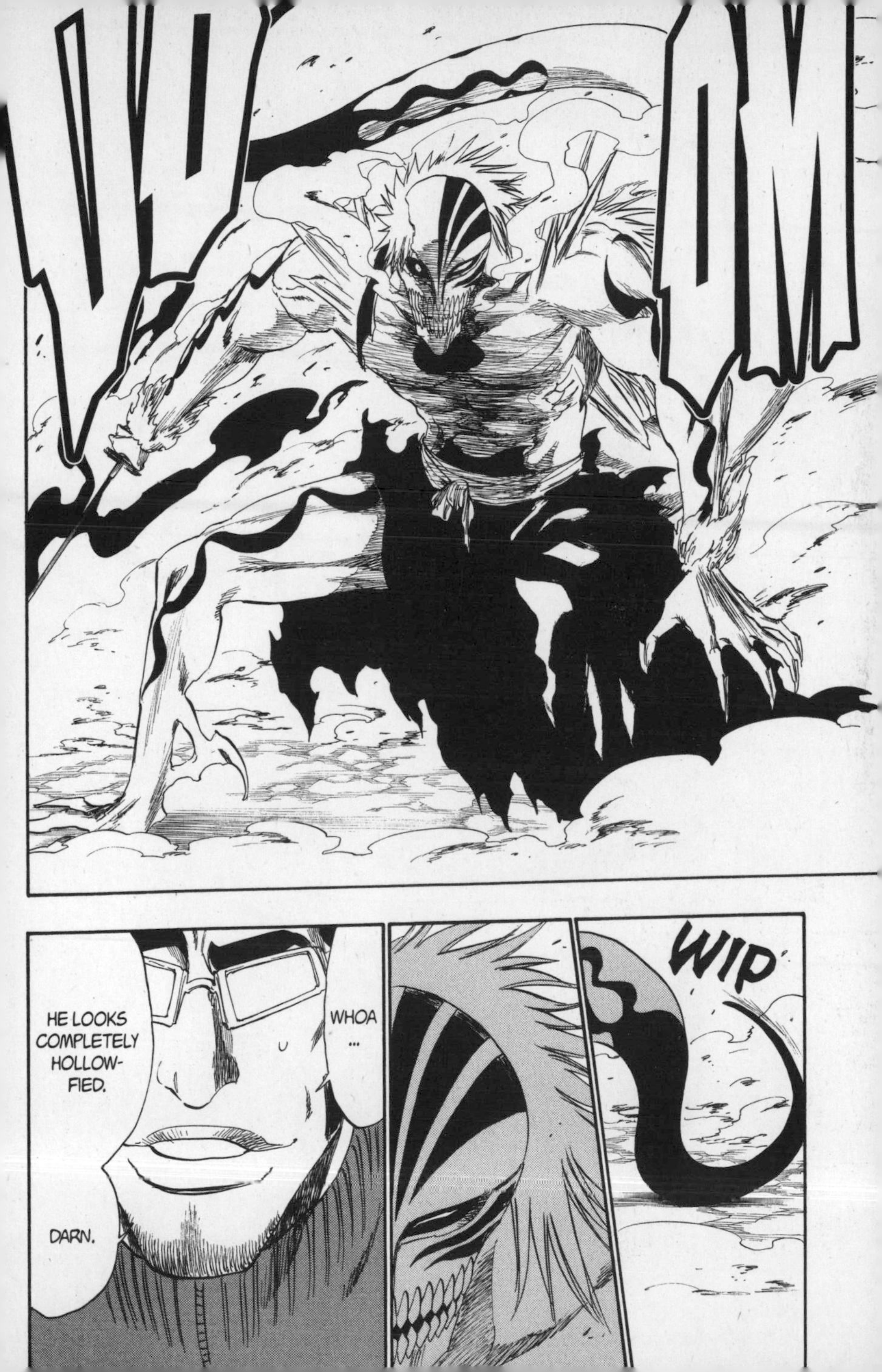
WIP
WHOA ...
HE LOOKS COMPLETELY HOLLOW-FIED.
DARN.

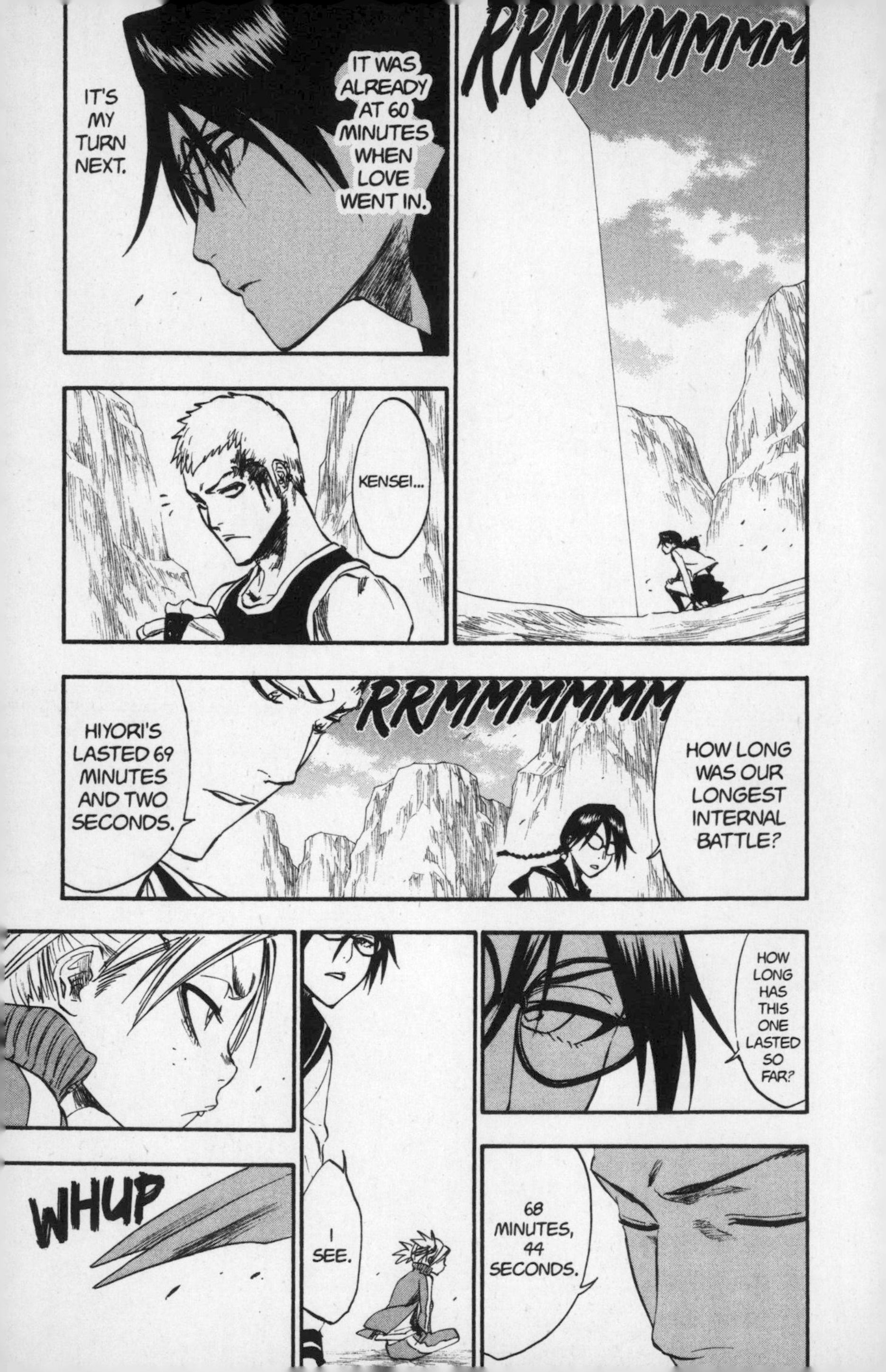
RRMMMMMMMM
IT WAS ALREADY AT 60 MINUTES WHEN LOVE WENT IN.
IT'S MY TURN NEXT.
KENSEI...
RRMMMMMMM
HOW LONG WAS OUR LONGEST INTERNAL BATTLE?
HIYORI'S LASTED 69 MINUTES AND TWO SECONDS.
HOW LONG HAS THIS ONE LASTED SO FAR?
68 MINUTES, 44 SECONDS.
I SEE.
WHUP

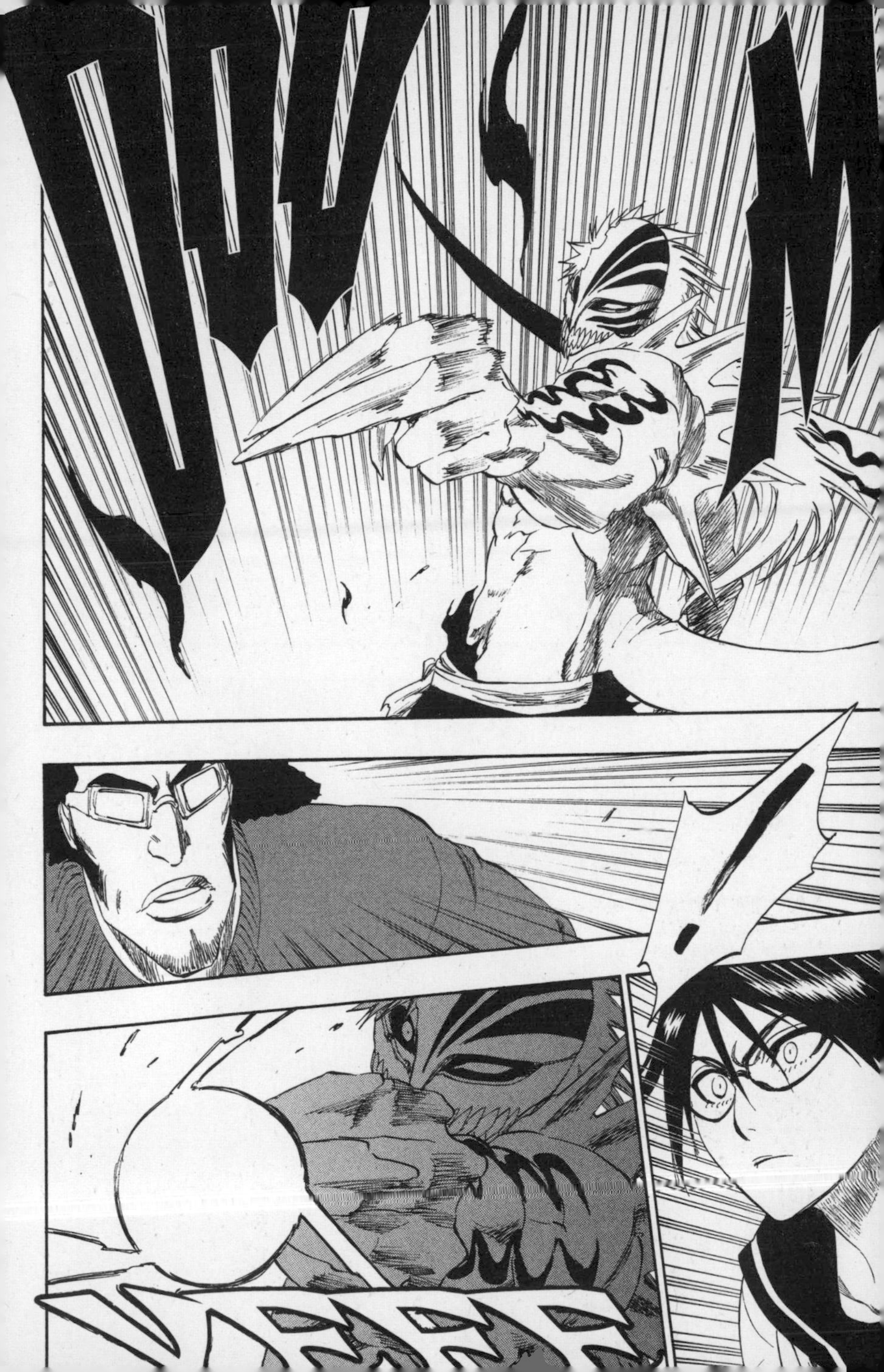

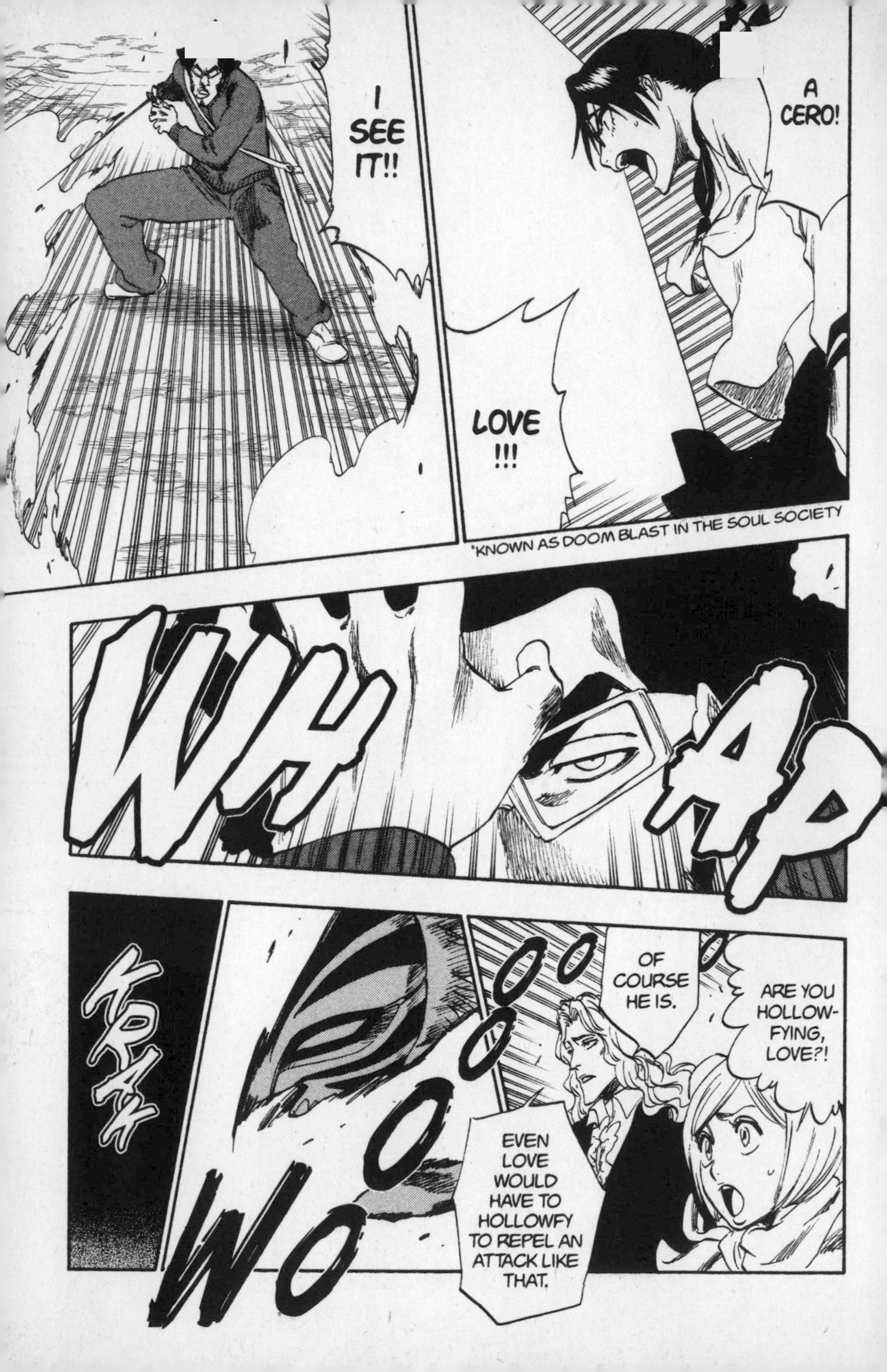
A CERO!
LOVE !!!
*KNOWN AS DOOM BLAST IN THE SOUL SOCIETY
I SEE IT!!
WHAP
ARE YOU HOLLOW-FYING, LOVE?!
OF COURSE HE IS.
EVEN LOVE WOULD HAVE TO HOLLOWFY TO REPEL AN ATTACK LIKE THAT.
WOOOOOO
KRAK

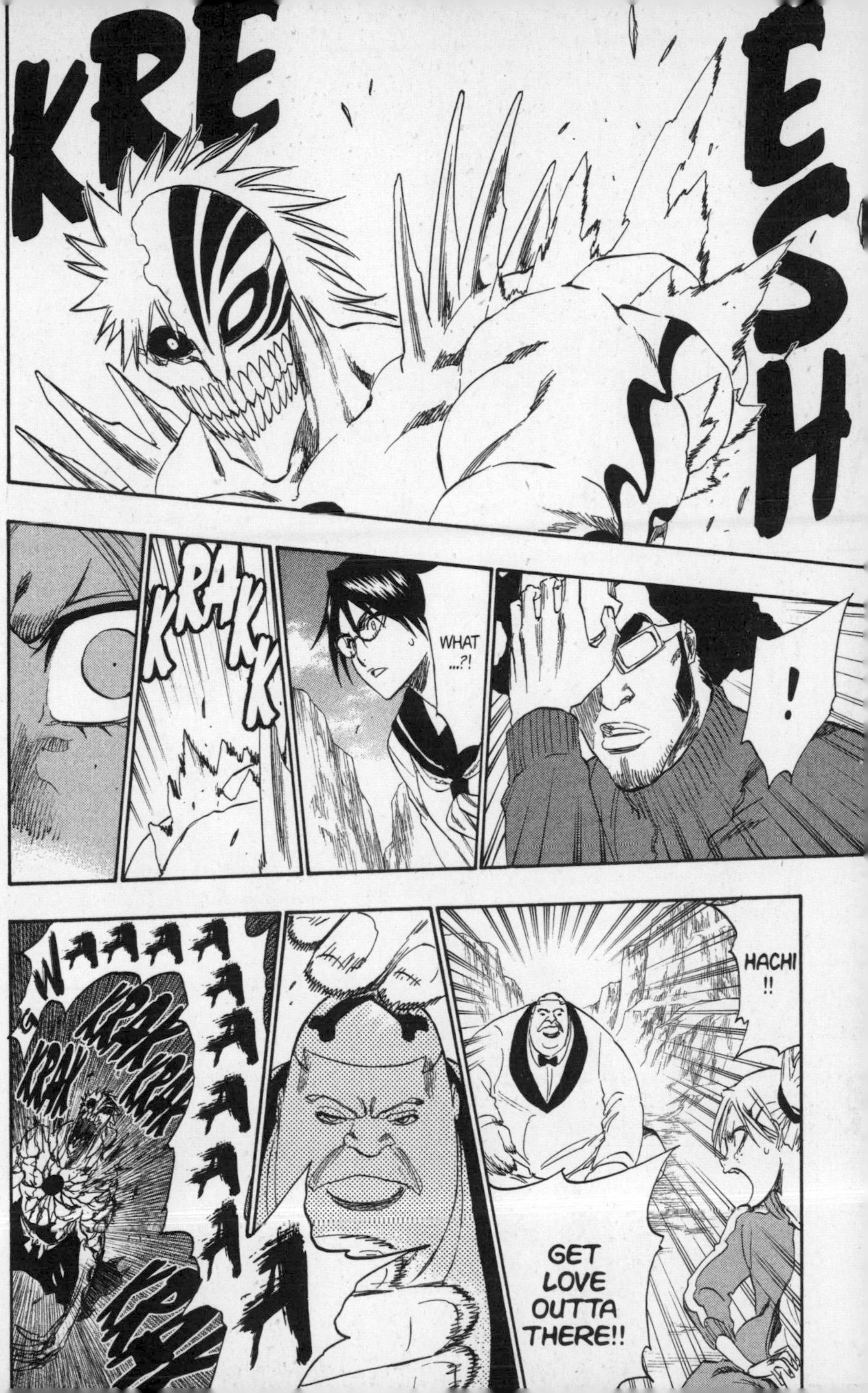
KREESH
!
WHAT ...?!
KRAKK
HACHI !!
GET LOVE OUTTA THERE!!
WAAAA
KRAK KRAK KRAK

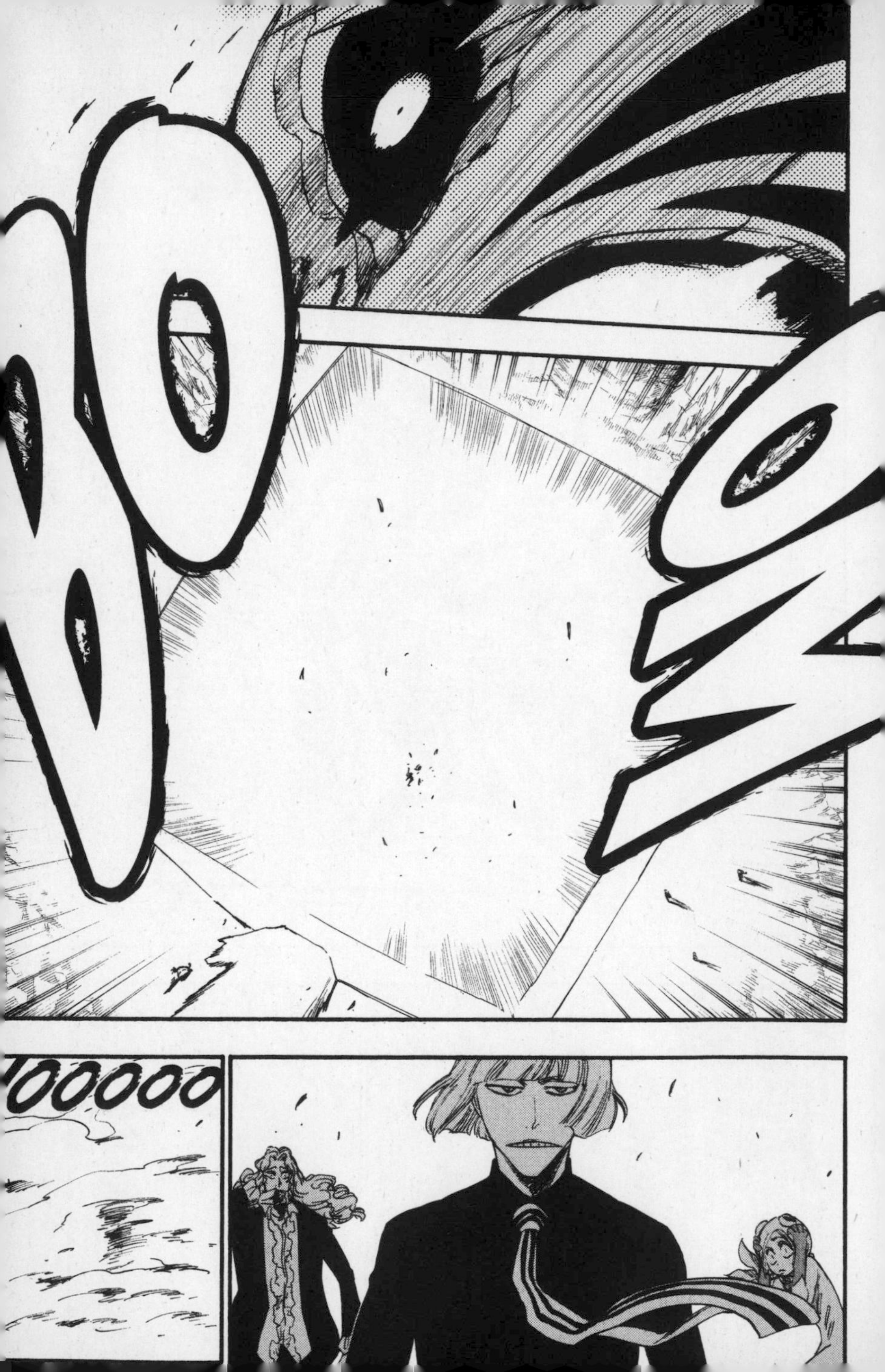
OOOOOO

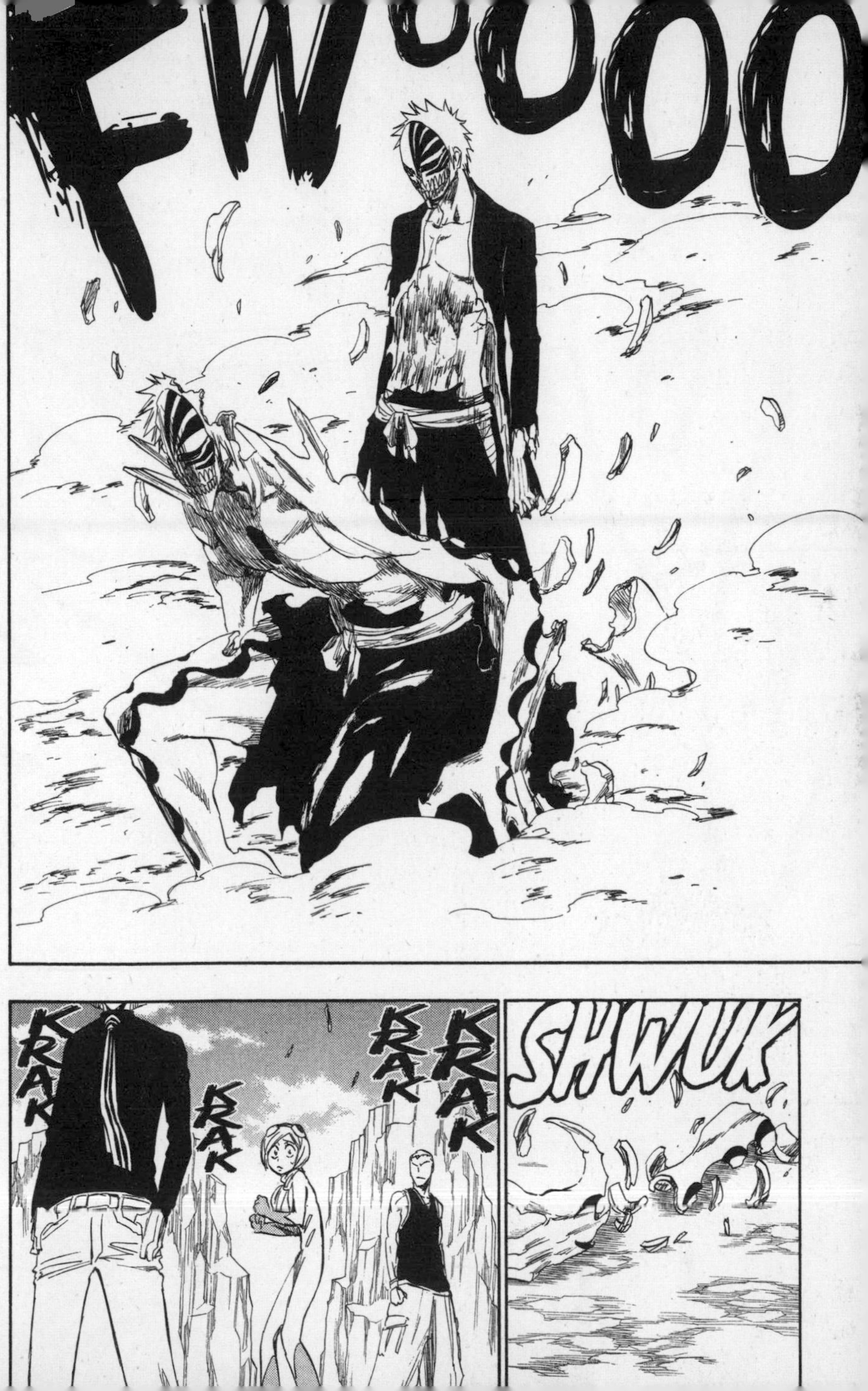
FWOOOO
SHWUK
KRAK
KRAK
KRAK
KRAK

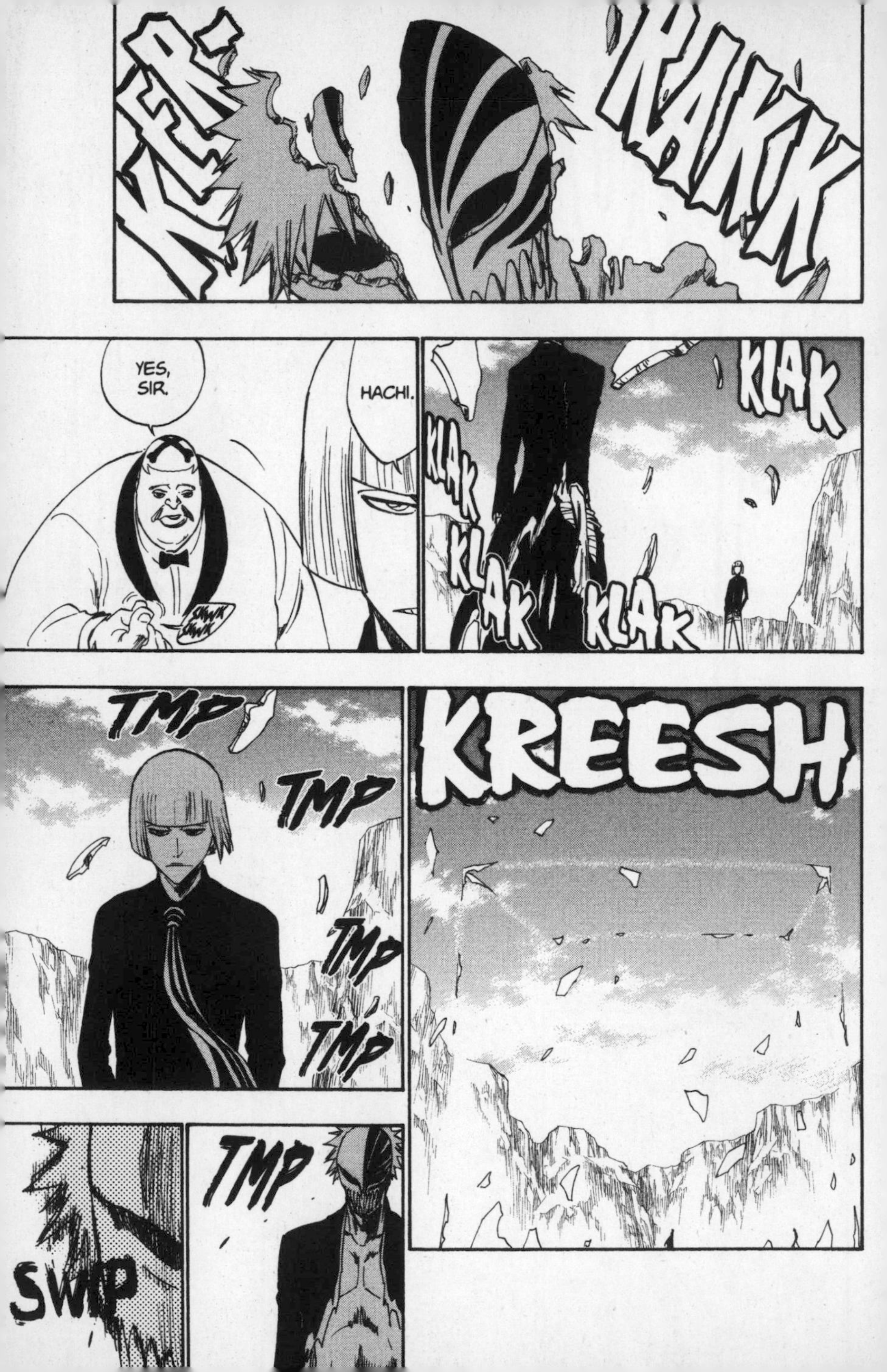
CR
RAKK
KLAK
KLAK
KLAK
KLAK
KLAK
HACHI.
YES, SIR.
KREESH
TMP
TMP
TMP
TMP
TMP
SWP

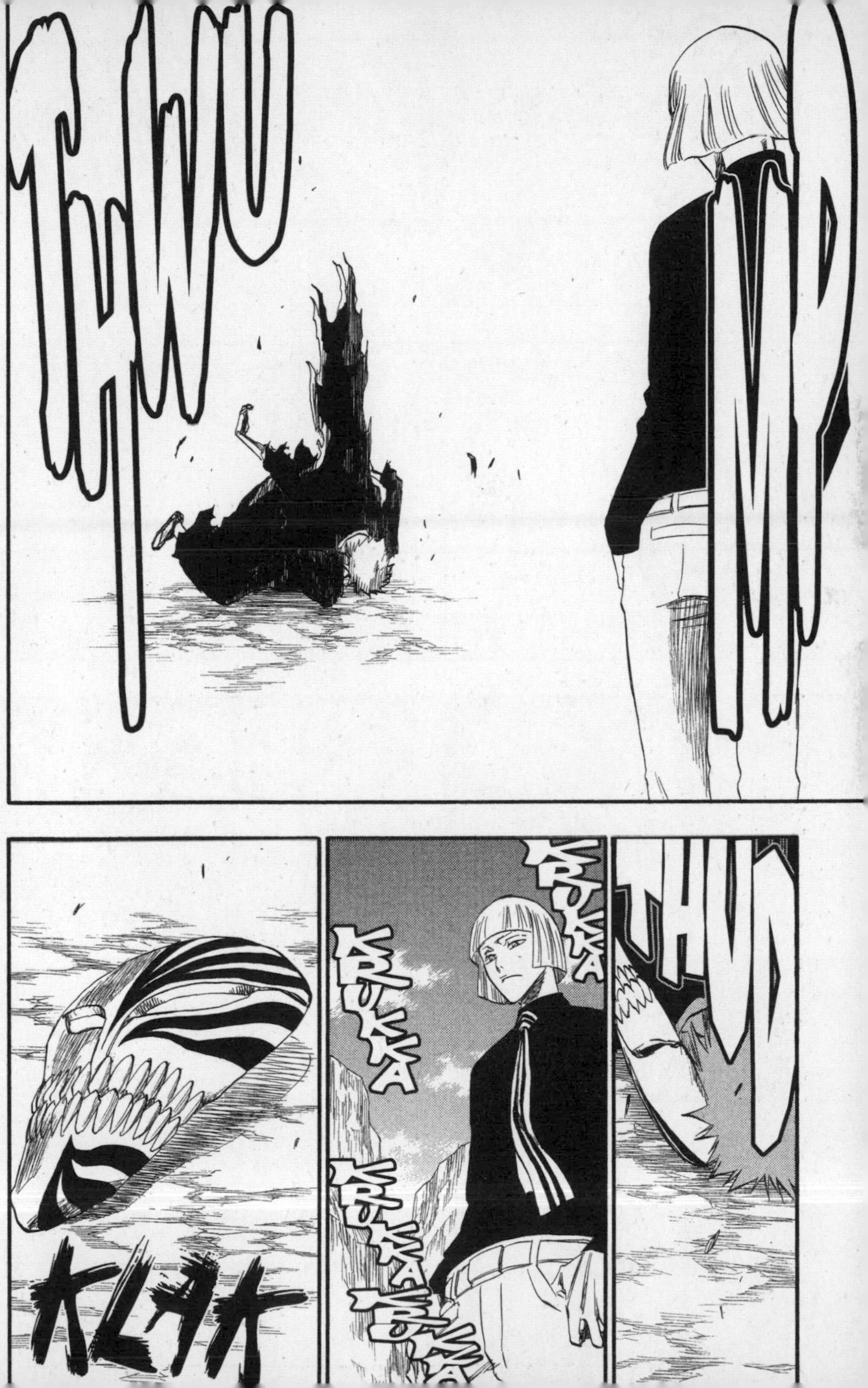
THWUMP
THUD
KRUKKA
KRUKKA
KRUKKA
KRUKKA
KLAK

READ THIS WAY

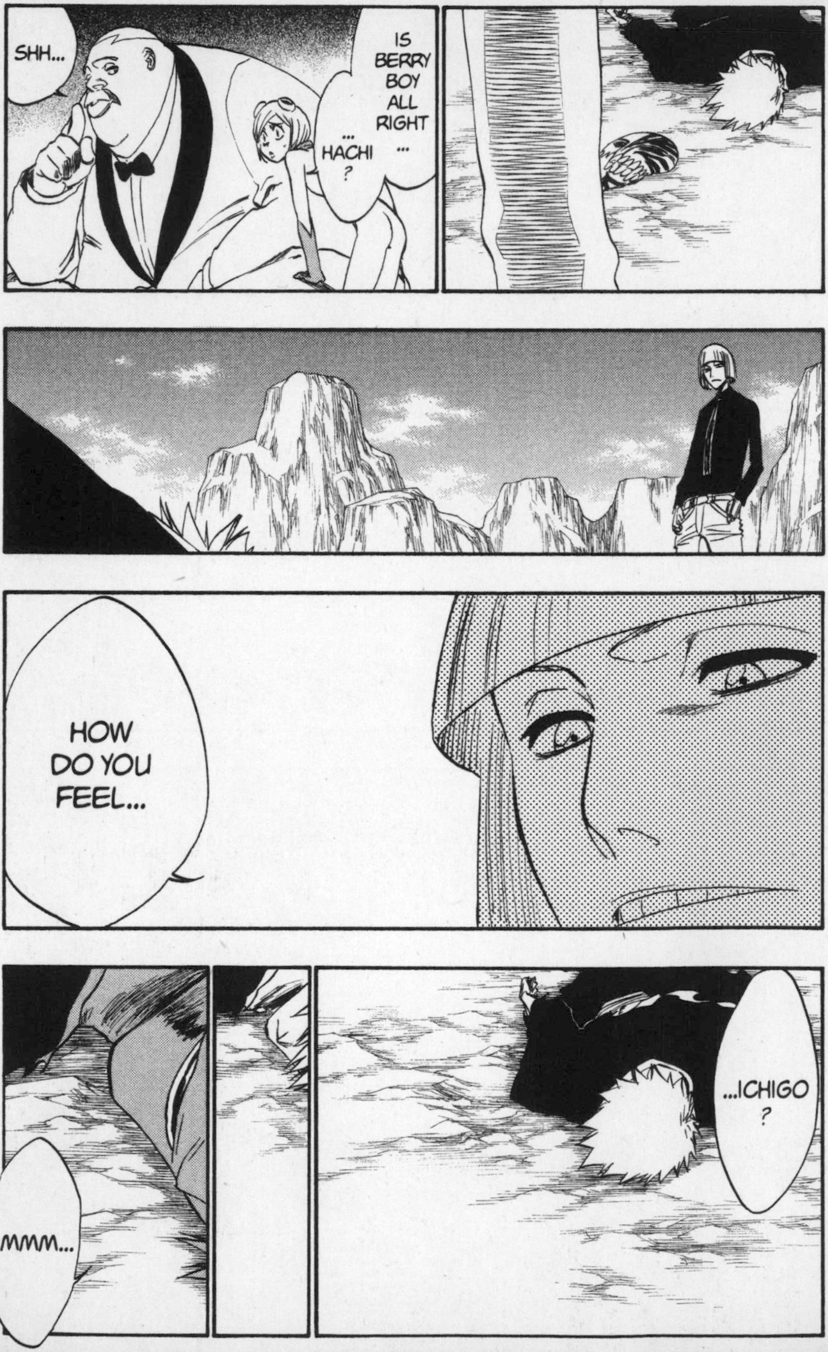
IS BERRY BOY ALL RIGHT ... ...HACHI ?
SHH...
HOW DO YOU FEEL...
...ICHIGO ?
MMM...

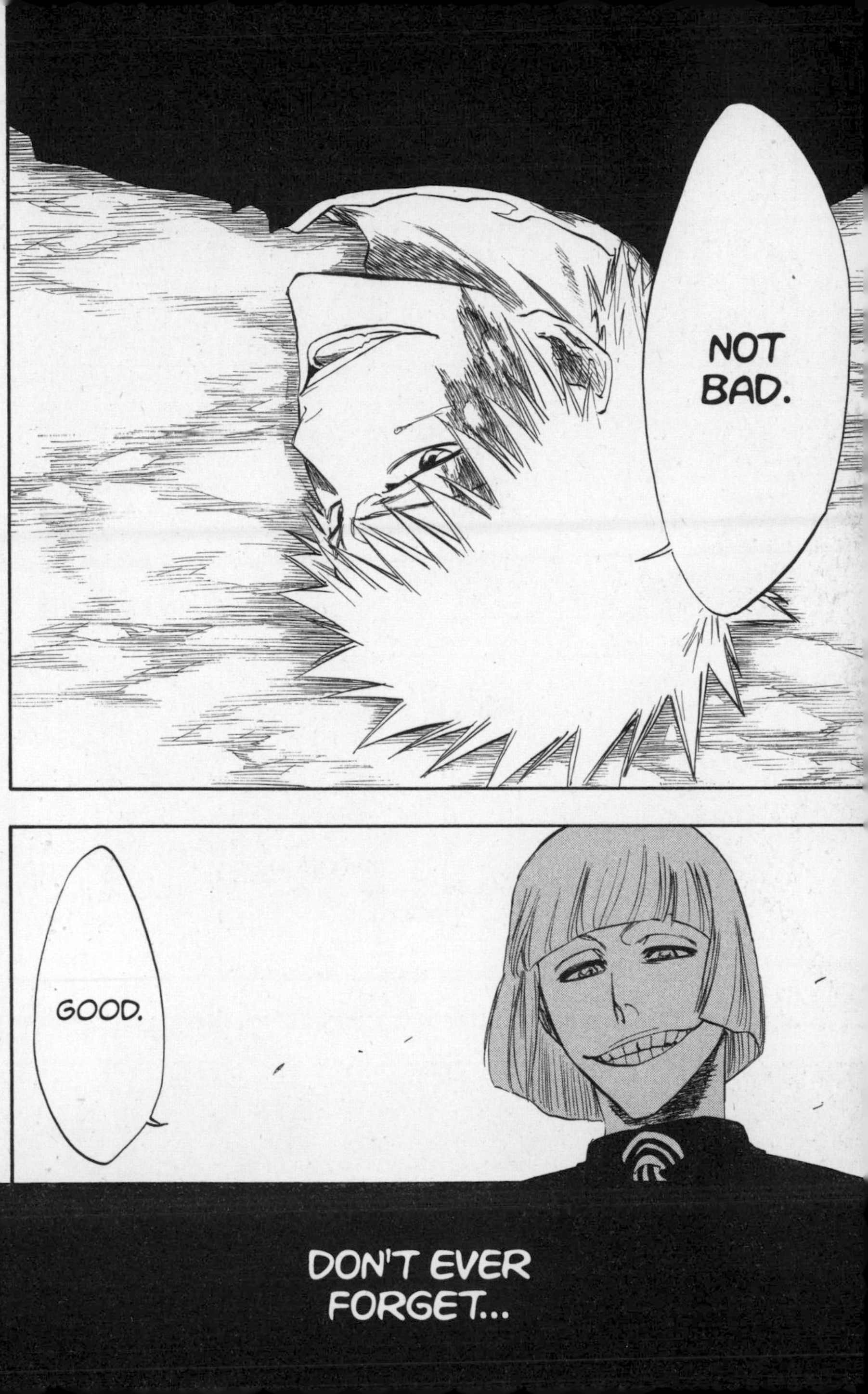
NOT BAD.
GOOD.
DON'T EVER FORGET...

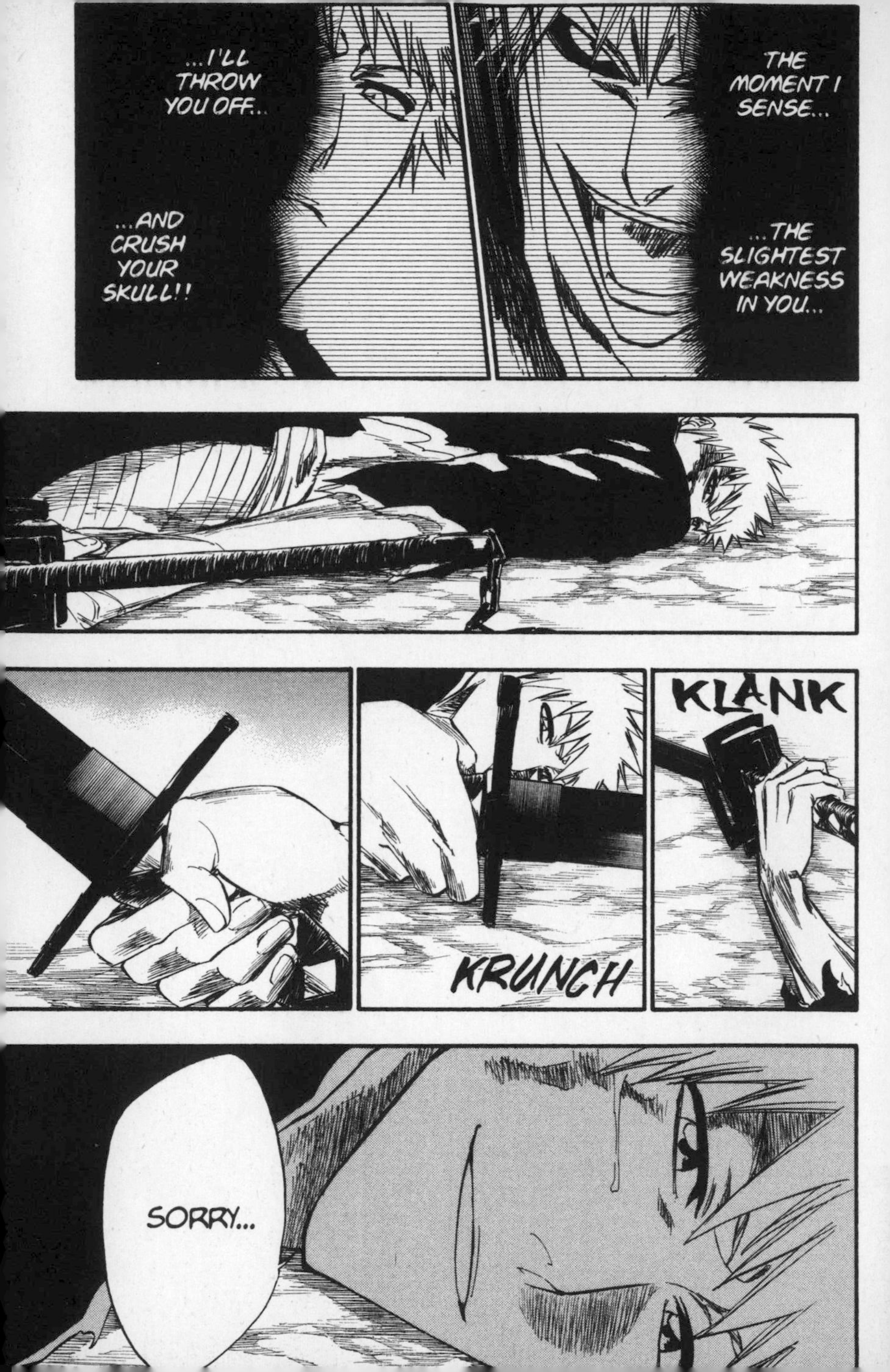
THE MOMENT I SENSE...
...THE SLIGHTEST WEAKNESS IN YOU...
...I'LL THROW YOU OFF...
...AND CRUSH YOUR SKULL!!
KLANK
KRUNCH
SORRY...

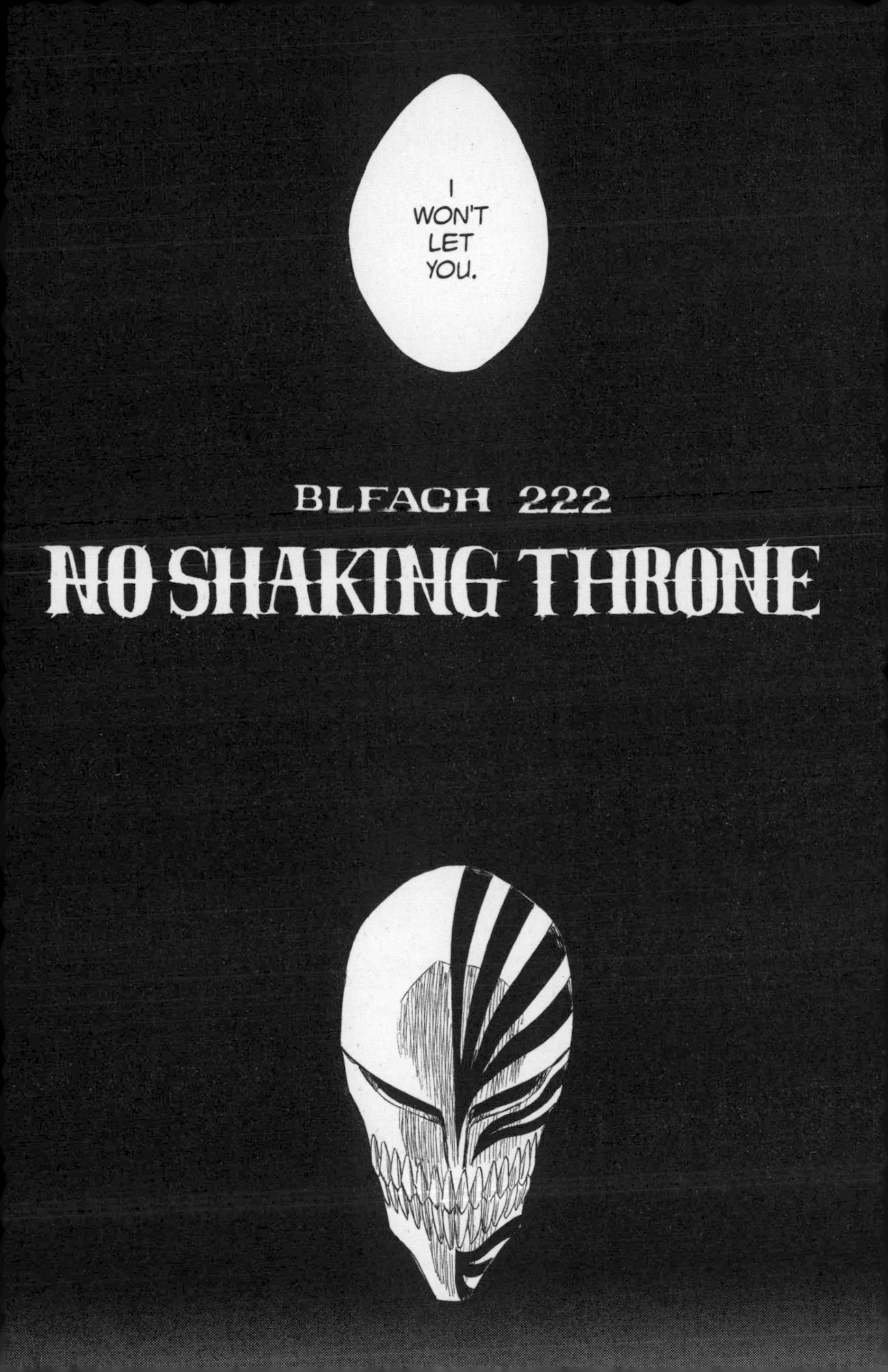
I WON'T LET YOU.
BLEACH 222
NO SHAKING THRONE

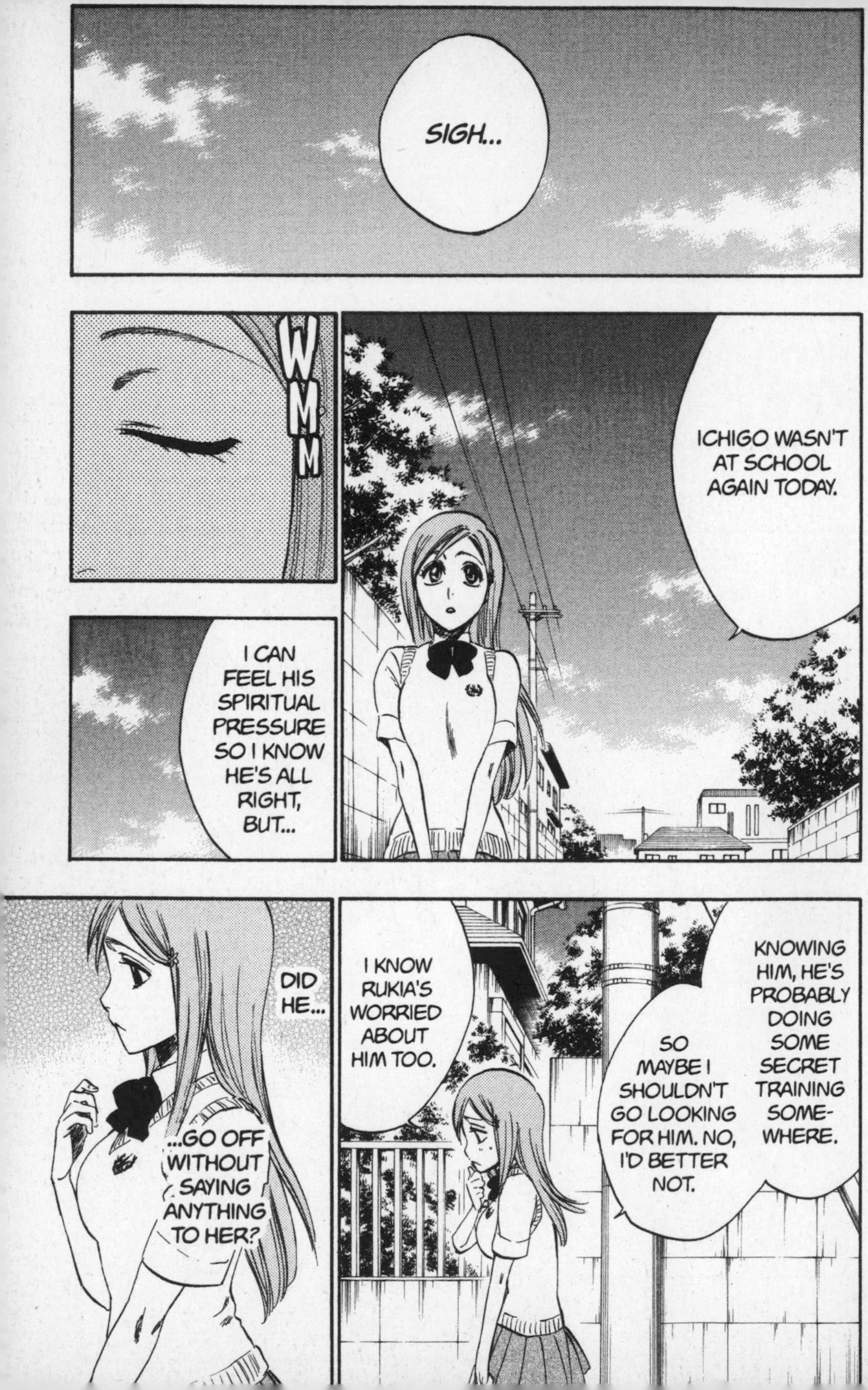
SIGH...
ICHIGO WASN'T AT SCHOOL AGAIN TODAY.
WMM
I CAN FEEL HIS SPIRITUAL PRESSURE SO I KNOW HE'S ALL RIGHT, BUT...
KNOWING HIM, HE'S PROBABLY DOING SOME SECRET TRAINING SOME-WHERE.
SO MAYBE I SHOULDN'T GO LOOKING FOR HIM. NO, I'D BETTER NOT.
I KNOW RUKIA'S WORRIED ABOUT HIM TOO.
DID HE...
...GO OFF WITHOUT SAYING ANYTHING TO HER?

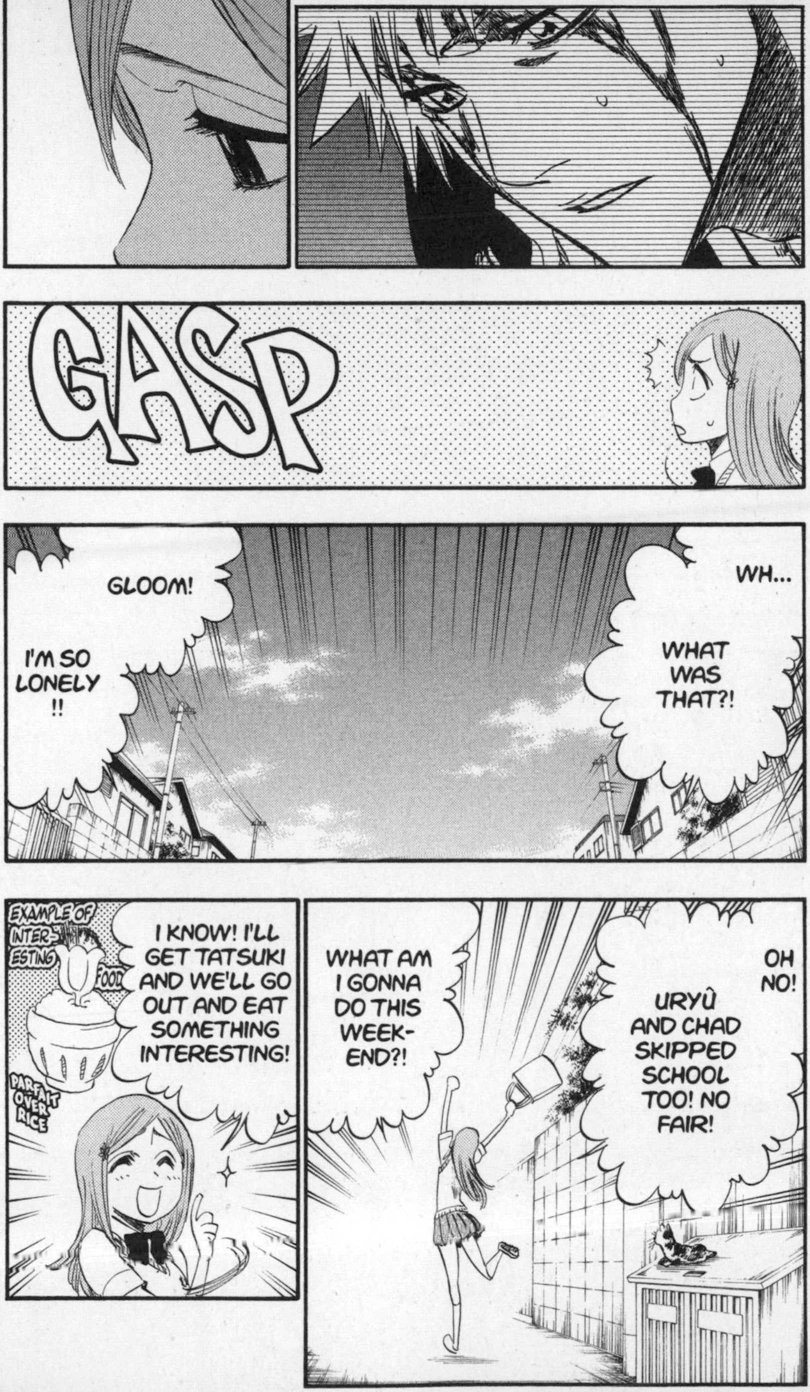
GASP
WH... WHAT WAS THAT?!
GLOOM! I'M SO LONELY!!
OH NO! URYÛ AND CHAD SKIPPED SCHOOL TOO! NO FAIR!
WHAT AM I GONNA DO THIS WEEK-END?!
I KNOW! I'LL GET TATSUKI AND WE'LL GO OUT AND EAT SOMETHING INTERESTING!
EXAMPLE OF INTER-ESTING FOOD
PARFAIT OVER RICE

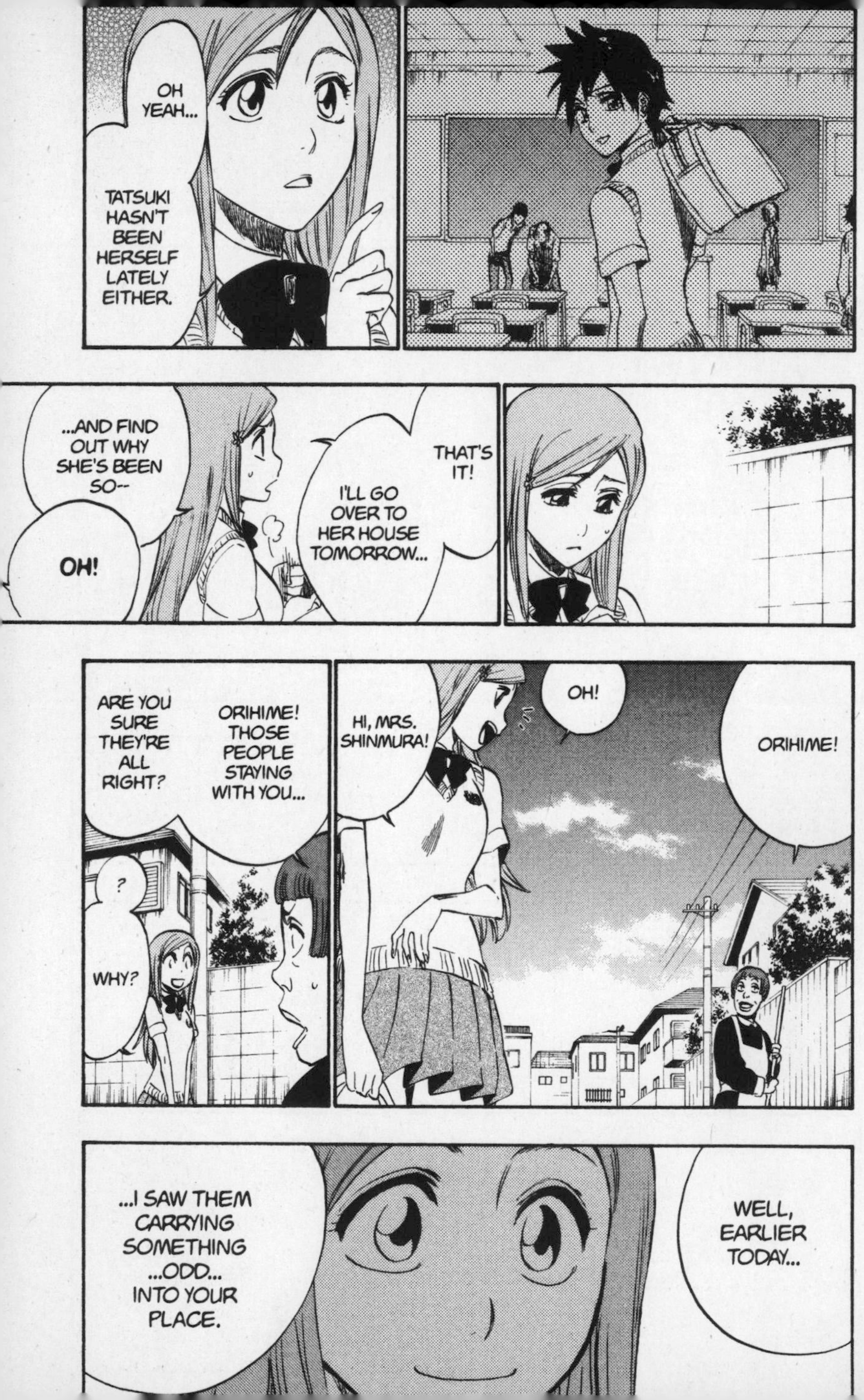
OH YEAH...
TATSUKI HASN'T BEEN HERSELF LATELY EITHER.
THAT'S IT!
I'LL GO OVER TO HER HOUSE TOMORROW...
...AND FIND OUT WHY SHE'S BEEN SO--
OH!
ORIHIME!
OH!
HI, MRS. SHINMURA!
ORIHIME! THOSE PEOPLE STAYING WITH YOU...
ARE YOU SURE THEY'RE ALL RIGHT?
?
WHY?
WELL, EARLIER TODAY...
...I SAW THEM CARRYING SOMETHING ...ODD... INTO YOUR PLACE.

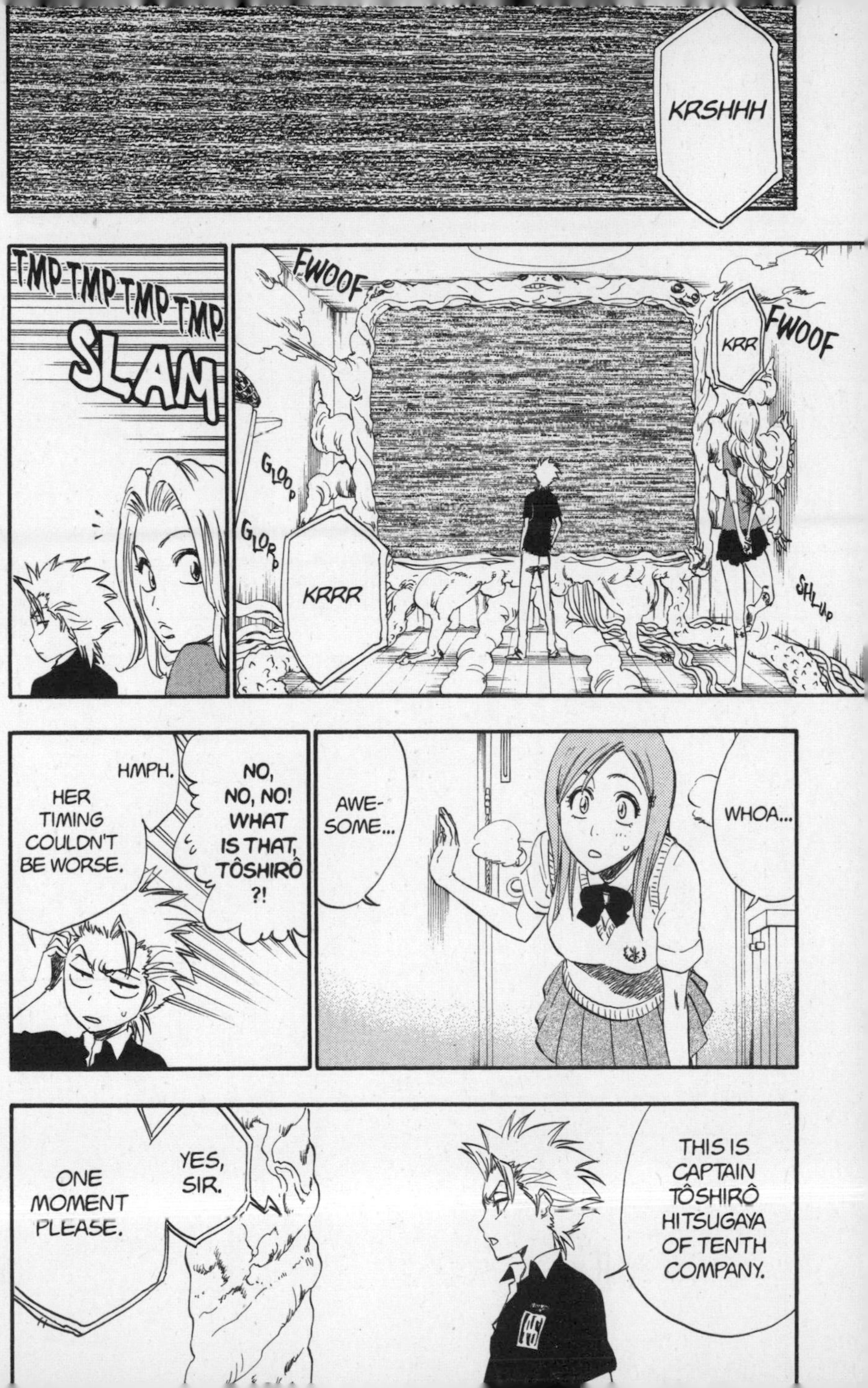
KRSHHH
FWOOF
KRR
FWOOF
GLOOP
GLORP
KRRR
SHLUP
TMP TMP TMP TMP
SLAM
WHOA...
AWE-SOME...
NO, NO, NO! WHAT IS THAT, TÔSHIRÔ?!
HMPH.
HER TIMING COULDN'T BE WORSE.
THIS IS CAPTAIN TÔSHIRÔ HITSUGAYA OF TENTH COMPANY.
YES, SIR.
ONE MOMENT PLEASE.

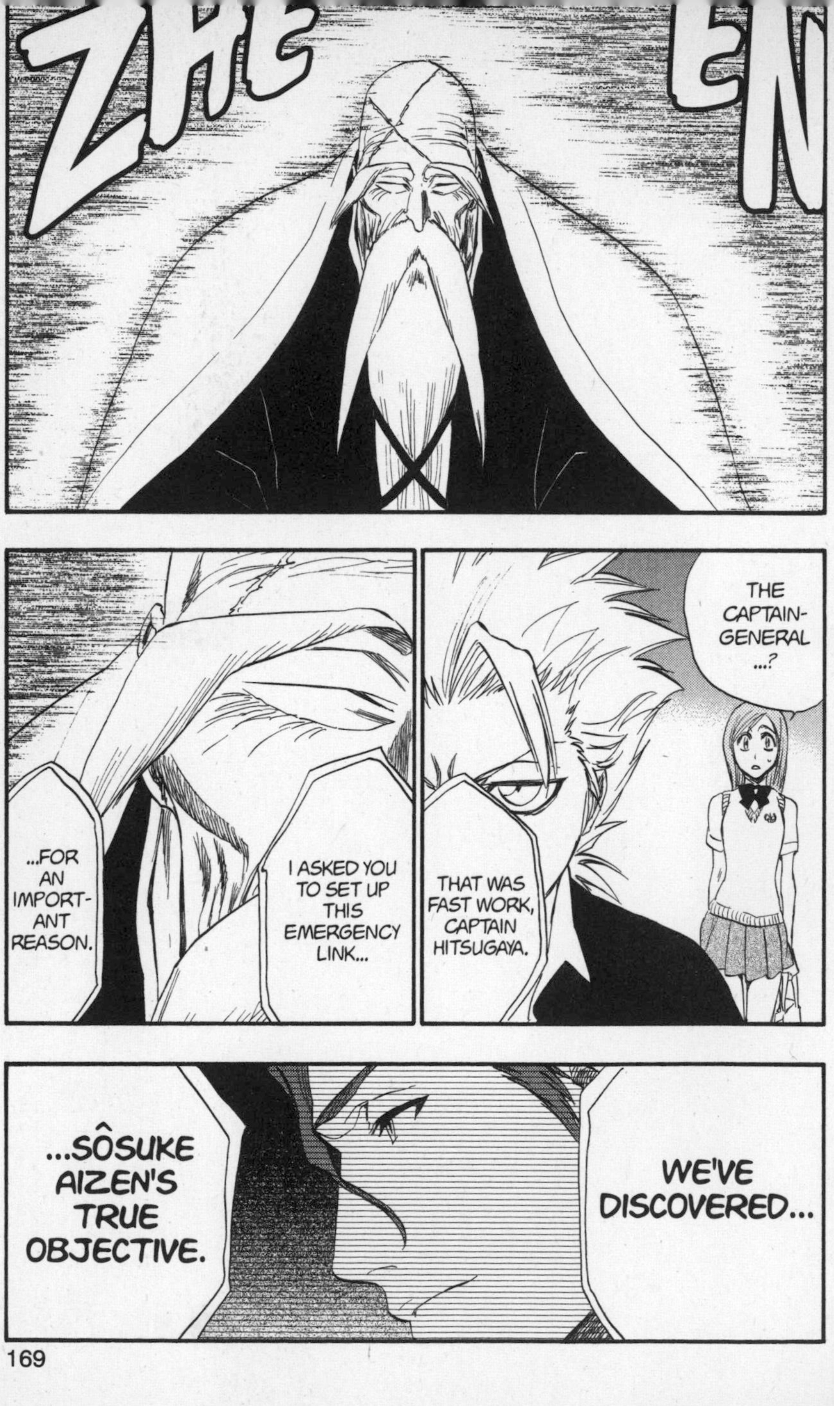
ZHE
EN
THE CAPTAIN-GENERAL ...?
THAT WAS FAST WORK, CAPTAIN HITSUGAYA.
I ASKED YOU TO SET UP THIS EMERGENCY LINK...
...FOR AN IMPORTANT REASON.
WE'VE DISCOVERED...
...SÔSUKE AIZEN'S TRUE OBJECTIVE.

SOUL CANDY "KING" (NEW)
HIDE SOME-WHERE SAFE...
HIDE SOME-WHERE SAFE...
MAKES YOU VERY DILIGENT, BUT...
...STUPID.
THIS SPOT HAS A 97% CHANCE OF BEING SAFE...
MAKES YOU SPOUT MEANING-LESS PERCENT-AGES.
I MEAN ...
REALLY SAFE!
Do.
WHAT TO SAY.

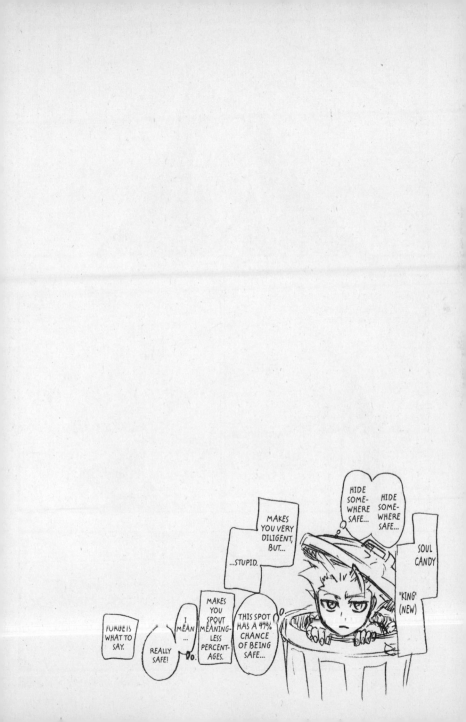

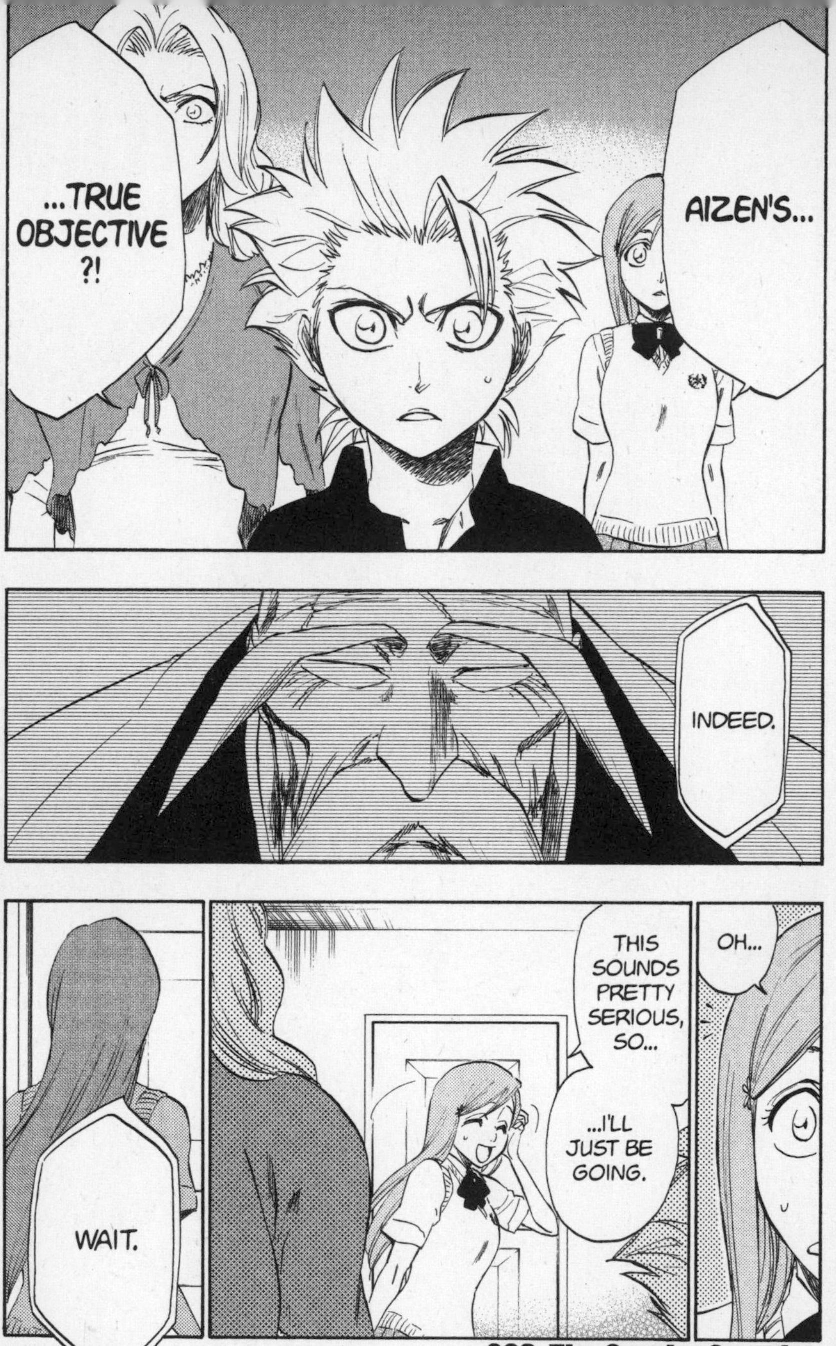
AIZEN'S...
...TRUE OBJECTIVE ?!
INDEED.
OH...
THIS SOUNDS PRETTY SERIOUS, SO...
...I'LL JUST BE GOING.
WAIT.

223. The Scarlet Creation

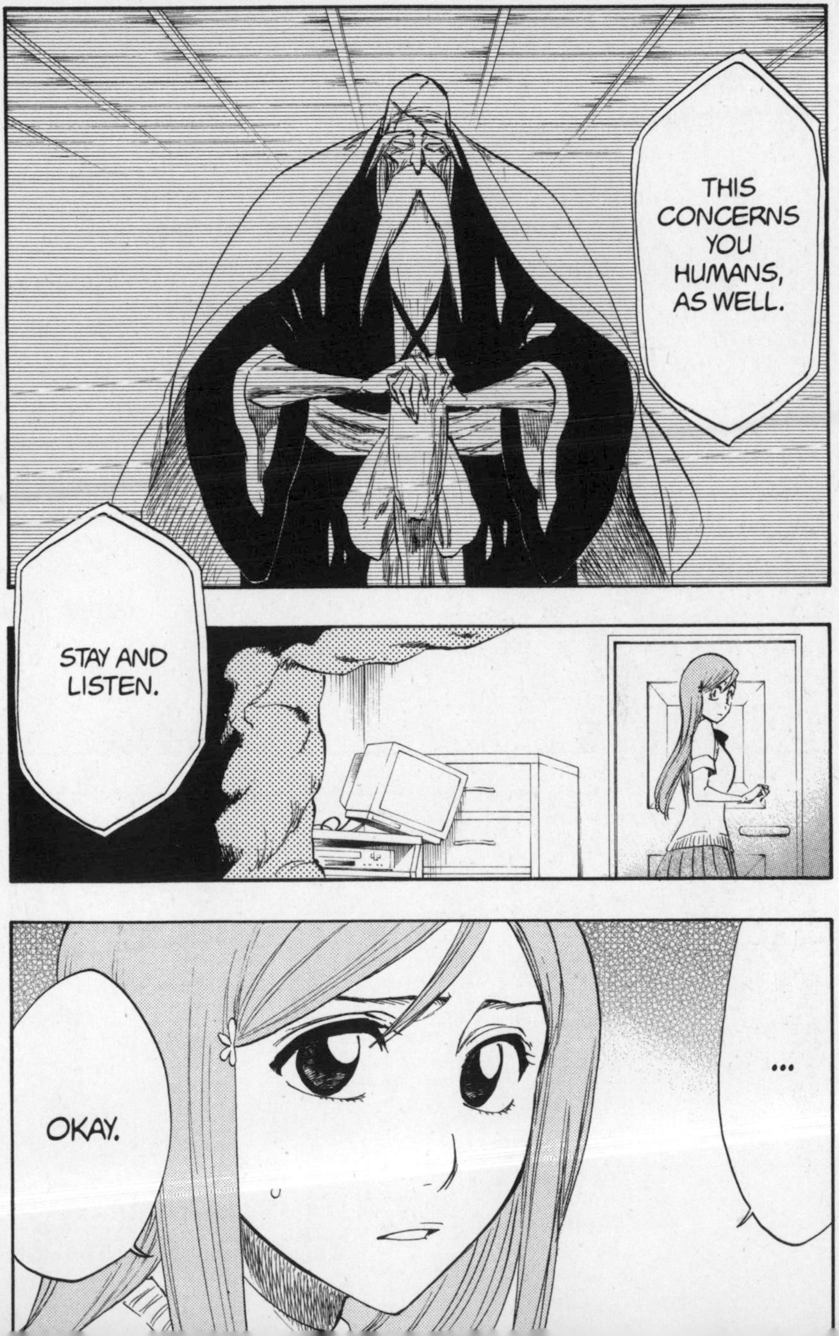
THIS CONCERNS YOU HUMANS, AS WELL.
STAY AND LISTEN.
...
OKAY.

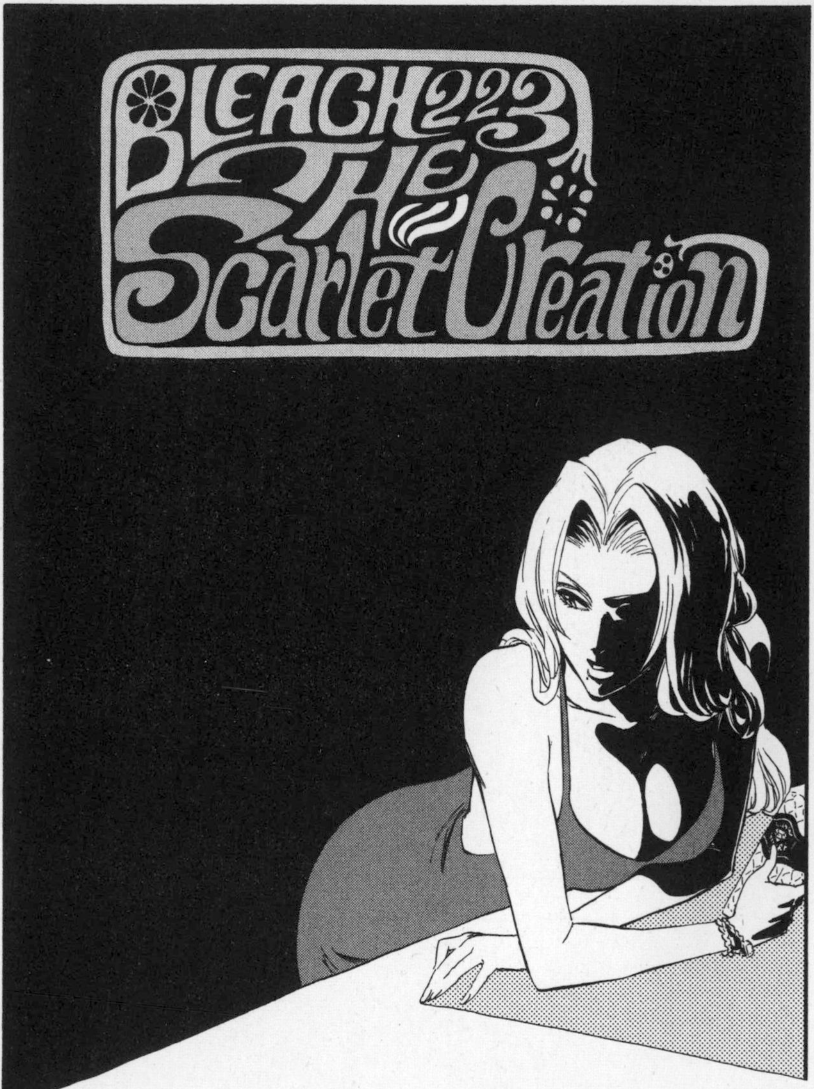
BLEACH 223
THE
Scarlet Creation

Bleach 223. The Scarlet Creation

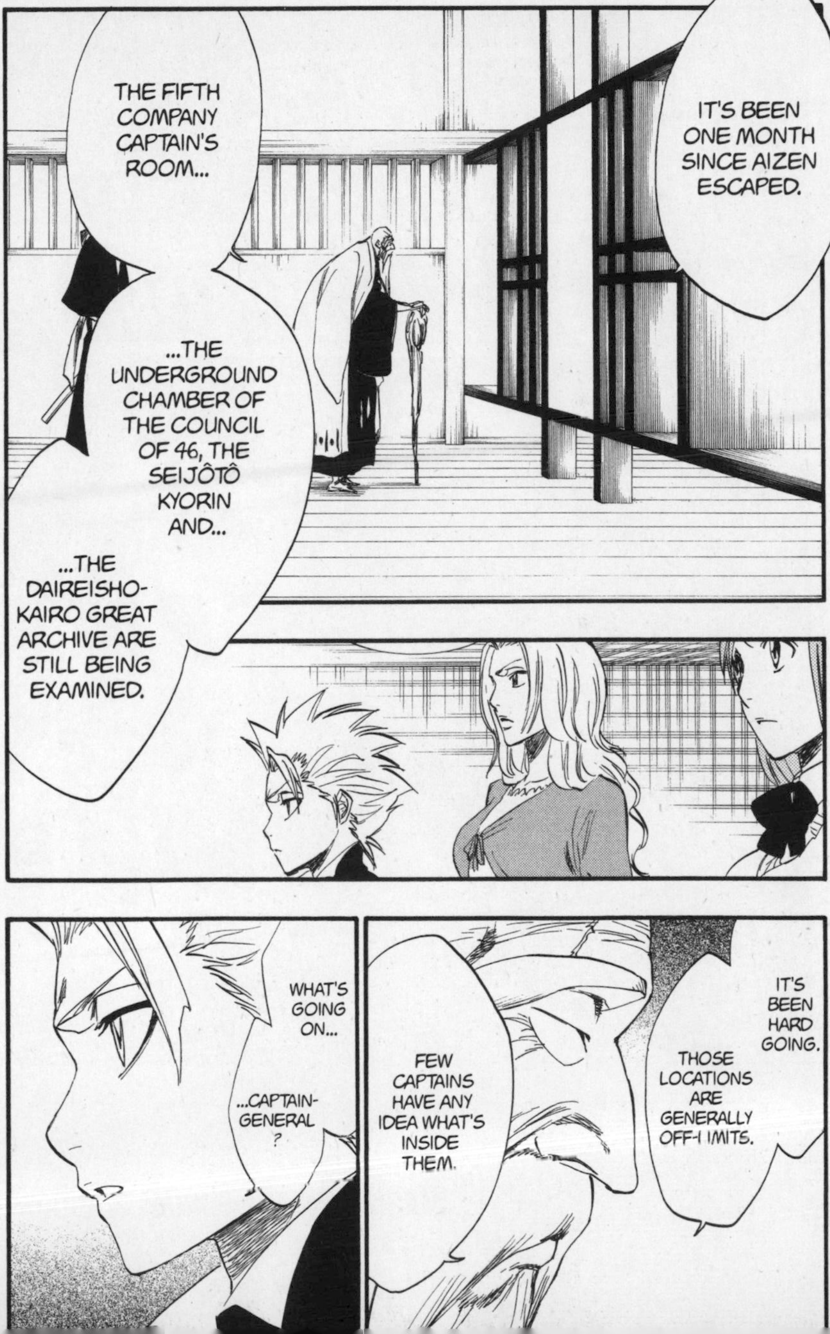
IT'S BEEN ONE MONTH SINCE AIZEN ESCAPED.
THE FIFTH COMPANY CAPTAIN'S ROOM...
...THE UNDERGROUND CHAMBER OF THE COUNCIL OF 46, THE SEIJÔTÔ KYORIN AND...
...THE DAIREISHO-KAIRO GREAT ARCHIVE ARE STILL BEING EXAMINED.
IT'S BEEN HARD GOING.
THOSE LOCATIONS ARE GENERALLY OFF-LIMITS.
FEW CAPTAINS HAVE ANY IDEA WHAT'S INSIDE THEM.
WHAT'S GOING ON...
...CAPTAIN-GENERAL ?

READ THIS WAY

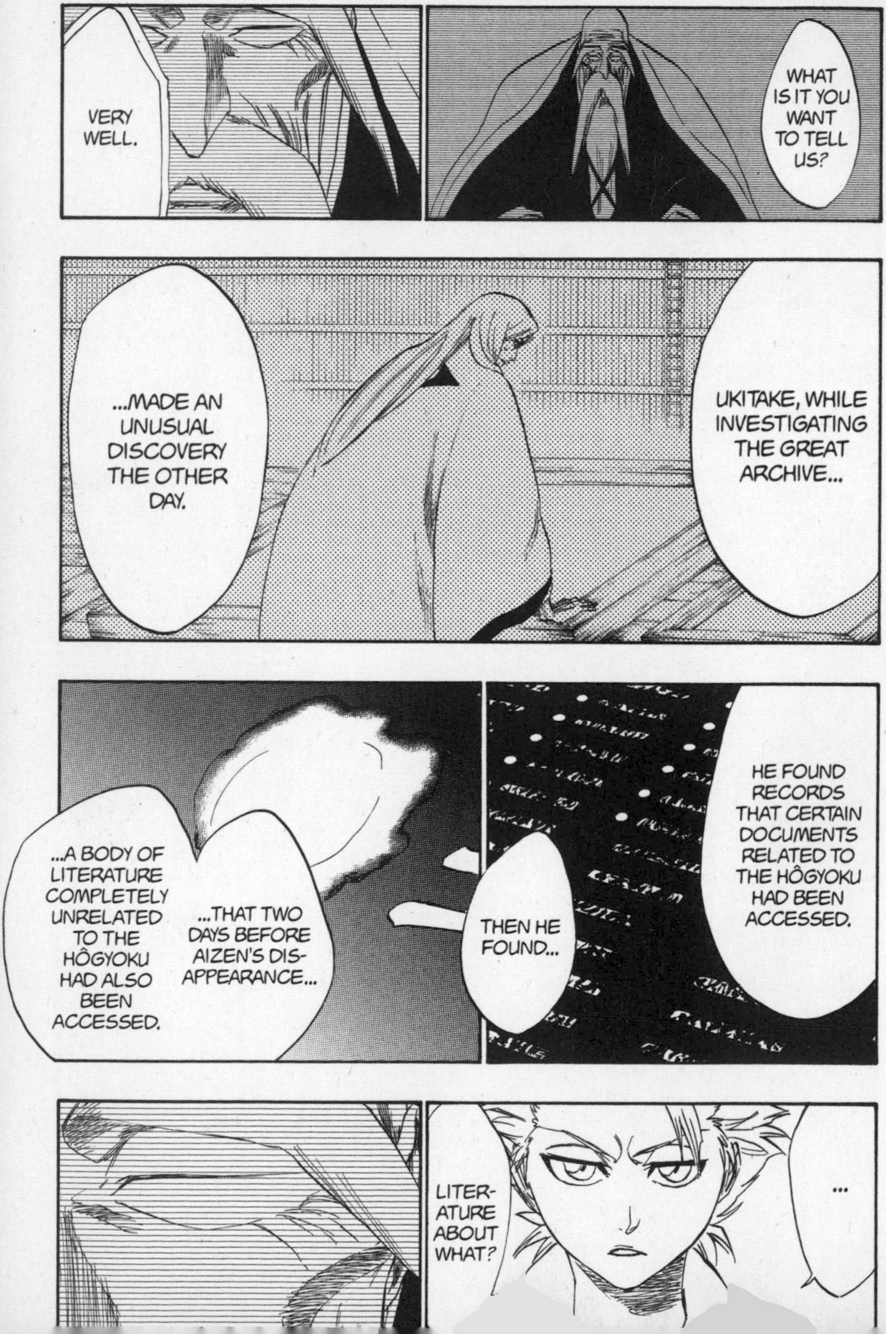
WHAT IS IT YOU WANT TO TELL US?
VERY WELL.
UKITAKE, WHILE INVESTIGATING THE GREAT ARCHIVE...
...MADE AN UNUSUAL DISCOVERY THE OTHER DAY.
HE FOUND RECORDS THAT CERTAIN DOCUMENTS RELATED TO THE HÔGYOKU HAD BEEN ACCESSED.
THEN HE FOUND...
...THAT TWO DAYS BEFORE AIZEN'S DIS-APPEARANCE...
...A BODY OF LITERATURE COMPLETELY UNRELATED TO THE HÔGYOKU HAD ALSO BEEN ACCESSED.
...
LITER-ATURE ABOUT WHAT?

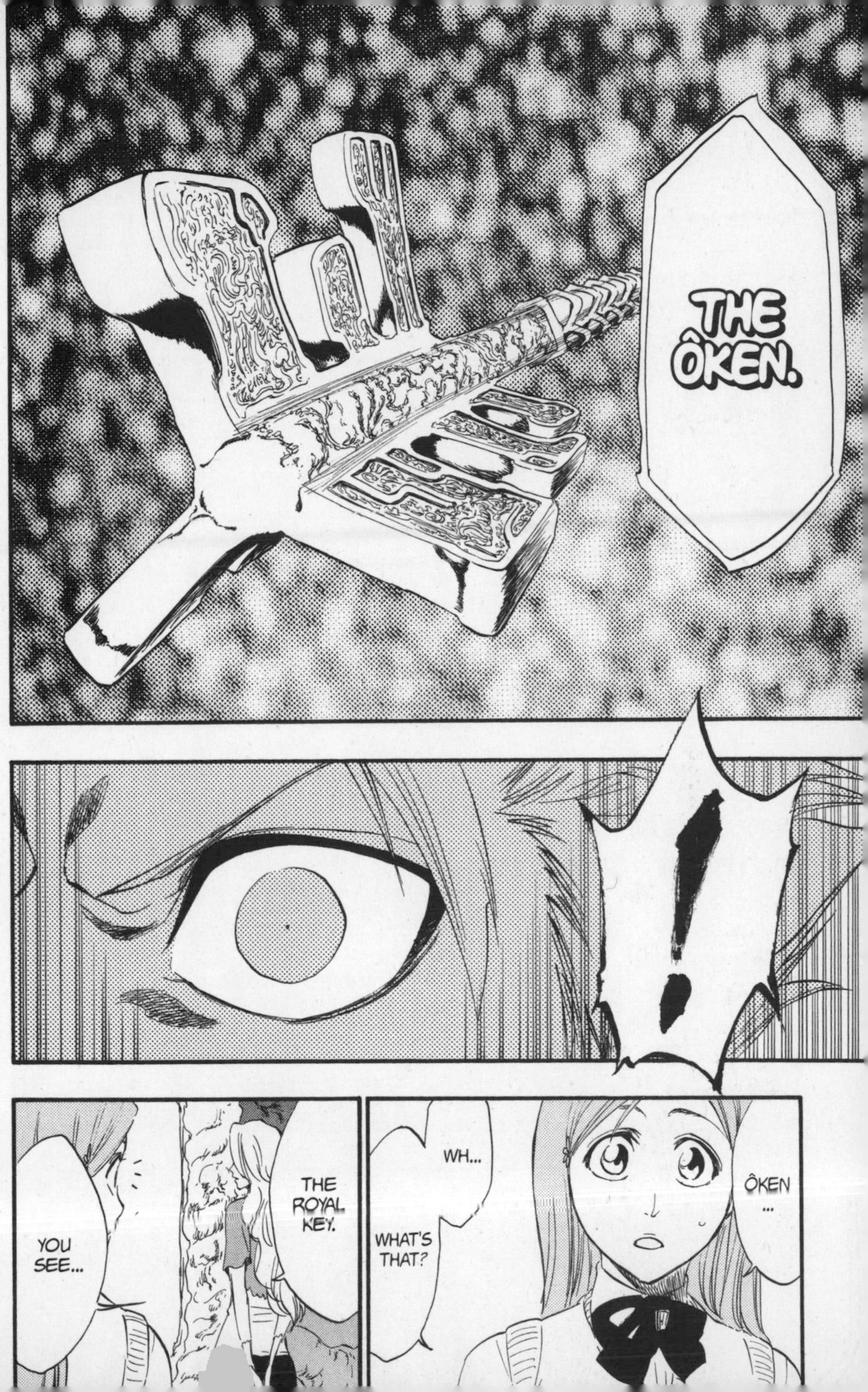
THE ÔKEN.
ÔKEN ...
WH...
WHAT'S THAT?
THE ROYAL KEY.
YOU SEE...

READ THIS WAY

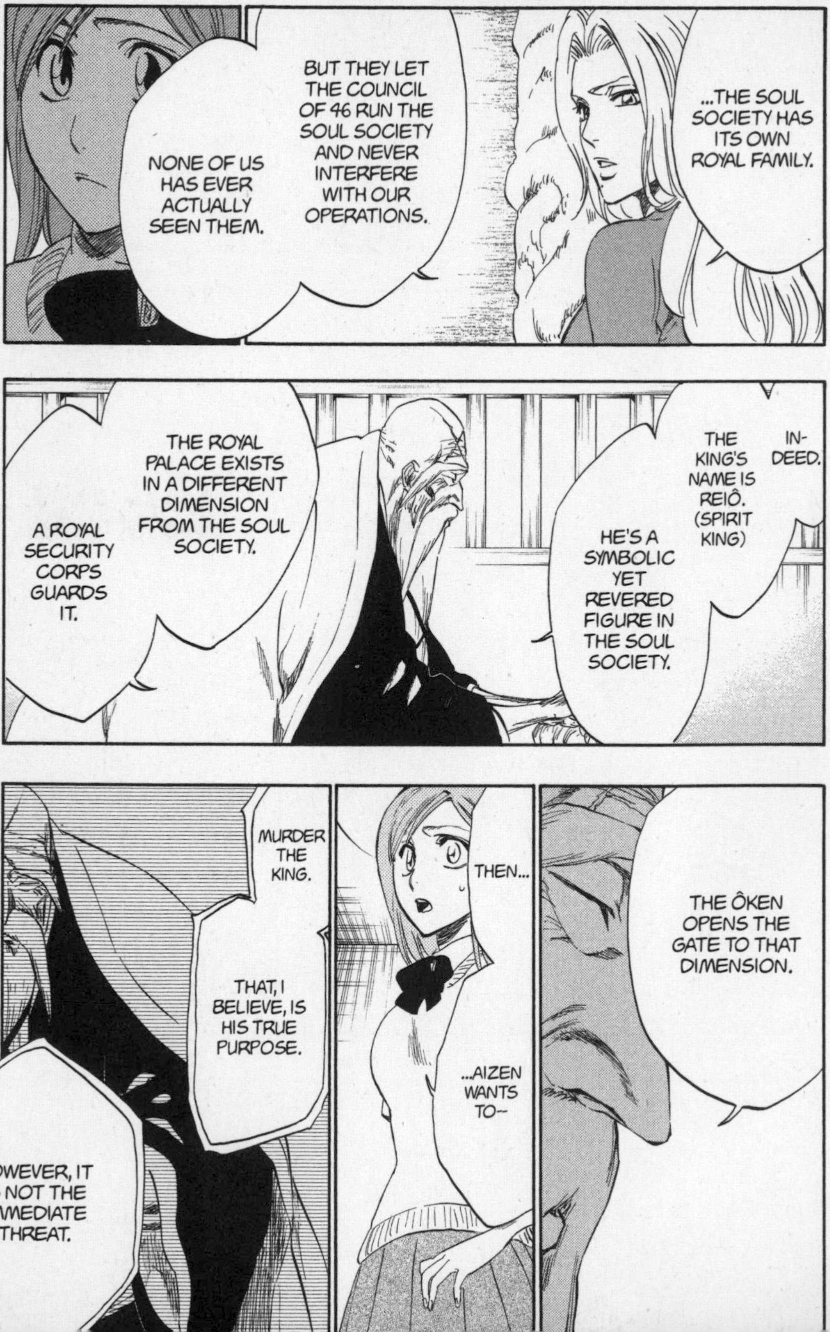
...THE SOUL SOCIETY HAS ITS OWN ROYAL FAMILY.
BUT THEY LET THE COUNCIL OF 46 RUN THE SOUL SOCIETY AND NEVER INTERFERE WITH OUR OPERATIONS.
NONE OF US HAS EVER ACTUALLY SEEN THEM.
IN-DEED.
THE KING'S NAME IS REIÔ. (SPIRIT KING)
HE'S A SYMBOLIC YET REVERED FIGURE IN THE SOUL SOCIETY.
THE ROYAL PALACE EXISTS IN A DIFFERENT DIMENSION FROM THE SOUL SOCIETY.
A ROYAL SECURITY CORPS GUARDS IT.
THE ÔKEN OPENS THE GATE TO THAT DIMENSION.
THEN...
...AIZEN WANTS TO--
MURDER THE KING.
THAT, I BELIEVE, IS HIS TRUE PURPOSE.
HOWEVER, IT IS NOT THE IMMEDIATE THREAT.

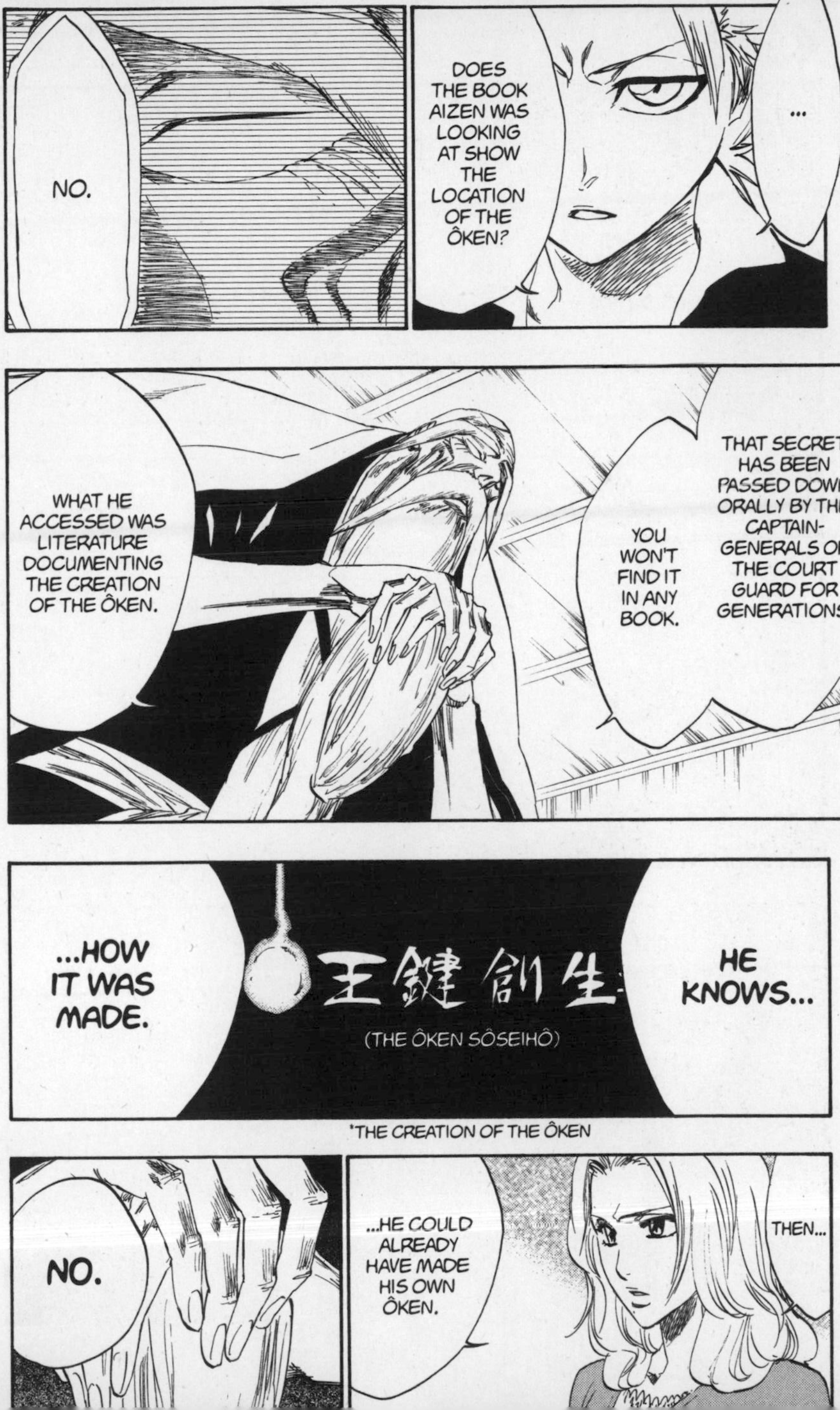
...
DOES THE BOOK AIZEN WAS LOOKING AT SHOW THE LOCATION OF THE ÔKEN?
NO.
THAT SECRET HAS BEEN PASSED DOWN ORALLY BY THE CAPTAIN-GENERALS OF THE COURT GUARD FOR GENERATIONS.
YOU WON'T FIND IT IN ANY BOOK.
WHAT HE ACCESSED WAS LITERATURE DOCUMENTING THE CREATION OF THE ÔKEN.
HE KNOWS...
王鍵創生
(THE ÔKEN SÔSEIHÔ)
...HOW IT WAS MADE.
*THE CREATION OF THE ÔKEN
THEN...
...HE COULD ALREADY HAVE MADE HIS OWN ÔKEN.
NO.

READ THIS WAY

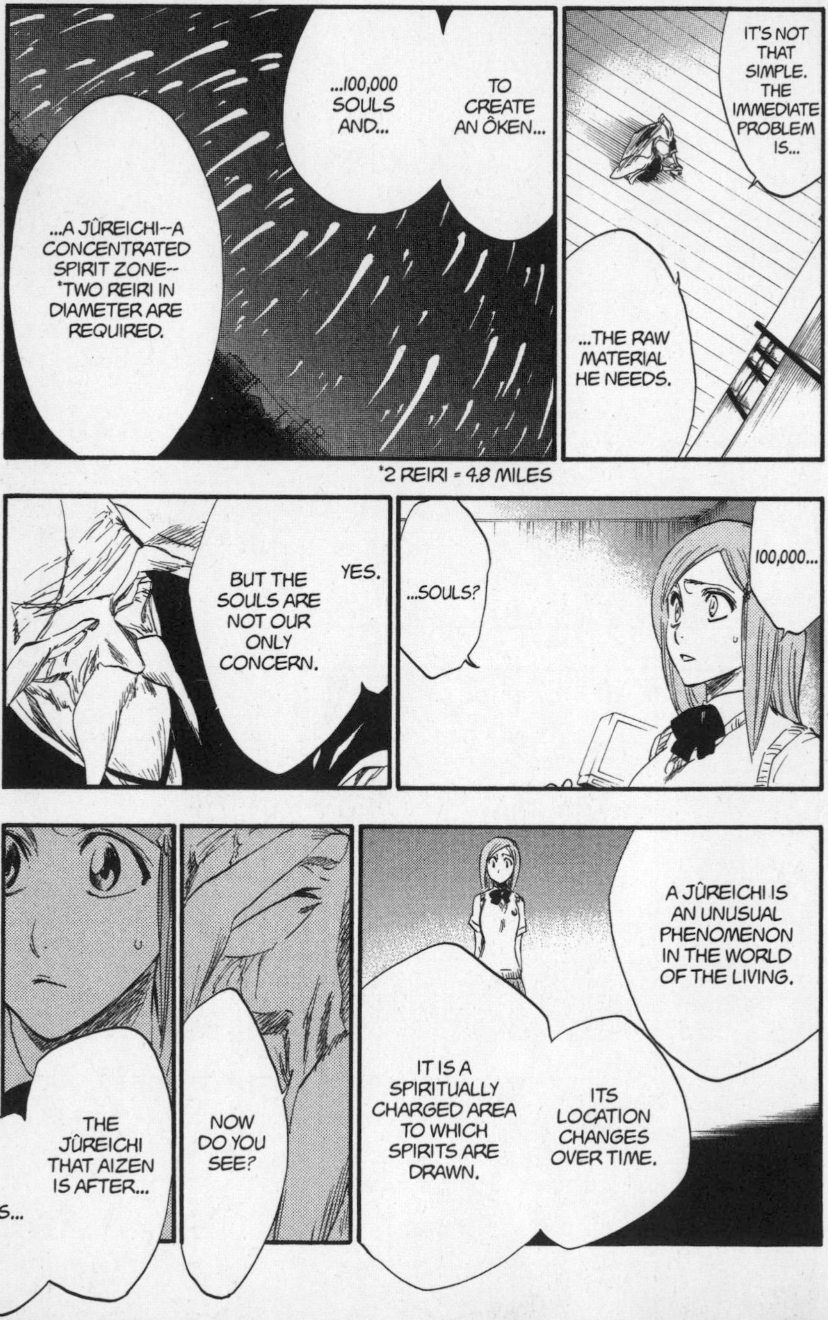
IT'S NOT THAT SIMPLE. THE IMMEDIATE PROBLEM IS...
...THE RAW MATERIAL HE NEEDS.
TO CREATE AN ÔKEN...
...100,000 SOULS AND...
...A JÛREICHI--A CONCENTRATED SPIRIT ZONE--*TWO REIRI IN DIAMETER ARE REQUIRED.
*2 REIRI = 4.8 MILES
100,000...
...SOULS?
YES.
BUT THE SOULS ARE NOT OUR ONLY CONCERN.
A JÛREICHI IS AN UNUSUAL PHENOMENON IN THE WORLD OF THE LIVING.
IT IS A SPIRITUALLY CHARGED AREA TO WHICH SPIRITS ARE DRAWN.
ITS LOCATION CHANGES OVER TIME.
NOW DO YOU SEE?
THE JÛREICHI THAT AIZEN IS AFTER...
...IS...

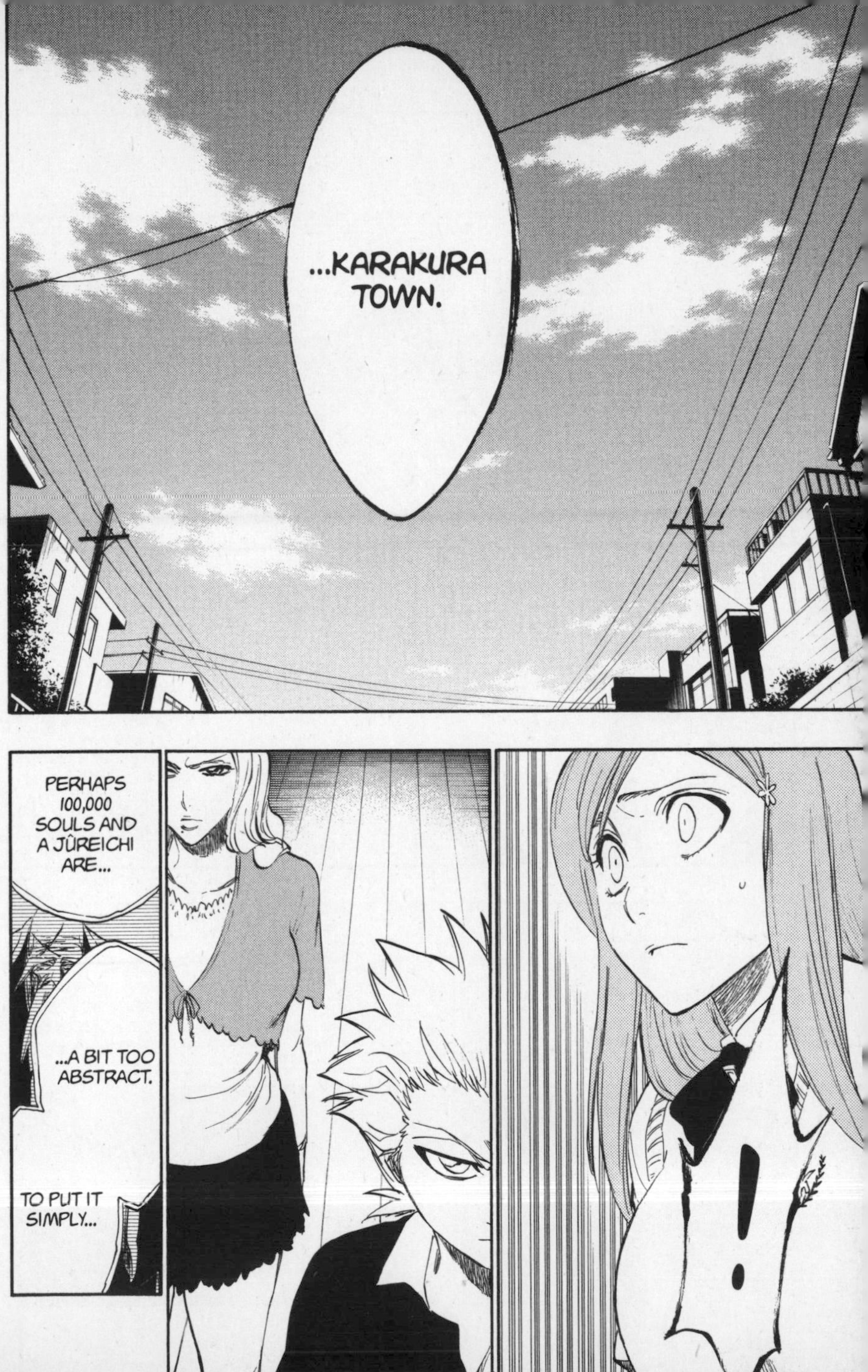
...KARAKURA TOWN.
!
PERHAPS 100,000 SOULS AND A JÛREICHI ARE...
...A BIT TOO ABSTRACT.
TO PUT IT SIMPLY...

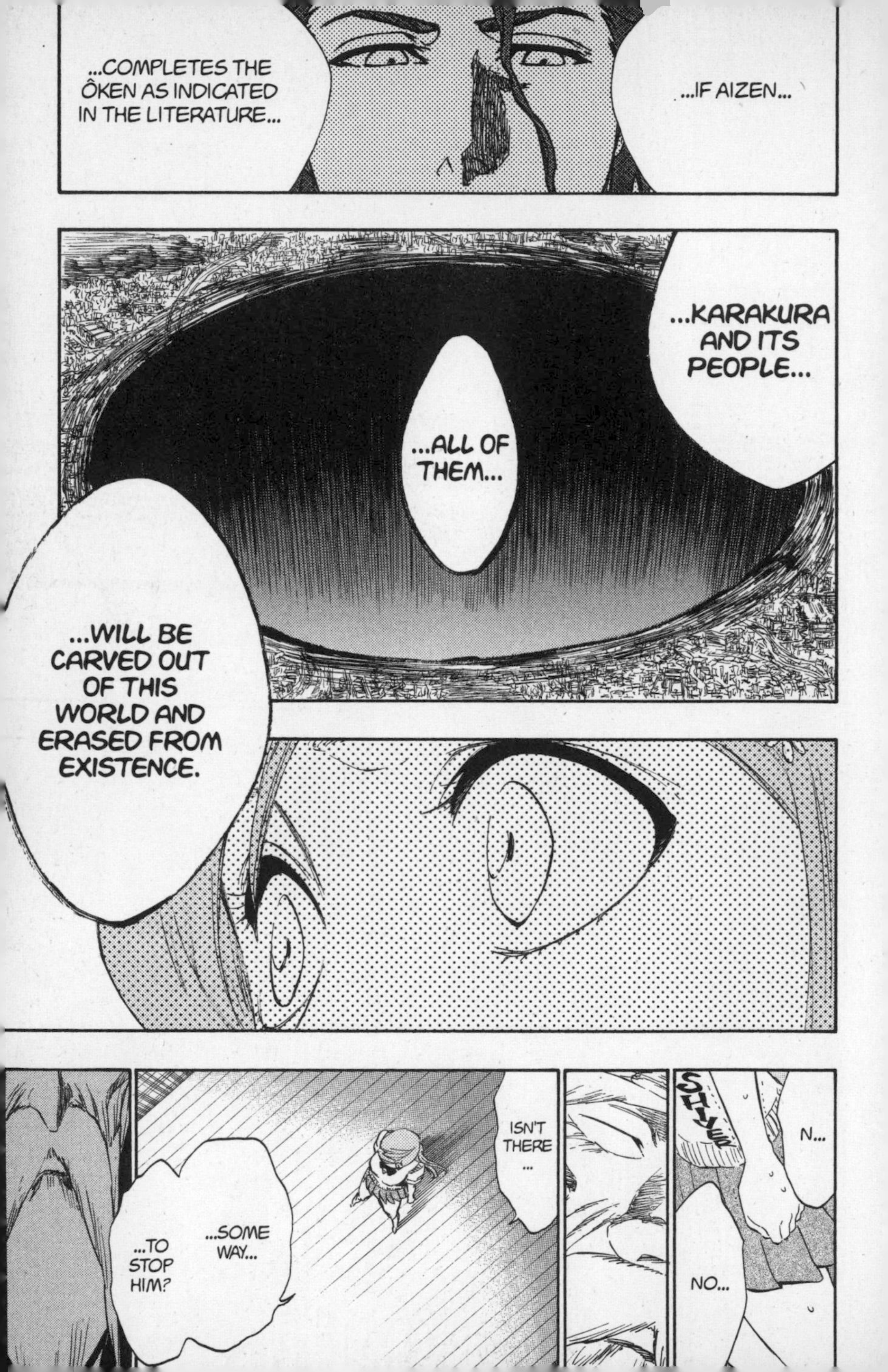
...IF AIZEN...
...COMPLETES THE ÔKEN AS INDICATED IN THE LITERATURE...
...KARAKURA AND ITS PEOPLE...
...ALL OF THEM...
...WILL BE CARVED OUT OF THIS WORLD AND ERASED FROM EXISTENCE.
N...
SHIVER
NO...
ISN'T THERE ...
...SOME WAY...
...TO STOP HIM?

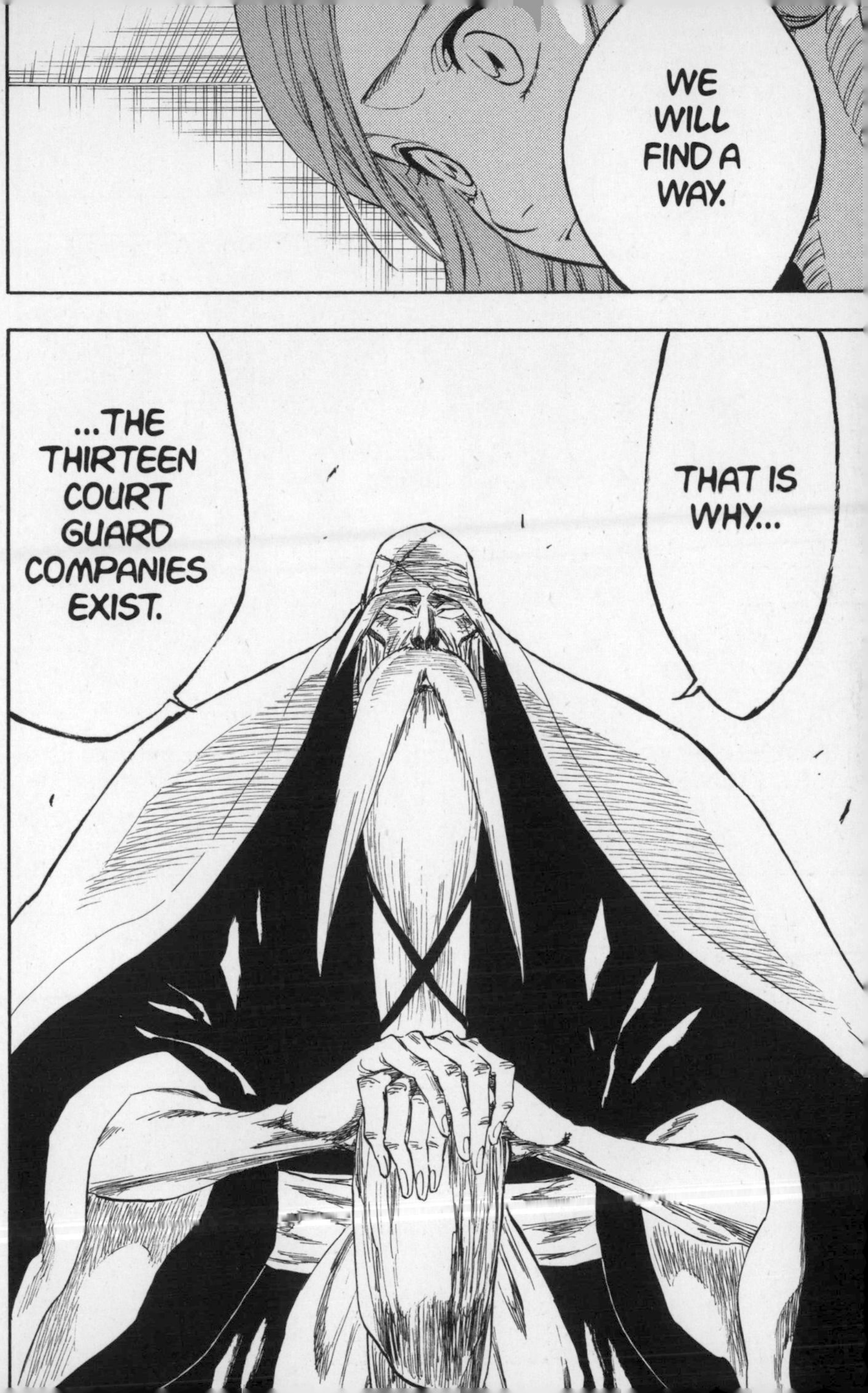
WE WILL FIND A WAY.
THAT IS WHY...
...THE THIRTEEN COURT GUARD COMPANIES EXIST.

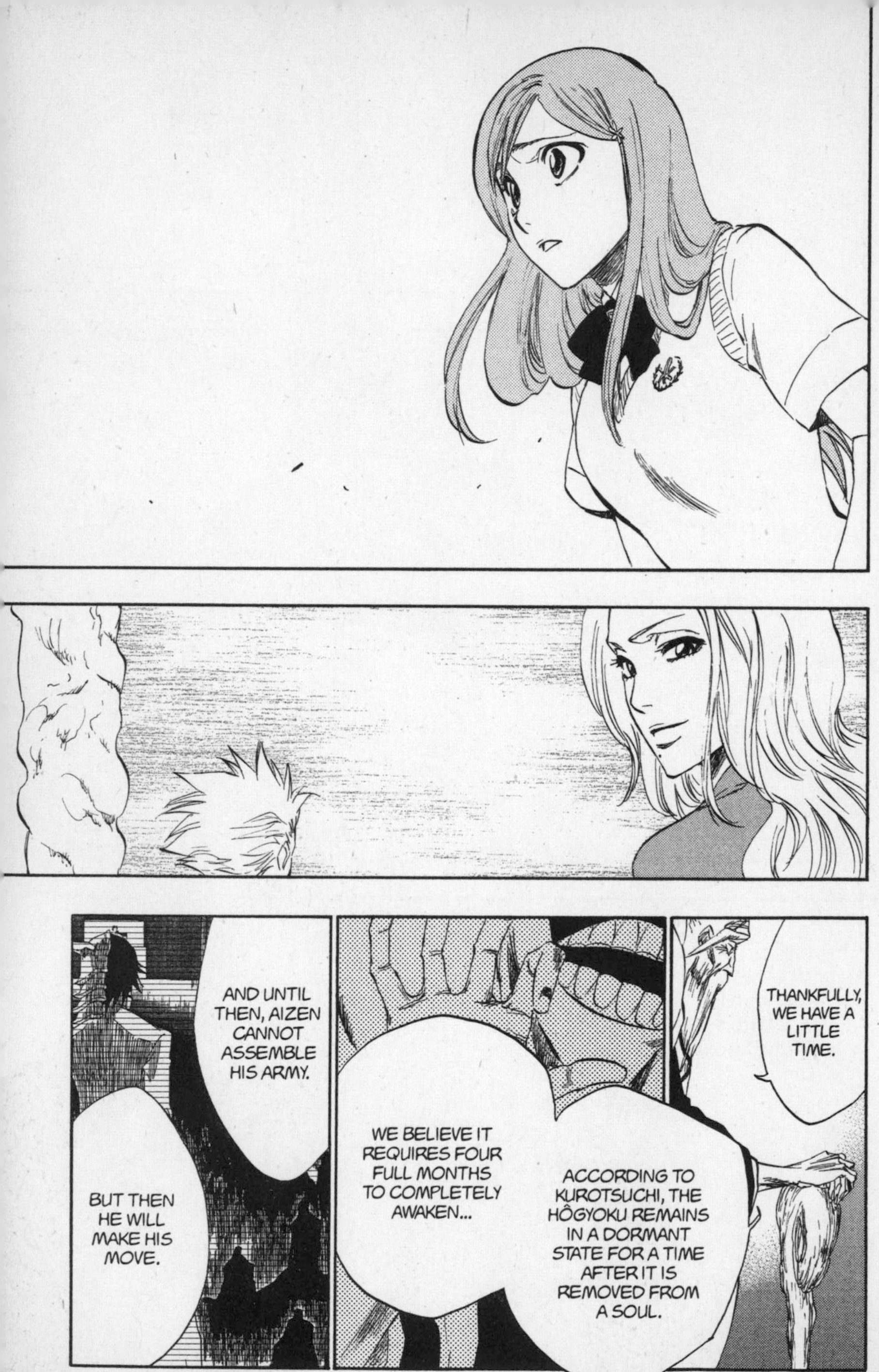
THANKFULLY, WE HAVE A LITTLE TIME.
ACCORDING TO KUROTSUCHI, THE HÔGYOKU REMAINS IN A DORMANT STATE FOR A TIME AFTER IT IS REMOVED FROM A SOUL.
WE BELIEVE IT REQUIRES FOUR FULL MONTHS TO COMPLETELY AWAKEN...
AND UNTIL THEN, AIZEN CANNOT ASSEMBLE HIS ARMY.
BUT THEN HE WILL MAKE HIS MOVE.

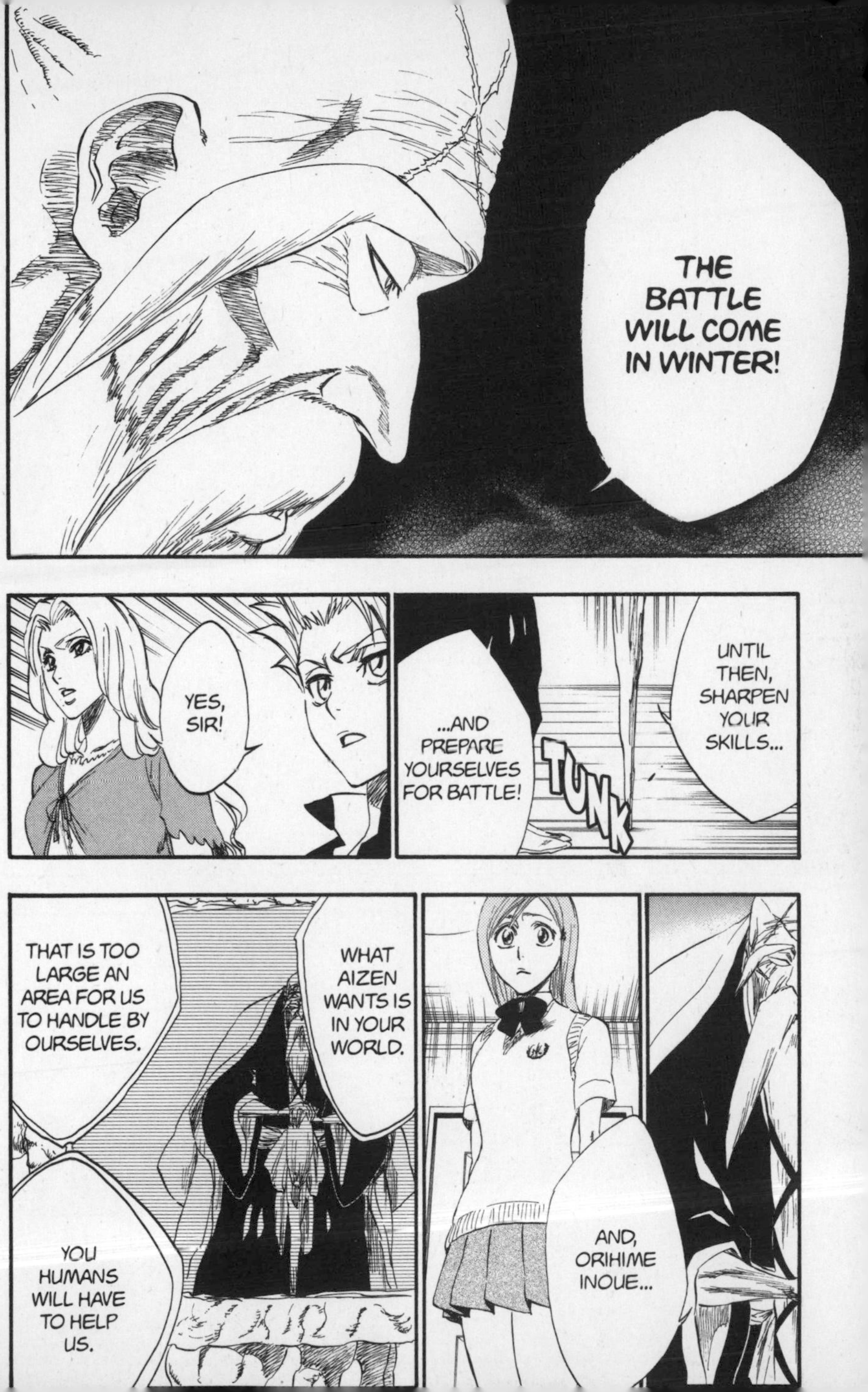
THE BATTLE WILL COME IN WINTER!
UNTIL THEN, SHARPEN YOUR SKILLS...
...AND PREPARE YOURSELVES FOR BATTLE!
TUNK
YES, SIR!
AND, ORIHIME INOUE...
WHAT AIZEN WANTS IS IN YOUR WORLD.
THAT IS TOO LARGE AN AREA FOR US TO HANDLE BY OURSELVES.
YOU HUMANS WILL HAVE TO HELP US.

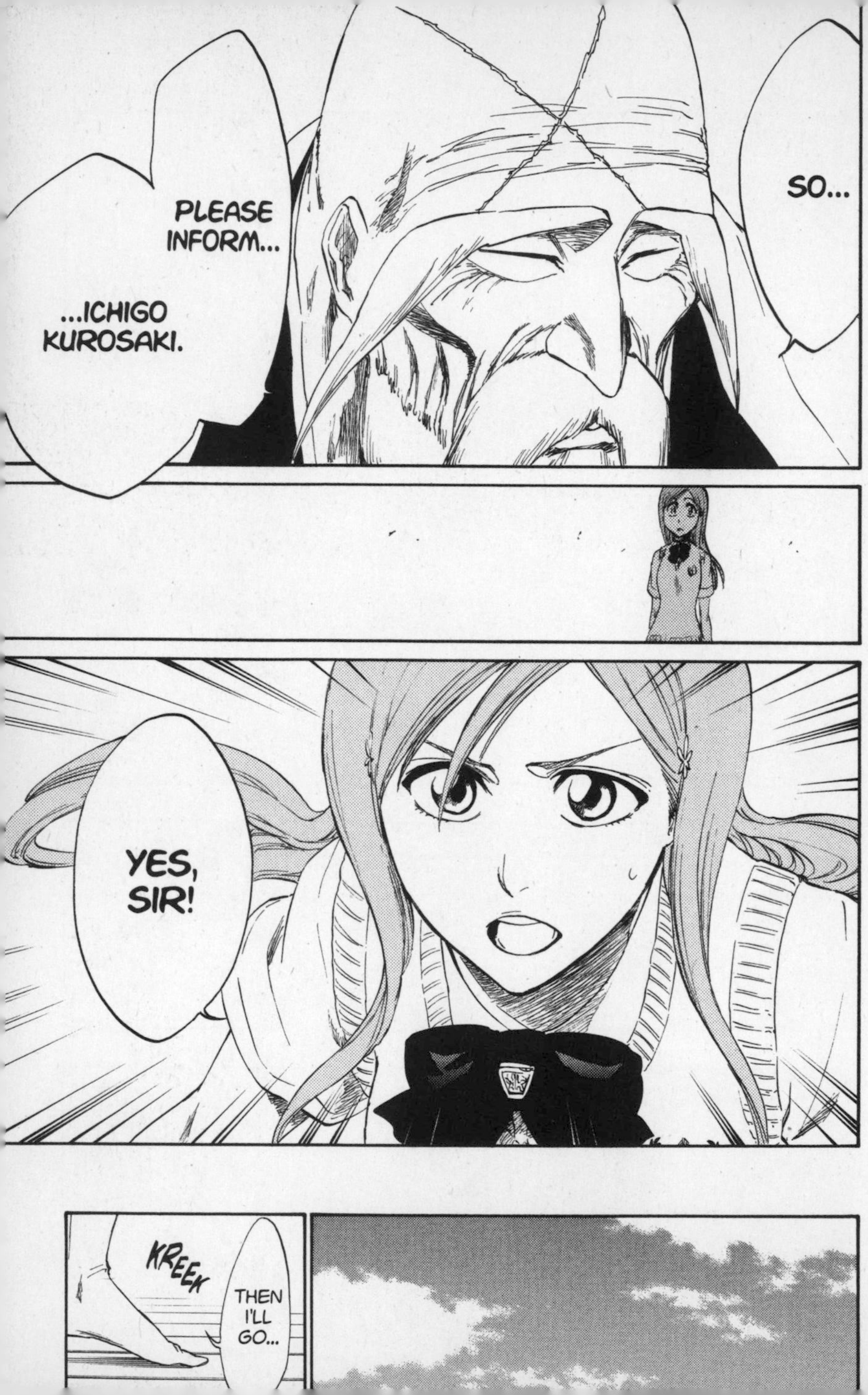
SO...
PLEASE INFORM...
...ICHIGO KUROSAKI.
YES, SIR!
KREEK
THEN I'LL GO...

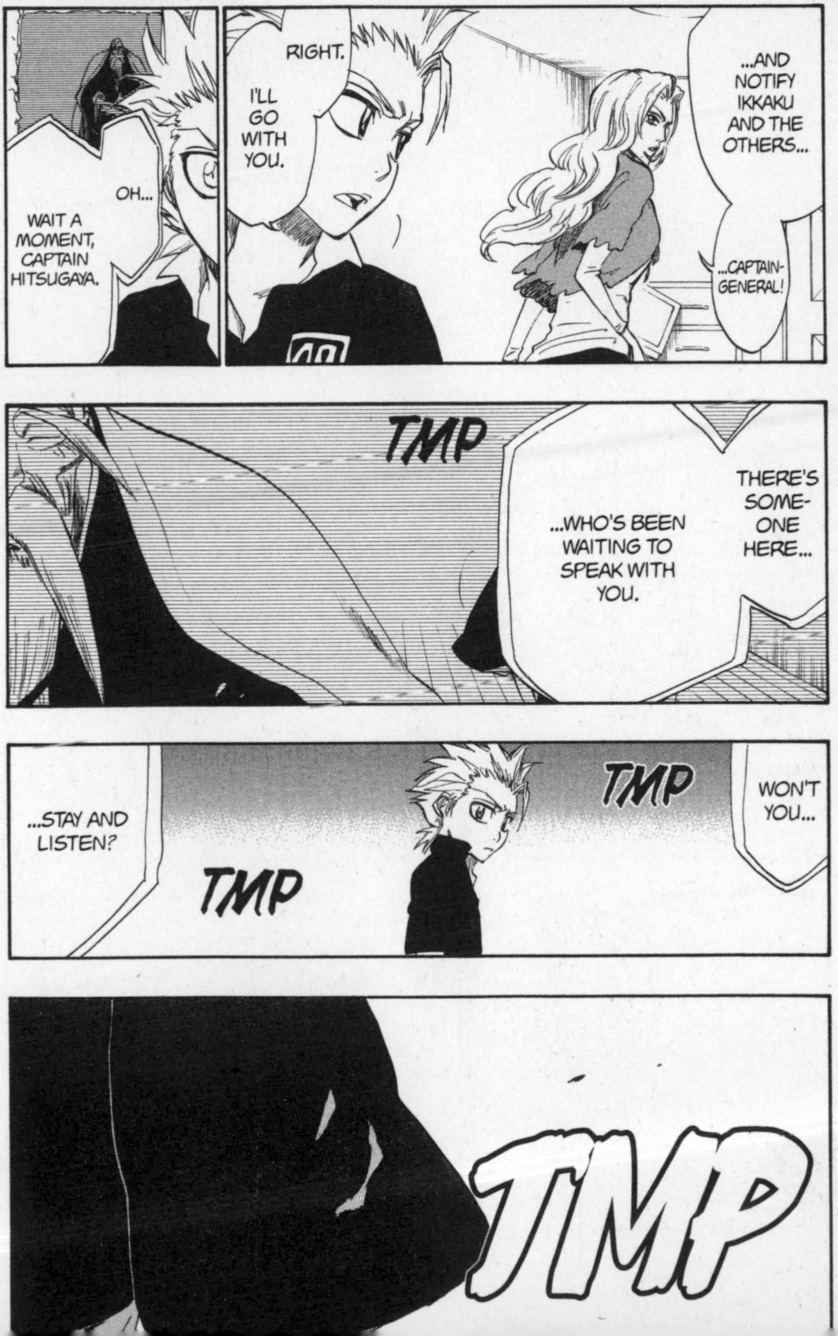
...AND NOTIFY IKKAKU AND THE OTHERS...
...CAPTAIN-GENERAL!
RIGHT.
I'LL GO WITH YOU.
OH...
WAIT A MOMENT, CAPTAIN HITSUGAYA.
TMP
THERE'S SOMEONE HERE...
...WHO'S BEEN WAITING TO SPEAK WITH YOU.
WON'T YOU...
TMP
TMP
...STAY AND LISTEN?
TMP

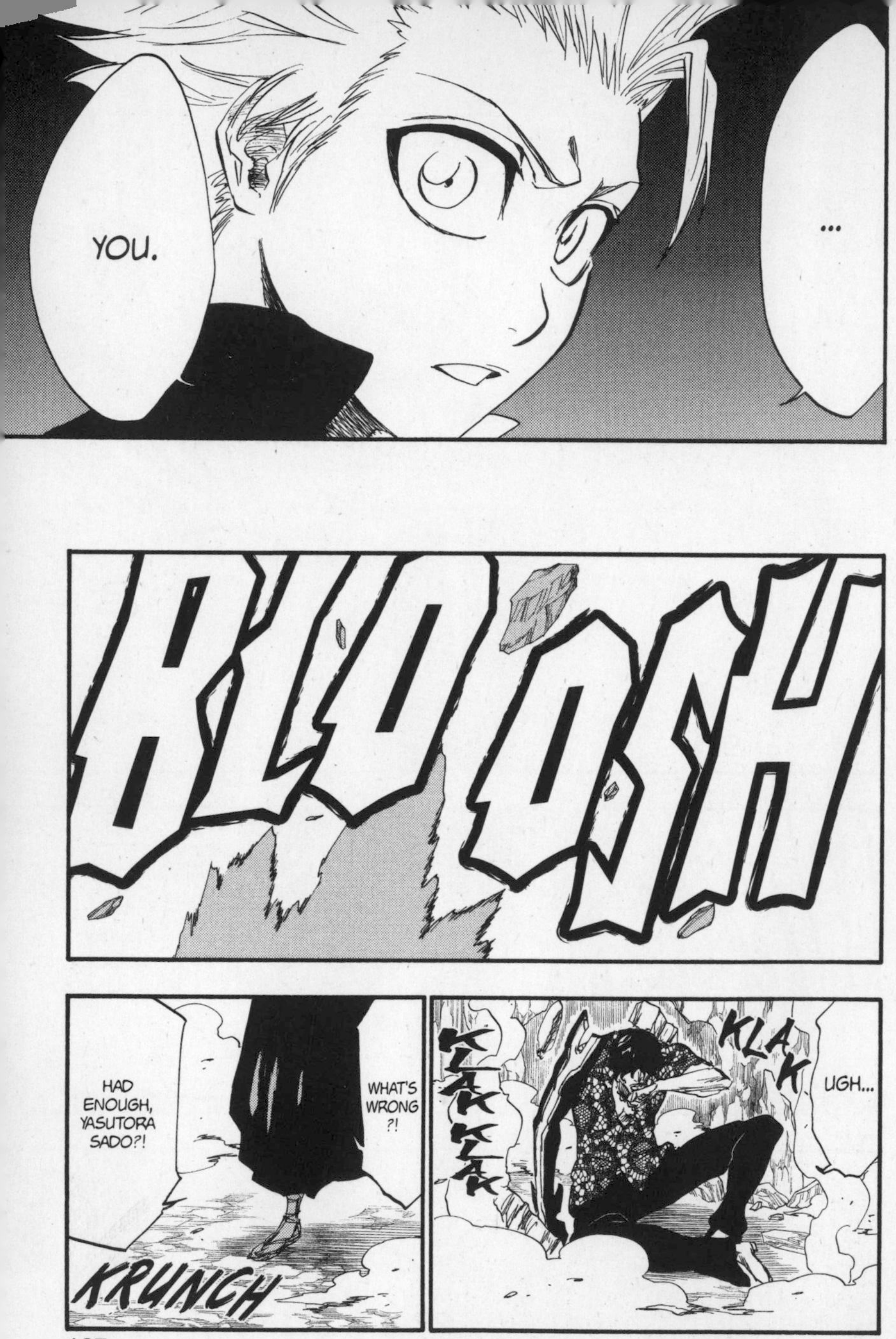
...
YOU.
BLOOSH
KLAK
UGH...
KLAK KLAK KLAK
WHAT'S WRONG?!
HAD ENOUGH, YASUTORA SADO?!
KRUNCH

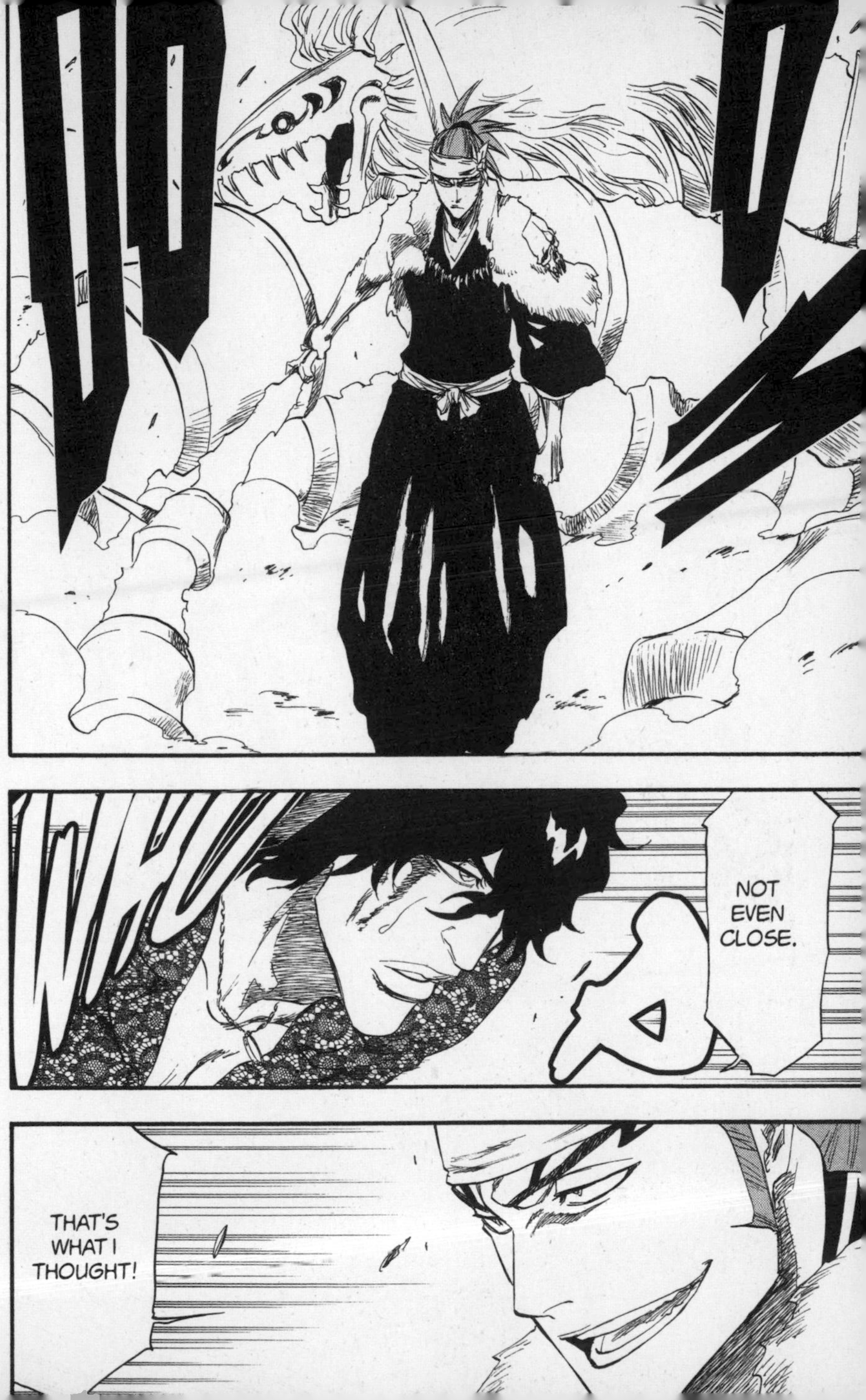
NOT EVEN CLOSE.
THAT'S WHAT I THOUGHT!

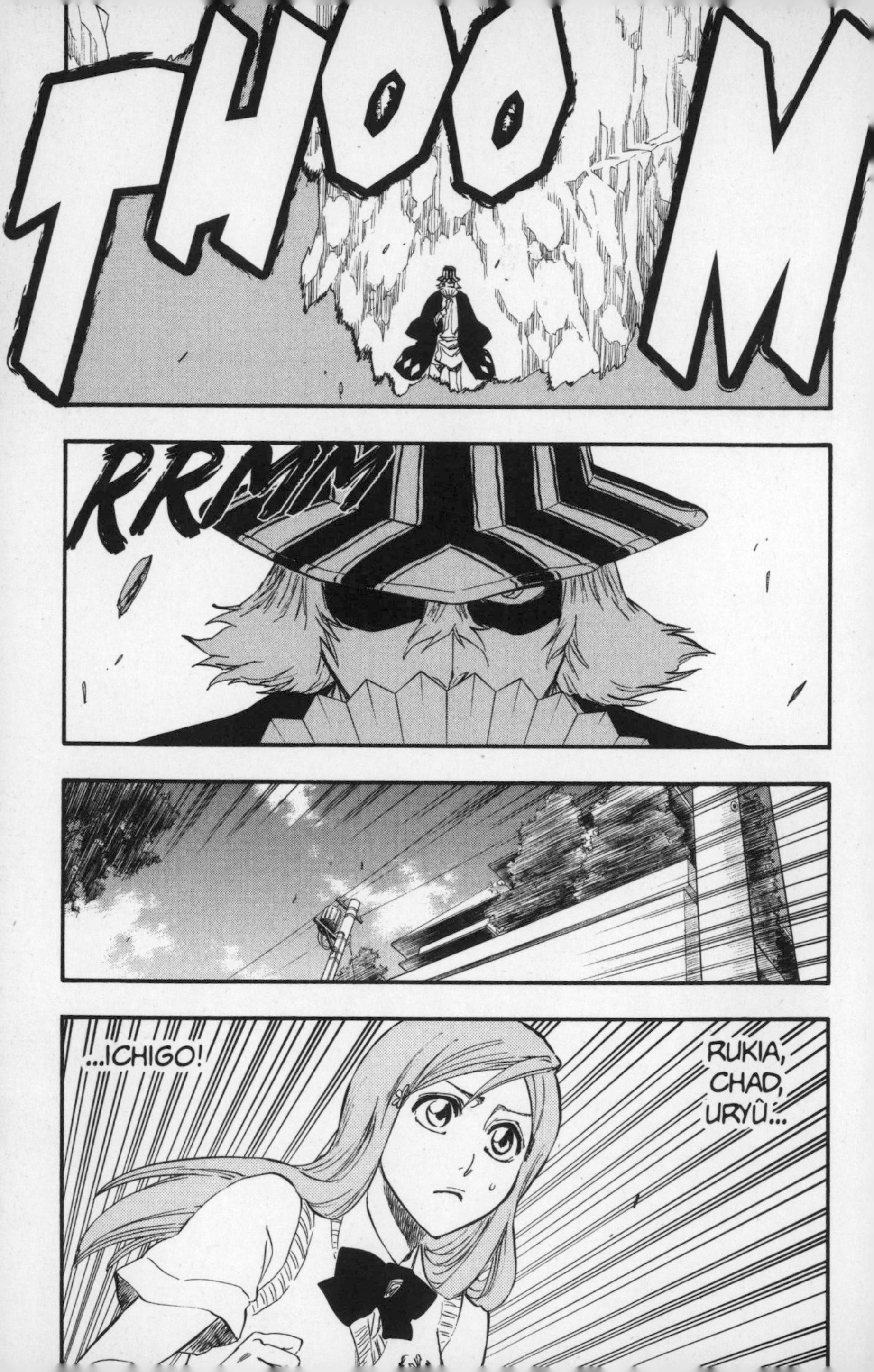
THOOM
RRMM
RUKIA, CHAD, URYÛ...
...ICHIGO!

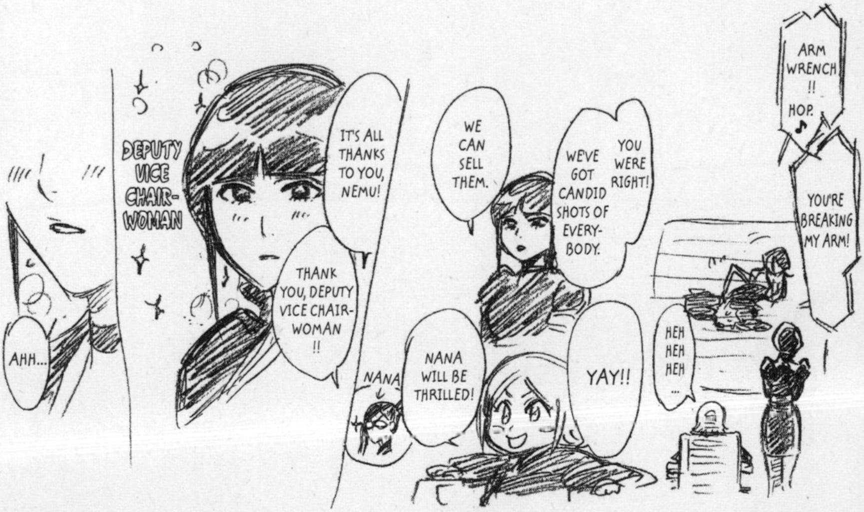
ARM WRENCH!!
HOP.
YOU'RE BREAKING MY ARM!
YOU WERE RIGHT!
WE'VE GOT CANDID SHOTS OF EVERYBODY.
WE CAN SELL THEM.
HEH HEH HEH...
YAY!!
NANA WILL BE THRILLED!
NANA
IT'S ALL THANKS TO YOU, NEMU!
THANK YOU, DEPUTY VICE CHAIR-WOMAN!!
DEPUTY VICE CHAIR-WOMAN
AHH...

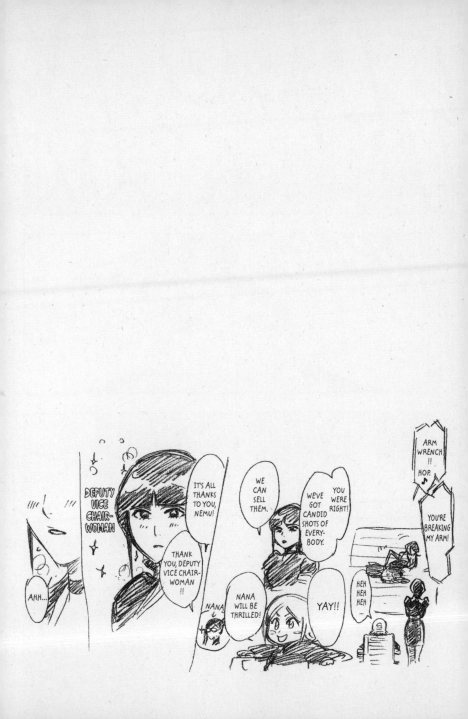

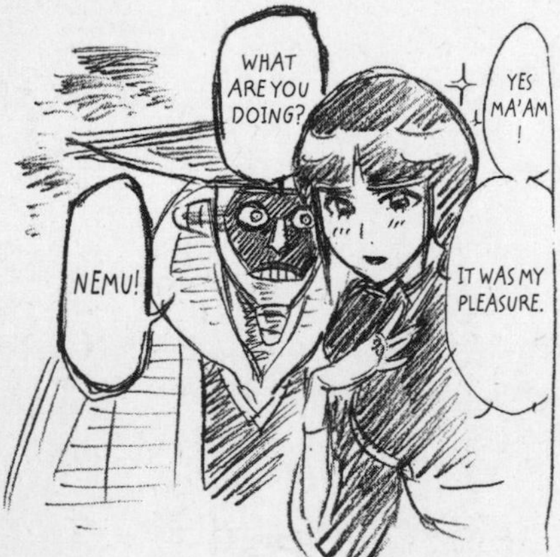
YES MA'AM!
WHAT ARE YOU DOING?
IT WAS MY PLEASURE.
NEMU!

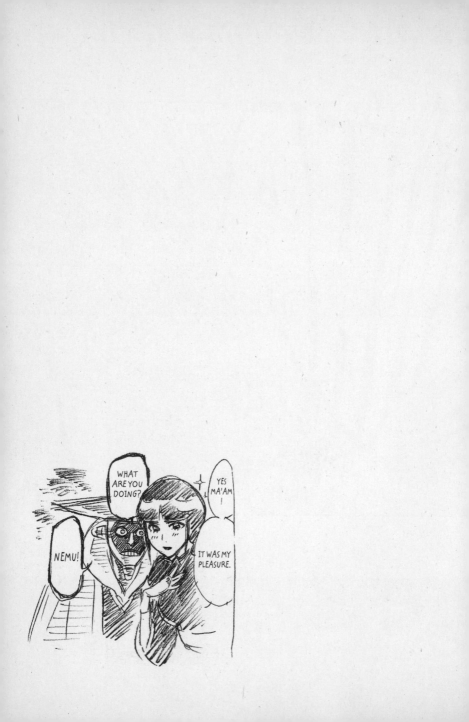

Next Volume Preview

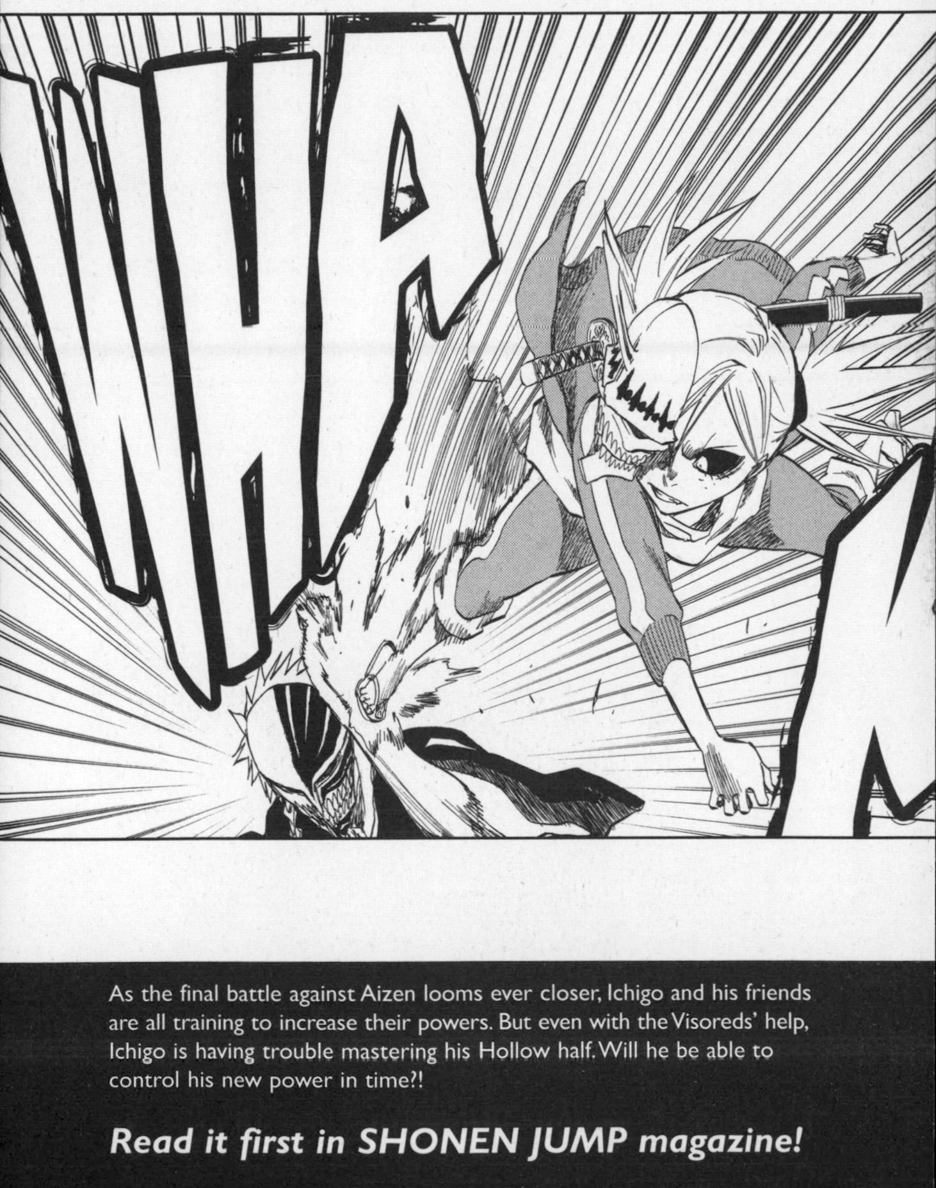
WHAP

As the final battle against Aizen looms ever closer, Ichigo and his friends are all training to increase their powers. But even with the Visoreds' help, Ichigo is having trouble mastering his Hollow half. Will he be able to control his new power in time?!

Read it first in SHONEN JUMP magazine!

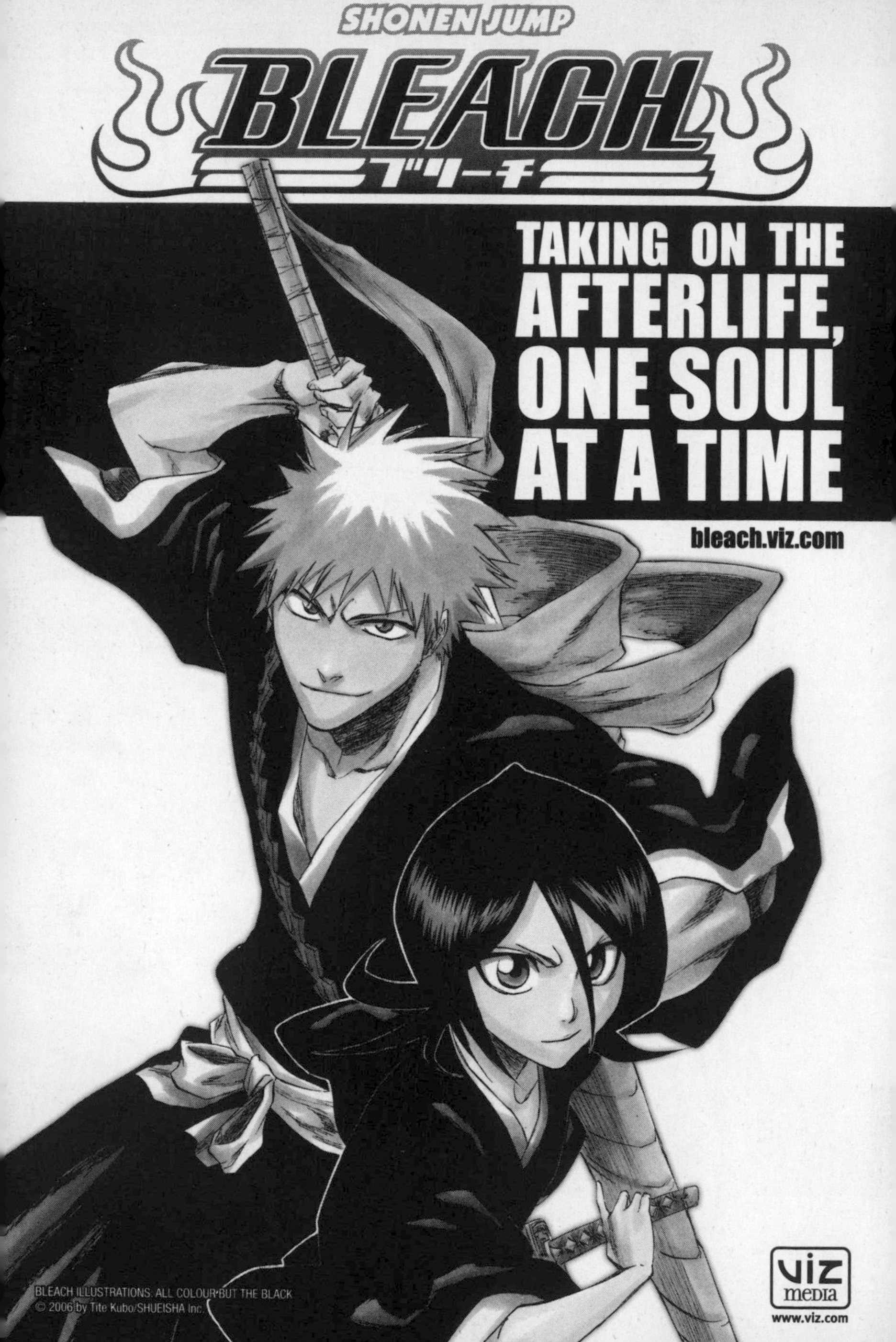
SHONEN JUMP
BLEACH
ブリーチ
TAKING ON THE AFTERLIFE, ONE SOUL AT A TIME
bleach.viz.com
BLEACH ILLUSTRATIONS: ALL COLOUR BUT THE BLACK
© 2006 by Tite Kubo/SHUEISHA Inc.
VIZ media
www.viz.com

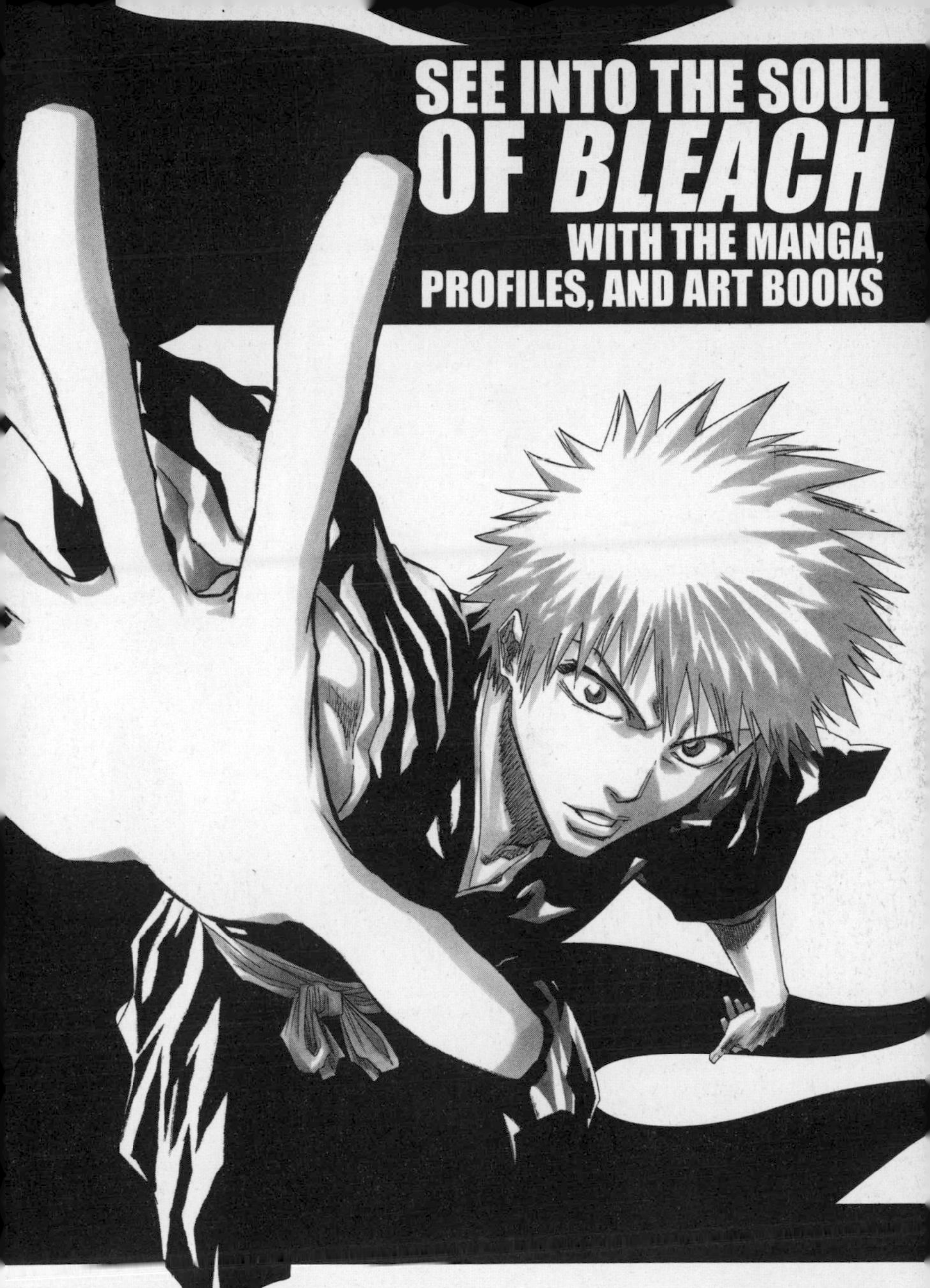
SEE INTO THE SOUL
OF *BLEACH*
WITH THE MANGA,
PROFILES, AND ART BOOKS

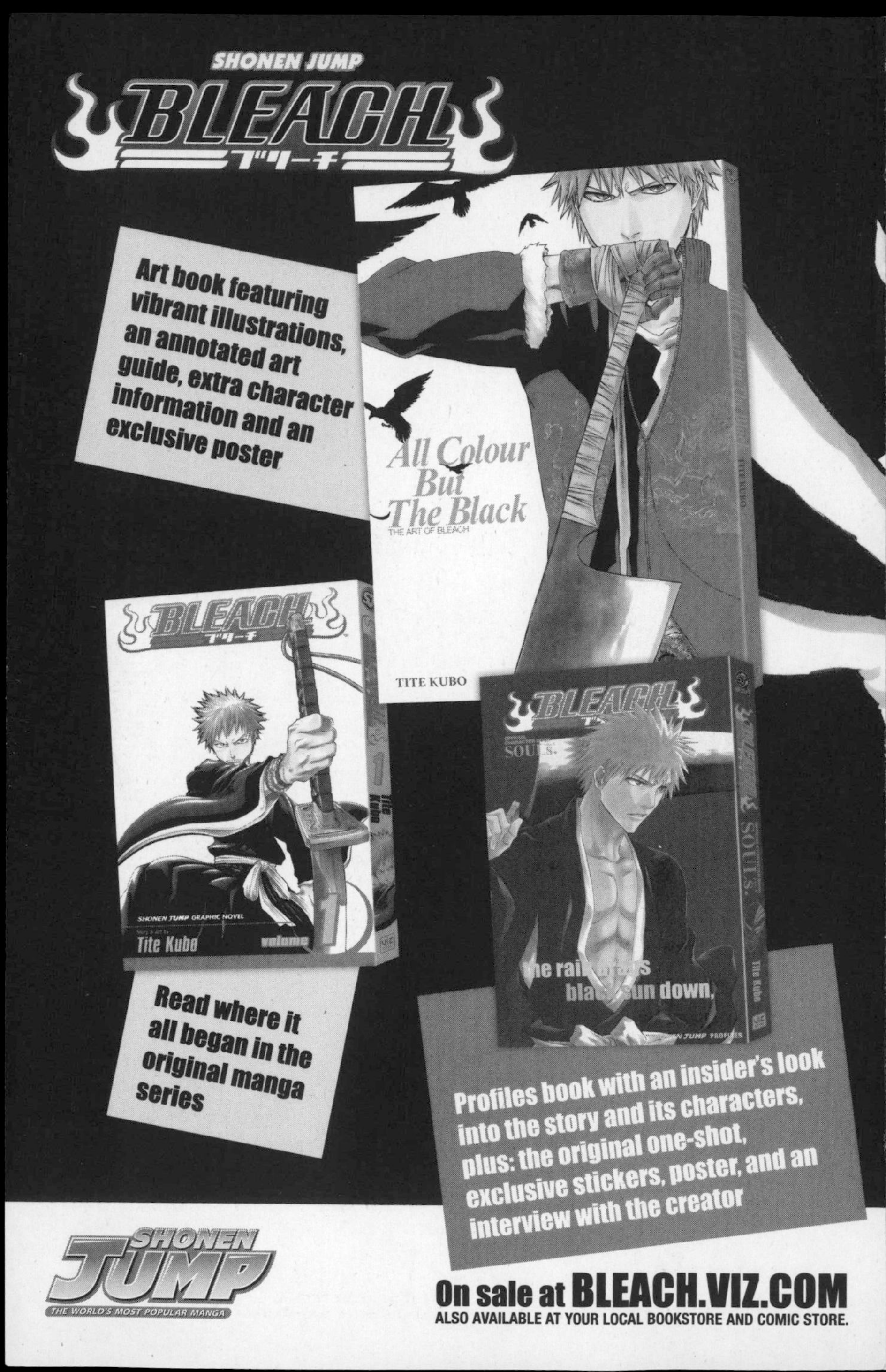
SHONEN JUMP
BLEACH
ブリーチ
Art book featuring vibrant illustrations, an annotated art guide, extra character information and an exclusive poster
All Colour But The Black
THE ART OF BLEACH
TITE KUBO
BLEACH
ブリーチ
SHONEN JUMP GRAPHIC NOVEL
Tite Kubo
Read where it all began in the original manga series
BLEACH
SOULS.
Profiles book with an insider's look into the story and its characters, plus: the original one-shot, exclusive stickers, poster, and an interview with the creator
SHONEN JUMP
THE WORLD'S MOST POPULAR MANGA
On sale at BLEACH.VIZ.COM
ALSO AVAILABLE AT YOUR LOCAL BOOKSTORE AND COMIC STORE.

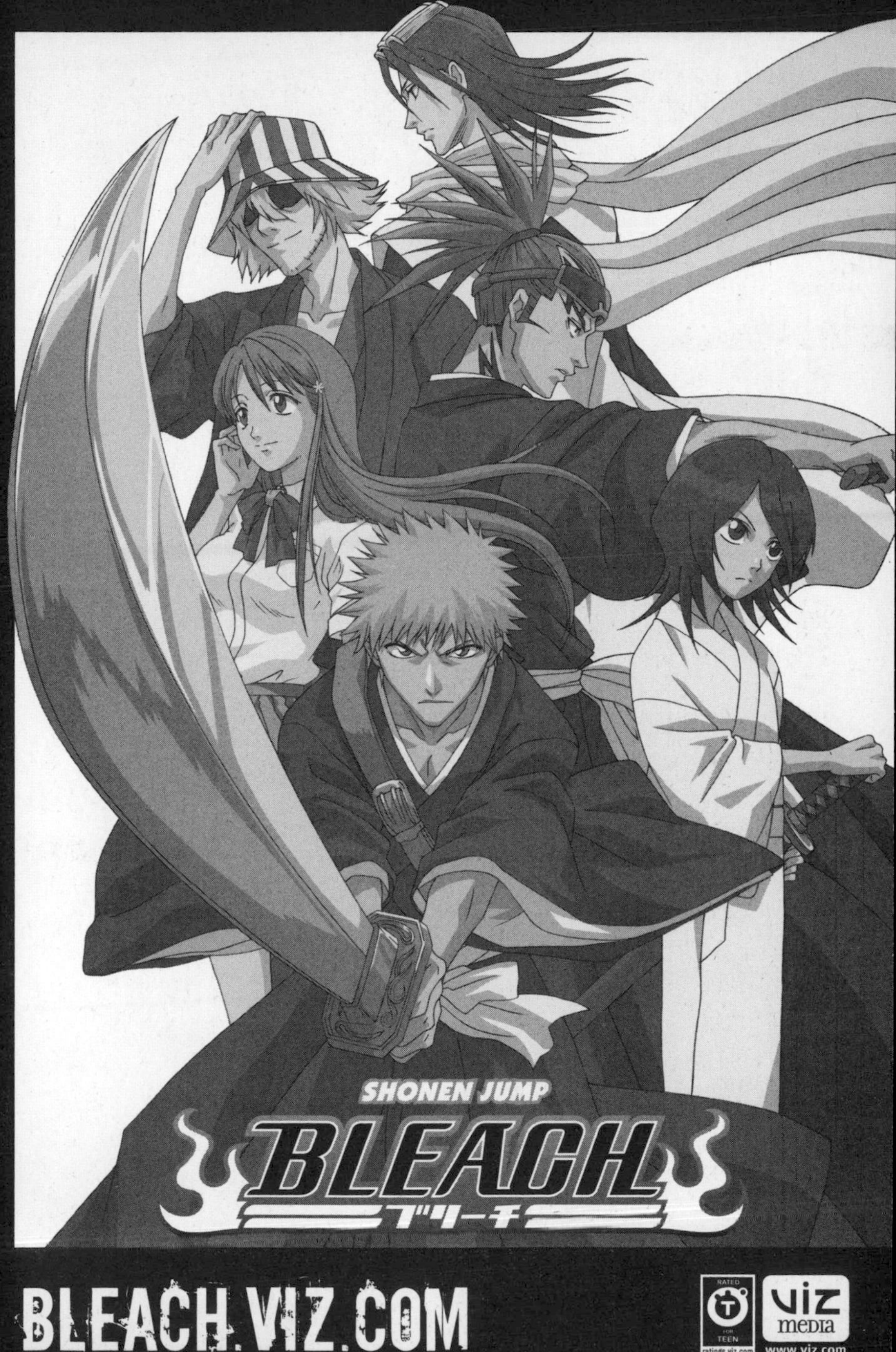
SHONEN JUMP
BLEACH
ブリーチ
BLEACH.VIZ.COM
RATED T FOR TEEN
ratings.viz.com
VIZ media
www.viz.com

JOURNEY TO THE SOUL SOCIETY WITH THE ANIME

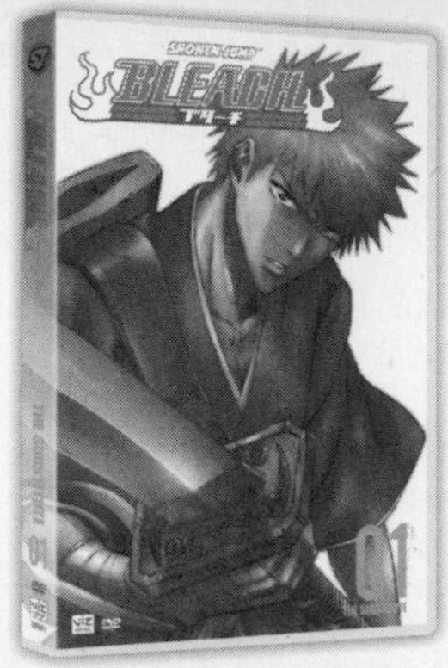
SHONEN JUMP
BLEACH
ブリーチ
01

ORIGINAL AND UNCUT EPISODES NOW ON DVD

GET AN ENTIRE TV SEASON IN ONE COLLECTIBLE DVD BOX SET

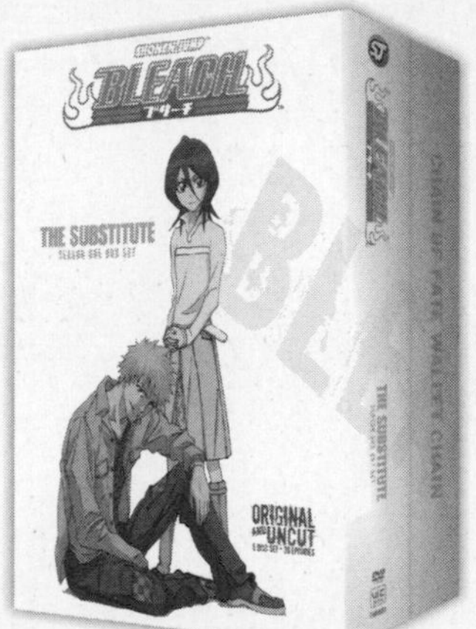
SHONEN JUMP
BLEACH
ブリーチ
THE SUBSTITUTE
ORIGINAL AND UNCUT
CHAIN OF FATE WALLET CHAIN

ANIME ALSO AVAILABLE FOR DOWNLOAD

FIND OUT MORE AT **bleach.viz.com**

SHONEN JUMP

BLEACH

ブリーチ

MEMORIES OF NOBODY

THE MOVIE

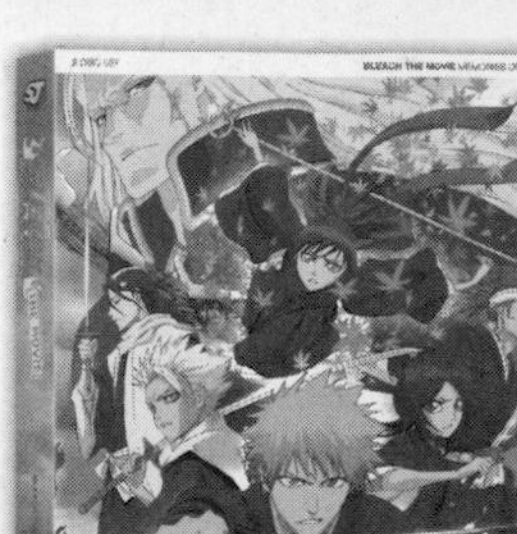
BLEACH THE MOVIE MEMORIES OF NOBODY
SHONEN JUMP
BLEACH
ブリーチ
MEMORIES OF NOBODY
THE MOVIE

CAN THE SOUL REAPERS SAVE TWO WORLDS FROM TOTAL ANNIHILATION? FIND OUT IN THE FIRST FULL-LENGTH FEATURE FILM!

SHONEN JUMP HOME VIDEO

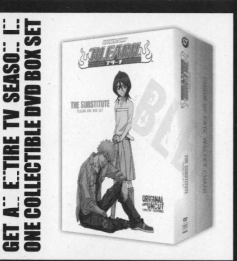

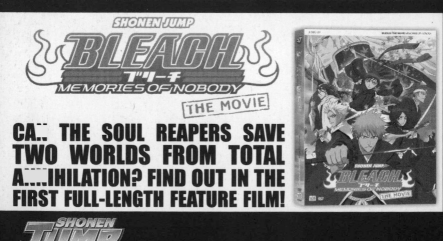

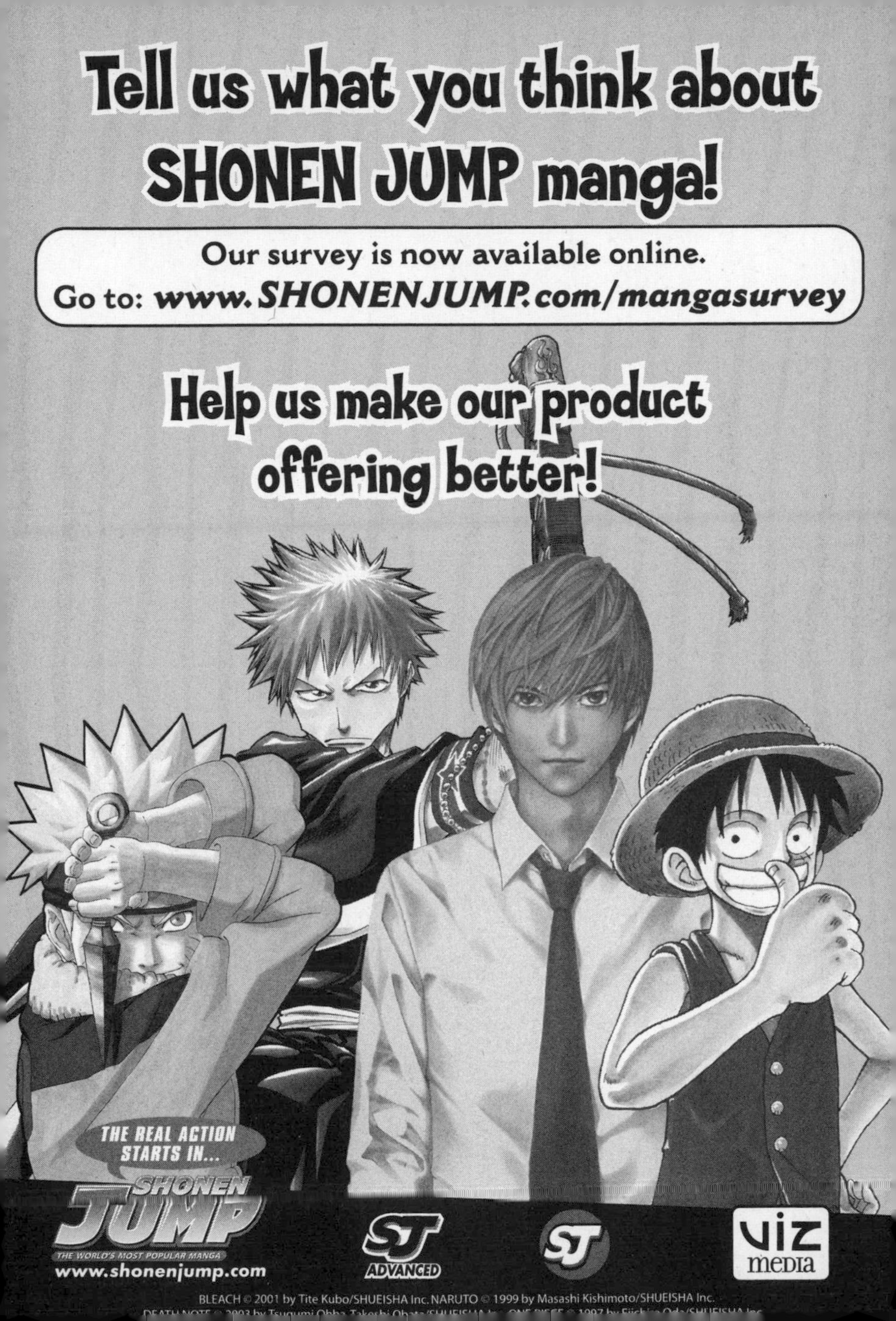
Tell us what you think about SHONEN JUMP manga!
Our survey is now available online.
Go to: www.SHONENJUMP.com/mangasurvey
Help us make our product offering better!
THE REAL ACTION STARTS IN...
SHONEN JUMP
THE WORLD'S MOST POPULAR MANGA
www.shonenjump.com
SJ ADVANCED
SJ
viz media
BLEACH © 2001 by Tite Kubo/SHUEISHA Inc. NARUTO © 1999 by Masashi Kishimoto/SHUEISHA Inc.